FIFTH EDITION

FROM CRITICAL THINKING to ARGUMENT

A Portable Guide

Sylvan Barnet
Professor of English, Late of Tufts University

Hugo Bedau
Professor of Philosophy, Late of Tufts University

John O'Hara
Associate Professor of Critical Thinking, Reading, and Writing, Stockton University

bedford/st.martin's
Macmillan Learning
Boston | New York

For Bedford /St. Martin's

Vice President, Editorial, Macmillan Learning Humanities: Edwin Hill
Editorial Director, English: Karen S. Henry
Senior Publisher for Composition, Business and Technical Writing, Developmental Writing: Leasa Burton
Executive Editor: John E. Sullivan III
Developmental Editor: Alicia Young
Senior Production Editor: Jessica Gould
Media Producers: Allison Hart and Rand Thomas
Production Supervisor: Victoria Anzalone
Marketing Manager: Joy Fisher Williams
Copy Editor: Alice Vigliani
Photo Editor: Martha Friedman
Photo Researcher: Jen Simmons
Permissions Editor: Elaine Kosta
Senior Art Director: Anna Palchik
Cover Design: John Callahan
Composition: Jouve
Printing and Binding: LSC Communications

Manufactured in the United States of America.

1   0   9   8
f   e   d   c   b

For information, write: Bedford/St. Martin's, 75 Arlington Street, Boston, MA 02116   (617-399-4000)

ISBN: 978-1-319-03544-0

Acknowledgments

Text acknowledgments and copyrights appear at the back of the book on page 406, which constitutes an extension of the copyright page. Art acknowledgments and copyrights appear on the same page as the art selections they cover.

Preface

This brief book is about reading other people's arguments and writing your own. Before we describe the sorts of essays we include here, we first want to mention our chief assumptions about the aims of a course that might use *From Critical Thinking to Argument: A Portable Guide*.

Probably most students and instructors would agree that, as *critical readers*, students should be able to

- summarize accurately an argument they have read;
- locate the thesis (the claim) of an argument;
- locate the assumptions, stated and unstated, of an argument;
- analyze and evaluate the strength of the evidence and the soundness of the reasoning offered in support of the thesis; and
- analyze, evaluate, and account for discrepancies among various readings on a topic (for example, explain why certain facts are used, why probable consequences of a proposed action are examined or are ignored, or why two sources might interpret the same facts differently).

Probably, too, students and instructors would agree that, as *thoughtful writers*, students should be able to

- imagine an audience and write effectively for it (for instance, by using the appropriate tone and providing the appropriate amount of detail);

- present information in an orderly and coherent way;
- be aware of their own assumptions;
- locate sources and incorporate them into their own writing, not simply by quoting extensively or by paraphrasing but also by having digested material so that they can present it in their own words;
- properly document all borrowings—not merely quotations and paraphrases but also borrowed ideas; and
- do all these things in the course of developing a thoughtful argument of their own.

In the first edition of this book we quoted Edmund Burke and John Stuart Mill. Burke said,

> He that wrestles with us strengthens our nerves, and sharpens our skill. Our antagonist is our helper.

Mill said,

> He who knows only his own side of the cause knows little.

These two quotations continue to reflect the view of argument that underlies this text: In writing an essay one is engaging in a serious effort to know what one's own ideas are and, having found them, to contribute to a multisided conversation. One is not setting out to trounce an opponent, and that is partly why such expressions as "marshaling evidence," "attacking an opponent," and "defending a thesis" are misleading. True, on television talk shows we see right-wingers and left-wingers who have made up their minds and who are concerned only with pushing their own views and brushing aside all others. But in an academic community, and indeed in our daily lives, we learn by listening to others and also by listening to ourselves.

We draft a response to something we have read, and in the very act of drafting we may find—if we think critically about the words we are putting down on paper—we are changing (perhaps slightly, perhaps radically) our own position. In short, one reason that we write is so that we can improve our ideas. And even if we do not drastically change our views, we and our readers at least come to a better understanding of why we hold the views we do.

FEATURES

In Part One, the first four chapters deal with recognizing and evaluating assumptions—in both texts and images—as a way to start annotating, summarizing, and analyzing arguments. Among the topics discussed are critical thinking, analysis, summary and paraphrase, reasoning, and the uses of humor, emotion, and images. Chapter 4, Visual Rhetoric: Thinking about Images as Arguments, not only helps students to analyze advertisements but also offers suggestions about using visuals such as maps, graphs, tables, and pie charts in their own arguments.

Chapters 5 and 6 focus principally on writing. Students are expected to apply the critical thinking and reading skills they have learned to writing analytical and argumentative papers. We include sample student papers as models. Chapter 7, on research, includes information on finding, evaluating, and documenting electronic and other sources and discusses ways to choose topics for research, take notes, avoid plagiarism, and integrate quotations. Two annotated student papers—one in MLA style and one in APA style—provide models for reading and reference. Part Two, a kind of appendix, presents alternative perspectives on argument: the Toulmin model, logical reasoning (a detailed discussion of induction, deduction, and fallacies), and a description of Rogerian argument (named for the psychologist Carl Rogers).

We trust that this book is brief enough and affordable enough to be assigned as an accompaniment to a separate anthology of readings or as a supplement to a selection of individual longer works that do not include necessary instruction in critical thinking and argument.

WHAT'S NEW IN THE FIFTH EDITION

This fifth edition brings highly significant changes. The authors of the previous four editions established a firm foundation for the book: Hugo Bedau, professor of philosophy, brought analytical rigor to the instruction in argumentation, and Sylvan Barnet, professor of English, contributed expertise in writing instruction. They have now turned the project over to John O'Hara, professor of critical thinking, to contribute a third dimension, augmenting and enriching the material on critical thinking throughout, especially in the early chapters. Other changes have been made to ensure practical instruction and current topics.

Expanded coverage of critical thinking. Chapters 1 through 4 have been heavily revised to help better show students how effective reading, analysis, and writing all begin with critical thinking. Enhancements include an expanded vocabulary for critical thinking, instruction on writing critical summaries, guidance on confronting unfamiliar issues in reading and writing, new strategies for generating essay topics, and extended critical reading approaches.

New "Thinking Critically" activities. Throughout the text, new exercises test students' ability to apply critical thinking, reading, and writing concepts.

Expanded discussion of developing thesis statements in Chapter 6. This updated section helps better illustrate for students what the difference is between taking a truly critical position versus resting on their laurels in argumentative essays.

Updated coverage of visual rhetoric in Chapter 4. The "Visual Rhetoric" chapter has been expanded to include discussion of how to analyze images rhetorically, including how to recognize and resist the meanings of images, how to identify visual emotional appeals, and what the difference is exactly between *seeing* passively and truly *looking* critically.

ACKNOWLEDGMENTS

Finally, the authors would like to thank those who have strengthened this book by their comments and advice on the fifth edition: Joshua Dickinson, Jefferson Community College; Christine Gray, Community College of Baltimore; Gregory Hagan, Madisonville Community College; Jennifer Hewerdine, Southern Illinois University Carbondale; Leslie Johnson, Lansing Community College; Vincent Lasnik, Rogue Community College; Meredith Love-Steinmetz, Francis Marion University; Karen Miller, University of Minnesota Crookston; Rick Rivera, Columbia College; Sandra Snow, Central Michigan University; Joseph Michael Sommers, Central Michigan University; Greg Winston, Husson University; and Susan Wright, Campbellsville University.

We are also deeply indebted to the people at Bedford/St. Martin's, especially to our editor, Alicia Young, who is wise, patient, supportive, and unfailingly helpful. Steve Scipione, Maura Shea, John Sullivan, and Adam Whitehurst, our editors for preceding editions, have left a lasting impression on us and on the book; without their work on the first four editions, there probably would not be a fifth.

We would also like to thank Kalina Ingham, Elaine Kosta, Martha Friedman, Angela Boehler, and Jen Simmons, who adeptly managed art research and text permissions. Others at Bedford/St. Martin's to whom we are deeply indebted include Edwin Hill, Leasa Burton, Karen Henry, Joy Fisher Williams, Jennifer Prince, Elise Kaiser, and Jessica Gould, all of whom have offered countless valuable (and invaluable) suggestions. Intelligent, informed, firm yet courteous, persuasive—all of these folks know how to think and how to argue.

WITH BEDFORD/ST. MARTIN'S, YOU GET MORE

At Bedford/St. Martin's, providing support to teachers and their students who use our books and digital tools is our top priority. The Bedford/St. Martin's English Community is now our home for professional resources, including Bedford *Bits*, our popular blog with new ideas for the composition classroom. Join us to connect with our authors and your colleagues at **community.macmillan.com**, where you can download titles from our professional resource series, review projects in the pipeline, sign up for webinars, or start a discussion. In addition to this dynamic online community and book-specific instructor resources, we offer digital tools, custom solutions, and value packages to support both you and your students. We are committed to delivering the quality and value that you've come to expect from Bedford/St. Martin's, supported as always by the power of Macmillan Learning. To learn more about or to order any of the following products, contact your Bedford/St. Martin's sales representative or visit the Web site at **macmillanlearning.com**.

Choose from Alternative Formats of *From Critical Thinking to Argument*

Bedford/St. Martin's offers a range of affordable formats, allowing students to choose the one that works best for them. For details about our e-book partners, visit **macmillanlearning.com/ebooks**.

Select Value Packages

Add value to your text by packaging one of the following resources with *From Critical Thinking to Argument*. To learn more about package options for any of the following products, contact your Bedford/St. Martin's sales representative or visit **macmillanlearning.com**.

LaunchPad Solo for Readers and Writers allows students to work on whatever they need help with the most. At home or in class, students learn at their own pace, with instruction tailored to each student's unique needs. *LaunchPad Solo for Readers and Writers* features:

- **Pre-built units that support a learning arc.** Each easy-to-assign unit is comprised of a pre-test check, multimedia instruction and assessment, and a post-test that assesses what students have learned about critical reading, writing process, using sources, grammar, style, and mechanics. Dedicated units also offer help for multilingual writers.

- **Diagnostics that help establish a baseline for instruction.** Assign diagnostics to identify areas of strength and areas for improvement on topics related to grammar and reading and to help students plan a course of study. Use visual reports to track performance by topic, class, and student as well as comparison reports that track improvement over time.

- **A video introduction to many topics.** Introductions offer an overview of the unit's topic, and many include a brief, accessible video to illustrate the concepts at hand.

- **Twenty-five reading selections with comprehension quizzes.** Assign a range of classic and contemporary essays, each of which includes a label indicating Lexile level to help you scaffold instruction in critical reading.

- **Adaptive quizzing for targeted learning.** Most units include LearningCurve, game-like adaptive quizzing that focuses on the areas in which each student needs the most help.

- **The ability to monitor student progress.** Use our gradebook to see which students are on track and which need additional help with specific topics.

- **Additional reading comprehension quizzes.** *From Critical Thinking to Argument* includes multiple-choice quizzes, which help you quickly gauge your students' understanding of the assigned reading. These are available in *LaunchPad Solo for Readers and Writers*.

Order ISBN 978-1-319-12324-6 to package *LaunchPad Solo for Readers and Writers* with *From Critical Thinking to Argument* at **a significant**

discount. Students who rent or buy a used book can purchase access and instructors may request free access at **macmillanlearning .com/readwrite**.

Writer's Help 2.0 is a powerful online writing resource that helps students find answers whether they are searching for writing advice on their own or as part of an assignment.

- **Smart search**. Built on research with more than 1,600 student writers, the smart search in Writer's Help 2.0 provides reliable results even when students use novice terms, such as *flow* and *unstuck*.

- **Trusted content from our best-selling handbooks.** Choose *Writer's Help 2.0, Hacker Version* or *Writer's Help 2.0, Lunsford Version* and ensure that students have clear advice and examples for all of their writing questions.

- **Diagnostics that help establish a baseline for instruction**. Assign diagnostics to identify areas of strength and areas for improvement on topics related to grammar and reading and to help students plan a course of study. Use visual reports to track performance by topic, class, and student as well as comparison reports that track improvement over time.

- **Adaptive exercises that engage students**. Writer's Help 2.0 includes LearningCurve, game-like online quizzing that adapts to what students already know and helps them focus on what they need to learn.

- **Reading comprehension quizzes.** *From Critical Thinking to Argument* includes multiple-choice quizzes, which help you quickly gauge your students' understanding of the assigned reading. These are available in Writer's Help 2.0.

Writer's Help 2.0 can be packaged with *From Critical Thinking to Argument* at **a significant discount**. For more information, contact your sales representative or visit **macmillanlearning.com /writershelp2**.

Macmillan Learning Curriculum Solutions

Curriculum Solutions brings together the quality of Bedford/St. Martin's content with Hayden-McNeil's expertise in publishing original custom print and digital products. Developed especially for writing courses, our ForeWords for English program contains a library of the most popular, requested content in easy-to-use modules to help you build the best possible text. Whether you are considering creating a custom version of *From Critical Thinking to Argument* or incorporating our content with your own, we can adapt and combine the resources that work best for your course or program. Some enrollment minimums apply. Contact your sales representative for more information.

Brief Contents

Contents

PART ONE

FROM CRITICAL THINKING to ARGUMENT and RESEARCH

1

Critical Thinking

What is the hardest task in the world? To think.

—RALPH WALDO EMERSON

In all affairs it's a healthy thing now and then to hang a question mark on the things you have long taken for granted.

—BERTRAND RUSSELL

Although Emerson said the hardest task in the world is simply "to think," he was using the word *think* in the sense of *critical thinking.* By itself, *thinking* can mean almost any sort of cognitive activity, from idle daydreaming ("I'd like to go camping") to simple reasoning ("but if I go this week, I won't be able to study for my chemistry exam"). Thinking by itself may include forms of deliberation and decision-making that occur so automatically they hardly register in our consciousness ("What if I do go camping? I won't be likely to pass the exam. Then what? I better stay home and study").

When we add the adjective *critical* to the noun *thinking,* we begin to examine this thinking process consciously. When we do this, we see that even our simplest decisions involve a fairly elaborate series of calculations. Just in choosing to study and not to go camping, for instance, we weighed the relative importance of each activity (both are important in different ways); considered our goals, obligations, and commitments (to ourselves, our parents, peers, and professors); posed questions and predicted outcomes (using experience and observation as evidence); and resolved to take the most prudent course of action.

Many people associate being critical with fault-finding and nit-picking. The word *critic* might conjure an image of a sneering art or food critic eager to gripe about everything that's wrong with a particular work of art or menu item. People's low estimation of the stereotypical critic comes to light humorously in Samuel Beckett's play *Waiting for Godot*, when the two vagabond heroes, Vladimir and Estragon, engage in a name-calling contest to see who can hurl the worst insult at the other. Estragon wins hands-down when he fires the ultimate invective:

V: Moron!

E: Vermin!

V: Abortion!

E: Morpion!

V: Sewer-rat!

E: Curate!

V: Cretin!

E: (*with finality*) Crritic!

V: Oh! (*He wilts, vanquished, and turns away.*)

However, being a good *critical* thinker isn't the same as being a "critic" in the derogatory sense. Quite the reverse: Because critical thinkers approach difficult questions and seek intelligent answers, they must be open-minded and self-aware, and they must interrogate *their own* thinking as rigorously as they interrogate others'. They must be alert to *their own* limitations and biases, the quality of evidence and forms of logic *they themselves* tentatively offer. In college, we may not aspire to become critics, but we all should aspire to become better critical thinkers.

Becoming more aware of our thought processes is a first step in practicing critical thinking. The word *critical* comes from the Greek word *krinein*, meaning "to separate, to choose"; above all, it implies *conscious* inquiry. It suggests that by breaking apart, or examining, our reasoning we can understand better the basis of our judgments and decisions—ultimately, so that we can make better ones.

THINKING THROUGH AN ISSUE: GAY MARRIAGE LICENSES

By way of illustration, let's examine a case from Kentucky that was reported widely in the news in 2015. After the U.S. Supreme Court's landmark decision making gay marriage legal in all fifty states, a Rowan County clerk, Kim Davis, refused to begin issuing marriage licenses to same-sex couples. Citing religious freedom as her reason, Davis contended that the First Amendment of the Constitution protects her from being forced to act against her religious convictions and conscience. As a follower of Apostolic Christianity, she believes gay marriage is not marriage at all. To act against her belief, she said, "I would be asked to violate a central teaching of Scripture and of Jesus Himself regarding marriage. . . . It is not a light issue for me. It's a Heaven or Hell decision."

Let's think critically about this—and let's do it in a way that's fair to all parties and not just a snap judgment. Critical thinking means questioning not only the beliefs and assumptions of others, but also *one's own* beliefs and assumptions. We'll discuss this point at some length later, but for now we'll say only that when writing an argument you ought to be *thinking*—identifying important problems, exploring relevant issues, and evaluating available evidence—not merely collecting information to support a preestablished conclusion.

In 2015, Kim Davis was an elected county official. She couldn't be fired from her job for not performing her duties because she had been placed in that position by the vote of her constituency. And as her lawyers pointed out, "You don't lose your conscience

Ty Wright/Getty Images

rights, or your religious freedom rights, or your constitutional rights just because you accept public employment." However, once the Supreme Court established the legality of same-sex marriage, Davis's right to exercise her religious freedom impinged upon others' abilities to exercise their equal right to marriage (now guaranteed to them by the federal government). And so there was a problem: Whose rights have precedence?

We may begin to identify important problems and explore relevant issues by using a process called *clustering*. (We illustrate clustering again on p. 15.) Clustering is a method of brainstorming, a way of getting ideas on paper to see what develops, what conflicts and issues exist, and what tentative conclusions you can draw as you begin developing an argument. To start clustering, take a sheet of paper, and in the center jot down the most basic issue you can think of related to the problem at hand. In our example, we wrote a sentence that we think gets at the heart of the matter. It's important to note that we conducted this demonstration in "real time"—just a few minutes—so if our thoughts seem incomplete or off-the-cuff, that's fine. The point of clustering is to get ideas on paper. Don't be afraid to write down whatever you think, because you can always go back, cross out, rethink. This process of working through an issue can be messy. In a sense, it involves conducting an argument with yourself.

At the top of our page we wrote, "The law overrides individual religious freedom." (Alternatively, we could have written from the perspective of Davis and her supporters, saying "Individual religious freedom supersedes the law," and seen where that might have taken us.) Once we have a central idea, we let our minds work and allow one thought to lead to another. We've added numbers to our thoughts so you can follow the progression of our thinking.

Notice that from our first idea about the law being more important than individual religious freedom, we immediately challenged our initial thinking. The law, in fact, protects religious freedom (2), and in some cases allows individuals to "break the law" if their religious rituals require it. We learned this when we wrote down a number of illegal activities sometimes associated with religion, and quickly looked up whether or not there was a legal precedent protecting these activities. We found the Supreme Court has allowed for the use of illegal drugs in some ceremonies (*Gonzalez v. O Centro Espirita*), and for the ritual sacrifice of animals in another (*Church of Lakumi Bablu Aye v. Hialeah*). Still, religions cannot do *anything they want* in the name of religious freedom. Religions cannot levy taxes, or incarcerate or kill people, for example. We then realized that what

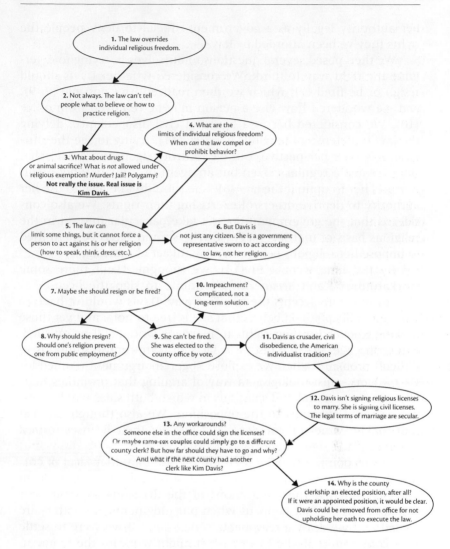

religions do as part of their ceremonies is not really the issue at all. The questions we are asking have to do with Kim Davis, her individual religious freedom, and what the law might force her to do (4).

Individuals cannot simply break the law and claim religious exemption. But the government cannot force people to act against their religious beliefs (5). Then (6) it occurred to us that Davis isn't just any citizen but a government employee whose job is to issue marriage licenses under the law. She may be free to believe what she wants and exercise her rights accordingly, but she cannot use her authority legally as a government official to deny people the rights they've been afforded by law.

We then posed several questions to ourselves in trying to determine the right way to think. We considered whether Davis should resign or be fired (7), which we then realized isn't possible (8, 9), and we wondered how else a person may be removed from office (10). We considered her as a figure of civil disobedience, defying the law in defense of religious liberties (11), trying to see the situation from her perspective. But we returned again to the idea that she isn't just a regular citizen but an agent of the law whose oath compels her to uphold the law (6). She shouldn't be able to use her authority to deprive others of exercising their rights. We also considered that the government doesn't take particular interest in the religious basis of marriage (12), so why should Davis be permitted to impose her religious beliefs on a lawful act of marriage?

By the time we got to (13), we thought, "Isn't there some workaround? Can't *deputy clerks* continue to sign the licenses as long as the state accepts them?" This way, Davis wouldn't have to violate the deeply held beliefs that she is free to hold, and yet those seeking to exercise their rights to marriage would still be satisfied. Later, on page 391, we discuss a facet of compromise solutions to difficult problems when we explore Rogerian argument (named for Carl Rogers, a psychologist), a way of arguing that promotes finding common ground and solutions in which both sides win by conceding some elements to the opposition. We also thought in (13) that maybe same-sex couples could just get their licenses from a different place, one where Davis doesn't work.

At this point, it may be useful to mention another facet of critical thinking and argument that we'll also explore in more detail later: considering the implications of the decisions to which our thinking leads. What happens when our judgments on matters are settled and we draw a reasonable conclusion? If we were to settle on a compromise in the Davis case, it might work for the moment, but what would happen if other clerks in the state held the same beliefs as Davis (13)? In (13), we also considered the implications if same-sex couples were simply asked to go to a different office. How far should a same-sex couple have to go to find someone willing to issue the license if all clerks can decide based on their religious convictions what kinds of marriage they will authorize? Additionally, and maybe even more important, why should same-sex couples be hindered in any way in acquiring their license or be treated as a different class of citizens?

Again, if you think with pencil and paper in hand and let your mind make associations by clustering, you'll find (perhaps to your surprise) that you have plenty of interesting ideas and that some can lead to satisfying conclusions. Doubtless you'll also have some ideas that represent gut reactions or poorly thought-out conclusions, but that's okay. When clustering, allow your thoughts to take shape without restriction; you can look them over again and organize them later. Originally, we wrote in our cluster (7) that Davis could be fired for not performing her job according to its requirements. We then realized that this wouldn't involve a simple process. Because she's an elected official, there would have to be a state legislative action to impeach her (9). This made us think, "The state of Kentucky could impeach Davis" (10). But then we also considered the consequences and decided this would not be a long-term solution. What if the next election cycle brought someone else who shares Davis's beliefs into the same position? In fact, what if citizens in Kentucky continued to elect county clerks in Rowan County—or any county—who refused to issue marriage licenses based on religious convictions? Would the state have to impeach clerks over and over again? We then thought, "Why is the county clerkship an elected position" (14)? Could it become an appointed position instead, such that governors could emplace county clerks, whose primary job is to administer legislative policy? Perhaps this is the argument we'll want to make. (Of course, it might open up new questions and issues that we would have to explore: What else does the clerk do? Is the autonomy of an elected position necessary? Do all states elect county clerks? And so on.)

At the time of this writing, Kim Davis had continued to refuse signing marriage licenses for same-sex couples. When ordered by a judge to do so or face contempt of court, she held firm to her position and spent six days in jail as a result. Her supporters cheered her act of civil disobedience (defined as breaking a law based on moral or religious conscience) and even compared her to Rosa Parks, Martin Luther King Jr., and other civil rights leaders who fought against unjust laws on the basis of religious principles.

A RULE FOR WRITERS One good way to start writing an essay is to generate ideas by clustering — and at this point not to worry that some ideas may be off-the-cuff or even nonsense. Just get ideas down on paper. You can evaluate them later.

Davis returned to her position as Rowan County clerk and authorized her deputy clerks to issue marriage licenses to same-sex couples, but without her signature. Time will tell how the case plays out.

TOPICS FOR CRITICAL THINKING AND WRITING

1. As noted, some of Kim Davis's supporters have compared her to celebrated figures from American history like Rosa Parks who practiced civil disobedience by breaking laws they believed were immoral, unfair, or unjust. What are the similarities and differences in the case of Rosa Parks, who violated the law in Montgomery, Alabama, in 1955 by refusing to move to the "black" section of a public bus, and that of Kim Davis, who has refused to abide by laws established by the U.S. Supreme Court regarding gay marriage? How do the similarities and differences justify or not justify Davis's actions?

2. On a Facebook page dedicated to Davis's case, one commenter wrote, "Davis is a hero for all of us Christians who feel this country is abandoning our God." Think critically about this statement by writing about the assumptions it reveals.

3. In denying Davis's appeal to a federal court to not be forced to authorize same-sex marriage licenses, Judge David Bunning wrote that individuals "cannot choose what orders they follow" and that religious conscience "is not a viable defense" for not adhering to the law. At the same time, the free exercise clause of the First Amendment of the U.S. Constitution says that Congress shall make no law prohibiting the free exercise of religion. What do you think about Kim Davis's exercise of religion? Is it fair that in order to keep her job after the Court's decision about the legality of gay marriage, she has to regularly violate one of her religion's central beliefs about marriage? Explain your response.

ON FLYING SPAGHETTI MONSTERS: ANALYZING AND EVALUATING FROM MULTIPLE PERSPECTIVES

Let's think critically about another issue related to religious freedom, equality, and the law—one that we hope brings some humor to the activity but also inspires careful thinking and debate.

In 2005, in response to pressure from some religious groups, the Kansas Board of Education gave preliminary approval for teaching alternatives to evolution in public school science classes. New policies would require science teachers to present "intelligent design"—the idea that the universe was created by an intentional, conscious force such as God—as an equally plausible explanation for natural selection and human development.

In a quixotic challenge to the legislation, twenty-four-year-old physics graduate Bobby Henderson wrote an open letter that quickly became popular on the Internet and then was published in the *New York Times*. Henderson appealed for recognition of another theory that he said was equally valid: that an all-powerful deity called the Flying Spaghetti Monster created the world. While clearly writing satirically on behalf of science, Henderson nevertheless kept a straight face and argued that if creationism were to be taught as a theory in science classes, then "Pastafarianism" must also be taught as another legitimate possibility. "I think we can all look forward to the time," he wrote, "when these three theories are given equal time in our science classes. . . . One third time for Intelligent Design; one third time for Flying Spaghetti Monsterism (Pastafarianism); and one third time for logical conjecture based on overwhelming observable evidence."

Since that time, the Church of the Flying Spaghetti Monster has become a creative venue where secularists and atheists construct elaborate mythologies, religious texts, and rituals, most of which involve cartoonish pirates and various noodle-and-sauce images. ("R'amen," they say at the end of their prayers.) However, although tongue-in-cheek, many followers have also used the organization seriously as a means to champion the First Amendment's establishment clause, which prohibits government institutions from *establishing*, or preferring, any one religion over another. Pastafarians have challenged policies and laws in various states that appear to discriminate among religions or to provide exceptions or exemptions based on religion. In Tennessee, Virginia, and Wisconsin, church members have successfully petitioned for permission to display statues or signs of the Flying

Brian Cahn/Newscom/ZUMA Press/Washington/District of Columbia/U.S.

Spaghetti Monster in places where other religious icons are permitted, such as on state government properties. One petition in Oklahoma argued that because the state allows a marble and granite Ten Commandments monument on the state courthouse lawn, then a statue of the Flying Spaghetti Monster must also be permitted; this effort ultimately forced the state to remove the Ten Commandments monument in 2015. In the past three years, individuals in California, Georgia, Florida, Texas, California, and Utah have asserted their right to wear religious head coverings in their driver's license photos—a religious exemption afforded to Muslims in those states—and have had their pictures taken with colanders on their heads.

Let's stop for a moment. Take stock of your initial reactions to the Church of the Flying Spaghetti Monster. Some responses might be quite uncritical, quite unthinking: "That's outrageous!" or "What a funny idea!" Others might be the type of snap judgment we discussed earlier: "These people are making fun of real religions!" or "They're just causing trouble." Think about it: If your hometown approved placing a Christmas tree on the town square during the holiday season, and the Church of the Flying Spaghetti Monster argued that it too should be allowed to set up its holiday symbol as a matter of religious equality—perhaps a statue—should it be afforded equal space? Why, or why not?

Be careful here, and exercise critical thinking. Can one simply say, "No, that belief is ridiculous," in response to a religious claim? What if members of a different religious group were asking for equal space? Should a menorah (a Jewish holiday symbol) be allowed? A mural celebrating Kwanzaa? A Native American symbol? Can some religious expressions be included in public spaces and not others? If so, why? If not, why not?

In thinking critically about a topic, we must try to see it from all sides before reaching a conclusion. We conduct an argument with ourselves, advancing and then questioning different opinions:

- What can be said *for* the proposition?
- What can be said *against* it?

Critical thinking requires us to support our position and also see the other side. The heart of critical thinking is a *willingness to face objections to one's own beliefs*, to adopt a skeptical attitude not only toward views opposed to our own but also toward our own common sense—that is, toward views that seem to us as obviously right. If we assume we have a monopoly on the truth and dismiss those who disagree with us as misguided fools, or if we say that our opponents are acting out of self-interest (or a desire to harass the community) and we don't analyze their views, we're being critical but we aren't engaging in critical thinking.

When thinking critically, it's important to ask key questions about any position, decision, or action we take and any regulation, policy, or law we support. We must ask:

- Is it fair?
- What is its purpose?
- Is it likely to accomplish its purpose?
- What will its effects be? Might it unintentionally cause some harm?
- If it might cause harm, to whom? What kind of harm? Can we weigh the potential harm against the potential good?
- Who gains something and who loses something as a result?
- Are there any compromises that might satisfy different parties?

What do you think? If you were on your hometown's city council, how would you answer the above questions in relation to a petition from the Church of the Flying Spaghetti Monster to permit a Spaghetti Monster display alongside the traditional Christmas tree on the town square? How would you vote, and why? What other questions and issues might arise from your engagement with this issue? (*Hint:* Try clustering. Place the central question in the middle of a sheet of a paper, and brainstorm the issues that flower from it.)

Call-Out: Obstacles to Critical Thinking   Because critical thinking requires engaging seriously with potentially difficult topics, topics about which you may already have strong opinions, and topics that elicit powerful emotional responses, it's important to recognize the ways in which your thinking may be compromised or clouded. Write down or discuss how each of the following attitudes might impede or otherwise negatively affect your critical thinking in real life. How might each one be detrimental in making conclusions?

1. The topic is too controversial and will never be resolved.
2. The topic hits "too close to home" (i.e., "I've had direct experience with this").
3. The topic disgusts me.

4. The topic angers me.
5. Everyone I know thinks roughly the same thing I do about this topic.
6. Others may judge me if I verbalize what I think.
7. My opinion on this topic is X because it benefits me, my family, or my kind the most.
8. My parents raised me to think X about this topic.
9. One of my favorite celebrities believes X about this topic, so I do too.
10. I know what I think, but my solutions are probably unrealistic. It's impossible to change the system.

Think of some more obstacles to critical thinking, and provide examples of how they might lead to unsound conclusions or poor solutions.

> **A RULE FOR WRITERS** Early in the process of jotting down your ideas on a topic, stop to ask yourself, "What might someone reasonably offer as an *objection* to my view?"

In short, as we will say several times (because the point is key), *argument is an instrument of learning* as well as of persuasion. In order to formulate a reasoned position and make a vote, you'll have to gather some information, find out what experts say, and examine the points on which they agree and disagree. You'll likely want to gather opinions from religious leaders, community members, and legal experts (after all, you wouldn't want the town to be sued for discrimination). You'll want to think beyond a knee-jerk value judgment like, "No, a Spaghetti Monster statue would be ugly."

Seeing the issue from multiple perspectives will require familiarizing yourself with current debates—perhaps about religious equality, free speech, or the separation of church and state—and considering the responsibility of public institutions to accommodate different viewpoints and various constituencies. Remember, the Church of the Flying Spaghetti Monster didn't gain so much traction by being easy to dismiss. Thus, you must do the following:

Survey, considering as many perspectives as possible.

Analyze, identifying and then separating out the parts of the problem, trying to see how its pieces fit together.

Evaluate, judging the merit of various ideas and claims and the weight of the evidence in their favor or against them.

If you survey, analyze, and evaluate comprehensively, you'll have better and more informed ideas; you'll generate a wide variety of ideas, each triggered by your own responses and the ideas your research brings to light. As you form an opinion and prepare to vote, you'll be constructing an argument to yourself at first, but also one you may have to present to the community, so you should be as thorough as possible and sensitive to the ideas and rights of many different people.

Critical Thinking at Work: From Jottings to a Short Essay

We have already seen an example of clustering on page 7, which illustrates the prewriting process of thinking through an issue and generating ideas by imagining responses—counterthoughts—to our initial thoughts. Here's another example, this time showing

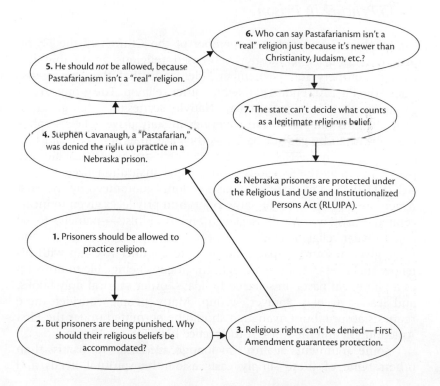

6. Who can say Pastafarianism isn't a "real" religion just because it's newer than Christianity, Judaism, etc.?

5. He should *not* be allowed, because Pastafarianism isn't a "real" religion.

7. The state can't decide what counts as a legitimate religious belief.

4. Stephen Cavanaugh, a "Pastafarian," was denied the right to practice in a Nebraska prison.

8. Nebraska prisoners are protected under the Religious Land Use and Institutionalized Persons Act (RLUIPA).

1. Prisoners should be allowed to practice religion.

2. But prisoners are being punished. Why should their religious beliefs be accommodated?

3. Religious rights can't be denied—First Amendment guarantees protection.

an actual student's thoughts about an issue related to the Church of the Flying Spaghetti Monster. The student, Alexa Cabrera, was assigned to write approximately 500 words about a specific legal challenge made by a member of the Church of the Flying Spaghetti Monster. She selected the case of Stephen Cavanaugh, a prisoner who made a complaint against the Nebraska State Penitentiary after being denied the right to practice Pastafarianism while incarcerated there. Because the Department of Corrections denied him those privileges, Cavanaugh filed suit citing civil rights violations and asked for his rights to be accommodated. Notice that in the essay—the product of several revised drafts—the student introduced points she had *not* thought of while clustering. The cluster, in short, was a *first* step, not a road map of the final essay.

A Student's Essay, Developed from a Cluster and a List

Stirred and Strained: Pastafarians Should Be Allowed to Practice in Prison

Stephen Cavanaugh is a member of the Church of the Flying Spaghetti Monster, a mostly Web-based religious group that has earned notoriety for its members' demands that they be treated under the First Amendment like any other religion. The group strives to show that if Christians can place Nativity scenes on public grounds, or if Muslims can wear head coverings in state driver's license photographs, then by god (or pasta, as the case may be), they can too. Cavanaugh is in the Nebraska State Penitentiary, where inmates are permitted under the Religious Land Use and Institutionalized Persons Act (RLUIPA) to exercise religious freedoms guaranteed by the First Amendment. He wants the same rights and privileges given to incarcerated Christians, Muslims, Jews, and Buddhists—namely, to be able to wear religious clothing, to eat specially prepared meals, and to be given resources, space, and time to conduct worship with his fellow "believers." For Cavanaugh, this means being able to dress up as a pirate, eat pasta on selected holidays, order satirical holy books, and lead a weekly "prayer" group. Many people consider these requests absurd, but Cavanaugh should be permitted under the First Amendment and the RLUIPA to practice his faith.

Some arguments against Cavanaugh are easier to dismiss than others. One of these simply casts aside the spiritual needs and concerns of prisoners: They are being punished, after all, so why should they receive any religious accommodations? This position is both immoral and unconstitutional. Religion is an important sustaining force for prisoners who might otherwise struggle to find meaning and purpose in life, and it is protected by the First Amendment *because* it helps prisoners find purpose and become rehabilitated—the fundamental goal of correctional facilities (even for those serving life without parole). Another argument sees religion as important as long as it conforms to Judeo-Christian belief structures, which has for a long time been the only spiritual path available in American prisons. But today, in our diverse society, the RLUIPA *requires* prisons to provide religious accommodations for all faiths equally unless an undue administrative, financial, or security burden can be proven. Obviously, many religious observances cannot be accommodated. Prisons cannot permit inmates to carry crosses and staves, construct temples and sweat lodges, or make required religious pilgrimages. However, as long as some religious accommodations can be and are made—such as Catholics being offered fish on Fridays, or Jewish and Muslim prisoners receiving kosher and halal meals—all religious groups must be similarly accommodated.

The more challenging question about the Church of the Flying Spaghetti Monster is whether it is a religion at all, whether it deserves equal treatment among more established religions. When Cavanaugh was first denied his request, the prison claimed that FSM was not a religion but a "parody" of religion. The Nebraska State Penitentiary suggested it could not grant privileges to anyone who presents his whimsical desires as part of a religious philosophy. In dealing with a humorous and politically motivated "religion" without a strong tradition and whose founder may write a new gospel at any time, should the prison have to keep up with the possibility of constantly changing prisoner demands? Can anyone just make up a religion and then expect to be accommodated?

For better or worse, the answer is yes—as long as the accommodations represent valid forms of observance, are reasonable, and do not pose a substantial burden to the institution. Many religions have councils that at times alter the tenets of their faith. The state does not have the authority to determine what is or is not a "real" religion or religious practice. It does have an obligation under the RLUIPA to accommodate not just some but all forms of faith for incarcerated persons. As long as individuals sincerely hold certain beliefs, and as long as the accommodations requested meet the standards of reasonability and equity, state prisons, like all other government agencies and institutions, cannot discriminate. Some might argue that Cavanaugh's faith is not sincere — that he does not *really* believe that the Earth was literally created by a ball of pasta with meatball-shaped eyes. But this is not the point. The government cannot apply a religious test to measure the degree of one's sincerity or faith. Like others in the Flying Spaghetti Monster movement — secularists, atheists, and professed believers — Cavanaugh should not be treated as an exploiter of religious freedom. In fact, in a pluralistic society with laws to ensure religious freedom and equality, his challenge helps protect all faiths.   ∎

The Essay Analyzed

The title, in its words *stirred* and *strained,* engages readers' attention by playing with words related to pasta, prison, and the frustration likely to be encountered by an individual who is denied religious freedom. The subtitle states the thesis. This introductory material — a paper begins with its title, not with its first paragraph — makes readers curious and lets them know where the essay will take them.

Paragraph 1 sets the stage. The first sentence clarifies what the Church is and uses a nifty turn of phrase, "by god (or by pasta)," to encourage engagement and make the author's voice, like the FSM, playful but dead serious. The second, third, and fourth sentences provide the basis for Cavanaugh's claims. The last sentence presents a clear thesis.

Paragraph 2 draws on the student's preliminary map. It sets forth objections to making religious accommodations for prisoners and disputes them, providing a citation of the law that guarantees religious freedom in prison, a definition of its limits, and a few examples of these limits. The last sentence sustains the thesis by arguing that accommodations must be equal among religions. However, it also anticipates that readers are likely to agree on this point but still not consider the FSM as a religion.

Paragraph 3 addresses the potential counterargument set up by paragraph 2 and highlights the most common criticism of the FSM: that it isn't *really* a religion at all. The writer raises the problematic question that if prisons must accommodate Cavanaugh, then where would the protest end? What new accommodations might he ask for in the future? Paragraph 3 in effect suggests the *implications* of granting Cavanaugh his request, inviting the reader to imagine a potentially slippery argumentative slope.

Paragraph 4 halts readers' imaginings, reminding them that the writer is still in the realm of talking about *reasonable* and *fair* treatment among inmates, not an "anything goes" proposition. It reminds readers that the state cannot determine a "real" or "unreal" religion, just as it cannot judge the depth, rigor, or literalness of an inmate's belief (Christian, Pastafarian, or otherwise). The fact is that our society has laws to ensure religious freedom and equality for all citizens. In this way, the writer makes a shrewd rhetorical move, presenting Cavanaugh's complaint not just as antagonistic but also as something essential to protecting prisoners of all faiths. Such an appeal to democratic insistence on fairness is normally effective, although in this instance a reader may wonder if the writer has demonstrated convincingly that fairness requires prisons to accommodate Pastafarians. Are you convinced that it would be *unfair* to deny Cavanaugh and other Pastafarian inmates their demands? Why, or why not?

GENERATING IDEAS: WRITING AS A WAY OF THINKING

We have already seen, in the clusters that students have generated, concise examples of how the act of writing helps thinkers to think better. "To learn to write," Robert Frost said, "is to learn to have ideas." But how does one "learn to have ideas"? Often we discover ideas while talking with others. A friend says *X* about some issue, and we—who have never really thought much about the matter—say,

- "Well, yes, I see what you're saying, but come to think of it, I'm not of your opinion. I see it differently—*not as* X *but as* Y."

Or maybe we say,

- "*Yes,* X, *sure, and also a bit of* Y, *too.*"

Mere chance—a friend's comment—has led us to an idea that we didn't know we had. This sort of discovery may seem like the one we make when reaching under the couch to retrieve the dog's ball and finding a ten-dollar bill instead: "How it got there, I'll never know, but I'm sure glad I found it."

In fact, learning to have ideas is not largely a matter of chance. Or if chance *is* involved, well, as Louis Pasteur put it, "Chance favors the prepared mind." This means that lurking in the mind are bits of information or hints or hunches that in the unexpected circumstance—when talking, when listening to a lecture or a class-room discussion, or especially when reading—are triggered and lead to useful thoughts. This is a sort of seat-of-the-pants knowl-edge that, when brought to the surface in the right circumstances, produces good results.

Consider the famous example of Archimedes, the ancient Greek mathematician who discovered a method to determine the volume of an irregularly shaped object. The problem: A king gave a goldsmith a specific weight of gold with which to make a crown in the shape of laurel leaves. When the job was finished, the king weighed the crown and found that it matched the weight of the gold he had provided, but he nevertheless suspected that the gold-smith might have substituted some silver for some of the gold. How could the king find out (without melting or otherwise damaging the crown) if the crown was pure gold? For Archimedes, medi-tating on this problem produced no ideas, but when he entered a bathtub he noticed that the water level rose as he immersed his body. He suddenly realized that he could thus determine the vol-ume of the crown—by measuring the amount of displaced water. Since silver is less dense than gold, it takes a greater volume of sil-ver to equal a given weight of gold. That is, a given weight of gold will displace less water than the same weight of silver. Archimedes then immersed the given weight of gold, measured the water it dis-placed, and found that indeed the crown displaced more water than the gold did. In his excitement at confirming his idea, Archimedes is said to have leaped out of the tub and run naked through the street, shouting "Eureka!" (Greek for "I have found [it]!").

Why do we tell this story? Partly because we like it, but chiefly because the word *eureka* comes from the same Greek word that has given our language the word **heuristic** (pronounced hyoo-RIS-tik), which refers to a method or process of discovering ideas—in short, of thinking. In this method, one thought triggers another. (*Note:* In computer science, *heuristic* has a more specialized meaning.) Of course, one of the best ways of generating ideas is to hear what's going on around you—and that is talk, both in and out of the class-room, as well as in the world of books. You'll find, as we said early in this discussion, that your response may be, "Well, yes, I see what you're saying, but come to think of it, I don't see it quite that way. I see it differently—not as *X* but as *Y*." As we've said, argument is an instrument of learning as well as of persuasion. For instance:

> *Yes*, solar power is a way of conserving energy, *but* do we
> need to despoil the Mojave Desert and endanger desert life

with—literally—fifty thousand solar mirrors so that folks in Los Angeles can heat their pools? Doesn't it make sense to reduce our use of energy, rather than develop sources of renewable energy that violate the environment? Some sites should be off-limits.

Maybe your response to the proposal (now at least fifteen years old) that wind turbines be placed in the waters off Cape Cod, Massachusetts, would go like this:

> Given our need for wind power, *how can a reasonable person object* to the proposal that we put 130 wind turbines in the waters off Cape Cod, Massachusetts? *Yes,* the view will be changed, *but* in fact the turbines are quite attractive. No one thinks that windmills in Holland spoil the landscape. So the view will be changed, but not spoiled; *and furthermore,* the verdict is still out on whether or not wind turbines pose a significant risk to birds or aquatic life.

When you're asked to write about something you've read in this book, if your first response is that you have no ideas, remember the responses that we have mentioned—"No, I don't see it that way" or "Yes, but" or "Yes, and moreover"—and see if one of them helps you respond to the work—helps you, in short, to develop ideas.

Confronting Unfamiliar Issues

Generating ideas can be a challenge when you, as a student, are asked to read about and respond to an unfamiliar issue. Sometimes, students wonder why they have to engage in particular topics and generate ideas about them. "I want to be a speech pathologist," you might say, "so why do I need to read essays and formulate ideas about capital punishment?"

One answer is that a college curriculum should spur students to think about pressing issues facing our society, so learning about capital punishment is important to all students. But this isn't the only answer. One could never study "all" the important social problems we face (anyway, many of them change very rapidly). Instead, colleges seek to equip students with tools, methods, and habits of mind that enable them to confront arguments about *any* potential issue or problem (including those within the field of speech pathology!). The primary goal of a college education (and of this book) is to help students develop an *intellectual apparatus*—a toolkit that can be applied to any subject matter, any issue.

The techniques presented in this book offer a practical framework for approaching issues, thinking about them carefully, asking good questions, identifying problems, and offering reasonable solutions—not necessarily because we want you to form opinions about the issues we have selected (though we hope you do), but because we want you to practice critical thinking, reading, and writing in ways that transfer to other aspects of your education as well as to your personal, professional, and civic life.

The playwright Edward Albee once said, "Good writers define reality; bad ones merely restate it." Rather than thinking that you must "agree or disagree" with the authors whose works you'll read in this book, imagine that you'll be practicing how to discover your unique point of view by finding pathways into debates, negotiating different positions, and generating new ideas. So when you confront an unfamiliar issue in this book (or elsewhere), consider the strategies discussed below as practical methods for generating new ideas. That is what critical thinking (and writing) is all about.

Topics

One way of generating ideas, practiced by the ancient Greeks and Romans and still regarded as among the best ways, is to consider what the ancients called **topics**—from the Greek *topos*, meaning "place," as in our word *topography* (a description or representation of a place). For the ancients, certain topics, when formulated as questions, were places where they went to find ideas. Among the classical topics were *definition, comparison, relationship*, and *testimony*. By prompting oneself with questions about these topics, one moves toward answers.

If you're at a loss for ideas when confronted with an issue (and an assignment to write about it), you might discover ideas by turning to the relevant classical topics and jotting down your responses. (In classical terminology, this means engaging in the process of invention, from the Latin *invenire*, "to come upon, to find.") Seeing your ideas on paper—even in the briefest form—will help bring other ideas to mind and will also help you evaluate them. For instance, after jotting down ideas as they come and your responses to them, you might do the following:

1. First, organize them into two lists, pro and con.
2. Next, delete ideas that, upon consideration, seem wrong or irrelevant.
3. Finally, develop the ideas that strike you as pretty good.

You probably won't know where you stand until you've gone through such a process. It would be nice to be able to make a quick decision, immediately justify it with three excellent reasons, and then give three further reasons showing why the opposing view is inadequate. In fact, however, people almost never can reach a reasoned decision without a good deal of preliminary thinking.

Consider the following brief essay about the Food and Drug Administration's approval, in 2015, of a genetically engineered salmon. Although GMO (genetically modified organisms) foods and medicines are common in the United States, this salmon will soon be the first genetically modified animal approved for food consumption in the United States. After you read the essay, refer to Thinking Critically: Generating Topics (pp. 26–27), which asks you to begin jotting down ideas on a sheet of paper along the lines of the classical topics. As an example of how to respond to the questions, we've included columns related to the Kim Davis and Stephen Cavanaugh cases. As you attempt to formulate ideas related to the essay about genetically engineered salmon, answer the questions related to the classical topics. There's no need to limit yourself to one answer per item as we did.

Nina Fedoroff

Nina Fedoroff (b. 1942) is the Evan Pugh professor emerita at Penn State University. She served as science and technology adviser to the U.S. secretary of state from 2007 to 2010. The following essay originally appeared in the New York Times *in December 2015.*

The Genetically Engineered Salmon Is a Boon for Consumers and Sustainability

This is great news for consumers and the environment. Wild salmon populations have long been in deep trouble because of overfishing, and open-water cage farming of salmon pollutes coastal waters, propagates fish diseases, and sacrifices a lot of wild-caught fish to be consumed as salmon feed.

The fish is virtually identical to wild salmon, but it is a more sustainable food source, growing faster to maturity.

But just imagine, you'll soon be able to eat salmon guilt-free. AquaBounty has spent more than 20 years developing and testing this faster-growing salmon that will require less feed to bring it to a marketable size. It can be farmed economically in closed, on-land facilities that recirculate water and don't dump waste into the sea. Since the fish live in clean, managed water, they don't get diseases that are spread among caged fish in the sea. And the growing facilities could be closer to markets, cutting shipping costs.

All of these elements take pressure off wild salmon and make salmon farming more sustainable.

Much of the concern about AquaBounty's salmon centers 5 around several bits of added DNA, taken from another fish, that let the salmon grow continuously, not just seasonally. That does not make them "unnatural" or dangerous, it just makes them grow to market size on less feed.

We've been tinkering with our plants and animals to serve our food needs for somewhere between 10 and 20 thousand years. We created corn, for example. The seed-bearing structure of the original "wild" version, called teosinte, looked very different from the modern-day ear, packed with hundreds of soft, starch-and-protein-filled kernels. And it's people who developed the tomatoes we eat today. Mother Nature's are tiny: A pioneering breeder described them in an 1893 grower's guide as "small, hollow, tough, watery" fruits.

But there's money (and fame) in being anti-G.M.O. The organic food marketers want to sell their food, which is over-priced because organic farming is inefficient—not because the food's better—so they tell scare stories about the dangers of G.M.O.s.

There is also no reason to fear that these genetically engineered salmon will escape and destroy wild populations. Only sterile females will be grown for food. And since the fish will be grown in contained facilities on land, escapees can't survive either.

AquaBounty's salmon is salmon, plain and simple. I, for one, can't wait to taste it. ∎

Here's an inner dialogue that you might engage in as you think critically about the question of genetically engineered salmon:

> The purpose of genetically engineered salmon is to protect against the ecological effects of overfishing—that seems to be a good thing.

> Another purpose is to protect consumers by ensuring that the price of salmon, one of the most commonly eaten fish, will not become so high that few people could afford it.

But other issues are apparent. Should we turn to altering the genes of animals to protect the environment or consumer prices? Are there other solutions, like eating less salmon or regulating overfishing?

Who gains and who loses, and what do they stand to gain or lose, by this FDA approval of genetically modified salmon?

The author says no one should worry about "several bits of DNA added"; but come to think of it, is this modification unethical or dangerous in any way? Is it okay to create a new type of animal by altering genes?

The author attacks anti-GMO activists, saying they're just after money (and fame — why fame?). Isn't money (and fame?) also the goal of AquaBounty and other GMO food producers?

Notice how part of the job is *analytic,* recognizing the elements or complexities of the whole, and part is *evaluative,* judging the adequacy of all the ideas, one by one. Both tasks require critical thinking in the form of analyzing and evaluating, and those processes themselves require a disciplined *imagination.*

So far we have jotted down a few thoughts and then immediately given some second thoughts contrary to the first. Be aware that your own counterthoughts might not come to mind right away. For instance, they might not occur until you reread your notes or try to explain the issue to a friend, or until you begin drafting an essay aimed at supporting or undermining the new FDA rules. Most likely, in fact, some good ideas won't occur until a second or third or fourth draft.

Here are some further thoughts on the genetically modified salmon. We list them more or less as they occurred to us and as we typed them into a computer—not sorted neatly into two groups, pro and con, or evaluated as you should do in further critical thinking of your own. Of course, a later step would be to organize the material into a useful pattern. As you read, try writing your responses in the margin.

According to one article, the FDA is not requiring companies to label the salmon as genetically engineered. Should this information at least be made available to consumers? Maybe their

THINKING CRITICALLY GENERATING TOPICS

Provide the relevant information for the topic of genetically engineered salmon.

Topics	Questions	Davis
Definition Categories Descriptions Definitions Explanations	*What is it?*	"The Kim Davis case involves one woman's dissent against the Supreme Court decision of 2015 legalizing gay marriage. The law says *X*, but Davis draws upon *Y*."
Comparison Similarities Differences Analogies Applications	*What is it like or unlike?*	"Other cases in which individuals defied the law because of conscience include *X*, *Y*, and *Z*. The Davis case is similar/different because . . ."
Relationship Antecedents Precedents Consequences Outcomes	*What caused it, and what will it cause?*	"The issue of gay marriage had been a state's rights issue but was unevenly applied across states. When the Court legalized it at the federal level, it required all public officials including judges and clerks to abide by the law, yet the result is . . ."
Testimony Statistics Maxims Laws Quotations	*What is known or said about it, especially by experts?*	"Supreme Court Justice Kennedy asserted in his opinion that the Constitution guarantees *X*, though Justice Scalia in his dissent said . . ."

Cavanaugh	Genetically Engineered Salmon
"The RLUIPA requires state prisons to provide religious accommodations under the First Amendment, which says X. Cavanaugh asserted his 'right' to . . ."	
"This case is like other challenges made by the FSM Church; however, since he is a prisoner asking for XYZ, Cavanaugh's case is different because . . ."	
"Prisoners deserve to exercise their religious freedom, but for most of U.S. history Christianity was the only available option, which violated the establishment clause . . ."	
"In American prisons, there are over X number of recognized religious groups, including Satanists and Wiccans. If they can have their rights, then . . ."	

religious, ethical, or personal preferences would be not to eat modified fish species. If the fish were properly labeled and people knew of any risks associated with eating it, they could avoid it if they wished.

Are there any animal rights issues at stake here? Is it okay to breed "only sterile females"? Critics say that scientists shouldn't create new kinds of animals. Is this even what AquaBounty is doing?

The author says we shouldn't worry about these fish breeding with other salmon, but is she understating the risks? I hadn't thought of the possibility, but clearly someone has. Is there an actual risk of threatening the natural species? If there was really zero risk, why are they bothering to breed only *sterile* females?

Maybe the FDA shouldn't have approved genetically modified salmon for food. If we start with the salmon, where will it end? What other foods are being reviewed for similar kinds of farming? Is this really the same as the development of corn and other vegetables, as the author suggests — or is animal life something different?

Doubtless there is much that we haven't asked or thought about, but we hope you'll agree that the issue deserves careful thought, given that the availability of genetically modified food animals has serious implications for the environment and the future of food production.

If you worked for the FDA and were part of this decision, you would *have* to think about these questions and issues. As a thought experiment, imagine you had to contribute to the decision about approving these fish. Try to put your tentative views into writing.

Note that you would want to get answers to questions such as the following:

- What sort of evidence exists about the safety of genetically engineered salmon? Who has studied it?
- What do biologists and bioethicists say about the genetically engineered salmon?

- What kind of people and organizations oppose the approval of this genetically engineered salmon, and what are their primary critiques?

Some of these questions require you to do **research** on the topic. Some raise issues of fact, and relevant evidence probably is available. In order to reach a conclusion in which you have confidence, you'll have to do some research to find out what the facts—the objective data—are. Merely explaining your position without giving the evidence will not be convincing.

Even without doing any research, however, you might want to look over the pros and cons, perhaps adding some new thoughts or modifying or even rejecting (for reasons that you can specify) some of those already given. If you do think further about this issue (and we hope that you will), notice an interesting point about *your own* thinking: It probably isn't *linear* (moving in a straight line from *A* to *B* to *C*) but *recursive*, moving from *A* to *C* and back to *B* or starting over at *C* and then back to *A* and *B*. By zigging and zagging almost despite yourself, you'll reach a conclusion that may finally seem correct. In retrospect, it might seem obvious; *now* you can chart a nice line from *A* to *B* to *C*—but that probably wasn't at all evident at the start.

✓ A CHECKLIST FOR CRITICAL THINKING

Attitudes:

☐ Does my thinking show imaginative open-mindedness and intellectual curiosity?

☐ Am I willing to examine my assumptions?

☐ Am I willing to entertain new ideas — both those that I encounter while reading and those that come to mind while writing?

☐ Am I willing to exert myself — for instance, to do research — to acquire information and to evaluate evidence?

Skills:

☐ Can I summarize an argument accurately?

☐ Can I evaluate assumptions, evidence, and inferences?

☐ Can I present my ideas effectively — for instance, by organizing and by writing in a manner appropriate to my imagined audience?

A SHORT ESSAY CALLING FOR CRITICAL THINKING

When reading an essay, we expect the writer to have thought carefully about the topic. We don't want to read every false start, every fuzzy thought, every ill-organized paragraph that the writer knocked off. Yes, writers make false starts, put down fuzzy thoughts, write ill-organized paragraphs; but then they revise and revise yet again, ultimately producing a readable essay that seems effortlessly written. Still—and this is our main point—writers of argumentative essays need to show readers that they have made some effort; they need to show *how* they got to their final (for the moment) views. It isn't enough for the writer to say, "I believe X"; rather, he or she must in effect say, "I believe X—and I hope you'll believe it also—because Y and Z, though attractive, just don't stand up to inquiry as well as X does. Y is superficially plausible, but . . . , and Z, which is an attractive alternative to Y, nevertheless fails because. . . ."

Notice in the following short essay—on employers using biometric devices to monitor employees' performance—that the author, Lynn Stuart Parramore, positions herself against these workplace technologies in a compelling way. As you read, think critically about how she presents her position, how she encourages readers to sympathize with her views. Ask questions about what she includes and excludes, whether she presents other perspectives amply or fairly, and what additional positions might be valid on these recent developments in the rapidly growing field of biometrics in business.

Lynn Stuart Parramore

Lynn Stuart Parramore is a contributing editor of AlterNet, *a frequent contributor to* Al-Jazeera America, Reuters, *and the* Huffington Post, *and a member of the editorial board of* Lapham's Quarterly. *Reprinted here is an essay published by* Al-Jazeera America *on September 18, 2015.*

Fitbits for Bosses

Imagine you've just arrived at your job with the Anywhere Bank call center. You switch on your computer and adjust the height of your chair. Then, you slide on the headset, positioning the mic in front of your lips. All that's left to do is to activate your behavior-monitoring device—the gadget hanging from your neck that tracks your tone of voice, your heart rate, and your physical movements throughout the day, sending real-time reports to your supervisor.

A scene from a dystopian movie? Nope. It's already happening in America. Welcome to the brave new world of workplace biosurveillance.

It's obvious that wearable tracking technology has gone mainstream: Just look at the explosion of smart watches and activity monitors that allow people to count steps and check their calorie intake. But this technology has simultaneously been creeping into workplaces: The military uses sensors that scan for injuries, monitor heart rate, and check hydration. More and more, professional athletes are strapping on devices that track every conceivable dimension of performance. Smart ice skates that measure a skater's jump. Clothes that measure an athlete's breathing and collect muscle data. At this year's tryouts in Indianapolis, some NFL hopefuls wore the "Adidas miCoach," a device that sends data on speed and acceleration straight to trainers' iPads. Over the objection of many athletes, coaches and team owners are keen to track off-the-field activity, too, such as sleep patterns and diet. With million-dollar players at stake, big money seems poised to trump privacy.

Now employers from industries that don't even require much physical labor are getting in on the game.

Finance is adopting sophisticated analytics to ensure business performance from high-dollar employees. Cambridge neuroscientist and former Goldman Sachs trader John Coates works with companies to figure out how monitoring biological signals can lead to trading success; his research focuses on measuring hormones that increase confidence and other desirable states as well as those that produce negative, stressful states. In a report for Bloomberg, Coates explained that he is working with "three or four hedge funds" to apply an "early-warning system" that would alert supervisors when traders are getting into the hormonal danger zone. He calls this process "human optimization." 5

People who do the most basic, underpaid work in our society are increasingly subject to physical monitoring, too—and it extends far beyond the ubiquitous urine test. Bank of America has started using smart badges that monitor the voice and behavior patterns of call-center workers, partnering with the creepily named Humanyze, a company specializing in "people analytics." Humanyze is the brainchild of the MIT Media Lab, the fancy research institute at the Massachusetts Institute of Technology dedicated to the "betterment of humanity," which, incidentally, receives a quarter of its funding from taxpayers. Humanyze concocted a computer dashboard complete with graphs and pie charts that can display the location of employees (Were you hanging out in the lounge today?) and their "social context" (Do you spend a lot of time alone?).

Humanyze founder Ben Waber points out that companies already spend enormous resources collecting analytics on their customers. Why not their employees?

A growing number of workers are being monitored by GPS, often installed on their smartphones. In the U.S. the Supreme Court ruled that law enforcement officials need a warrant to use GPS devices to track a suspect. But employers don't worry over such formalities in keeping tabs on employees, especially those who are mobile, such as truck drivers. A *Washington Post* report on GPS surveillance noted a 2012 study by the research firm Aberdeen Group, which showed that 62 percent of "field employees"—those who regularly perform duties away from the office—are tracked this way. In May, a California woman filed a lawsuit against her former employer, Intermex Wire Transfer, for forcing her to install a tracking app on her phone, which she was required to keep on 24/7. She described feeling like a prisoner wearing an ankle bracelet. After removing the app, the woman was fired.

Sensitive to Big Brother accusations, the biosurveillance industry is trying to keep testing and tool evaluations under the radar. Proponents of the technology point to its potential to improve health conditions in the workplace and enhance public safety. Wouldn't it be better, they argue, if nuclear power plant operators, airline pilots, and oil rig operatives had their physical state closely monitored on the job?

Young Americans nurtured in a digital world where their 10 behavior is relentlessly collected and monitored by advertisers may shrug at an employer's demands for a biosurveillance badge. In a world of insecure employment, what choice do they have, anyway? Despite the revelations of alarming National Security Agency spying and increased government and corporate surveillance since 9/11, the young haven't had much experience yet with what's at stake for them personally. What could possibly go wrong?

A lot: Surveillance has a way of dehumanizing workers. It prevents us from experimenting and exercising our creativity on the job because it tends to uphold the status quo and hold back change. Surveillance makes everyone seem suspicious, creating perceptions and expectations of dishonesty. It makes us feel manipulated. Some researchers have found that increased monitoring actually decreases productivity.

Philosopher and social theorist Michel Foucault observed that the relationship between the watcher and the watched is mostly about power. The power of the observer is enhanced, while the person observed feels more powerless. When an employer or manager interprets our personal data, she gets to make categorical judgments about us and determine how to predict our behavior.

What if she uses the information to discriminate? Coerce? Selectively apply the rules? The data she uses to make her judgments may not even be telling the truth: Researchers have warned that big data can produce big errors. People looking at numbers tend to use them to confirm their own biases, cherry-picking the information that supports their beliefs and ditching the rest. And since algorithms are constructed by human beings, they are not immune to human biases, either. A consumer might be labeled "unlikely to pay a credit card bill" because of an ethnic name, thus promulgating a harmful stereotype.

As Americans, we like to tell ourselves that we value freedom and undue interference from authority. But when we are subjected to surveillance, we feel disempowered and disrespected. We may be more inclined to accept the government getting involved because of fears about terrorism—but when it comes to surveillance on the job, our tendency to object may be chilled by weakened worker protections and increased employment insecurity.

Instead of producing an efficient and productive workplace, 15 biosurveillance may instead deliver troops of distracted, apathetic employees who feel loss of control and decreased job satisfaction. Instead of feeling like part of a team, surveilled workers may develop an us-versus-them mentality and look for opportunities to thwart the monitoring schemes of Big Boss.

Perhaps what we really need is biosurveillance from the bottom up—members of Congress and CEOs could don devices that could, say, detect when they are lying or how their hormones are behaving. Colorful PowerPoints could display the results of data collection on public billboards for the masses to pore over. In the name of safety and efficiency, maybe we ought to ensure that those whose behavior can do society the most harm do not escape the panopticon.   ■

Overall View of the Essay

Before we comment in detail on Parramore's essay, we need to say that in terms of the length of some of its paragraphs, it isn't necessarily a model for you to imitate. Material in print or online news sources is typically presented in very short paragraphs (notice Parramore's one-sentence-long paragraph 4). This is partly because people read it while eating breakfast or commuting to work, and in the case of print newspapers partly because the columns are narrow (a paragraph of only two or three sentences may still be an inch or two deep).

The title, "Fitbits for Bosses," is provocative, captures readers' attention, and leaves them with a sense of where Parramore's argument is heading.

Paragraph 1 compels readers by asking them to imagine an ordinary day at work, presenting the routine activities of getting work under way—turning on the computer, adjusting the chair—before throwing in the "behavior-monitoring device" almost as an afterthought, as if to shock us with the possibility that such devices could become routine.

Paragraph 2 presses the idea of invasion of privacy, almost aggressively, by using words like *dystopian* and a reference to a science fiction novel ("brave new world") whose title has become a shorthand for technological intrusions into individuals' lives.

Paragraph 3 presents as "obvious" the fact that self-monitoring technology has gone mainstream. (One of the authors of this book just purchased a new mobile device that came preinstalled with an application that records the number of steps and miles the user walks in a day. Going deeper into the menu, it includes functions for recording everything from nutrient intake to sexual activity.) The writer is clearly drawing on readers' familiarity with these technologies. Then she presents the portent of these devices "creeping" into the workplace, first by showing how such technologies have already been used in military applications and in businesses like professional sports. "So what?" we might think, but Parramore is about tell us.

Paragraph 4 is a single-sentence paragraph, turning the essay's focus from two specialized fields to the everyday jobs that millions of people hold. Notice how the language ("getting in on the game") reveals Parramore's position that this trend signals something new and troubling.

Paragraph 5 turns to the finance industry to show how some industries are beginning to monitor not just employee health but hormonal flows that have been correlated to emotional and psychological states. The dystopian theme is extended here as these technologies are presented as reaching into new realms where independent action and decision-making occur. Phrases like "human optimization" and references to an "early warning system" that would "alert supervisors" hint at potential limitations on human independence and deeper control of employees by managers.

Paragraph 6 focuses on Bank of America's partnership with Humanyze and shows more ways in which biosurveillance technologies could be used to monitor employees. Parramore is enhancing her argument through careful language use. In fact, her position is arguably coming most strongly through tone. What language cues indicate her position on these technologies? What specific words and phrases does she use ironically or sardonically?

Paragraph 7 quotes Humanyze's founder, Ben Waber, who rationally states that companies spend enormous amounts of money tracking consumers, so why not track employees too? But Parramore presents this statement as anything but appealing; instead, it comes across as a kind of dangerous rationality.

Paragraph 8 starts out by noting that the government doesn't permit law enforcement to do what employers regularly do in various industries. It cites a study showing how widespread the use of these devices is, and a case in which a woman lost her job by refusing to be monitored.

Paragraph 9 provides the defense offered by the industries that create these technologies, pointing out that some highly sensitive jobs such as power plant operator and airline pilot require the closest scrutiny of individuals' physical conditions.

Paragraph 10 mentions "Young Americans," raised in a digital world, who may just "shrug" at the latest developments in surveillance technology without realizing the implications to them personally. "What could go wrong?" Parramore asks.

Paragraph 11 answers that question, first with the word *dehumanizing*, then by claiming that surveillance dampens creativity and change, encourages suspicion, presumes dishonesty, and hurts productivity.

Paragraph 12 brings into the mix a philosopher, Michel Foucault—one of the twentieth century's most recognized theorists of power. Foucault leads Parramore to wonder about what kinds of power may be exercised by using the information gained from surveillance technology.

Paragraph 13 considers hypothetical scenarios in which a manager might be able to discriminate or coerce an employee by using collected data. Parramore seems to be asking how employees are protected from such strict oversight.

Paragraph 14 reminds readers that measurements are just measurements, prone to error and to biases that could lead to unfair or discriminatory uses of data.

Paragraph 15 presents a summary of the potentially harmful outcomes of widespread implementation of biometric surveillance of employees, pointing especially to decreased job satisfaction and an "us-versus-them" mentality among employees and employers.

Paragraph 16 drives home the author's point by offering a reversal of the expected order of surveillance arrangements. What if, Parramore suggests, the public demanded surveillance of those in power, especially since those in important managerial positions are presumably the ones whose behaviors and actions might impact the most people? The essay finishes with a suggestion that it is those in power who most need to be watched "in the name of safety and efficiency"—ostensibly the terms used to justify the practice as applied to workers.

TOPICS FOR CRITICAL THINKING AND WRITING

1. Do you think biometric measurement by employers is ever justified, or do the privacy and security of one's own body always trump the concerns of employers? Why, or why not?

2. If your teachers or parents could monitor the time you spent, and how you felt, while doing homework and studying, what benefits and drawbacks might result? What types of personal monitoring are already in place (or possible) in schools and homes, and are these different from biometric surveillance?

3. Do you think Lynn Parramore fairly portrays the founder of Humanyze and others who see potential in the possibilities for biometric monitoring? Why, or why not? In what other ways might biometric measurements help employees and employers?

4. List some examples of Parramore's use of language, word choice, and phrasing that would influence readers to be suspicious of biometric monitoring. How does this language make the essay more or less effective or convincing?

5. In what way does Parramore's recommendation in the final paragraph support or contradict her argument about individuals' basic rights to privacy?

EXAMINING ASSUMPTIONS

In Chapter 3, we will discuss **assumptions** in some detail, but here we introduce the topic by emphasizing the importance of *identifying* and *examining* assumptions—those you'll encounter in the writings of others and those you'll rely on in your own essays.

With this in mind, let's again consider some of the assumptions suggested in this chapter's earlier readings. The student who wrote about Stephen Cavanaugh's case pointed out that Nebraska prison officials simply did not see the Church of the Flying Spaghetti Monster as a real religion. Their assumption was that some religions can be more or less "real" than others or can make more sense than others. Assumptions may be *explicit* or *implicit*, stated or unstated. In this case, the prison officials were forthright about their assumptions in their stated claim about the Church, perhaps believing their point was obvious to anyone who thought seriously about the idea of a Flying Spaghetti Monster. It didn't occur to them to consider that even major and mainstream religions honor stories, claims, and rituals that seem absurd to others.

An implicit assumption is one that is not stated but, rather, is taken for granted. It works like an underlying belief that structures an argument. In Lynn Stuart Parramore's essay on workplace biometric devices, the unstated assumption is that these sorts of technology in the workplace represent a kind of evil "big brother" intent on subduing and exploiting employees with newer and newer forms of invasion of privacy. Parramore's assumption, while not stated directly, is evident in her choice of language, as we've pointed out above. Another way to discern her assumption is by looking at the scenarios and selections of examples she chooses. For example, in imagining a company that would seek to know how much time an employee spends in the lounge area or alone, Parramore sees only obsessive monitoring of employees for the purposes of regulating their time. But what if these technologies could enable a company to discover that productivity or worker satisfaction increases in proportion to the amount of time employees spend collaborating in the lounge? Maybe workplace conditions would improve instead of deteriorating (a bigger lounge, more comfortable chairs), and

✓ A CHECKLIST FOR EXAMINING ASSUMPTIONS

☐ What assumptions does the writer's argument presuppose?

☐ Are these assumptions explicit or implicit?

☐ Are these assumptions important to the author's argument, or are they only incidental?

☐ Does the author give any evidence of being aware of the hidden assumptions in her or his argument?

☐ Would a critic be likely to share these assumptions, or are they exactly what a critic would challenge?

☐ What sort of evidence would be relevant to supporting or rejecting these assumptions?

☐ Am I willing to grant the author's assumptions? Would most readers grant them?

☐ If not, why not?

maybe more efforts would be made for team-building and improving interpersonal employee relations.

Consider now two of the assumptions involved in the Kim Davis case. Thanks to the clustering exercise (p. 7), these and other assumptions are already on display. Perhaps the most important and fundamental assumption Davis and her supporters made is this:

> Where private religious beliefs conflict with duly enacted laws, the former should prevail.

This assumption is widely held in our society; it is by no means unique to Davis and her supporters. Opponents, however, probably assumed a very different but equally fundamental proposition:

> Private religious practices and beliefs must yield to the demands of laws guaranteeing citizens equal rights.

Obviously, these two assumptions are opposed to each other, and neither side can prevail so long as the key assumption of the other side is ignored.

Assumptions can be powerful sources of ideas and opinions, and understanding our own and others' assumptions is a major part of critical thinking. Assumptions about race, class, disability, sex, and gender are among the most powerful sources of social inequality. The following essay arguing that women should be permitted to serve in combat roles in the military was published in 2012, well before the Department of Defense lifted the ban on women in combat roles in the armed forces in 2013. More recently, Defense Secretary Ashton Carter further lifted exclusions pertaining to women by granting them access to serve in all capacities in combat, including in elite special forces units. Following that development, General Lori J. Robinson made history as the first female combatant commander when she was appointed leader of the North American Aerospace Defense Command and U.S. Northern Command in Colorado in May 2016. Still, we reprint McGregor's essay because it compels readers to consider some of their assumptions about women (and men). Topics for discussion appear after the essay.

Jena McGregor

Jena McGregor, a graduate of the University of Georgia, is a freelance writer and a daily columnist for the Washington Post. *This article was published on May 25, 2012.*

Military Women in Combat: Why Making It Official Matters

It's been a big couple of weeks for women in the military.

Last week, female soldiers began formally moving into jobs in previously all-male battalions, a program that will later go Army-wide. The move is a result of rule changes following a February report that opened some 14,000 new positions to women in critical jobs much closer to the front lines. However, some 250,000 combat jobs still remain officially closed to them.

The same week, Rep. Loretta Sanchez (D, Calif.) and Sen. Kirsten Gillibrand (D, N.Y.) introduced legislation in both houses of Congress that would encourage the "repeal of the Ground Combat Exclusion policy" for women in the armed forces. Then this Wednesday, two female U.S. Army reservists filed a lawsuit that seeks to overturn the remaining restrictions on women in combat, saying they limit "their current and future earnings, their potential for promotion and advancement, and their future retirement benefits." (A Pentagon spokesperson told Bloomberg News that Defense Secretary Leon Panetta "is strongly committed to examining the expansion of roles for women in the U.S. military, as evidenced by the recent step of opening up thousands of more assignments to women.")

One of the arguments behind both the lawsuit and the new legislation is that the remaining restrictions hurt women's opportunities for advancement. Advocates for women in the military say that even if women like Gen. Ann Dunwoody have reached four-star general status, she and women like her without official frontline combat experience apparently haven't been considered for the military's very highest posts. "If women remain restricted to combat service and combat service support specialties, we will not see a woman as Commandant of the Marine Corps, or CENTCOM commander, or Chairman of the Joint Chiefs of Staff," writes Greg Jacob, policy director for the Service Women's Action Network. "Thus women in the military are being held back simply because they are women. Such an idea is not only completely at odds with military ethics, but is distinctly un-American."

Women have been temporarily "attached" to battalions for the 5 last decade; still, allowing women to formally serve in combat operations could help to break down the so-called brass ceiling.

Another way to break down the ceiling would be to consider talented women for top military leadership positions, whether or not they've officially held certain combat posts. Presidents have chosen less-senior officers for Joint Chiefs roles, which are technically staff jobs, wrote Laura Conley and Lawrence Korb, a former assistant defense secretary in the Reagan administration and a senior fellow at the Center for American Progress, in the *Armed Forces Journal* last year. They argue that putting a woman on the Joint Chiefs would help the military grapple with rising sexual harassment issues, bring nontraditional expertise (which women have developed because of some of their role exclusions) at a time when that's increasingly critical, and send the signal that the military is not only open to women, but puts no barriers in their way.

Yes, putting women in combat roles beyond those that have been recently formalized would require many adjustments, both logistical and psychological, for the military and for its male troops. There are plenty of women who may not be interested in these jobs, or who do not meet the physical demands required of them. And gradual change may be prudent. The recent openings are a start; Army Chief of Staff Ray Odierno's acknowledgment last week that if women are allowed into infantry, they will at some point probably go through Ranger School, is encouraging.

But at a time when experience like the infantry is reportedly crucial for getting top posts, it's easy to see how official and sizable policy changes are needed in order to create a system that lets talented women advance to the military's highest echelons. In any field where there are real or perceived limitations for women's advancement, it's that much harder to attract the best and brightest. Indeed, the Military Leadership Diversity Commission recommended last March that the services end combat exclusion policies for women, along with other "barriers and inconsistencies, to create a level playing field for all qualified service members." As the commission chairman, Retired Air Force Gen. Lester L. Lyles, told the American Forces Press Service at the time, "we know that [the exclusion] hinders women from promotion."

For the military to achieve the diverse workforce it seeks, interested and capable women should either not face exclusions, or the culture of the armed forces needs to change so that women without that particular experience can still reach the very top. Both changes may be difficult, but the latter is extraordinarily so. Ending the restrictions is the shortest route to giving the military the best pool of talent possible and the most diverse viewpoints for leading it.   ■

TOPICS FOR CRITICAL THINKING AND WRITING

1. How would you characterize Jena McGregor's tone (her manner)? Is it thoughtful? Pushy? Identify passages that support your view.

2. Explain the term *brass ceiling* (para. 5).

3. One argument *against* sending women onto an actual battlefield, as infantry or as members of a tank crew, is that if they're captured they might be gang-raped. In your view, how significant is this argument? Explain your response.

4. Here is a second argument against sending women into direct combat: Speaking generally, women do not have the upper-body strength that men have, and a female soldier (again, speaking generally, not about a particular individual) would thus be less able to pull a wounded companion out of a burning tank or off a battlefield. To put the matter differently: Male soldiers might feel that they couldn't count on their female comrades in a time of need. What is your reply?

5. In her final paragraph, McGregor suggests that if the armed forces were to change their policy and not require battlefield experience for the very highest jobs, the military would achieve diversity at the top and women would have an opportunity for top pay. What are your thoughts? For instance, is the idea that the top officers should have experienced hand-to-hand combat out of date, romantic, hopelessly macho, or irrelevant to modern warfare? Explain.

6. What do you make of the following question? Since women are now permitted to serve in all military combat positions, should all women, like all men, have to register for Selective Service and be subject to the military draft, if one were needed? Construct an argument to defend your position on this question.

Four Exercises in Critical Thinking

As you draft essays for one or more of the assignments, consider typing your notes in a Google document or in Microsoft OneNote, or using another collaborative application or service (perhaps offered free by your school), so that you can easily share your thoughts and writing on the topic. As always, submit and complete assignments in the way that your instructor directs. However, remember that services such as Google and OneNote can be good places to maintain copies of your notes and essays for later consultation.

1. Think further about the issues of privacy and surveillance raised by Lynn Parramore's essay. Consider several different kinds of work, types of employers, and the various types of employee monitoring that do or may occur. Jot down pros and cons, and then write a balanced dialogue between two imagined speakers who hold opposing views on the issue. You'll doubtless have to revise your dialogue several times, and in revising your drafts you'll likely come up with further ideas. Present *both* sides as strongly as possible. (You may want to give the two speakers distinct characters; for instance, one may be an employer seeking to introduce a new technology, and the other may be an employee intent on protecting his privacy and freedom. Alternatively, one could be an employee looking forward to a new "healthy workplace" initiative using biometrics, and the other could be a colleague suspicious of the new program.)

2. Choose one of the following topics, and write down all the pro and con arguments you can think of in, say, ten minutes. Then, at

least an hour or two later, return to your notes and see whether you can add to them. Finally, as in Exercise 1, write a balanced dialogue, presenting each idea as strongly as possible. (If none of these topics interests you, ask your instructor about the possibility of choosing a topic of your own.) Suggested topics:

a. Colleges with large athletic programs should pay student athletes a salary or stipend.

b. Bicyclists and motorcyclists should be required by law to wear helmets.

c. High school teachers should have the right to carry concealed firearms in schools.

d. Smoking should be prohibited on all college campuses, including in all buildings *and* outdoors.

e. College students should have the right to request alternative assignments from their professors if class material is offensive or traumatic.

f. Students should have the right to drop out of school at any age.

g. Sororities and fraternities should be coeducational (allowing both males and females).

h. The government should tax sugary foods and drinks in order to reduce obesity.

3. In April 2012, Williams College in Williamstown, Massachusetts, hosted a lecture and film screening of work by Jiz Lee, described in campus advertisements as a "genderqueer porn star." After inviting the adult entertainer to campus, the college came under fire by some students and members of the public (especially after the story was reported by national media). Opponents questioned the appropriateness and academic value of the event, which was brought to campus by the Mike Dively Committee, an endowment established to help "develop understanding of human sexuality and sexual orientation and their impact on culture." Proponents argued that (1) pornography is a subject that deserves critical analysis and commentary; (2) the Dively series is intended to create conversations about sexuality and sexual orientation in society and culture; and (3) treating any potential subject in an academic setting under the circumstances of the program is appropriate. What are your views? Should adult film stars ever be invited to college campuses? Should pornography constitute a subject of analysis on campus? Why, or why not?

Imagine you're a student member of the campus programming board, and the Gender and Sexuality Program comes to your committee seeking funds to invite a female former adult film star to campus to lecture on "The Reality of Pornography." Faculty and student sponsors have assured your committee that the visit by the actress in question is part of an effort to educate students and the public about the adult film industry and its impact on popular culture. Images and short film clips may be shown. Pose as many questions as you can about the potential benefits and risks of approving this invitation. How would you vote, and why? (If you can find a peer who has an opposing view, construct a debate on the issue.)

4. In 1985, the U.S. Congress passed the National Minimum Drinking Age Act, mandating that all states implement and enforce raising the minimum drinking age from eighteen to twenty-one years. Through this legislation, the United States became one of a handful of developed countries to have such a high drinking age. In 2009, John McCardell, president of Middlebury College in Vermont, wrote a declaration signed by 135 college presidents supporting returning the drinking age to eighteen. McCardell's organization, Choose Responsibly, says that people age eighteen to twenty should be treated as the adults they are—for example, in terms of voting, serving on juries and in the military, or buying legal weapons. The organization encourages educational programs and awareness efforts that would introduce alcohol-related issues to young college students and demystify and discourage problem drinking. Such a move is opposed by Mothers Against Drunk Drivers (MADD), whose members argue that raising the drinking age to twenty-one has curbed traffic accidents and fatalities caused by drunk driving. Opponents to lowering the drinking age also claim that it would introduce alcohol to even younger people, as many eighteen-year-olds would inevitably interact in social situations with underage peers. Argue for the age you think might be the best legal minimum—eighteen, or twenty-one, or something in between?—trying to anticipate and address the counterarguments that will be made against your position.

2

Critical Reading: Getting Started

> *Some books are to be tasted, others to be swallowed, and some few to be chewed and digested.*
>
> —FRANCIS BACON

ACTIVE READING

In the passage that we quote above, Bacon makes two good points. One is that books are of varying worth; the second is that a taste of some books may be enough.

But even a book (or an essay) that you will chew and digest is one that you first may want to taste. How can you get a taste—that is, how can you get some sense of a piece of writing—*before* you sit down to read it carefully?

Previewing

Even before reading a work, you may have some ideas about it, perhaps because you already know something about the **author**. You know, for example, that a work by Martin Luther King Jr. will probably deal with civil rights. You know, too, that it will be serious and eloquent. In contrast, if you pick up an essay by Stephen King, you'll probably expect it to be about fear, the craft of writing, or his experiences as a horror novelist. It may be about something else, but it's probable the essay will follow your expectations. For one thing, you know that King writes for a broad audience, so his essay won't be terribly difficult to understand.

In short, a reader who has knowledge of the author probably has some idea of what the subject will be and what the writing will be like, so the reader approaches it in a certain light. But even if you don't know the author, you can often discern important information about him or her by looking at biographical information provided in the text or by doing a quick Internet search. You can use this information to predict not only the essay's subject and style but also the author's approach to the topic, which helps when trying to diagnose assumptions and biases, among other things.

The **place of publication** may also reveal something about the essay in terms of its subject, style, and approach. For instance, the *National Review* is a conservative journal. If you notice that an essay on affirmative action was published in the *National Review*, you're probably safe in tentatively assuming that the essay will not endorse affirmative action. In contrast, *Ms.* magazine is a liberal publication, and an essay on affirmative action published there will probably be an endorsement. You often can learn a good deal about a journal or magazine simply by flipping through it and noticing the kinds of articles and advertisements in it.

The **title** of an essay, too, may give an idea of what to expect. Of course, a title may announce only the subject and not the author's thesis or point of view ("On Gun Control"; "Should Drugs Be Legal?"), but fairly often it will indicate the thesis too (as in "Give Children the Vote" or "We Need Campaign Finance Reform Now"). By knowing more or less what to expect, you can probably take in some of the major points even on a quick reading.

When engaging with an essay, you can also consider the role of **context**—the situational conditions in which it was written. Context can refer to the time period, geographical location, cultural climate, political environment, or any other setting for a piece of writing. Recognizing the context of any piece of writing can reveal a lot about how an author treats a subject. For example, an essay written before September 11, 2001, about how to contain global terrorism might have a less urgent approach and advocate more lenient measures than one written today. An article about transgender identity or police brutality might convey different assumptions about those topics depending on whether it was written before or after Bruce Jenner publicly became Caitlyn Jenner, for instance, or before or after the events of Ferguson, Missouri, brought the issue of race and police violence into the public's consciousness in new ways.

Anything you read exists in at least two broad contexts: the context of its *production* (where and when it was written or published) and the context of its *consumption* (where and when it is encountered and read). One thing all good critical thinkers do when considering the validity of claims and arguments is to take *both* types of context into account. This means asking questions not only about the approach, assumptions, and beliefs that were in place when an essay was written, but also about how current events and understandings generate new issues and challenges within the subject of the essay. The state of affairs in the time and place in which that argument is made *and received* shapes the questions you might ask, the evidence you might consider, and the responses you might produce.

Notice that you can apply these previewing techniques before reading a single word of the essay. And once you have a good sense of the what, who, where, and when of an essay, you should keep them in mind while reading.

Your first reading might involve another previewing technique, **skimming**. Sometimes, you can find the **thesis** (the main point or major claim) of an essay by looking at the first paragraph. Other times, especially if the paragraphs are short, you can locate the thesis within the first several paragraphs. Depending on what you discover while skimming, you can speed up or slow down your reading as needed while you locate the thesis and get a sense of how the argument for it is structured. If the essay has sections, pay attention to *headings* and *subheadings*. Look for key expressions that indicate an author's conclusive statements, such as "Finally, then, it is time that we . . ." or "Given this evidence, it is clear that. . . ." These kinds of sentences frequently appear at the beginnings or endings of paragraphs and sections. Final paragraphs are particularly important because they often summarize the argument and restate the thesis.

By previewing and skimming effectively, you can quickly ascertain quite a bit of information about an article or essay. You can detect the author's claims and methods, see the evidence he or she uses (experience, statistics, quotations, etc.), ascertain the tone and difficulty level, and determine whether the piece of writing offers useful ideas for you. This strategy works well if you're researching a topic and need to review many essays—you can read efficiently to find those that are most important or relevant to you, or those that offer different perspectives. Of course, if you do find an essay to be compelling during previewing, you can begin "chewing and digesting," as Francis Bacon put it—reading more closely and carefully (or else putting it aside for later when you can give it more time).

Call-out: Critical Reading Tip   Instead of imagining previewing and close reading as two separate stages to be completed consecutively, think of previewing as an activity that might at any time develop into close reading.

A Short Essay for Previewing Practice

Before skimming the following essay, apply the previewing techniques discussed above, and complete the Thinking Critically: Previewing activity on page 53.

Sanjay Gupta

Dr. Sanjay Gupta (b. 1969) is a neurosurgeon and multiple Emmy award–winning television personality. As a leading public health expert, he has appeared widely on television, including the Oprah Winfrey Show, *the* Late Show with David Letterman, *the* Jon Stewart Show, *and* 60 Minutes. *He is most well known as CNN's chief medical correspondent. In 2011, Forbes magazine named him one of the ten most influential celebrities in America. The essay reprinted below originally appeared on CNN.com in August 2013.*

Why I Changed My Mind on Weed

Over the last year, I have been working on a new documentary called "Weed." The title "Weed" may sound cavalier, but the content is not.

I traveled around the world to interview medical leaders, experts, growers and patients. I spoke candidly to them, asking tough questions. What I found was stunning.

Long before I began this project, I had steadily reviewed the scientific literature on medical marijuana from the United States and thought it was fairly unimpressive. Reading these papers five years ago, it was hard to make a case for medicinal marijuana. I even wrote about this in a *Time* magazine article, back in 2009, titled "Why I Would Vote No on Pot."

Well, I am here to apologize.

I apologize because I didn't look hard enough, until now. I   5
didn't look far enough. I didn't review papers from smaller labs in other countries doing some remarkable research, and I was too dismissive of the loud chorus of legitimate patients whose symptoms improved on cannabis.

Instead, I lumped them with the high-visibility malingerers, just looking to get high. I mistakenly believed the Drug Enforcement Agency listed marijuana as a Schedule 1 substance because of sound scientific proof. Surely, they must have quality reasoning as to why marijuana is in the category of the most dangerous drugs that have "no accepted medicinal use and a high potential for abuse."

They didn't have the science to support that claim, and I now know that when it comes to marijuana neither of those things are true. It doesn't have a high potential for abuse, and there are very legitimate medical applications. In fact, sometimes marijuana is the only thing that works. Take the case of Charlotte Figi, whom I met in Colorado. She started having seizures soon after birth. By age 3, she was having 300 a week, despite being on 7 different medications. Medical marijuana has calmed her brain, limiting her seizures to 2 or 3 per month.

I have seen more patients like Charlotte first hand, spent time with them and come to the realization that it is irresponsible not to provide the best care we can as a medical community, care that could involve marijuana.

We have been terribly and systematically misled for nearly 70 years in the United States, and I apologize for my own role in that.

I hope this article and upcoming documentary will help set the 10 record straight.

On August 14, 1970, the Assistant Secretary of Health, Dr. Roger O. Egeberg, wrote a letter recommending the plant, marijuana, be classified as a Schedule 1 substance, and it has remained that way for nearly 45 years. My research started with a careful reading of that decades-old letter. What I found was unsettling. Egeberg had carefully chosen his words:

"Since there is still a considerable void in our knowledge of the plant and effects of the active drug contained in it, our recommendation is that marijuana be retained within Schedule 1 at least until the completion of certain studies now under way to resolve the issue."

Not because of sound science, but because of its absence, marijuana was classified as a Schedule 1 substance. Again, the year was 1970. Egeberg mentions studies that are under way, but many were never completed. As my investigation continued, however, I realized Egeberg did in fact have important research already available to him, some of it from more than 25 years earlier.

HIGH RISK OF ABUSE

In 1944, New York mayor Fiorello LaGuardia commissioned research to be performed by the New York Academy of Science. Among their conclusions: they found marijuana did not lead to significant addiction in the medical sense of the word. They also did not find any evidence marijuana led to morphine, heroin or cocaine addiction.

We now know that while estimates vary, marijuana leads to 15 dependence in around 9 to 10% of its adult users. By comparison, cocaine, a Schedule 2 substance "with less abuse potential than Schedule 1 drugs," hooks 20% of those who use it. Around 25% of heroin users become addicted.

The worst is tobacco, where the number is closer to 30% of smokers, many of whom go on to die because of their addiction.

There is clear evidence that in some people marijuana use can lead to withdrawal symptoms, including insomnia, anxiety and nausea. Even considering this, it is hard to make a case that it has a high potential for abuse. The physical symptoms of marijuana addiction are nothing like those of the other drugs I've mentioned. I have seen the withdrawal from alcohol, and it can be life threatening.

I do want to mention a concern that I think about as a father. Young, developing brains are likely more susceptible to harm from marijuana than adult brains. Some recent studies suggest that regular use in teenage years leads to a permanent decrease in IQ. Other research hints at a possible heightened risk of developing psychosis.

Much in the same way I wouldn't let my own children drink alcohol, I wouldn't permit marijuana until they are adults. If they are adamant about trying marijuana, I will urge them to wait until they're in their mid-20s, when their brains are fully developed.

MEDICAL BENEFIT

While investigating, I realized something else quite impor- 20 tant. Medical marijuana is not new, and the medical community has been writing about it for a long time. There were in fact hundreds of journal articles, mostly documenting the benefits. Most of those papers, however, were written between the years 1840 and 1930. The papers described the use of medical marijuana to treat "neuralgia, convulsive disorders, emaciation," among other things.

A search through the U.S. National Library of Medicine this past year pulled up nearly 20,000 more recent papers. But the majority were research into the harm of marijuana, such as "Bad trip due to anticholinergic effect of cannabis," or "Cannabis induced pancreatitis" and "Marijuana use and risk of lung cancer."

In my quick running of the numbers, I calculated about 6% of the current U.S. marijuana studies investigate the benefits of medical marijuana. The rest are designed to investigate harm. That imbalance paints a highly distorted picture.

THE CHALLENGES OF MARIJUANA RESEARCH

To do studies on marijuana in the United States today, you need two important things.

First of all, you need marijuana. And marijuana is illegal. You see the problem. Scientists can get research marijuana from a special farm in Mississippi, which is astonishingly located in the middle of the Ole Miss campus, but it is challenging. When I visited this year, there was no marijuana being grown.

The second thing you need is approval, and the scientists I 25 interviewed kept reminding me how tedious that can be. While a cancer study may first be evaluated by the National Cancer Institute, or a pain study may go through the National Institute for Neurological Disorders, there is one more approval required for marijuana: NIDA, the National Institute on Drug Abuse. It is an organization that has a core mission of studying drug abuse, as opposed to benefit.

Stuck in the middle are the legitimate patients who depend on marijuana as a medicine, oftentimes as their only good option.

Keep in mind that up until 1943, marijuana was part of the United States drug pharmacopeia. One of the conditions for which it was prescribed was neuropathic pain. It is a miserable pain that's tough to treat. My own patients have described it as "lancinating, burning and a barrage of pins and needles." While marijuana has long been documented to be effective for this awful pain, the most common medications prescribed today come from the poppy plant, including morphine, oxycodone and dilaudid.

Here is the problem. Most of these medications don't work very well for this kind of pain, and tolerance is a real problem.

Most frightening to me is that someone dies in the United States every 19 minutes from a prescription drug overdose, mostly accidental. Every 19 minutes. It is a horrifying statistic. As much as

I searched, I could not find a documented case of death from marijuana overdose.

It is perhaps no surprise then that 76% of physicians recently 30 surveyed said they would approve the use of marijuana to help ease a woman's pain from breast cancer.

When marijuana became a Schedule 1 substance, there was a request to fill a "void in our knowledge." In the United States, that has been challenging because of the infrastructure surrounding the study of an illegal substance, with a drug abuse organization at the heart of the approval process. And yet, despite the hurdles, we have made considerable progress that continues today.

Looking forward, I am especially intrigued by studies like those in Spain and Israel looking at the anti-cancer effects of marijuana and its components. I'm intrigued by the neuro-protective study by Lev Meschoulam in Israel, and research in Israel and the United States on whether the drug might help alleviate symptoms of PTSD. I promise to do my part to help, genuinely and honestly, fill the remaining void in our knowledge.

Citizens in 20 states and the District of Columbia have now voted to approve marijuana for medical applications, and more states will be making that choice soon. As for Dr. Roger Egeberg, who wrote that letter in 1970, he passed away 16 years ago.

I wonder what he would think if he were alive today.   ■

The "First and Last" Rule   As noted previously, authors often place main points of emphasis at the beginnings and endings of *essays*. They also place important material at the beginnings and endings of *paragraphs* and *sentences*.

When writing, you can emphasize main points by using the first and last rule. Don't bury your most important material in the middle of sentences, paragraphs, or entire papers. Make it stand out.

Consider the following observations. Select two that you find to be most important.

1. Gupta is one of the most respected voices in public health.
2. Gupta argues for the legalization of medical marijuana.
3. Gupta's article was written for CNN News in 2011.
4. Gupta rejects his previous position on medical marijuana and apologizes for his oversight.
5. The article was important because it represented a shift in approach by a leading doctor.

THINKING CRITICALLY PREVIEWING

Provide the missing information for Sanjay Gupta and his essay "Why I Changed My Mind on Weed."

Previewing Strategies	Types of Questions	Answers
Author	Who is he? What expertise does he have? What credibility does he have? How difficult is the writing likely to be?	
Title	What does the title reveal about the essay's content? Does it give any clues about how the argument will take shape?	
Place of Publication	How does the place of publication help you understand the argument? What type of audiences will it be likely to target?	
Context	By placing the article in the context of its time — given trends in the conversations about or popular understandings of the subject — what can you expect about the author's position?	
Skimming	As you skim over the first several paragraphs, where do you first realize the purpose of the essay? What is Gupta's argument? What major forms of evidence does he offer?	

Now arrange these statements in a short paragraph, using the first and last rule to emphasize the two that you selected as most important. Compare your paragraph to your classmates' paragraphs. How do they compare?

Reading with a Careful Eye: Underlining, Highlighting, Annotating

Once you have a general idea of the work—not only an idea of its topic and thesis but also a sense of the way in which the thesis is argued—you can go back and start reading it carefully.

As you read, **underline** or **highlight** key passages, and make **annotations** in the margins. Because you're reading actively, or interacting with the text, you won't simply let your eye rove across the page.

- Highlight what seem to be the chief points, so that later when reviewing the essay you can easily locate the main passages.
- But don't overdo a good thing. If you find yourself highlighting most of a page, you're probably not thinking carefully enough about what the key points are.
- Similarly, your marginal annotations should be brief and selective. They will probably consist of hints or clues, comments like "doesn't follow," "good," "compare with Jones," "check this," and "really?"
- In short, in a paragraph you might highlight a key definition, and in the margin you might write "good," or "in contrast," or "?" if you think the definition is unclear or incorrect.
- With many electronic formats, you can use tools to highlight or annotate. Also consider copying and pasting passages that you would normally highlight in a Google document. Include a link to the piece, and create an RSS feed to the journal's Web site. Having your notes in an electronic format makes it easy to access and use them later.

In all these ways, you interact with the text and lay the groundwork for eventually writing your own essay on what you have read.

What you annotate will depend largely on your **purpose**. If you're reading an essay in order to see how the writer organizes an argument, you'll annotate one sort of thing. If you're reading in order to challenge the thesis, you'll annotate other things. Here is a passage from an essay entitled "On Racist Speech," with a student's rather skeptical, even aggressive, annotations. But notice that the student apparently made at least one of the annotations—"Definition of 'fighting words'"—chiefly in order to remind herself to locate where the definition of an important term appears in the essay. The essay is by Charles R. Lawrence III, a professor of law at Georgetown University. It originally appeared in the *Chronicle of Higher Education* (October 25, 1989), a publication read chiefly by college and university faculty members and administrators.

Example of such a policy?

University officials who have formulated <u>policies</u> to respond to incidents of racial harassment have been characterized in the press as "thought police," but such policies generally do nothing more than impose ⟨sanctions⟩ against intentional face-to-face insults. When <u>racist speech</u> takes the form of <u>face-to-face insults</u>, catcalls, or other assaultive speech aimed at an individual or small group of persons, it falls directly within the "<u>fighting words</u>" exception to First Amendment protection. The Supreme Court has held that <u>words "which 'by their very utterance inflict</u> injury or tend to incite an immediate breach of the peace'"</u> are not protected by the First Amendment.

?

Example?

What about sexist speech?

Definition of "fighting words"

If the purpose of the First Amendment is to foster the greatest amount of speech, racial insults disserve that purpose. Assaultive racist speech functions as a preemptive strike. The <u>invective is experienced as a blow, not as a proffered idea,</u> and once the blow is struck, it is unlikely that a dialogue will follow. Racial insults are particularly undeserving of First Amendment protection because the perpetrator's <u>intention is not to discover truth</u> or initiate dialogue but to injure the victim. <u>In most situations,</u> members of minority groups realize that they are likely to lose if they respond to epithets by fighting and are forced to remain silent and submissive.

Really? Probably depends on the individual.

Why must speech always seek "to discover truth"?

How does he know?

"This; Therefore, That"

To arrive at a coherent thought or series of thoughts that will lead to a reasonable conclusion, a writer has to go through a good deal of preliminary effort. When we discussed heuristics in Chapter 1 (p. 20), we talked about patterns of thought that stimulate initial ideas. The path to sound conclusions involves similar thought patterns that carry forward the arguments presented in the essay:

- While these arguments are convincing, they fail to consider . . .
- While these arguments are convincing, they must also consider . . .
- These arguments, rather than being convincing, instead prove . . .
- While these authors agree, in my opinion . . .
- Although it is often true that . . .

- Consider also . . .
- What sort of audience would agree with such an argument?
- What sort of audience would be opposed?
- What are the differences in values between these two kinds of audiences?

All of these patterns can serve as heuristics or prompts — that is, they can stimulate the creation of ideas.

Moreover, for the writer to convince the reader that the conclusion is sound, the reasoning behind the conclusion must be set forth in detail, with a good deal of "This; therefore, that"; "If this, then that"; and "Others might object at this point that. . . ." The arguments in this book require more comment than President Calvin Coolidge supposedly provided when his wife, who hadn't been able to attend church one Sunday, asked him what the preacher talked about in his sermon. "Sin," Coolidge said. His wife persisted: "What did the preacher say about it?" Coolidge's response: "He was against it."

But, again, when we say that most of the arguments in this book are presented at length and require careful reading, we don't mean that they are obscure; we mean, rather, that you have to approach the sentences thoughtfully, one by one. In this vein, recall an episode from Lewis Carroll's *Through the Looking-Glass:*

> "Can you do Addition?" the White Queen asked. "What's one and one and one and one and one and one and one and one and one and one?"
>
> "I don't know," said Alice. "I lost count."
>
> "She can't do Addition," the Red Queen said.

Universal Images Group/Getty Images

Alice with the Red Queen and the White Queen

It's easy enough to add one and one and one and so on, and of course Alice can do addition — but not at the pace that the White Queen sets. Fortunately, you can set your own pace in reading the cumulative thinking set forth in the essays we reprint in this book. Skimming won't work, but slow reading—and thinking about what you're reading—will.

When you first pick up an essay, you may indeed want to skim it, for some of the reasons mentioned on page 53, but sooner or later you have to settle down to read it and think about it. The effort will be worthwhile. Consider what John Locke, a seventeenth-century English philosopher, said:

> *Reading* furnishes the mind with materials of knowledge; it is *thinking* [that] makes what we read ours. We are of the ruminating kind, and it is not enough to cram ourselves with a great load of collections; unless we chew them over again they will not give us strength and nourishment.

Often students read an essay just once, supposing that to reread would be repetitious. But much can be gleaned from a second reading, as new details will likely emerge and new ideas will be generated. Roland Barthes, a twentieth-century philosopher, warned against accepting a first reading as final. Far from being repetitive, "[r]e-reading," he wrote, "*saves* the text from repetition, multiplies it in its variety and plurality." What may actually be repetitious is reading something only once and, thinking you have it pinned down, repeating it (in your writing) and thereby sticking to your first and only impression.

Defining Terms and Concepts

Suppose you're reading an argument about whether a certain set of images is pornography or art. For the present purpose, let's use a famous example from 1992, when American photographer Sally Mann published *Immediate Family*, a controversial book featuring numerous images of her three children (then ages 12, 10, and 7) in various states of nakedness during their childhood on a rural Kentucky farm. Mann is considered a great photographer and artist ("America's Best Photographer," according to *Time* magazine in 2001), and *Immediate Family* is very well regarded in the art community ("one of the great photograph books of our time," according to the *New Republic*). But some critics couldn't separate the images of Mann's own naked children from the label "child pornography."

When reading, attend carefully to how terms and concepts are used for the purposes of advancing an argument. In this case, you might begin by asking, "What is *pornography*? What is *art*?" If writers and readers cannot agree on basic definitions of the terms and concepts that structure the debate, then argument is futile. And if an author doesn't share *your* definition of a term or concept, then you might challenge the premise of his or her argument. If someone were to define pornography to include *any* images of nude children, that definition would include photographs taken for any reason—medical, sociological, anthropological, scientific—and would include even the innocent photographs taken by proud parents of their children swimming, bathing, and so on. It would also apply to some of the world's great art. Most people do not seriously think the mere image of the naked body, adult or child, is pornography.

Pornography is often defined according to its intended effect on the viewer ("genital commotion," Father Harold Gardiner, S.J., called it in *Catholic Viewpoint on Censorship*). In this definition, if images are eroticized (i.e., made erotic through style or symbolism), if they invite a sexual gaze, they are pornographic. This seems to be the definition that novelist Mary Gordon applied in a 1996 critique of Sally Mann:

> Unless we believe it is ethically permissible for adults to have sex with children, we must question the ethics of an art which allows the adult who has the most power over these children—a parent, in this case a mother—to place them in a situation where they become the imagined sexual partner of adults. . . . It is inevitable that Sally Mann's photographs arouse the sexual imaginations of strangers.

But is it enough to say something is pornographic if it "arouses the sexual imagination"? No, you might contend, because there is no way to predict what will arouse people's sexual imaginations. Many kinds of images might arouse the sexual imaginations of different people. You might say in rebutting Gordon, "These are just pictures of children. Sure, they're naked in some of them, but children have been symbols of purity and innocence in art since the dawn of civilization. If some people see these images as sexual, that's their problem, not Mann's."

A RULE FOR WRITERS Be alert to how terms and concepts are defined both in your source material and in your own writing. Are your terms broadly, narrowly, or technically construed?

THINKING CRITICALLY DEFINING TERMS AND CONCEPTS

Examine each claim, and note the terms and concepts used. Provide a terminological (strict, codified by an authoritative source) or a conceptual (loose, self-generated) definition for each. What sources did you use? Compare your answers to those of your peers to see if they are similar or different.

Statement	Definition	Type of Definition
Video games are **addictive**.		
Poor people will suffer most from the new law.		
The **epidemic of obesity** needs to be solved.		
We must send troops to protect **the national interest**.		
The Internet has ushered in a new age of **progress**.		

Writers often attempt to provide a provisional definition of important terms and concepts in their arguments. They may write, for example, "For the purposes of this argument, let's define terrorism as *X*" (a broad definition) or "According to federal law, the term 'international terrorism' means *A, B,* and *C*" (a technical definition). If you do this and a reader wants to challenge your ideas, he must argue on your terms or else offer a different definition.

So that we are consistent with our own recommendations, allow us to define the difference between a "term" and a "concept." A rule of thumb is that a *term* is more concrete and fixed than a *concept*. You may be able to find an authoritative source (like a federal law or an official policy) to help define a *term*. A *concept* is more open-ended and may have a generally agreed-upon definition, but rarely a strict or unchanging one. Concepts can be abstract but can also function powerfully in argumentation; love, justice, morality, psyche, health, freedom, bravery, obscenity, masculinity—these are all concepts. You may look up such words in the dictionary for general definitions, but the source won't say much about how to apply the concepts.

Since you cannot assume that everyone has a shared understanding of concepts you may be using, it's prudent for the purposes of effective writing to define them. You may find a useful definition of a concept given by an authoritative person, such as an expert in a field, as in "Stephen Hawking defines time as. . . ." You might cite a respected authority, as in "Mahatma Gandhi defines love as. . . ." Alternatively, you can combine several views and insert your own provisional definition. See "Thinking Critically: Defining Terms and Concepts" for an exercise.

SUMMARIZING AND PARAPHRASING

After a first reading, perhaps the best approach to a fairly difficult essay is to reread it and simultaneously take notes on a sheet of paper, summarizing each paragraph in a sentence or two. Writing a summary will help you to:

- understand the contents and
- see the strengths and weaknesses of the piece.

Don't confuse a summary with a paraphrase. A paraphrase is a word-by-word or phrase-by-phrase rewording of a text, a sort of translation of the author's language into your own. A paraphrase is therefore as long as the original or even longer; a summary is much shorter. An entire essay, even a whole book, may be summarized in a page, in a paragraph, even in a sentence. Obviously, the summary will leave out most details, but it will accurately state the essential thesis or claim of the original.

Why would anyone summarize, and why would anyone paraphrase? Because, as we've already said, these two activities—in different ways—offer a way to introduce other authors' ideas into your arguments in a way that readers can follow. You may do this for a number of reasons. Summaries and paraphrases can accomplish the following:

- **validate** the basis of your argument by providing an instance in which someone else wrote about the same topic

- **clarify** in short order the complex ideas contained in another author's work

- **support** your argument by showing readers where someone else "got it right" (corroborating your ideas) or "got it wrong" (countering your ideas, but giving you a chance to refute that position in favor of your own)

- **lend authority** to your voice by showing readers that you have considered the topic carefully by consulting other sources

- **help you build new ideas** from existing ideas on the topic, enabling you to insert your voice into an ongoing debate made evident by the summary or paraphrase

When you summarize, you're standing back, saying briefly what the whole adds up to; you're seeing the forest, as the saying goes, not the individual trees. **When you paraphrase**, you're inching through the forest, scrutinizing each tree—finding a synonym for almost every word in the original in an effort to ensure you know exactly what the original is saying. (*Caution:* Do not incorporate a summary or a paraphrase into your own essay without acknowledging the source and stating that you are summarizing or paraphrasing.)

Let's examine the distinction between summary and paraphrase in connection with the first two paragraphs of Paul Goodman's essay "A Proposal to Abolish Grading," excerpted from Goodman's book *Compulsory Miseducation and the Community of Scholars* (1966).

> Let half a dozen of the prestigious universities—Chicago, Stanford, the Ivy League—abolish grading, and use testing only and entirely for pedagogic purposes as teachers see fit.

> Anyone who knows the frantic temper of the present schools will understand the transvaluation of values that would be effected by this modest innovation. For most of the students, the competitive grade has come to be the essence. The naive teacher points to the beauty of the subject and the ingenuity of the research; the shrewd student asks if he is responsible for that on the final exam.

A **summary** of these two paragraphs might read like this:

> If some top universities used tests only to help students to learn and not for grades, students would stop worrying about whether they got an A, B or C and might begin to share the teacher's interest in the beauty of the subject.

Notice that the summary doesn't convey Goodman's style or voice (e.g., the wry tone in his pointed contrast between "the naive teacher" and "the shrewd student"). That is not the purpose of summary.

Now for a **paraphrase**. Suppose you're not sure what Goodman is getting at, maybe because you're uncertain about the meanings of some words (e.g., *pedagogic* and *transvaluation*), or else you just want to make sure you understand the point. In such a case, you may want to move slowly through the sentences, restating them in your own words. You might turn Goodman's "pedagogic purposes" into "goals in teaching," "attempts to help students to learn," or something else. Here is a paraphrase—not a summary, but a rewording—of Goodman's paragraphs:

> Suppose some of the top universities—such as Chicago, Stanford, Harvard, Yale, and others in the Ivy League—stopped using grades and instead used tests only in order to help students to learn.
>
> Everyone who is aware of the rat race in schools today will understand the enormous shift in values about learning that would come about by this small change. At present, idealistic instructors talk about how beautiful their subjects are, but smart students know that grades are what count. They only want to know if it will be on the exam.

In short, you may decide to paraphrase an important text if you want the reader to see the passage itself but you know that the full passage will be puzzling. In this situation, you offer help, *paraphrasing* before making your own point about the author's claim.

A second good reason to offer a paraphrase is if there is substantial disagreement about what the text says. The Second Amendment to the U.S. Constitution is a good example of this sort of text:

> A well regulated Militia being necessary to the security of a free State, the right of the people to keep and bear Arms shall not be infringed.

Exactly what, one might ask, is a "Militia"? What does it mean for a militia to be "well regulated"? And does "the people" mean each individual or the citizenry as a unified group? After all, elsewhere in the document, where the Constitution speaks of individuals, it speaks of a "man" or a "person," not "the people." To speak of "the people" is to use a term (some argue) that sounds like a reference to a unified group— perhaps the citizens of each of the thirteen states—rather than a reference to individuals. However, if Congress did mean a unified

Gun control supporters marching in 2013 at the Washington Monument in Washington, D.C.

group rather than individuals, why didn't it say, "Congress shall not prohibit the states from organizing militias"? In fact, thousands of pages have been written about this sentence, and if you're going to talk about it, you certainly have to let readers know exactly how you interpret each word. In short, you almost surely will paraphrase the sentence, going word by word, giving readers your own sense of what each word or phrase means. Here is one possible paraphrase:

> Because an independent society needs the protection of an armed force if it is to remain free, the government may not limit the right of the individuals (who may someday form the militia needed to keep the society free) to possess weapons.

In this interpretation, the Constitution grants individuals the right to possess weapons, and that is that.

Other students of the Constitution, however, offer very different paraphrases, usually along these lines:

> Because each state that is now part of the United States may need to protect its freedom (from the new national government), the national government may not infringe on the right of each state to form its own disciplined militia.

This paraphrase says that the federal government may not prevent each state from having a militia; it says nothing about every individual person having a right to possess weapons.

The first paraphrase might be offered by the National Rifle Association or any other group that interprets the Constitution as guaranteeing individuals the right to own guns. The second paraphrase might be offered by groups that seek to limit the ownership of guns.

Why paraphrase? Here are two reasons why you might paraphrase a passage:

- To help yourself to understand it. In this case, the paraphrase does not appear in your essay.

- To help your reader to understand a passage that is especially important but that is not immediately clear. In this case, you paraphrase to let the reader know exactly what the passage means. This paraphrase does appear in your essay.

PARAPHRASE, PATCHWRITING, AND PLAGIARISM

We have indicated that only rarely will you have reason to introduce a paraphrase into your essays. But in your preliminary work, when taking notes, you might sometimes do one or more of the following: copy word for word, paraphrase (usually to establish an author's idea clearly in your mind), summarize, and/or produce a medley of borrowed words and original words. The latter strategy is known as *patchwriting*, and it can be dangerous: If you submit such a medley in your final essay, you risk the charge of **plagiarism** *even if you have rearranged the phrases and clauses, and even if you have cited your source.*

Here's an example. First, we give the source: a paragraph from Jena McGregor's essay on whether women serving in the armed forces should be allowed to participate directly in combat. (The entire essay is printed on pp. 39–41.)

> Last week, female soldiers began formally moving into jobs in previously all-male battalions, a program that will later go Army-wide. The move is a result of rule changes following a February report that opened some 14,000 new positions to women in critical jobs much closer to the front lines. However, some 250,000 combat jobs still remain officially closed to them.

Here is a student's patchwriting version:

> Women in the army recently began to formally move into jobs in battalions that previously were all-male. This program later will go

throughout the Army. According to author Jena McGregor, the move comes from changes in the rules following a February report that opened about 14,000 new jobs to women in critical jobs that are much closer to the front lines. About 250,000 jobs, however — as McGregor points out — continue to be officially closed to women.

As you can see, the student writer has followed the source almost phrase by phrase — certainly, sentence by sentence — making small verbal changes, such as substituting *Women in the army recently* for McGregor's *Last week, female soldiers* and substituting *the move comes from changes in the rules* for McGregor's *The move is a result of rule changes. . . .*

What the student should have done is either (1) *quote the passage exactly,* setting it off to indicate that it's a quotation and indicating the source, or (2) *summarize it briefly* and credit the source — maybe in a sentence such as this:

Jena McGregor points out that although a recent change in army rules has resulted in new jobs being opened for women in the military, some 250,000 jobs "continue to be officially closed."

As opposed to the above example of a sentence that frankly summarizes a source, patchwriting is *not* the student's writing but, rather, the source material thinly disguised. In a given paragraph of patchwriting, usually some of the words are copied from the source, and all or most of the rest consists of synonyms substituted for the source's words, with minor rearrangement of phrases and clauses. That is, the sequence of ideas and their arrangement, as well as most of the language, are entirely or almost entirely derived from the source, even if some of the words are different.

The fact that you may cite a source is not enough to protect you from the charge of plagiarism. Citing a source tells the reader that some fact or idea — or some groups of words enclosed within quotation marks or set off by indentation — comes from the named source; it does *not* tell the reader that almost everything in the paragraph is, in effect, someone else's writing with a few words changed, a few words added, and a few phrases moved.

The best way to avoid introducing patchwriting into your final essay is to make certain that when taking notes you indicate, *in the notes themselves,* what sorts of notes they are. For example:

- When quoting word for word, put the passage within quotation marks, and cite the page number(s) of the source.

- When paraphrasing—perhaps to ensure that you understand the writer's idea, or because your readers won't understand the source's highly technical language unless you put it into simpler language—use some sign, perhaps (*par*), to remind yourself later that this passage is a paraphrase and thus is not really *your* writing.

- When summarizing, use a different key, such as (*sum*), and cite the page(s) of the source.

Make certain that your notes indicate the degree of indebtedness to your source, and again, do *not* think that if you name a source in a paraphrase you're not plagiarizing. The reader assumes that the name indicates the source of a fact or an idea—not that the paragraph is a rewriting of the original with an occasional phrase of your own inserted here and there.

If you have taken notes properly, with indications of the sort we've mentioned, when writing your paper you can say things like the following:

X's first reason is simple. He says, " . . ." (here you quote *X*'s words, putting them within quotation marks).

X's point can be summarized thus . . . (here you cite the page).

X, writing for lawyers, uses some technical language, but we can paraphrase her conclusion in this way: . . . (here you give the citation).

In short:

- Avoid patchwriting; it is *not* acceptable.

- Enclose direct quotations within quotation marks, or, if the quotations are long, set them off as a block quotation. (Consult your specific style guide for instructions on how to set off block quotations.)

- If you offer a paraphrase, tell readers that you are paraphrasing and explain *why* you are doing so rather than quoting directly or summarizing.

For additional information about plagiarism, see pages 264–68.

Strategies for Summarizing

As with paraphrases, summaries can be useful for helping you to establish your understanding of an essay or article. Summarizing each paragraph or each group of closely related paragraphs will

✓ **A CHECKLIST FOR A PARAPHRASE**

☐ Do I have a good reason for offering a paraphrase rather than a summary?

☐ Is the paraphrase entirely in my own words — a word-by-word "translation" — rather than a patchwork of the source's words and my own, with some of my own rearrangement of phrases and clauses?

☐ Do I not only cite the source but also explicitly say that the entire passage is a paraphrase?

enable you to follow the threads of the argument and will ultimately provide a useful map of the essay. Then, when rereading the essay, you may want to underline passages that you now realize are the author's key ideas — for instance, definitions, generalizations, summaries. You may also want to jot notes in the margins, questioning the logic, expressing your uncertainty, or calling attention to other writers who see the matter differently.

Summaries are also useful for your readers, for the reasons noted on page 60. How long should your summaries be? They can be as short as a single sentence or as long as an entire paragraph. Here's a one-sentence summary of Martin Luther King Jr.'s famous essay "Letter from Birmingham Jail." King wrote this essay after his arrest for marching against racial segregation and injustice in Birmingham, Alabama.

> In his letter, King argues that the time is ripe for nonviolent protest throughout the segregated South, dismissing claims by local clergymen who opposed him, and arguing that unjust laws need to be challenged by black people who have been patient and silent for too long.

King's essay, however, is quite long. Obviously, our one-sentence summary cannot convey substantial portions of King's eloquent arguments, sacrificing almost all the nuance of his rationale, but it serves as an efficient summation and allows the writer to move on to his own analysis promptly.

A longer summary might try to capture more nuance, especially if, for the purposes of your essay, you need to capture more. How much you summarize depends largely on the *purpose* of your

A RULE FOR WRITERS Your essay is *likely to include brief summaries* of points of view with which you agree or disagree, but it will *rarely include a paraphrase* unless the original is obscure and you feel compelled to present a passage at length in words that are clearer than those of the original. If you do paraphrase, explicitly identify the material as a paraphrase. Never submit patchwriting.

summary (see again our list of reasons to summarize on p. 60). Here is a longer summary of King's letter:

In his letter, King argues that the time is ripe for nonviolent pro-test in the segregated South despite the criticism he and his fellow civil rights activists received from various authorities, especially the eight local clergymen who wrote a public statement against him. King addresses their criticism point by point, first claiming his essential right to be in Birmingham with his famous state-ment, "injustice anywhere is a threat to justice everywhere," and then saying that those who see the timing of his group's nonviolent direct action as inconvenient must recognize at least two things: one, that his "legitimate and unavoidable impatience" resulted from undelivered promises by authorities in the past; and two, that African Americans had long been told over and over again to wait for change with no change forthcoming. "This 'wait' has almost always meant 'never,'" King writes. For those who criticized his lead-ership, which encouraged people to break laws prohibiting their march, King says that breaking *unjust* laws may actually be con-strued as a *just* act. For those who called him an extremist, he rev-els in the definition ("was not Jesus an extremist in love?" he asks) and reminds them of the more extremist groups who call for vio-lence in the face of blatant discrimination and brutality (and who will surely rise, King suggests, if no redress is forthcoming for the peaceful southern protestors he leads). Finally, King rails against "silence," saying that to hold one's tongue in the face of segrega-tion is tantamount to supporting it—a blow to "white moderates" who believe in change but do nothing to help bring it about.

This summary, obviously much longer than the first, raises numerous points from King's argument and preserves through quotation some of King's original tone and substance. It sacrifices much, of course, but seeks to provide a thorough account of a long and complex document containing many primary and secondary claims.

If your instructor asks for a summary of an essay, most often he or she won't want you to include your own thoughts about the content. Of course, you'll be using your own words, but try to "put yourself in the original author's shoes" and provide a summary that reflects the approach taken by the source. It should *not* contain ideas that the original piece doesn't express. If you use exact words and phrases drawn from the source, enclose them in quotation marks.

Summaries may be written for exercises in reading comprehension, but the point of summarizing when writing an essay is to assist your own argument. A faithful summary—one without your own ideas interjected—can be effective when using a source as an example or showing another writer's concordance with your argument. Consider the following paragraph written by a student who was arguing that if a person today purchases goods manufactured in sweatshops or under other inadequate labor conditions, then he or she is just as responsible for the abuses of labor as the companies who operate them. Notice how the student provides a summary (underlined) along the way and how it assists her argument.

Americans today are so disconnected from the source and origins of the products they buy that it is entirely possible for them one day to march against global warming and the next to collect a dividend in their 401k from companies that are the worst offenders. It is possible to weep over a news report on child labor in China and then post an emotional plea for justice on Facebook using a mobile device made by Chinese child laborers. <u>In 1849, Henry David Thoreau wrote in "Resistance to Civil Government" how ironic it was to see his fellow citizens in Boston opposed to slavery in the South, yet who read the daily news and commodity prices and "fall asleep over them both," not recognizing their own investments in, or patronage of, the very thing that offends their consciences. To Thoreau, such "gross inconsistency" makes even well-intentioned people "agents of injustice."</u> Similarly, today we do not see the connections between our consumer habits and the various kinds of oppression that underlie our purchases—forms of oppression we would never support directly and outright.

The embedded short summary addresses only one point of Thoreau's original essay, but it shows how summaries may serve in an integrative way—as analogy, example, or illustration—to support an argument even without adding the writer's own commentary or analysis.

Critical Summary

When writing a longer summary that you intend to integrate into your argument, you may interject your own ideas; the appropriate term for this is **critical summary**. It signifies that you're offering more than a thorough and accurate account of an original source, because you're adding your evaluation of it as well. Think of this as weaving together your neutral summary with your own argument so that the summary meshes seamlessly with your overall writing goal. Along the way, during the summary, you may appraise the original author's ideas, commenting on them as you go—even while being faithful to the original.

How can you faithfully account for an author's argument while commenting on its merits or shortcomings? One way is to offer examples from the original. In addition, you might assess the quality of those examples or present others that the author didn't consider. Remember, being critical doesn't necessarily mean refuting the author. Your summary can refute, support, or be more balanced, simply recognizing where the original author succeeds and fails.

A Strategy for Writing a Critical Summary   Follow these five steps when writing a critical summary:

1. **Introduce** the summary. You don't have to provide all these elements, but consider offering the *author's name* and *expertise*, the *title* of the source, the *place* of publication, the *year* of publication, or any other relevant information. You may also start to explain the author's main point that you are summarizing:

Pioneering feminist Betty Friedan, in her landmark book *The Feminine Mystique* (1963), argued that . . .

In an <u>essay on the state of higher education today</u>, University of Illinois English professor <u>Cary Nelson</u> complains about . . .

2. **Explain** the major point the source makes. Here you have a chance to tell your readers what the original author is saying, so be faithful to the original but also highlight the point you're summarizing:

Pioneering feminist Betty Friedan, in her landmark book *The Feminine Mystique* (1963), argued that <u>women of the early 1960s were falling victim to a media-created image of ideal femininity that pressured them to prioritize homemaking, beauty, and maternity above almost all other concerns.</u>

Here you can control the readers' understanding through simple adjectives such as *pioneering* and *landmark*. (Compare how *"stalwart* feminist Betty Friedan, in her *provocative* book" might dispose the reader to interpret your material differently.)

In a *blunt critique* of the state of higher education today, University of Illinois professor Cary Nelson complains that universities are underpaying and overworking part-time, adjunct teachers.

3. **Exemplify** by offering one or more representative examples or evidence on which the original author draws. Feel free to quote if needed, though it is not required in a summary.

Friedan examines post–World War II trends that included <u>the lowering of the marriage age</u>, <u>the rise of the mass media</u>, and what she calls <u>"the problem that has no name"</u> — that of feminine un-fulfillment, or what we might today call "depression."

4. **Problematize** by placing your assessment, analysis, or question into the summary.

While the word *depression* never comes up in Friedan's work, <u>one could assume</u> that terms like *malaise, suffering,* and *housewives' fatigue* <u>signal an emerging understanding of the relationship between stereotypical media representations of social identity and mental health.</u>

If you're working toward a balanced critique or rebuttal, here is a good place to insert your ideas or those of someone with a slightly different view.

Nelson is right to say that schools should model themselves on the ideals being taught in classrooms, <u>but having a flexible workforce is perfectly logical for a large organization</u> (something probably also taught in many business classes).

5. **Extend** by tying the summary to your argument, helping transition out of the critical summary and back into your own analysis.

Friedan's work should raise questions about how women are portrayed in the media today, and about what mental health consequences are attributable to the ubiquitous and consistent messages given to women about their bodies, occupations, and social roles.

The biggest problem with using too many contingent faculty is with preserving the quality of undergraduate education and the basic principles of academic freedom. Paying contingent faculty more money while increasing the number of tenure-track positions is not just a question of principles but a hallmark of the investment a university makes in its students.

It is possible to use this method—**Introduce, Explain, Exemplify, Problematize,** and **Extend**—in many ways, but essentially it is a way of providing a critical summary, any element of which can be enhanced or built upon as needed.

Having insisted earlier that you should read the essays in this book slowly because the writers build one reason on another, we will now seem to contradict ourselves by presenting an essay that you can almost skim. Susan Jacoby's piece originally appeared in the *New York Times*, a thoroughly respectable newspaper but not one that requires readers to linger over every sentence. Still, compared with most news accounts, Jacoby's essay requires close reading. Notice that it zigs and zags, not because Jacoby is careless but because in building a strong case to support her point of view, she must consider some widely held views that she does *not* accept; she must set these forth and then give her reasons for rejecting them.

A RULE FOR WRITERS Remember that when writing a summary you are putting yourself into the author's shoes.

Susan Jacoby

Susan Jacoby (b. 1946), a journalist since the age of seventeen, is well known for her feminist writings. "A First Amendment Junkie" (our title) appeared in the Hers column in the New York Times *in 1978.*

A First Amendment Junkie

It is no news that many women are defecting from the ranks of civil libertarians on the issue of obscenity. The conviction of Larry Flynt, publisher of *Hustler* magazine—before his metamorphosis into a born-again Christian—was greeted with unabashed feminist approval. Harry Reems, the unknown actor who was convicted by a Memphis jury for conspiring to distribute the movie *Deep Throat,* has carried on his legal battles with almost no support from women who ordinarily regard themselves as supporters of the First Amendment. Feminist writers and scholars have even discussed the possibility of making common cause against pornography with adversaries of the women's movement—including opponents of the Equal Rights Amendment and "right-to-life" forces.

All of this is deeply disturbing to a woman writer who believes, as I always have and still do, in an absolute interpretation of the First Amendment. Nothing in Larry Flynt's garbage convinces me that the late Justice Hugo L. Black was wrong in his opinion that "the Federal Government is without any power whatsoever under the Constitution to put any type of burden on free speech and expression of ideas of any kind (as distinguished from conduct)." Many women I like and respect tell me I am wrong; I cannot remember having become involved in so many heated discussions of a public issue since the end of the Vietnam War. A feminist writer described my views as those of a "First Amendment junkie."

Many feminist arguments for controls on pornography carry the implicit conviction that porn books, magazines, and movies pose a greater threat to women than similarly repulsive exercises of free speech pose to other offended groups. This conviction has, of course, been shared by everyone—regardless of race, creed, or sex—who has ever argued in favor of abridging the First Amendment. It is the argument used by some Jews who have withdrawn their support from the American Civil Liberties Union because it has defended the right of American Nazis to march through a community inhabited by survivors of Hitler's concentration camps.

If feminists want to argue that the protection of the Constitution should not be extended to *any* particularly odious or threatening form of speech, they have a reasonable argument (although I don't agree with it). But it is ridiculous to suggest that the porn shops on 42nd Street are more disgusting to women than a march of neo-Nazis is to survivors of the extermination camps.

The arguments over pornography also blur the vital distinc-   5
tion between expression of ideas and conduct. When I say I believe unreservedly in the First Amendment, someone always comes back at me with the issue of "kiddie porn." But kiddie porn is not a First Amendment issue. It is an issue of the abuse of power—the power adults have over children—and not of obscenity. Parents and promoters have no more right to use their children to make porn movies than they do to send them to work in coal mines. The responsible adults should be prosecuted, just as adults who use children for back-breaking farm labor should be prosecuted.

Susan Brownmiller, in *Against Our Will: Men, Women, and Rape,* has described pornography as "the undiluted essence of antifemale propaganda." I think this is a fair description of some types of pornography, especially of the brutish subspecies that equates sex with death and portrays women primarily as objects of violence.

The equation of sex and violence, personified by some glossy rock record album covers as well as by *Hustler,* has fed the illusion that censorship of pornography can be conducted on a more rational basis than other types of censorship. Are all pictures of naked women obscene? Clearly not, says a friend. A Renoir nude is art, she says, and *Hustler* is trash. "Any reasonable person" knows that.

But what about something between art and trash—something, say, along the lines of *Playboy* or *Penthouse* magazines? I asked five women for their reactions to one picture in *Penthouse* and got responses that ranged from "lovely" and "sensuous" to "revolting" and "demeaning." Feminists, like everyone else, seldom have rational reasons for their preferences in erotica. Like members of juries, they tend to disagree when confronted with something that falls short of 100 percent vulgarity.

In any case, feminists will not be the arbiters of good taste if it becomes easier to harass, prosecute, and convict people on obscenity charges. Most of the people who want to censor girlie magazines are equally opposed to open discussion of issues that are of vital concern to women: rape, abortion, menstruation, contraception, lesbianism—in fact, the entire range of sexual experience from a woman's viewpoint.

Feminist writers and editors and filmmakers have limited 10 financial resources: Confronted by a determined prosecutor, Hugh Hefner[1] will fare better than Susan Brownmiller. Would the Memphis jurors who convicted Harry Reems for his role in *Deep Throat* be inclined to take a more positive view of paintings of the female genitalia done by sensitive feminist artists? *Ms.* magazine has printed color reproductions of some of those art works; *Ms.* is already banned from a number of high school libraries because someone considers it threatening and / or obscene.

Feminists who want to censor what they regard as harmful pornography have essentially the same motivation as other would-be censors: They want to use the power of the state to accomplish what they have been unable to achieve in the marketplace of ideas and images. The impulse to censor places no faith in the possibilities of democratic persuasion.

It isn't easy to persuade certain men that they have better uses for $1.95 each month than to spend it on a copy of *Hustler*. Well, then, give the men no choice in the matter.

I believe there is also a connection between the impulse toward censorship on the part of people who used to consider themselves civil libertarians and a more general desire to shift responsibility from individuals to institutions. When I saw the movie *Looking for Mr. Goodbar*, I was stunned by its series of visual images equating sex and violence, coupled with what seems to me the mindless message (a distortion of the fine Judith Rossner novel) that casual sex equals death. When I came out of the movie, I was even more shocked to see parents standing in line with children between the ages of ten and fourteen.

I simply don't know why a parent would take a child to see such a movie, any more than I understand why people feel they can't turn off a television set their child is watching. Whenever I say that, my friends tell me I don't know how it is because I don't have children. True, but I do have parents. When I was a child, they did turn off the TV. They didn't expect the Federal Communications Commission to do their job for them.

I am a First Amendment junkie. You can't OD on the First 15 Amendment, because free speech is its own best antidote. ∎

[1]**Hugh Hefner** Founder and longtime publisher of *Playboy* magazine.

Summarizing Jacoby

Suppose we want to make a *rough summary*, more or less paragraph by paragraph, of Jacoby's essay. Our summary might look like this:

Paragraph 1. Although feminists usually support the First Amendment, when it comes to pornography many feminists take pretty much the position of those who oppose the Equal Rights Amendment and abortion and other causes of the women's movement.

Paragraph 2. Larry Flynt produces garbage, but I think his conviction represents an unconstitutional limitation of freedom of speech.

Paragraphs 3, 4. Feminists who want to control (censor) pornography argue that it poses a greater threat to women than similar repulsive speech poses to other groups. If feminists want to say that all offensive speech should be restricted, they can make a case, but it is absurd to say that pornography is a "greater threat" to women "than a march of neo-Nazis is to survivors of the extermination camps."

Paragraph 5. Trust in the First Amendment is not refuted by kiddie porn; kiddie porn is not a First Amendment issue but an issue of child abuse.

Paragraphs 6, 7, 8. Some feminists think censorship of pornography can be more "rational" than other kinds of censorship, but a picture of a nude woman strikes some women as base and others as "lovely." There is no unanimity.

Paragraphs 9, 10. If feminists censor girlie magazines, they will find that they are unwittingly helping opponents of the women's movement to censor discussions of rape, abortion, and so on. Some of the art in the feminist magazine *Ms.* would doubtless be censored.

Paragraphs 11, 12. Like other would-be censors, feminists want to use the power of the state to achieve what they have not achieved in "the marketplace of ideas." They display a lack of faith in "democratic persuasion."

Paragraphs 13, 14. This attempt at censorship reveals a "desire to shift responsibility from individuals to institutions." The responsibility—for instance, to keep young people from equating sex with violence—is properly the parents'.

Paragraph 15. We can't have too much of the First Amendment.

Jacoby's **thesis** (i.e., major claim or chief proposition)—that any form of censorship of pornography is wrong—is clear enough, even as early as the end of paragraph 1, but it gains force from the **reasons** she offers throughout the essay. If we want to reduce our summary further, we might say that she supports her thesis by arguing several subsidiary points. Here we'll merely assert them briefly, but Jacoby **argues** them—that is, she gives reasons:

- Pornography can scarcely be thought of as more offensive than Nazism.
- Women disagree about which pictures are pornographic.
- Feminists who want to censor pornography will find that they help antifeminists to censor discussions of issues advocated by the women's movement.
- Feminists who favor censorship are in effect turning to the government to achieve what they haven't achieved in the free marketplace.
- One sees this abdication of responsibility in the fact that parents allow their children to watch unsuitable movies and television programs.

If we want to present a *brief summary* in the form of one coherent paragraph—perhaps as part of an essay arguing for or against—we might write something like the one shown in the paragraph below. (Of course, we would **introduce** it with a lead-in along these lines: "Susan Jacoby, writing in the *New York Times,* offers a forceful argument against censorship of pornography. Jacoby's view, briefly, is. . . .")

> When it comes to censorship of pornography, some feminists take a position shared by opponents of the feminist movement. They argue that pornography poses a greater threat to women than other forms of offensive speech offer to other groups, but this interpretation is simply a mistake. Pointing to kiddie porn is also a mistake, for kiddie porn is an issue involving not the First Amendment but child abuse. Feminists who support censorship of pornography will inadvertently aid those who wish to censor discussions of abortion and rape or censor art that is published in magazines such as *Ms.* The solution is not for individuals to turn to institutions (i.e., for the government to limit the First Amendment) but for individuals to accept the responsibility for teaching young people not to equate sex with violence.

In contrast, a *critical summary* of Jacoby—an evaluative summary in which we introduce our own ideas and examples—might look like this:

> Susan Jacoby, writing for the *New York Times* in 1978, offers a forceful argument against censorship of pornography, but one that does not have foresight of the Internet age and the new availability of extreme and exploitative forms of pornography. While she dismisses claims by feminists that pornography should be censored because it constitutes violence against women, what would Jacoby think of such things as "revenge porn" and "voyeuristic porn" today, or the array of elaborate sadistic fantasies readily available to anyone with access to a search engine? Jacoby says that censoring pornography is a step toward censoring art, and she proudly wears the tag "First Amendment junkie," ostensibly to protect what she finds artistic (such as images of female genitalia in *Ms.* Magazine). However, her argument does not help us account for these new forms of exploitation and violence disguised as art or "free speech." Perhaps she would see revenge porn and voyeur porn in the same the way she sees kiddie porn—not so much as an issue of free speech but as an issue of other crimes. Perhaps she would hold her position that we can avoid pornography by just "turning off the TV," but the new Internet pornography is intrusive, entering our lives and the lives of our children whether we like it or not. Education is part of the solution, Jacoby would agree, but we could also consider. . . .

The example above not only summarizes and applies the other techniques presented in this chapter (e.g., accounting for context and questioning definitions of terms and concepts) but also weaves them together with a central argument that offers a new response and a practicable solution.

TOPICS FOR CRITICAL THINKING AND WRITING

1. What does Susan Jacoby mean by saying she is a "First Amendment junkie" (para. 15)?

2. The essay is primarily an argument against the desire of some feminists to censor the sort of pornography that appealed to some heterosexual adult males in 1978. How does the context of the article's publication reflect events and perspectives of that period? How are conditions different now, and how do these new contexts offer ways to support or challenge Jacoby's argument?

3. Evaluate the final paragraph as a conclusion. (Effective final paragraphs are not all of one sort. Some round off the essay by echoing one or more points from the opening; others suggest that the reader, having now seen the problem, should think further about it or act on it. No matter what form it takes, a good final paragraph should make the reader feel that the essay has come to a satisfactory conclusion, not a sudden breaking-off of the argument.)

4. This essay originally appeared in the *New York Times*. If you're unfamiliar with this newspaper, consult an issue or two in your school library. Next, in a paragraph, try to characterize the paper's readers—that is, Jacoby's audience.

5. Jacoby claims in paragraph 2 that she "believes . . . in an absolute interpretation of the First Amendment." What does such an interpretation involve? Would it permit shouting "Fire!" in a crowded theater even when there is no fire? Posting racist insults on the Internet? Spreading untruths about someone's past? (*Does* the First Amendment, as actually interpreted by the Supreme Court today, permit any or all of these claims? Consult your reference librarian for help in answering this question.)

6. Jacoby implies that permitting prosecution of persons on obscenity charges will lead eventually to censorship of "open discussion" of important issues such as "rape, abortion, menstruation, contraception, lesbianism" (para. 9). Do you find her fears convincing? Does she give evidence to support her claim? Explain your responses.

✓ A CHECKLIST FOR GETTING STARTED

☐ Have I adequately previewed the work?

☐ Can I state the thesis?

☐ If I have written a summary, is it accurate?

☐ Does my summary mention all the chief points?

☐ If there are inconsistencies, are they in the summary or the original selection?

☐ Will my summary be clear and helpful?

☐ Have I considered the audience for whom the author is writing?

ESSAYS FOR ANALYSIS

Zachary Shemtob and David Lat

Zachary Shemtob teaches criminal justice at Central Connecticut State University; David Lat is a former federal prosecutor. Their essay originally appeared in the New York Times *in 2011.*

Executions Should Be Televised

Earlier this month, Georgia conducted its third execution this year. This would have passed relatively unnoticed if not for a controversy surrounding its videotaping. Lawyers for the condemned inmate, Andrew Grant DeYoung, had persuaded a judge to allow the recording of his last moments as part of an effort to obtain evidence on whether lethal injection caused unnecessary suffering.

Though he argued for videotaping, one of Mr. DeYoung's defense lawyers, Brian Kammer, spoke out against releasing the footage to the public. "It's a horrible thing that Andrew DeYoung had to go through," Mr. Kammer said, "and it's not for the public to see that."

We respectfully disagree. Executions in the United States ought to be made public.

Right now, executions are generally open only to the press and a few select witnesses. For the rest of us, the vague contours are provided in the morning paper. Yet a functioning democracy demands maximum accountability and transparency. As long as executions remain behind closed doors, those are impossible. The people should have the right to see what is being done in their name and with their tax dollars.

This is particularly relevant given the current debate on 5 whether specific methods of lethal injection constitute cruel and unusual punishment and therefore violate the Constitution.

There is a dramatic difference between reading or hearing of such an event and observing it through image and sound. (This is obvious to those who saw the footage of Saddam Hussein's hanging in 2006 or the death of Neda Agha-Soltan during the protests in Iran in 2009.) We are not calling for opening executions completely to the public—conducting them before a live crowd—but rather for broadcasting them live or recording them for future release, on the Web or TV.

When another Georgia inmate, Roy Blankenship, was executed in June, the prisoner jerked his head, grimaced, gasped, and lurched, according to a medical expert's affidavit. The *Atlanta Journal-Constitution* reported that Mr. DeYoung, executed in the same manner, "showed no violent signs in death." Voters should not have to rely on media accounts to understand what takes place when a man is put to death.

Cameras record legislative sessions and presidential debates, and courtrooms are allowing greater television access. When he was an Illinois state senator, President Obama successfully pressed for the videotaping of homicide interrogations and confessions. The most serious penalty of all surely demands equal if not greater scrutiny.

Opponents of our proposal offer many objections. State lawyers argued that making Mr. DeYoung's execution public raised safety concerns. While rioting and pickpocketing occasionally marred executions in the public square in the eighteenth and nineteenth centuries, modern security and technology obviate this concern. Little would change in the death chamber; the faces of witnesses and executioners could be edited out, for privacy reasons, before a video was released.

Of greater concern is the possibility that broadcasting execu-   10
tions could have a numbing effect. Douglas A. Berman, a law professor, fears that people might come to equate human executions with putting pets to sleep. Yet this seems overstated. While public indifference might result over time, the initial broadcasts would undoubtedly get attention and stir debate.

Still others say that broadcasting an execution would offer an unbalanced picture—making the condemned seem helpless and sympathetic, while keeping the victims of the crime out of the picture. But this is beside the point: the defendant is being executed precisely because a jury found that his crimes were so heinous that he deserved to die.

Ultimately the main opposition to our idea seems to flow from an unthinking disgust—a sense that public executions are archaic, noxious, even barbarous. Albert Camus related in his essay "Reflections on the Guillotine" that viewing executions turned him against capital punishment. The legal scholar John D. Bessler suggests that public executions might have the same effect on the public today; Sister Helen Prejean, the death penalty abolitionist, has urged just such a strategy.

That is not our view. We leave open the possibility that making executions public could strengthen support for them; undecided viewers might find them less disturbing than anticipated.

Like many of our fellow citizens, we are deeply conflicted about the death penalty and how it has been administered. Our focus is on accountability and openness. As Justice John Paul Stevens wrote in *Baze v. Rees*, a 2008 case involving a challenge to lethal injection, capital punishment is too often "the product of habit and inattention rather than an acceptable deliberative process that weighs the costs and risks of administering that penalty against its identifiable benefits."

A democracy demands a citizenry as informed as possible about   15
the costs and benefits of society's ultimate punishment.   ■

Topics for Critical Thinking and Writing

1. In paragraphs 9–13, the authors discuss objections to their position. Are you satisfied with their responses to the objections, or do you think they do not satisfactorily dispose of one or more of the objections? Explain.

2. In paragraph 4, the authors say that "[t]he people should have the right to see what is being done in their name and with their tax dollars." But in terms of *rights*, should the person being executed have a right to die in privacy? Articulate a position that weighs the public's right to see what is being done with its tax dollars against death row prisoners' rights to privacy.

3. In the concluding paragraph, the authors imply that their proposal, if enacted, will help to inform citizens "about the costs and benefits of society's ultimate punishment." Do you agree? Why, or why not? What reasons do the authors offer to support their proposal?

4. In your view, what is the strongest argument the authors give on behalf of their proposal? What is the weakest? Explain why you made these choices.

Gwen Wilde

This essay was written for a composition course at Tufts University.

Why the Pledge of Allegiance Should Be Revised (Student Essay)

All Americans are familiar with the Pledge of Allegiance, even if they cannot always recite it perfectly, but probably relatively few know that the *original* Pledge did *not* include the words "under God." The original Pledge of Allegiance, published in the September 8, 1892, issue of the *Youth's Companion*, ran thus:

> I pledge allegiance to my flag, and to the Republic for which it stands: one Nation indivisible, with Liberty and justice for all. (Djupe 329)

In 1923, at the first National Flag Conference in Washington, D.C., it was argued that immigrants might be confused by the words "my Flag," and it was proposed that the words be changed to "the Flag of the United States." The following year it was changed again, to "the Flag of the United States of America," and this wording became the official—or, rather, unofficial—wording, unofficial because no wording had ever been nationally adopted (Djupe 329).

In 1942, the United States Congress included the Pledge in the United States Flag Code (4 USC 4, 2006), thus for the first time officially sanctioning the Pledge. In 1954, President Dwight D. Eisenhower approved adding the words "under God." Thus, since 1954 the Pledge reads:

> I pledge allegiance to the flag of the United States of America, and to the Republic for which it stands: one nation under God, indivisible, with Liberty and Justice for all. (Djupe 329)

In my view, the addition of the words "under God" is inappropriate, and they are needlessly divisive—an odd addition indeed to a nation that is said to be "indivisible."

Very simply put, the Pledge in its latest form requires all Americans to say something that some Americans do not believe. I say "requires" because although the courts have ruled that students may not be compelled to recite the Pledge, in effect peer pressure does compel all but the bravest to join in the recitation. When President Eisenhower authorized the change, he said, "In this way we are reaffirming the transcendence of religious faith in America's heritage and future; in this way we shall constantly strengthen those spiritual weapons which forever will be our country's most powerful resource in peace and war" (Sterner).

Exactly what did Eisenhower mean when he spoke of "the transcendence of religious faith in America's heritage" and when he spoke of "spiritual weapons"? I am not sure what "the transcendence of religious faith in America's heritage" means. Of course, many Americans have been and are deeply religious—no one doubts it—but the phrase certainly goes far beyond saying that many Americans have been devout. In any case, many Americans have *not* been devout, and many Americans have *not* believed in "spiritual weapons," but they have nevertheless been patriotic Americans. Some of them have fought and died to keep America free.

In short, the words "under God" cannot be uttered in good faith by many Americans. True, something like 70 or even 80% of Americans say they are affiliated with some form of Christianity, and approximately another 3% say they are Jewish. I don't have the figures for persons of other faiths, but in any case we can surely all agree that although a majority of Americans say they have a religious affiliation, nevertheless several million Americans do *not* believe in God.

If one remains silent while others are reciting the Pledge, or even if one remains silent only while others are speaking the words "under God," one is open to the charge that one is unpatriotic, is "unwilling to recite the Pledge of Allegiance." In the Pledge, patriotism is connected with religious belief, and it is this connection that makes it divisive and (to be blunt) un-American. Admittedly, the belief is not very specific: one is not required to say that one believes in the divinity of Jesus, or in the power of Jehovah, but the fact remains, one is required to express belief in a divine power, and if one doesn't express this belief one is — according to the Pledge — somehow not fully an American, maybe even un-American.

Please notice that I am not arguing that the Pledge is unconstitutional. I understand that the First Amendment to the Constitution says that "Congress shall make no law respecting an establishment of religion, or prohibiting the free exercise thereof." I am not arguing that the words "under God" in the Pledge add up to the "establishment of religion," but they certainly do assert a religious doctrine. Like the words "In God we trust," found on all American money, the words "under God" express an idea that many Americans do not hold, and there is no reason why these Americans — loyal people who may be called upon to defend the country with their lives — should be required to say that America is a nation "under God."

It has been argued, even by members of the Supreme Court, that the words "under God" are not to be taken terribly seriously, not to be taken to say what they seem to say. For instance, Chief Justice Rehnquist wrote:

> To give the parent of such a child a sort of "heckler's veto" over
> a patriotic ceremony willingly participated in by other students,
> simply because the Pledge of Allegiance contains the descriptive

10

phrase "under God," is an unwarranted extension of the establishment clause, an extension which would have the unfortunate
effect of prohibiting a commendable patriotic observance. (qtd. in
Stephens et al. 104)

Chief Justice Rehnquist here calls "under God" a "descriptive
phrase," but descriptive of *what*? If a phrase is a "descriptive phrase,"
it describes something, real or imagined. For many Americans, this
phrase does *not* describe a reality. These Americans may perhaps be
mistaken—if so, they may learn of their error at Judgment Day—
but the fact is, millions of intelligent Americans do not believe
in God.

Notice, too, that Chief Justice Rehnquist goes on to say that
reciting the Pledge is "a commendable patriotic observance."
Exactly. That is my point. It is a *patriotic* observance, and it should
not be connected with religion. When we announce that we
respect the flag—that we are loyal Americans—we should not also
have to announce that we hold a particular religious belief, in this
case a belief in monotheism, a belief that there is a God and that
God rules.

One other argument defending the words "under God" is
often heard: The words "In God We Trust" appear on our money.
It is claimed that these words on American money are analogous
to the words "under God" in the Pledge. But the situation really
is very different. When we hand some coins over, or some paper
money, we are concentrating on the business transaction, and we
are not making any affirmation about God or our country. But
when we recite the Pledge—even if we remain silent at the point
when we are supposed to say "under God"—we are very conscious
that we are supposed to make this affirmation, an affirmation that
many Americans cannot in good faith make, even though they
certainly can unthinkingly hand over (or accept) money with the
words "In God We Trust."

Because I believe that *reciting* the Pledge is to be taken seriously, with a full awareness of the words that is quite different
from when we hand over some money, I cannot understand the
recent comment of Supreme Court Justice Souter, who in a case
said that the phrase "under God" is "so tepid, so diluted, so far from
compulsory prayer, that it should, in effect, be beneath the constitutional radar" (qtd. in "Guide"). I don't follow his reasoning
that the phrase should be "beneath the constitutional radar," but
in any case I am willing to put aside the issue of constitutionality.

I am willing to grant that this phrase does not in any significant sense signify the "establishment of religion" (prohibited by the First Amendment) in the United States. I insist, nevertheless, that the phrase is neither "tepid" nor "diluted." It means what it says—it *must* and *should* mean what it says, to everyone who utters it—and, since millions of loyal Americans cannot say it, it should not be included in a statement in which Americans affirm their loyalty to our great country.

In short, the Pledge, which ought to unite all of us, is divisive; it   15
includes a phrase that many patriotic Americans cannot bring themselves to utter. Yes, they can remain silent when others recite these two words, but, again, why should they have to remain silent? The Pledge of Allegiance should be something that *everyone* can say, say out loud, and say with pride. We hear much talk of returning to the ideas of the Founding Fathers. The Founding Fathers did not create the Pledge of Allegiance, but we do know that they never mentioned God in the Constitution. Indeed, the only reference to religion, in the so-called establishment clause of the First Amendment, says, again, that "Congress shall make no law respecting an establishment of religion, or prohibiting the free exercise thereof." Those who wish to exercise religion are indeed free to do so, but the place to do so is not in a pledge that is required of all schoolchildren and of all new citizens.   ■

WORKS CITED

Djupe, Paul A. "Pledge of Allegiance." *Encyclopedia of American Religion and Politics*. Edited by Paul A. Djupe and Laura R. Olson, Facts on File, 2003.

"Guide to Covering 'Under God' Pledge Decision." *ReligionLink*, 17 Sept. 2005, religionlink.com/database/guide-to-covering-under-god/.

Stephens, Otis H., et al., editors. *American Constitutional Law*. 6th ed., vol. 1, Cengage Learning, 2014.

Sterner, Doug. "The Pledge of Allegiance." *Home of Heroes*, homeofheroes .com/hallofheroes/1st_floor/flag/1bfc_pledge_print.html. Accessed 13 Apr. 2016.

TOPICS FOR CRITICAL THINKING AND WRITING

1. Summarize the essay in a paragraph.

2. What terms and concepts are defined in this essay? Explain how one term or concept is defined.

3. Does the writer, Gwen Wilde, give enough weight to the fact that no one is compelled to recite the Pledge? Explain your answer.

4. What arguments does Wilde offer in support of her position?

5. Does Wilde show an adequate awareness of counterarguments? Identify one place where she raises and refutes a counterargument.

Spencer Platt/Getty Images

6. What is Wilde's strongest argument? Are any of her arguments notably weak? If so, how could they be strengthened?

7. What assumptions—tacit or explicit—does Wilde make? Do you agree or disagree with them? Explain your response.

8. What do you take the words "under God" to mean? Do they mean "under God's special protection"? Or "acting in accordance with God's rules"? Or "accountable to God"? Or something else? Explain.

9. Chief Justice Rehnquist wrote that the words "under God" are a "descriptive phrase." What do you think he meant by this?

10. What is the purpose of the Pledge of Allegiance? Does the phrase "under God" promote or defeat that purpose? Explain your answer.

11. What do you think about substituting "with religious freedom" for "under God"? Set forth your response, supported by reasons, in about 250 words.

12. Wilde makes a distinction between the reference to God on U.S. money and the reference to God in the Pledge. Do you agree with her that the two cases are not analogous? Explain.

13. What readers might *not* agree with Wilde's arguments? What values do they hold? How might you try to persuade an audience who disagrees with Wilde to consider her proposal?

14. Putting aside your own views on the issue, what grade would you give this essay as a work of argumentative writing? Support your evaluation with reasons.

3

Critical Reading: Getting Deeper into Arguments

He that wrestles with us strengthens our nerves, and sharpens our skill. Our antagonist is our helper.

—EDMUND BURKE

PERSUASION, ARGUMENT, DISPUTE

When we think seriously about an argument, not only do we encounter ideas that may be unfamiliar but also we are forced to examine our own cherished opinions—and perhaps for the first time really see the strengths and weaknesses of what we believe. As John Stuart Mill put it, "He who knows only his own side of the case knows little."

It is useful to distinguish between **persuasion** and **argument**. Persuasion has the broader meaning. To **persuade** is to convince someone else to accept or adopt your position, which can be accomplished in a number of ways, including

- by giving reasons (i.e., by argument, by logic),
- by appealing to the emotions, or
- by using torture.

Argument, we mean to say, represents only one form of persuasion, one that relies on the cognitive or intellectual capacity for reason. Rhetoricians often use the Greek word *logos*, which means "word" or "reason," to denote this aspect of persuasive writing. An appeal to reason may by conducted by using such things as

- physical evidence,
- the testimony of experts,
- common sense, and
- probability.

We can put it this way: The goal of *argument* is to convince by demonstrating the truth (or probable truth) of an assertion, whereas the goal of *persuasion* is simply to convince by one means or another. *Logos*, the root word of *logic*, means appealing to the intellect to make rational claims and reasoned judgments.

The appeal to the emotions is known as **pathos**. Strictly speaking, *pathos* is Greek for "feeling." It covers all sorts of emotional appeals—for instance, appeals that elicit pity or sympathy (derived from the Greek for "feeling with"), or one's sense of duty or patriotism.

Notice that an argument doesn't require two speakers or writers with opposing positions. In practice, of course, they may, but it is not a requirement that arguments advance claims in opposition to another position. **Dispute** is a special kind of argument in which two or more people express views that are at odds. But the Declaration of Independence is also an argument, setting forth the colonists' reasons for declaring their independence. An essay showing indecisiveness to be Hamlet's tragic flaw would present an argument. Even when writing only for oneself, trying to clarify one's thinking by setting forth reasons and justifications for an idea, the result is an argument.

Most of this book is about argument in the sense of presenting reasonable support of claims, but reason is not the whole story. If an argument is to be effective, it must be presented persuasively. For instance, the writer's **tone** (presentation of self, topic, and audience) must be appropriate if the discourse is to persuade the reader. The careful presentation of the self is not something disreputable, nor is it something that publicity agents or advertising agencies invented. Aristotle (384–322 B.C.E.) emphasized the importance of impressing on the audience that the speaker is a person of good sense and high moral character. (He called this aspect of persuasion *ethos*, the Greek word for "character," a basis of persuasion different from *logos*, which involves persuasion by appealing to reason, and *pathos*, which persuades by appealing to emotion.)

Writers convey their *ethos*, their good character or trustworthiness, by doing the following:

- using language appropriate to the setting, avoiding vulgar language, slang, and colloquialism;

- showing an awareness of the issue's complexity (e.g., by offering other points of view in goodwill and by recognizing that contrary points of view may have some merit); and
- showing attention to detail (e.g., by citing relevant statistics).

In short, writers who are concerned with *ethos*—and all writers should be—employ devices that persuade readers that the writers are reliable, fair-minded, intelligent persons in whom their readers can have confidence.

THINKING CRITICALLY ESTABLISHING TRUSTWORTHINESS AND CREDIBILITY

For each method listed, provide your own example of a sentence that helps to establish trustworthiness and credibility. (Pick a topic that interests you. If you need ideas, look at the topics addressed by the authors presented in this chapter.) Be sure to use a tone and language that are appropriate and respectful of your audience.

Method	Example	Your Turn
Acknowledge weaknesses, exceptions, and complexities.	"Although the unemployment rate continues to decline, further investigation into underemployment and the loss of jobless benefits is necessary in order to truly understand the unemployment crisis in the United States."	
Use personal experience when appropriate.	"As a student who works and attends school full-time, I can speak firsthand about the importance of increased availability of financial aid."	
Mention the qualifications of any sources as a way to boost your own credibility.	"Acording to Deborah Tannen, author and noted professor of linguistics at Georgetown University, . . ."	

We talk at length about tone, along with other matters such as the organization of an argument, in Chapter 5, Writing an Analysis of an Argument, but here we deal with some of the chief devices used in reasoning, and we glance at emotional appeals.

We should note at once, however, that an argument presupposes a fixed **topic**. Suppose we're arguing about Thomas Jefferson's assertion, in the Declaration of Independence, that "all men are created equal." Jones subscribes to this statement, but Smith says it's nonsense and argues that some people are obviously brighter than others, or healthier, or better coordinated, and so on. Jones and Smith, if they intend to argue the point, will do well to examine what Jefferson actually wrote:

> We hold these truths to be self-evident, that all men are created equal: that they are endowed by their Creator with certain unalienable rights; and that among these are life, liberty, and the pursuit of happiness.

There is room for debate over what Jefferson really meant and whether he is right, but clearly he was talking about *equality of rights.* If Smith and Jones wish to argue about Jefferson's view of equality—that is, if they wish to offer their reasons for accepting, rejecting, or modifying it—they must first agree on what Jefferson said or probably meant to say. Jones and Smith may still hold different views; they may continue to disagree on whether Jefferson was right and proceed to offer arguments and counterarguments to settle the point. But only if they can agree on *what* they disagree about will their dispute get somewhere.

REASON VERSUS RATIONALIZATION

Reason may not be the only way of finding the truth, but it is a way on which we often rely. "The subway ran yesterday at 6:00 A.M. and the day before at 6:00 A.M. and the day before that, so I infer from this evidence that it will also run today at 6:00 A.M." (a form of reasoning known as **induction**). "Bus drivers require would-be passengers to present the exact change; I don't have the exact change; therefore, I infer I cannot ride on the bus" (**deduction**). (The terms *deduction* and *induction* are discussed in more detail on pp. 101 and 106.)

We also know that if we set our minds to a problem, we can often find reasons (not always necessarily sound ones) for almost anything we want to justify. Here's an entertaining example from Benjamin Franklin's *Autobiography:*

I believe I have omitted mentioning that in my first voyage from Boston, being becalmed off Block Island, our people set about catching cod and hauled up a great many. Hitherto I had stuck to my resolution of not eating animal food, and on this occasion, I considered with my master Tryon the taking of every fish as a kind of unprovoked murder, since none of them had or ever could do us any injury that might justify the slaughter. All this seemed very reasonable. But I had formerly been a great lover of fish, and when this came hot out of the frying pan, it smelt admirably well. I balanced some time between principle and inclination, till I recollected that when the fish were opened I saw smaller fish taken out of their stomachs. Then thought I, if you eat one another, I don't see why we mayn't eat you. So I dined upon cod very heartily and continued to eat with other people, returning only now and then occasionally to a vegetable diet. So convenient a thing it is to be a *reasonable creature,* since it enables one to find or make a reason for everything one has a mind to do.

Franklin is being playful; he is *not* engaging in critical thinking. He tells us that he loved fish and that this fish "smelt admirably well," so we're prepared for him to find a reason (here one as weak as "Fish eat fish, therefore people may eat fish") to abandon his vegetarianism. (But think: Fish also eat their own young. May we therefore eat ours?)

Still, Franklin touches on a truth: If necessary, we can find reasons to justify whatever we want. That is, instead of reasoning, we may *rationalize* (devise a self-serving but dishonest reason), like the fox in Aesop's fables who, finding the grapes he desired were out of reach, consoled himself with the thought that they were probably sour.

Perhaps we can never be certain that we aren't rationalizing, except when being playful like Franklin. But we can seek to think critically about our own beliefs, scrutinizing our assumptions, looking for counterevidence, and wondering if it's reasonably possible to draw different conclusions.

SOME PROCEDURES IN ARGUMENT

Definition

Definition, we mentioned in Chapter 1, is one of the classical topics, a "place" to which one goes with questions; in answering the questions, one finds ideas. When we define, we're answering the question "What is it?" In answering this question as precisely as we can, we will find, clarify, and develop ideas.

We have already glanced at an argument over the proposition that "all men are created equal," and we saw that the words needed clarification. *Equal* meant, in the context, not physically or mentally equal but something like "equal in rights," equal politically and legally. (And, of course, *men* meant "white men and women.") Words don't always mean exactly what they seem to mean: There's no lead in a lead pencil, and a standard 2-by-4 is currently 1⁵/₈ inches in thickness and 3³/₈ inches in width.

Definition by Synonym   Let's return for a moment to *pornography*, a word that is not easy to define. One way to define a word is to offer a **synonym**. Thus, pornography can be defined, at least roughly, as "obscenity" (something indecent). But definition by synonym is usually only a start because then we have to define the synonym; besides, very few words have exact synonyms. (In fact, *pornography* and *obscenity* are not exact synonyms.)

Definition by Example   A second way to define a word is to point to an example (this is often called **ostensive definition**, from the Latin *ostendere*, "to show"). This method can be very helpful, ensuring that both writer and reader are talking about the same thing, but it also has limitations. A few decades ago, many people pointed to James Joyce's *Ulysses* and D. H. Lawrence's *Lady Chatterley's Lover* as examples of obscene novels, but today these books are regarded as literary masterpieces. It's possible that they can be obscene and also be literary masterpieces. (Joyce's wife is reported to have said of her husband, "He may have been a great writer, but . . . he had a very dirty mind.")

One of the difficulties of using an example, however, is that the example is richer and more complex than the term it's being used to define, and this rich-ness and complex-ity get in the way of achieving a clear definition. Thus, if one cites *Lady Chatterley's Lover* as an example of pornography, a reader may erroneously think that pornography has something to do

"It all depends on how you define 'chop.'"

with British novels (because Lawrence was British) or with heterosexual relationships outside of marriage. Yet neither of these ideas
relates to the concept of pornography.

We are not trying here to formulate a satisfactory definition of
pornography. Our object is to make the following points clear:

- An argument will be most fruitful if the participants first
  agree on what they are talking about.
- One way to secure such agreement is to define the topic
  ostensively.
- Choosing the right example, one that has all the central or
  typical characteristics, can make a topic not only clear but
  also vivid.

Definition by Stipulation   Arguments frequently involve matters of
definition. In a discussion of gun control, for instance, you probably will hear one side speak of *assault weapons* and the other side
speak instead of *so-called assault weapons*. In arguing, you can hope
to get agreement—at least on what the topic of argument is—by
offering a **stipulative definition** (from a Latin verb meaning "to
bargain"). For instance, you and a representative of the other side
can agree on a definition of *assault weapon* based on the meaning of
the term in the ban approved by Congress in 1994, which expired
in 2004, and which President Obama in 2013 asked Congress to
renew. Although the renewal of the ban was unsuccessful, the
definition was this: a semiautomatic firearm (the spent cartridge
case is automatically extracted, and a new round is automatically
reloaded into the chamber but isn't fired until the trigger is pulled
again) with a detachable magazine *and at least two of the following five
characteristics*:

- collapsible or folding stock
- pistol grip (thus allowing the weapon to be fired from the hip)
- bayonet mount
- grenade launcher
- flash suppressor (to keep the shooter from being blinded by
  muzzle flashes)

Again, this was the agreed-upon definition for the purposes of the
legislation. Congress put *fully* automatic weapons into an entirely
different category, and the legislatures of California and of New York

each agreed on a stipulation different from that of Congress: In these two states, an assault weapon is defined as a semiautomatic firearm with a detachable magazine and with any *one* (not two) of the five bulleted items. The point is that for an argument to proceed rationally, and especially in the legal context, the key terms need to be precisely defined and agreed upon by all parties.

Let's now look at stipulative definitions in other contexts. Who is a *Native American*? In discussing this issue, you might stipulate that *Native American* means any person with any Native American blood; or you might say, "For the purpose of the present discussion, I mean that a *Native American* is any person who has at least one grandparent of pure Native American blood." A stipulative definition is appropriate in the following cases:

- when no fixed or standard definition is available, and
- when an arbitrary specification is necessary to fix the meaning of a key term in the argument.

Not everyone may accept your stipulative definition, and there will likely be defensible alternatives. In any case, when you stipulate a definition, your audience knows what *you* mean by the term.

It would *not* be reasonable to stipulate that by *Native American* you mean anyone with a deep interest in North American aborigines. That's too idiosyncratic to be useful. Similarly, an essay on Jews in America will have to rely on a definition of the key idea. Perhaps the writer will stipulate the definition used in Israel: A Jew is a person who has a Jewish mother or, if not born of a Jewish mother, a person who has formally adopted the Jewish faith. Perhaps the writer will stipulate another meaning: Jews are people who consider themselves to be Jews. Some sort of reasonable definition must be offered.

To stipulate, however, that *Jews* means "persons who believe that the area formerly called Palestine rightfully belongs to the Jews" would hopelessly confuse matters. Remember the old riddle: If you call a dog's tail a leg, how many legs does a dog have? The answer is four. Calling a tail a leg doesn't make it a leg.

In an essay titled "When 'Identity Politics' Is Rational," the author, Stanley Fish, begins by stipulating a definition. His first paragraph begins thus:

> If there's anything everyone is against in these election times, it's "identity politics," a phrase that covers a multitude of sins. Let

me start with a definition. (It may not be yours, but it will at least allow the discussion to be framed.) You're practicing identity politics when you vote for or against someone because of his or her skin color, ethnicity, religion, gender, sexual orientation, or any other marker that leads you to say yes or no independently of a candidates' ideas or policies.

Fish argues in later paragraphs that sometimes identity politics makes very good sense, that it is *not* irrational, is *not* logically indefensible; but here we simply want to make two points—one about how a definition helps the writer, and one about how it helps the reader:

- A definition is a good way to get started when drafting an essay, a useful stimulus (idea prompt, pattern, template, heuristic) that will help *you* to think about the issue, a device that will stimulate your further thinking.
- A definition lets readers be certain that they understand what the author means by a crucial word.

Readers may disagree with Fish, but at least they know what he means when he speaks of identity politics.

A stipulation may be helpful and legitimate. Here's the opening paragraph of a 1975 essay by Richard B. Brandt titled "The Morality and Rationality of Suicide." Notice that the author does two things:

- He first stipulates a definition.
- Then, aware that the definition may strike some readers as too broad and therefore unreasonable or odd, he offers a reason on behalf of his definition.

"Suicide" is conveniently defined, for our purposes, as doing something which results in one's death, either from the intention of ending one's life or the intention to bring about some other state of affairs (such as relief from pain) which one thinks it certain or highly probable can be achieved only by means of death or will produce death. It may seem odd to classify an act of heroic self-sacrifice on the part of a soldier as suicide. It is simpler, however, not to try to define "suicide" so that an act of suicide is always irrational or immoral in some way; if we adopt a neutral definition like the above we can still proceed to ask when an act of suicide in that sense is rational, morally justifiable, and so on, so that all evaluations anyone might wish to make can still be made. (61)

Sometimes, a definition that at first seems extremely odd can be made acceptable by offering strong reasons in its support. Sometimes, in fact, an odd definition marks a great intellectual step forward. For instance, in 1990 the U.S. Supreme Court recognized that *speech* includes symbolic nonverbal expression such as protesting against a war by wearing armbands or by flying the American flag upside down. Such actions, because they express ideas or emotions, are now protected by the First Amendment. Few people today would disagree that *speech* should include symbolic gestures.

A definition that seems notably eccentric to many readers and thus far has not gained much support is from Peter Singer's *Practical Ethics*, in which the author suggests that a nonhuman being can be a *person*. He admits that "it sounds odd to call an animal a person" but says that it seems so only because of our habit of sharply separating ourselves from other species. For Singer, *persons* are "rational and self-conscious beings, aware of themselves as distinct entities with a past and a future." Thus, although a newborn infant is a human being, it isn't a person; however, an adult chimpanzee isn't a human being but probably is a person. You don't have to agree with Singer to know exactly what he means and where he stands. Moreover, if you read his essay, you may even find that his reasons are plausible and that by means of his unusual definition he has broadened your thinking.

The Importance of Definitions   Trying to decide on the best way to define a key idea or a central concept is often difficult as well as controversial. *Death,* for example, has been redefined in recent years. Traditionally, a person was considered dead when there was no longer any heartbeat. But with advancing medical technology, the medical profession has persuaded legislatures to redefine death as cessation of cerebral and cortical functions—so-called brain death.

Some scholars have hoped to bring clarity into the abortion debate by redefining *life*. Traditionally, human life has been seen as beginning at birth or perhaps at viability (the capacity of a fetus to live independently of the uterine environment). However, others have proposed a *brain birth* definition in the hope of resolving the abortion controversy. Some thinkers want abortion to be prohibited by law at the point where "integrated brain functioning begins to emerge," allegedly about seventy days after conception. Whatever the merits of such a redefinition may be, the debate is convincing evidence of just how important the definition of certain terms can be.

Last Words about Definition   Since Plato's time in the fourth century B.C.E, it has often been argued that the best way to give a definition is to state the *essence* of the thing being defined. Thus, the classic example defines *man* as "a rational animal." (Today, to avoid sexist implications, instead of *man* we would say *human being* or *person.*) That is, the property of *rational animality* is considered to be the essence of every human creature, so it must be mentioned in the definition of *man.* This statement guarantees that the definition is neither too broad nor too narrow. But philosophers have long criticized this alleged ideal type of definition on several grounds, one of which is that no one can propose such definitions without assuming that the thing being defined has an essence in the first place—an assumption that is not necessary. Thus, we may want to define *causality,* or *explanation,* or even *definition* itself, but it's doubtful whether it is sound to assume that any of these concepts has an essence.

A much better way to provide a definition is to offer a set of **sufficient and necessary conditions**. Suppose we want to define the word *circle* and are conscious of the need to keep circles distinct from other geometric figures such as rectangles and spheres. We might express our definition by citing sufficient and necessary conditions as follows: "Anything is a circle *if and only if* it is a closed plane figure and all points on the circumference are equidistant from the center." Using the connective "if and only if" (called the *biconditional*) between the definition and the term being defined helps to make the definition neither too exclusive (too narrow) nor too inclusive (too broad). Of course, for most ordinary purposes we don't require such a formally precise definition. Nevertheless, perhaps the best criterion to keep in mind when assessing a proposed definition is whether it can be stated in the "if and only if" form, and whether, if so stated, it is true; that is, if it truly specifies *all and only* the things covered by the word being defined. The Thinking Critically exercise that follows provides examples.

We aren't saying that the four sentences in the table below are incontestable. In fact, they are definitely arguable. We offer them merely to show ways of defining, and the act of defining is one way of helping to get your own thoughts going. Notice, too, that the fourth example, a "statement of necessary and sufficient

THINKING CRITICALLY GIVING DEFINITIONS

In the spaces provided, define one of the "new terms" provided according to the definition type stipulated.

Definition Type	Example	New Term	Your Definition
Synonym	"*Pornography*, simply stated, is obscenity."	Police brutality Helicopter parenting Alternative music Organic foods	
Example	"*Pornography* can be seen, for example, in D. H. Lawrence's *Lady Chatterley's Lover*, in the scene where . . ."	Police brutality Helicopter parenting Alternative music Organic foods	
Stipulation	"For the purposes of this essay, *pornography* means any type of media that . . ."	Police brutality Helicopter parenting Alternative music Organic foods	
Statement of necessary and sufficient conditions	"Something can be called *pornography* if and only if it presents sexually stimulating material without offering anything of redeeming social value."	Police brutality Helicopter parenting Alternative music Organic foods	

conditions" (indicated by *if and only if*), is a bit stiff for ordinary writing. An informal prompt along this line might begin, "Essentially, something can be called *pornography* if it presents. . . ."

Assumptions

In Chapter 1, we discussed the **assumptions** made by the authors of two essays on religious freedoms. But we have more to say about assumptions. We've already said that in the form of discourse known as argument, certain statements are offered as reasons for other statements. But even the longest and most complex chain of reasoning or proof is fastened to assumptions—one or more *unexamined beliefs*. (Even if writer and reader share such a belief, it is no less an assumption.) Benjamin Franklin argued against paying salaries to the holders of executive offices in the federal government on the grounds that men are moved by ambition (love of power) and by avarice (love of money) and that powerful positions conferring wealth incite men to do their worst. These assumptions he stated, although he felt no need to argue them at length because he assumed that his readers shared them.

An assumption may be unstated. A writer, painstakingly arguing specific points, may choose to keep one or more of the argument's assumptions tacit. Or the writer may be completely unaware of an underlying assumption. For example, Franklin didn't even bother to state another assumption. He must have assumed that persons of wealth who accept an unpaying job (after all, only persons of wealth could afford to hold unpaid government jobs) will have at heart the interests of all classes of people, not only the interests of their own class. Probably Franklin didn't state this assumption because he thought it was perfectly obvious, but if you think critically about it, you may find reasons to doubt it. Surely one reason we pay our legislators is to ensure that the legislature does not consist only of people whose incomes may give them an inadequate view of the needs of others.

As another example, here are two assumptions in the argument for permitting abortion:

1. Ours is a pluralistic society, in which we believe that the religious beliefs of one group should not be imposed on others.
2. Personal privacy is a right, and a woman's body is hers, not to be violated by laws that forbid her from doing certain things to her body.

But these (and other) arguments *assume* that a fetus is not—or not yet—a person and therefore is not entitled to the same protection against assaults that we are. Virtually all of us assume that it is usually wrong to kill a human being. Granted, there may be instances in which we believe it's acceptable to take a human life, such as self-defense against a would-be murderer. But even here we find a shared assumption that persons are ordinarily entitled not to be killed.

The argument about abortion, then, usually depends on opposed assumptions. For one group, the fetus is a human being and a potential person—and this potentiality is decisive. For the other group, it is not. Persons arguing one side or the other of the abortion issue ought to be aware that opponents may not share their assumptions.

Premises and Syllogisms

Premises are stated assumptions that are used as reasons in an argument. (The word comes from a Latin word meaning "to send before" or "to set in front.") A premise thus is a statement set down—assumed—before the argument begins. The joining of two premises—two statements taken to be true—to produce a conclusion, a third statement, is a **syllogism** (from the Greek for "a reckoning together"). The classic example is this:

Major premise:	All human beings are mortal.
Minor premise:	Socrates is a human being.
Conclusion:	Socrates is mortal.

Deduction

The mental process of moving from one statement ("All human beings are mortal") through another ("Socrates is a human being") to yet a further statement ("Socrates is mortal") is **deduction**, from the Latin for "lead down from." In this sense, deductive reasoning doesn't give us any new knowledge, although it's easy to construct examples that have so many premises, or premises that are so complex, that the conclusion really does come as news to most who examine the argument. Thus, the great fictional detective Sherlock Holmes was credited by his admiring colleague, Dr. Watson, with having unusual powers of deduction. Watson meant in part that Holmes could see the logical consequences of apparently disconnected reasons, the number and complexity of which left others

at a loss. What is common in all cases of deduction is that the reasons or premises offered are supposed to contain within themselves, so to speak, the conclusion extracted from them.

Often a syllogism is abbreviated. Martin Luther King Jr., defending a protest march, wrote in "Letter from Birmingham Jail":

> You assert that our actions, even though peaceful, must be condemned because they precipitate violence.

Fully expressed, the argument that King attributes to his critics would be stated thus:

> Society must condemn actions (even if peaceful) that precipitate violence.
>
> This action (though peaceful) will precipitate violence.
>
> Therefore, society must condemn this action.

An incomplete or abbreviated syllogism in which one of the premises is left unstated, of the sort found in King's original quotation, is an **enthymeme** (from the Greek for "in the mind").

Here is another, more whimsical example of an enthymeme, in which both a premise and the conclusion are left implicit. Henry David Thoreau remarked that "circumstantial evidence can be very strong, as when you find a trout in the milk." The joke, perhaps intelligible only to people born before 1930 or so, depends on the fact that milk used to be sold "in bulk"—that is, ladled out of a big can directly to the customer by the farmer or grocer. This practice was prohibited in the 1930s because for centuries the sellers, seeking to increase their profit, were diluting the milk with water. Thoreau's enthymeme can be fully expressed thus:

> Trout live only in water.
>
> This milk has a trout in it.
>
> Therefore, this milk has water in it.

These enthymemes have three important properties: Their premises are *true*, the form of their argument is *valid*, and they leave *implicit* either the conclusion or one of the premises.

Sound Arguments

The purpose of a syllogism is to present reasons that establish its conclusion. This is done by making sure that the argument satisfies both of two independent criteria:

- First, all of the premises must be *true*.
- Second, the syllogism must be *valid*.

Once these criteria are satisfied, the conclusion of the syllogism is guaranteed. Any such argument is said to establish or to prove its conclusion—to use another term, it is said to be **sound**. Here's an example of a sound argument, a syllogism that proves its conclusion:

> Extracting oil from the Arctic Wildlife Refuge would adversely affect the local ecology.
>
> Adversely affecting the local ecology is undesirable, unless there is no better alternative fuel source.
>
> Therefore, extracting oil from the Arctic Wildlife Refuge is undesirable, unless there is no better alternative fuel source.

Each premise is **true**, and the syllogism is **valid**, so it establishes its conclusion.

But how do we tell in any given case that an argument is sound? We perform two different tests, one for the truth of each of the premises and another for the validity of the argument.

The basic test for the **truth** of a premise is to determine whether what it asserts corresponds with reality; if it does, then it is true, and if it doesn't, then it is false. Everything depends on the premise's content—what it asserts—and the evidence for it. (In the preceding syllogism, it's possible to test the truth of the premises by checking the views of experts and interested parties, such as policymakers, environmental groups, and experts on energy.)

The test for **validity** is quite different. We define a valid argument as one in which the conclusion follows from the premises, so that if all the premises are true, then the conclusion *must* be true, too. The general test for validity, then, is this: If one grants the premises, one must also grant the conclusion. In other words, if one grants the premises but denies the conclusion, is one caught in a self-contradiction? If so, the argument is valid; if not, the argument is invalid.

The preceding syllogism passes this test. If you grant the information given in the premises but deny the conclusion, you contradict yourself. Even if the information were in error, the conclusion in this syllogism would still follow from the premises—the hallmark of a valid argument! The conclusion follows because the validity of an argument is a purely formal matter concerning the *relation* between premises and conclusion based on what they mean.

It's possible to see this relationship more clearly by examining an argument that is valid but that, because one or both of the premises are false, does *not* establish its conclusion. Here's an example of such a syllogism:

> The whale is a large fish.
>
> All large fish have scales.
>
> Therefore, whales have scales.

We know that the premises and the conclusion are false: Whales are mammals, not fish, and not all large fish have scales (sharks have no scales, for instance). But in determining the argument's validity, the truth of the premises and the conclusion is beside the point. Just a little reflection assures us that *if* both premises were true, then the conclusion would have to be true as well. That is, anyone who grants the premises of this syllogism yet denies the conclusion contradicts herself. So the validity of an argument does not in any way depend on the truth of the premises or the conclusion.

A sound argument, as we said, is one that passes both the test of true premises and the test of valid inference. To put it another way, a sound argument does the following:

- It passes the test of content (the premises are true, as a matter of fact).

- It passes the test of form (its premises and conclusion, by virtue of their very meanings, are so related that it is impossible for the premises to be true and the conclusion false).

Accordingly, an unsound argument, one that fails to prove its conclusion, suffers from one or both of two defects:

- Not all the premises are true.

- The argument is invalid.

Usually, we have in mind one or both defects when objecting to someone's argument as "illogical." In evaluating a deductive argument, therefore, you must always ask: Is it vulnerable to criticism on the grounds that one (or more) of its premises is false? Or is the inference itself vulnerable because even if all the premises are true, the conclusion still wouldn't follow?

A deductive argument proves its conclusion if and only if *two conditions* are satisfied: (1) All the premises are true, and (2) it would be inconsistent to assert the premises and deny the conclusions.

A Word about False Premises

Suppose that one or more of a syllogism's premises are false but the syllogism itself is valid. What does that indicate about the truth of the conclusion? Consider this example:

> All Americans prefer vanilla ice cream to other flavors.
>
> Jimmy Fallon is an American.
>
> Therefore, Jimmy Fallon prefers vanilla ice cream to other flavors.

The first (or major) premise in this syllogism is false. Yet the argument passes our formal test for validity; if one grants both premises, then one must accept the conclusion. So we can say that the conclusion *follows from* its premises, even though the premises *do not prove* the conclusion. This is not as paradoxical as it may sound. For all we know, the argument's conclusion may in fact be true; Jimmy Fallon may indeed prefer vanilla ice cream, and the odds are that he does because consumption statistics show that a majority of Americans prefer vanilla. Nevertheless, if the conclusion in this syllogism is true, it's not because this argument proved it.

A Word about Invalid Syllogisms

Usually, one can detect a false premise in an argument, especially when the suspect premise appears in someone else's argument. A trickier business is the invalid syllogism. Consider this argument:

> All terrorists seek publicity for their violent acts.
>
> John Doe seeks publicity for his violent acts.
>
> Therefore, John Doe is a terrorist.

In this syllogism, let's grant that the first (major) premise is true. Let's also grant that the conclusion may well be true. Finally, the person mentioned in the second (minor) premise could indeed be a terrorist. But it's also possible that the conclusion is false; terrorists aren't the only ones who seek publicity for their violent acts—consider, for example, the violence committed against doctors, clinic workers, and patients at clinics where abortions are performed. In short, the truth of the two premises is no guarantee that the conclusion is also true. It's possible to assert both premises and deny the conclusion without being self-contradictory.

How do we tell, in general and in particular cases, whether a syllogism is valid? Chemists use litmus paper to determine instantly whether the liquid in a test tube is an acid or a base. Unfortunately, logic has no litmus test to tell us instantly whether an argument is valid or invalid. Logicians beginning with Aristotle have developed techniques to test any given argument, no matter how complex or subtle, to determine its validity. But the results of their labors cannot be expressed in a paragraph or even a few pages; this is why entire semester-long courses are devoted to teaching formal deductive logic. Apart from advising you to consult Chapter 9, A Logician's View: Deduction, Induction, Fallacies, all we can do here is repeat two basic points.

First, the validity of deductive arguments is a matter of their *form* or *structure*. Even syllogisms like the one on the Arctic Wildlife Refuge on page 127 come in a large variety of forms (256 forms, to be precise), and only some of these forms are valid. Second, all valid deductive arguments (and only such arguments) pass this test: If one accepts all the premises, then one must accept the conclusion as well. Hence, if it's possible to accept the premises but reject the conclusion (without self-contradiction, of course), then the argument is invalid.

Let's exit from further discussion of this important but difficult subject on a lighter note. Many illogical arguments masquerade as logical. Consider this example: If it takes a horse and carriage four hours to go from Pinsk to Chelm, does it follow that a carriage with two horses will get there in two hours?

Note: In Chapter 9, we discuss at some length other kinds of deductive arguments, as well as **fallacies**, which are kinds of invalid reasoning.

Induction

Whereas deduction takes beliefs and assumptions and extracts their hidden consequences, **induction** uses information about observed cases to reach a conclusion about unobserved cases. (The word comes from the Latin *in ducere,* "to lead into" or "to lead up to.") If we observe that the bite of a certain snake is poisonous, we may conclude on the basis of this evidence that the bite of another snake of the same general type is also poisonous. Our inference might be even broader: If we observe that snake after snake of a certain type has a poisonous bite and that these snakes are all rattlesnakes, then we're tempted to **generalize** that all rattlesnakes are poisonous.

By far the most common way to test the adequacy of a generalization is to consider one or more **counterexamples**. If the counterexamples are genuine and reliable, then the generalization must be false. For example, an essay by Ronald Takaki on the "myth" of Asian racial superiority is full of examples that contradict the alleged superiority of Asians; they are counterexamples to that thesis, and they help to expose it as a "myth." What is true of Takaki's reasoning is true generally in argumentative writing: We constantly test our generalizations by considering them against actual or possible counterexamples, or by doing research on the issue.

Unlike deduction, induction yields conclusions that go beyond the information contained in the premises used in their support. It's not surprising that the conclusions of inductive reasoning are not always true, even when all the premises are true. On page 91, we gave as an example our observation that on previous days a subway has run at 6:00 A.M. and that therefore we conclude that it runs at 6:00 A.M. every day. Suppose, following this reasoning, we arrive at the subway platform just before 6:00 A.M. on a given day and wait for an hour without seeing a single train. What inference should we draw to explain this? Possibly today is Sunday, and the subway doesn't run before 7:00 A.M. Or possibly there was a breakdown earlier this morning. Whatever the explanation might be, we relied on a sample that wasn't large enough (a larger sample might have included some early morning breakdowns) or representative enough (a more representative sample would have included the later starts on Sundays and holidays).

A Word about Samples When we reason inductively, much depends on the size and the quality of the sample (we say "sample" because a writer probably cannot examine every instance). If, for example, we're offering an argument concerning the politics of members of sororities and fraternities, we probably cannot interview *every* member. Rather, we select a sample. But is the sample a fair one? Is it representative of the larger group? We may interview five members of Alpha Tau Omega and find that all five are Republicans, yet we cannot legitimately conclude that all members of ATO are Republicans. The problem doesn't always involve failing to interview an adequately large sample group. For example, a poll of ten thousand college students tells us very little about "college students" if all ten thousand are white males at the University of Texas. Because such a sample leaves out women and minority males, it isn't sufficiently *representative* of "college students" as a group. Further, though not all students at the University of Texas are from Texas or even from the Southwest, it's quite likely that the student body is not fully representative (e.g., in race and in income) of American college students. If this conjecture is correct, even a truly representative sample of University of Texas students wouldn't enable us to draw firm conclusions about American college students.

In short: An argument that uses samples ought to tell the reader how the samples were chosen. If it doesn't provide this information, the reader should treat the argument with suspicion.

Evidence: Experimentation, Examples, Authoritative Testimony, Statistics

Different disciplines use different kinds of evidence:

- In literary studies, the texts are usually the chief evidence.
- In the social sciences, field research (interviews, surveys) usually provides evidence.
- In the sciences, reports of experiments are the usual evidence; if an assertion cannot be tested—if one cannot show it to be false—it is a *belief*, an *opinion*, not a scientific hypothesis.

Experimentation   Induction is obviously useful in arguing. If, for example, one is arguing that handguns should be controlled, one will point to specific cases in which handguns caused accidents or were used to commit crimes. In arguing that abortion has a traumatic effect on women, one will point to women who testify to that effect. Each instance constitutes **evidence** for the relevant generalization.

In a courtroom, evidence bearing on the guilt of the accused is introduced by the prosecution, and evidence to the contrary is introduced by the defense. Not all evidence is admissible (e.g., hearsay is not, even if it's true), and the law of evidence is a highly developed subject in jurisprudence. In the forum of daily life, the sources of evidence are less disciplined. Daily experience, a particularly memorable observation, an unusual event—any or all of these may serve as evidence for (or against) some belief, theory, hypothesis, or explanation. Science involves the systematic study of what experience can yield, and one of the most distinctive features of the evidence that scientists can marshal on behalf of their claims is that it is the result of **experimentation**. Experiments are deliberately contrived situations, often complex in their technology, that are designed to yield particular observations. What the ordinary person does with unaided eye and ear, the scientist does, much more carefully and thoroughly, with the help of laboratory instruments.

The variety, extent, and reliability of the evidence obtained in daily life are quite different from those obtained in the laboratory. It's no surprise that society attaches much more weight to the "findings" of scientists than to the corroborative (much less the contrary) experiences of ordinary people. No one today would seriously argue that the sun really does go around the earth just because it looks that way; nor would we argue that because viruses are invisible to the naked eye they cannot cause symptoms such as swellings and fevers, which are plainly evident.

Examples   One form of evidence is the **example**. Suppose we argue that a candidate is untrustworthy and shouldn't be elected to public office. We point to episodes in his career—his misuse of funds in 2008 and the false charges he made against an opponent in 2016—as examples of his untrustworthiness. Or if we're arguing that President Truman ordered the atom bomb dropped to save American (and, for that matter, Japanese) lives that otherwise would have been lost in a hard-fought invasion of Japan, we point to the stubbornness of the Japanese defenders in battles on the islands of Saipan, Iwo Jima, and Okinawa, where Japanese soldiers fought to the death rather than surrender.

These examples, we say, indicate that the Japanese defenders of the main islands would have fought to their deaths without surrendering, even though they knew defeat was certain. Or if we argue that the war was nearly won when Truman dropped the bomb, we can cite secret peace feelers as examples of the Japanese willingness to end the war.

An *example* is a *sample*. These two words come from the same Old French word, *essample*, from the Latin *exemplum*, which means "something taken out"—that is, a selection from the group. A Yiddish proverb shrewdly says, "'For example' is no proof," but the evidence of well-chosen examples can go a long way toward helping a writer to convince an audience.

In arguments, three sorts of examples are especially common:

* real events
* invented instances (artificial or hypothetical cases)
* analogies

We will treat each of these briefly.

REAL EVENTS   In referring to Truman's decision to drop the atom bomb, we've already touched on examples drawn from real events—the battles at Saipan and elsewhere. And we've also seen Ben Franklin pointing to an allegedly real happening, a fish that had consumed a smaller fish. The advantage of an example drawn from real life, whether a great historical event or a local incident, is that its reality gives it weight. It cannot simply be brushed off.

Yet an example drawn from reality may not be as clear-cut as we would like. Suppose, for instance, that someone cites the Japanese army's behavior on Saipan and on Iwo Jima as evidence that the Japanese later would have fought to the death in an American invasion of Japan and would therefore have inflicted terrible losses on themselves and on the Americans. This example is open to the response that in June and July 1945 certain Japanese diplomats sent out secret peace feelers, so that in August 1945, when Truman authorized dropping the bomb, the situation was very different.

Similarly, in support of the argument that nations will no longer resort to using atomic weapons, some people have offered as evidence the fact that since World War I the great powers have not used poison gas. But the argument needs more support than this fact provides. Poison gas wasn't decisive or even highly effective in World War I. Moreover, the invention of gas masks made its use obsolete.

In short, any *real* event is so entangled in historical circumstances that it might not be adequate or relevant evidence in the case being argued. In using a real event as an example (a perfectly valid strategy), the writer must demonstrate that the event can be taken out of its historical context for use in the new context of argument. Thus, in an argument against using atomic weapons in warfare, the many deaths and horrible injuries inflicted on the Japanese at Hiroshima and Nagasaki can be cited as effects of nuclear weapons that would invariably occur and did not depend on any special circumstances of their use in Japan in 1945.

INVENTED INSTANCES **Artificial** or **hypothetical cases—invented instances**—have the great advantage of being protected from objections of the sort we have just given. Recall Thoreau's trout in the milk; that was a colorful hypothetical case that illustrated his point well. An invented instance ("Let's assume that a burglar promises not to shoot a householder if the householder swears not to identify him. Is the householder bound by the oath?") is something like a drawing of a flower in a botany textbook or a diagram of the folds of a mountain in a geology textbook. It is admittedly false, but by virtue of its simplifications it sets forth the relevant details very clearly. Thus, in a discussion of rights, the philosopher Charles Frankel says:

> Strictly speaking, when we assert a right for X, we assert that Y has a duty. Strictly speaking, that Y has such a duty presupposes that Y has the capacity to perform this duty. It would be nonsense to say, for example, that a nonswimmer has a moral duty to swim to the help of a drowning man.

This invented example is admirably clear, and it is immune to charges that might muddy the issue if Frankel, instead of referring to a wholly abstract person, Y, talked about some real person, Jones, who did not rescue a drowning man. For then Frankel would get bogged down over arguing about whether Jones *really* couldn't swim well enough to help, and so on.

Yet invented examples have drawbacks. First and foremost, they cannot serve as evidence. A purely hypothetical example can illustrate a point or provoke reconsideration of a generalization, but it cannot substitute for actual events as evidence supporting an inductive inference. Sometimes, such examples are so fanciful that they fail to convince the reader. Thus, the philosopher Judith Jarvis Thomson, in the course of an argument entitled "A Defense of Abortion," asks the reader to imagine waking up one day and finding that against her will a celebrated violinist whose body is not adequately functioning has been hooked up into her body for life support. Does she have the right to unplug the violinist? As you read the essays we present in this textbook, you'll have to decide for yourself whether the invented cases proposed by various authors are helpful or whether they are so remote that they hinder thought. Readers will have to decide, too, about when they can use invented cases to advance their own arguments.

But we add one point: Even a highly fanciful invented case can have the valuable effect of forcing us to see where we stand. A person may say that she is, in all circumstances, against vivisection—the practice of performing operations on live animals for the purpose of research. But what would she say if she thought that an experiment on one mouse would save the life of someone she loves? Conversely, if she approves of vivisection, would she also approve of sacrificing the last giant panda to save the life of a senile stranger, a person who in any case probably wouldn't live longer than another year? Artificial cases of this sort can help us to see that we didn't really mean to say such-and-such when we said so-and-so.

ANALOGIES   The third sort of example, **analogy**, is a kind of comparison. An analogy asserts that things that are alike in some ways are alike in yet another way as well. Here's an example:

> Before the Roman Empire declined as a world power, it exhibited a decline in morals and in physical stamina; our society today shows a decline in both morals (consider the high divorce rate and the crime rate) and physical culture (consider obesity in children). America, like Rome, will decline as a world power.

Strictly speaking, an analogy is an extended comparison in which different things are shown to be similar in several ways. Thus, if one wants to argue that a head of state should have extraordinary power during wartime, one can argue that the state at such a time is like a ship in a storm: The crew is needed to lend its help, but the decisions are best left to the captain. (Notice that an analogy compares things that are relatively *un*like. Comparing the plight of

Gahan Wilson, The New Yorker Collection/The Cartoon Bank

"Do you mind if I use yet another sports analogy?"

one ship to another or of one government to another isn't an analogy; it's an inductive inference from one case of the same sort to another such case.)

Let's consider another analogy. We have already glanced at Judith Thomson's hypothetical case in which the reader wakes up to find herself hooked up to a violinist in need of life support. Thomson uses this situation as an analogy in an argument about abortion. The reader stands for the mother; the violinist, for the unwanted fetus. You may want to think about whether this analogy is close enough to pregnancy to help illuminate your own thinking about abortion.

The problem with argument by analogy is this: Two admittedly different things are agreed to be similar in several ways, and the arguer goes on to assert or imply that they are also similar in another way—the point being argued. (That's why Thomson argues that if something is true of the reader-hooked-up-to-a-violinist, it is also true of the pregnant-mother-hooked-up-to-a-fetus.) But the two things that are said to be analogous and that are indeed similar in characteristics *A, B,* and *C* are also different—let's say in characteristics *D* and *E.* As Bishop Butler is said to have remarked in the early eighteenth century, "Everything is what it is, and not another thing."

Analogies can be convincing, especially because they can make complex issues seem simple. "Don't change horses in midstream" isn't a statement about riding horses across a river but, rather, about choosing new leaders in critical times. Still, in the end, analogies don't necessarily prove anything. What may be true about riding horses across a stream may not be true about choosing new leaders in troubled times. Riding horses across a stream and choosing new leaders are fundamentally different things, and however much they may be said to resemble each other, they remain different. What is true for one need not be true for the other.

Analogies can be helpful in developing our thoughts and in helping listeners or readers to understand a point we're trying to make. It is sometimes argued, for instance—on the analogy of the doctor–patient, the lawyer–client, or the priest–penitent relationship—that newspaper and television reporters should not be required to reveal their confidential sources. That is worth thinking about: Do the similarities run deep enough, or are there fundamental differences? Consider another example: Some writers who support abortion argue that the fetus is not a person any more than the acorn is an oak. That is also worth thinking about. But one should also think about this response: A fetus is not a person, just as an acorn is not an oak; but an acorn is a potential oak, and a fetus is a potential person, a potential adult human being. Children, even newborn infants, have rights, and one way to explain this claim is to call attention to their potentiality to become mature adults. Thus, some people argue that the fetus, by analogy, has the rights of an infant, for the fetus, like the infant, is a potential adult.

Three analogies for consideration: First, let's examine a brief comparison made by Jill Knight, a member of the British Parliament, speaking about abortion:

> Babies are not like bad teeth, to be jerked out because they cause suffering.

Her point is effectively put; it remains for the reader to decide whether fetuses are *babies* and if a fetus is not a baby, *why* it can or cannot be treated like a bad tooth.

Now a second bit of analogical reasoning, again about abortion: Thomas Sowell, an economist at the Hoover Institute, grants that women have a legal right to abortion, but he objects to a requirement that the government pay for abortions:

> Because the courts have ruled that women have a legal right to
> an abortion, some people have jumped to the conclusion that
> the government has to pay for it. You have a constitutional right
> to privacy, but the government has no obligation to pay for your
> window shades. (*Pink and Brown People*, 1981, p. 57)

We leave it to you to decide whether the analogy is compelling— that is, if the points of resemblance are sufficiently significant to allow you to conclude that what's true of people wanting window shades should be true of people wanting abortions.

And one more: A common argument on behalf of legalizing gay marriage drew an analogy between gay marriage and interracial marriage, a practice that was banned in sixteen states until 1967, when the Supreme Court declared miscegenation statutes unconstitutional. The gist of the analogy was this: Racism and discrimination against gay and lesbian people are the same. If marriage is a fundamental right—as the Supreme Court held in its 1967 decision striking down bans on miscegenation—then it is a fundamental right for gay and lesbian people as well as heterosexual people.

Authoritative Testimony   Another form of evidence is **testimony**, the citation or quotation of authorities. In daily life, we rely heavily on authorities of all sorts: We get a doctor's opinion about our health, we read a book because an intelligent friend recommends it, we see a movie because a critic gave it a good review, and we pay at least a little attention to the weather forecaster.

In setting forth an argument, one often tries to show that one's view is supported by notable figures—perhaps Jefferson, Lincoln, Martin Luther King Jr., or scientists who won the Nobel Prize. You may recall that in Chapter 2, in talking about medical marijuana legalization, we presented an essay by Sanjay Gupta. To make certain that you were impressed by his ideas, we described him as CNN's chief medical correspondent and a leading public health expert. In our Chapter 2 discussion of Sally Mann, we qualified our description of her controversial photographs by noting that *Time* magazine called her "America's Best Photographer" and the *New Republic* called her book "one of the great photograph books of our time." But heed some words of caution:

- Be sure that the authority, however notable, is *an authority on the topic in question.* (A well-known biologist might be an authority on vitamins but not on the justice of war.)

- Be sure that the authority is *unbiased.* (A chemist employed by the tobacco industry isn't likely to admit that smoking may be harmful, and a producer of violent video games isn't likely to admit that playing those games stimulates violence.)

- Beware of *nameless* authorities: "a thousand doctors," "leading educators," "researchers at a major medical school." (If possible, offer at least one specific name.)

- Be careful when using authorities who indeed were great authorities in their day but *who now may be out of date.* (Examples would include Adam Smith on economics, Julius Caesar on the art of war, Louis Pasteur on medicine.)

- Cite authorities *whose opinions your readers will value.* (William F. Buckley Jr.'s conservative/libertarian opinions mean a good deal to readers of the magazine that he founded, the *National Review*, but probably not to most liberal thinkers. Gloria Steinem's liberal/feminist opinions carry weight with readers of the magazines that she cofounded, *New York* and *Ms.* magazine, but probably not with most conservative thinkers.) When writing for the general reader—your usual audience—cite authorities whom the general reader is likely to accept.

One other point: *You* may be an authority. You probably aren't nationally known, but on some topics you might have the authority of personal experience. You may have been injured on a motorcycle while riding without wearing a helmet, or you may have escaped injury because you wore a helmet. You may have dropped out of school and then returned. You may have tutored a student whose native language isn't English, you may be such a student who has received tutoring, or you may have attended a school with a bilingual education program. In short, your personal testimony on topics relating to these issues may be invaluable, and a reader will probably consider it seriously.

Statistics   The last sort of evidence we discuss here is quantitative, or statistical. The maxim "More is better" captures a basic idea of quantitative evidence: Because we know that 90 percent is greater than 75 percent, we're usually ready to grant that any claim supported by experience in 90 percent of cases is more likely to be true than an alternative claim supported by experience in only 75 percent of cases. The greater the difference, the greater our confidence. Consider an example. Honors at graduation from college are often computed on the basis of a student's cumulative grade-point average (GPA). The undisputed assumption is that the nearer a student's GPA is to a perfect record (4.0), the better scholar he or she is and therefore the more deserving of highest honors. Consequently, a student with a GPA of 3.9 at the end of her senior year is a stronger candidate for graduating summa cum laude than another student with a GPA of 3.6. When faculty members on the honors committee argue over the relative academic merits of graduating seniors, we know that these quantitative, statistical differences in student GPAs will be the basic (if not the only) kind of evidence under discussion.

GRAPHS, TABLES, NUMBERS   Statistical information can be presented in many forms, but it tends to fall into two main types: the graphic and the numerical. Graphs, tables, and pie charts are familiar ways of presenting quantitative data in an eye-catching manner. (See pp. 171–72.) To prepare the graphics, however, one first has to decide how best to organize and interpret the numbers, and for some purposes it may be more appropriate to directly present the numbers themselves.

But is it better to present the numbers in percentages or in fractions? Should a report say that the federal budget (1) underwent a twofold increase over the decade; (2) increased by 100 percent; (3) doubled; or (4) at the beginning of the decade was one-half what it was at the end? These are equivalent ways of saying the same thing. Making a choice among them, therefore, will likely rest on whether one's aim is to dramatize the increase (a 100 percent increase looks larger than a doubling) or to play down its size.

THINKING ABOUT STATISTICAL EVIDENCE   Statistics often get a bad name because it's so easy to misuse them (unintentionally or not) and so difficult to be sure that they were gathered correctly in the first place. (One old saying goes, "There are lies, damned lies, and statistics.") Every branch of social science and natural science needs statistical information, and countless decisions in public and private life are based on quantitative data in statistical form. It's important, therefore, to be sensitive to the sources and reliability of the statistics and to develop a healthy skepticism when you confront statistics whose parentage is not fully explained.

Consider statistics that pop up in conversations about wealth distribution in the United States. In 2014, the Census Bureau calculated that the **median** household income in the United States was $53,657, meaning that half of households earned less than this amount and half earned above it. However, the **average**— technically, the **mean**—household income in the same year was $72,641, about $19,000 (or 39 percent) higher. Which number more accurately represents the typical household income? Both are "correct," but both are calculated with different measures, median and mean. If a politician wanted to argue that the United States has a strong middle class, he might use the average (mean) income as evidence, a number calculated by dividing the total income of all households by the total number of households. If another politician wished to make a rebuttal, she could point out that the average income paints a rosy picture because the wealthiest households skew the average higher. The median income (representing the number above and below which two halves of all households fall) should be the measure we use, the rebutting politician could argue, because it helps reduce the effect of the limitless ceiling of higher incomes and the finite floor of lower incomes at zero.

Consider the following statistics: Suppose in a given city in 2014, 1 percent of the victims in fatal automobile accidents were bicyclists. In the same city in 2015, the percentage of bicyclists killed in automobile accidents was 2 percent. Was the increase 1 percent (not an alarming figure), or was it 100 percent (a staggering figure)? The answer is both, depending on whether we're comparing (1) bicycle deaths in automobile accidents *with all deaths in automobile accidents* (that's an increase of 1 percent), or (2) bicycle deaths in automobile accidents *only with other bicycle deaths in automobile accidents* (an increase of 100 percent). An honest statement would say that bicycle deaths due to automobile accidents doubled in 2015, increasing from 1 to 2 percent. But here's another point: Although every such death is lamentable, if there was one such death in 2014 and two in 2015, the increase from one death to two (an increase of 100 percent!) hardly suggests a growing problem that needs attention. No one would be surprised to learn that in the next year there were no deaths at all, or only one or two.

If it's sometimes difficult to interpret statistics, it's often at least equally difficult to establish accurate statistics. Consider this example:

> Advertisements are the most prevalent and toxic of the mental pollutants. From the moment your radio alarm sounds in the morning to the wee hours of late-night TV, microjolts of commercial pollution flood into your brain at the rate of about three thousand marketing messages per day. (Kalle Lasn, *Culture Jam* [1999], 18–19)

Lasn's book includes endnotes as documentation, so, being curious about the statistics, we turn to the appropriate page and find this information concerning the source of his data:

> "three thousand marketing messages per day." Mark Landler, Walecia Konrad, Zachary Schiller, and Lois Therrien, "What Happened to Advertising?" *BusinessWeek*, September 23, 1991, page 66. Leslie Savan in *The Sponsored Life* (Temple University Press, 1994), page 1, estimated that "16,000 ads flicker across an individual's consciousness daily." I did an informal survey in March 1995 and found the number to be closer to 1,500 (this included all marketing messages, corporate images, logos, ads, brand names, on TV, radio, billboards, buildings, signs, clothing, appliances, in cyberspace, etc., over a typical twenty-four hour period in my life). (219)

Well, this endnote is odd. In the earlier passage, the author asserted that about "three thousand marketing messages per day" flood into a person's brain. In the documentation, he cites a source for that statistic from *BusinessWeek*—though we haven't the faintest idea how the authors of the *BusinessWeek* article came up with that figure. Oddly, he goes on to offer a very different figure (16,000 ads) and then, to our confusion, offers yet a third figure, 1,500, based on his own "informal survey."

Probably the one thing we can safely say about all three figures is that none of them means very much. Even if the compilers of the statistics explained exactly how they counted—let's say that among countless other criteria they assumed that the average person reads one magazine per day and that the average magazine contains 124 advertisements—it would be hard to take them seriously. After all, in leafing through a magazine, some people may read many ads and some may read none. Some people may read some ads carefully—but perhaps just to enjoy their absurdity. Our point: Although the author in his text said, without implying any uncertainty, that "about three thousand marketing messages per day" reach an individual, it's evident (by checking the endnote) that even he is confused about the figure he gives.

UNRELIABLE STATISTICS   We'd like to make a final point about the unreliability of some statistical information—data that looks impressive but that is, in fact, insubstantial. For instance, Marilyn Jager Adams studied the number of hours that families read to their children in the five or so years before the children start attending school. In her book *Beginning to Read: Thinking and Learning about Print* (1994), she pointed out that in all those preschool years, poor families read to their children only 25 hours, whereas in the same period middle-income families read 1,000 to 1,700 hours. The figures were much quoted in newspapers and by children's advocacy groups. Adams could not, of course, interview every family in these two groups; she had to rely on samples. What were her samples? For poor families, she selected 24 children in 20 families, all in Southern California. Ask yourself: Can families from only one geographic area provide an adequate sample for a topic such as this? Moreover, let's think about Adams's sample of middle-class families. How many families constituted that sample? Exactly one—her own. We leave it to you to judge the validity of her findings.

✓ A CHECKLIST FOR EVALUATING STATISTICAL EVIDENCE

Regard statistical evidence (like all other evidence) cautiously, and don't accept it until you have thought about these questions:

☐ Was it compiled by a disinterested (impartial) source? The source's name doesn't always reveal its particular angle (e.g., People for the American Way), but sometimes it lets you know what to expect (e.g., National Rifle Association, American Civil Liberties Union).

☐ Is it based on an adequate sample?

☐ Is the statistical evidence recent enough to be relevant?

☐ How many of the factors likely to be relevant were identified and measured?

☐ Are the figures open to a different and equally plausible interpretation?

☐ If a percentage is cited, is it the average (or *mean*), or is it the median?

We are not suggesting that everyone who uses statistics is trying to deceive or is unconsciously being deceived by them. We suggest only that statistics are open to widely different interpretations and that often those columns of numbers, which appear to be so precise with their decimal points, may actually be imprecise and possibly worthless if they're based on insufficient or biased samples.

QUIZ

What is wrong with the following statistical proof that children do not have time for school?

> One-third of the time they are sleeping (about 122 days).
> One-eighth of the time they are eating (three hours a day, totaling 45 days).
> One-fourth of the time they are on summer and other vacations (91 days).
> Two-sevenths of the year is weekends (104 days).
> Total: 362 days—so how can a kid have time for school?

NONRATIONAL APPEALS

Satire, Irony, Sarcasm, Humor

In talking about definition, deduction, and evidence, we've been talking about means of rational persuasion. However, as mentioned earlier, there are also other means of persuasion. Force is an example. If X kicks Y, threatens to destroy Y's means of livelihood, or threatens Y's life, X may persuade Y to cooperate. But writers, of course, cannot use such kinds of force on their readers. Instead, one form of irrational but sometimes highly effective persuasion is **satire**—that is, witty ridicule. A cartoonist may persuade viewers that a politician's views are unsound by caricaturing (thus ridiculing) her appearance or by presenting a grotesquely distorted (funny, but unfair) picture of the issue she supports.

Satiric artists often use caricature; satiric writers, also seeking to persuade by means of ridicule, often use **verbal irony**. This sort of irony contrasts what is said and what is meant. For instance, words of praise may actually imply blame (when Shakespeare's Cassius says, "Brutus is an honorable man," he wants his hearers to think that Brutus is dishonorable), and words of modesty may actually imply superiority ("Of course, I'm too dumb to understand this problem"). Such language, when heavy-handed, is **sarcasm** ("You're a great guy," said to someone who won't lend the speaker ten dollars). If it's witty and clever, we call it irony rather than sarcasm.

Although ridicule isn't a form of argument (because it isn't a form of reasoning), passages of ridicule, especially verbal irony, sometimes appear in argument essays. These passages, like reasons or like appeals to the emotions, are efforts to persuade the reader to accept the writer's point of view. The key to using humor in an argument is, on the one hand, to avoid wisecracking like a smart aleck, and on the other hand, to avoid mere clownishness. Later in this chapter (p. 127), we print an essay by George F. Will that is (or seeks to be) humorous in places. You be the judge.

Emotional Appeals

It is sometimes said that good argumentative writing appeals only to reason, never to emotion, and that any emotional appeal is illegitimate and irrelevant. "Tears are not arguments," the Brazilian writer Machado de Assis said. Logic textbooks may even stigmatize with

Latin labels the various sorts of emotional appeal—for instance, *argumentum ad populam* (appeal to the prejudices of the mob, as in "Come on, we all know that schools don't teach anything anymore") and *argumentum ad misericordiam* (appeal to pity, as in "No one ought to blame this poor kid for stabbing a classmate because his mother was often institutionalized for alcoholism and his father beat him").

True, appeals to emotion may distract from the facts of the case; they may blind the audience by, in effect, throwing dust in its eyes or by provoking tears.

Learning from Shakespeare   A classic example is in Shakespeare's *Julius Caesar*, when Marc Antony addresses the Roman populace after Brutus, Cassius, and others have assassinated Caesar. The real issue is whether Caesar was becoming tyrannical (as the assassins claim) and would have curtailed the freedom of the Roman people. Antony turns from the evidence and stirs the mob against the assassins by appealing to its emotions. In the ancient Roman biographical writing that Shakespeare drew on, Sir Thomas North's translation of Plutarch's *Lives of the Noble Grecians and Romans*, Plutarch says this about Antony:

> perceiving that his words moved the common people to compassion, . . . [he] framed his eloquence to make their hearts yearn [i.e., grieve] the more, and, taking Caesar's gown all bloody in his hand, he laid it open to the sight of them all, showing what a number of cuts and holes it had upon it. Therewithal the people fell presently into such a rage and mutiny that there was no more order kept.

Here are a few extracts from Antony's speeches in Shakespeare's play. Antony begins by asserting that he will speak only briefly:

> Friends, Romans, countrymen, lend me your ears;
> I come to bury Caesar, not to praise him.

After briefly offering insubstantial evidence that Caesar gave no signs of behaving tyrannically (e.g., "When that the poor have cried, Caesar hath wept"), Antony begins to play directly on his hearers' emotions. Descending from the platform so that he may be in closer contact with his audience (like a modern politician, he wants to work the crowd), he calls attention to Caesar's bloody toga:

> If you have tears, prepare to shed them now.
> You all do know this mantle; I remember

The first time ever Caesar put it on:
'Twas on a summer's evening, in his tent,
That day he overcame the Nervii.
Look, in this place ran Cassius' dagger through;
See what a rent the envious Casca made;
Through this, the well-belovèd Brutus stabbed. . . .

In these few lines, Antony accomplishes the following:

- He prepares the audience by suggesting to them how they should respond ("If you have tears, prepare to shed them now").
- He flatters them by implying that they, like Antony, were intimates of Caesar (he credits them with being familiar with Caesar's garment).
- He then evokes a personal memory of a specific time ("a summer's evening")—not just any specific time, but a very important one, the day that Caesar won a battle against the Nervii (a particularly fierce tribe in what is now France).

In fact, Antony was not at the battle, and he did not join Caesar until three years later.

Antony doesn't mind being free with the facts; his point here is not to set the record straight but to stir the mob against the assassins. He goes on, daringly but successfully, to identify one particular slit in the garment with Cassius's dagger, another with Casca's, and a third with Brutus's. Antony cannot know which dagger made which slit, but his rhetorical trick works.

Notice, too, that Antony arranges the three assassins in climactic order, since Brutus (Antony claims) was especially beloved by Caesar:

Judge, O you gods, how dearly Caesar loved him!
This was the most unkindest cut of all;
For when the noble Caesar saw him stab,
Ingratitude, more strong than traitor's arms,
Quite vanquished him. Then burst his mighty heart. . . .

Nice. According to Antony, the noble-minded Caesar—Antony's words have erased all thought of the tyrannical Caesar—died not from wounds inflicted by daggers but from the heartbreaking perception of Brutus's ingratitude. Doubtless there wasn't a dry eye in the house. Let's all hope that if we are ever put on trial, we'll have a lawyer as skilled in evoking sympathy as Antony.

Are Emotional Appeals Fallacious?   Antony's oration was obviously successful in the play and apparently was successful in real life, but it is the sort of speech that prompts logicians to write disapprovingly of attempts to stir feeling in an audience. (As mentioned earlier, the evocation of emotion in an audience is **pathos,** from the Greek word for "emotion" or "suffering.") There is nothing inherently wrong in stimulating an audience's emotions when attempting to establish a claim, but when an emotional appeal confuses the issue being argued or shifts attention away from the facts, we can reasonably speak of the fallacy of emotional appeal.

No fallacy is involved, however, when an emotional appeal heightens the facts, bringing them home to the audience rather than masking them. In talking about legislation that would govern police actions, for example, it's legitimate to show a photograph of the battered, bloodied face of an alleged victim of police brutality. True, such a photograph cannot tell the whole truth; it cannot tell if the subject threatened the officer with a gun or repeatedly resisted an order to surrender. But it can demonstrate that the victim was severely beaten and (like a comparable description in words) evoke emotions that may properly affect the audience's decision about the permissible use of police evidence. Similarly, an animal rights activist who argues that calves are cruelly confined might reasonably talk about the inhumanely small size of their pens, in which they cannot turn around or even lie down. Others may argue that calves don't care about turning around or have no right to turn around, but the evocative verbal description of their pens, which makes an emotional appeal, cannot be called fallacious or irrelevant.

In appealing to emotions, then, important strategies are as follows:

- Do not falsify (especially by oversimplifying) the issue.
- Do not distract attention from the facts of the case.
- Do think ethically about how emotional appeals may affect the audience.

You should focus on the facts and offer reasons (essentially, statements linked with "because"), but you may also legitimately bring the facts home to your readers by seeking to provoke appropriate emotions. Your words will be fallacious only if you stimulate emotions that aren't connected with the facts of the case.

DOES ALL WRITING CONTAIN ARGUMENTS?

Our answer to the question above is no—however, *most* writing probably *does* contain an argument of sorts. The writer wants to persuade the reader to see things the way the writer sees them—at least until the end of the essay. After all, even a recipe for a cherry pie in a food magazine—a piece of writing that's primarily expository (how to do it) rather than argumentative (how a reasonable person ought to think about this topic)—probably starts out with a hint of an argument, such as *"Because* [a sign that a *reason* will be offered] this pie can be made quickly and with ingredients (canned cherries) that are always available, give it a try. It will surely become one of your favorites." Clearly, such a statement cannot stand as a formal argument—a discussion that addresses counter-arguments, relies chiefly on logic and little if any emotional appeal, and draws a conclusion that seems irrefutable.

Still, the statement is an argument on behalf of making a pie with canned cherries. In this case, we can identify a claim (the pie will become a favorite) and two *reasons* in support of the claim:

- It can be made quickly.
- The chief ingredient—because it is canned—can always be at hand.

There are two underlying *assumptions*:

- Readers don't have a great deal of time to waste in the kitchen.
- Canned cherries are just as tasty as fresh cherries and even if they aren't, no one who eats the pie will know the difference.

When we read a lead-in to a recipe, then, we won't find a formal argument, but we'll probably see a few words that seek to persuade us to keep reading. And most writing does contain such material—sentences that engage our interest and give us a reason to keep reading. If the recipe is difficult and time consuming, the lead-in may say:

> Although this recipe for a cherry pie, using fresh cherries that you will have to pit, is a bit more time consuming than the usual recipes that call for canned cherries, once you have tasted it you will never go back to canned cherries.

✓ A CHECKLIST FOR ANALYZING AN ARGUMENT

What is the writer's claim or thesis? Ask yourself:
☐ What claim is asserted?
☐ What evidence is imagined?
☐ What assumptions are being made — and are they acceptable?
☐ Are important terms satisfactorily defined?

What support (evidence) is offered on behalf of the claim? Ask yourself:
☐ Are the examples relevant and convincing?
☐ Are the statistics (if any) relevant, accurate, and complete? Do they allow only the interpretation that is offered in the argument?
☐ If authorities are cited, are they indeed authorities on this topic, and can they be considered impartial?
☐ Is the logic — deductive and inductive — valid?
☐ If there is an appeal to emotion (e.g., if satire is used to ridicule the opposing view), is this appeal acceptable?

Does the writer seem to be fair? Ask yourself:
☐ Are counterarguments adequately considered?
☐ Is there any evidence of dishonesty or of a discreditable attempt to manipulate the reader?
☐ How does the writer establish the image of himself or herself that readers sense in the essay? What is the writer's tone, and is it appropriate?

Again, although the logic is scarcely compelling, the persuasive element is evident. The assumption is that readers have a discriminating palate; once they've tasted a pie made with fresh cherries, they'll never again enjoy the canned stuff. The writer isn't making a formal argument with abundant evidence and detailed refutation of counterarguments, but we know where he stands and how he wishes us to respond.

In short, almost all writers are trying to persuade readers to see things *their* way.

AN EXAMPLE: AN ARGUMENT AND A LOOK AT THE WRITER'S STRATEGIES

This essay concerns President George W. Bush's proposal to allow drilling in part of the Arctic National Wildlife Refuge (ANWR, pronounced "An-war"). The ANWR section where drilling is proposed is called the 1002 area, as defined by Section 1002 of the Alaska National Interest Lands Conservation Act of 1980. In March 2003, the Senate rejected the Bush proposal, but the issue remains alive.

We follow George F. Will's essay with some comments about the ways in which he constructs his argument.

George F. Will

George F. Will (b. 1941), a syndicated columnist whose writing appears in 460 newspapers, was born in Champaign, Illinois, and educated at Trinity College (in Hartford), Oxford University, and Princeton University. Will has served as the Washington, D.C., editor of the National Review *and now writes a regular column for* Newsweek. *His essays have been collected in several books.*

This essay was originally published in 2002, so it is in some respects dated—for instance, in its reference to the price of gasoline—but it still serves as an excellent model of certain ways to argue.

Being Green at Ben and Jerry's

Some Environmental Policies Are Feel-Good Indulgences for an Era of Energy Abundance

If you have an average-size dinner table, four feet by six feet, put a dime on the edge of it. Think of the surface of the table as the Arctic National Wildlife Refuge in Alaska. The dime is larger than the piece of the coastal plain that would have been opened to drilling for oil and natural gas. The House of Representatives voted for drilling, but the Senate voted against access to what Sen. John Kerry, Massachusetts Democrat and presidential aspirant, calls "a few drops of oil." ANWR could produce, for twenty-five years, at least as much oil as America currently imports from Saudi Arabia.

Six weeks of desultory Senate debate about the energy bill reached an almost comic culmination in . . . yet another agriculture subsidy. The subsidy is a requirement that will triple the amount of ethanol, which is made from corn, that must be put in gasoline, ostensibly to clean America's air, actually to buy farmers' votes.

Over the last three decades, energy use has risen about 30 percent. But so has population, which means per capita energy use is unchanged. And per capita GDP has risen substantially, so we are using 40 percent less energy per dollar output. Which is one reason there is no energy crisis, at least none as most Americans understand such things—a shortage of, and therefore high prices of, gasoline for cars, heating oil for furnaces and electricity for air conditioners.

In the absence of a crisis to concentrate the attention of the inattentive American majority, an intense faction—full-time environmentalists—goes to work. Spencer Abraham, the secretary of Energy, says "the previous administration . . . simply drew up a list of fuels it *didn't* like—nuclear energy, coal, hydropower, and oil—which together account for 73 percent of America's energy supply." Well, there are always windmills.

Sometimes lofty environmentalism is a cover for crude poli- 5 tics. The United States has the world's largest proven reserves of coal. But Mike Oliver, a retired physicist and engineer, and John Hospers, professor emeritus of philosophy at USC, note that in 1996 President Clinton put 68 billion tons of America's cleanest-burning coal, located in Utah, off-limits for mining, ostensibly for environmental reasons. If every existing U.S. electric power plant burned coal, the 68 billion tons could fuel them for forty-five years at the current rate of consumption. Now power companies must import clean-burning coal, some from mines owned by Indonesia's Lippo Group, the heavy contributor to Clinton, whose decision about Utah's coal vastly increased the value of Lippo's coal.

The United States has just 2.14 percent of the world's proven reserves of oil, so some people say it is pointless to drill in places like ANWR because "energy independence" is a chimera.[1] Indeed it is. But domestic supplies can provide important insurance against uncertain foreign supplies. And domestic supplies can mean exporting hundreds of billions of dollars less to oil-producing nations, such as Iraq.

Besides, when considering proven reserves, note the adjective. In 1930 the United States had proven reserves of 13 billion barrels. We then fought the Second World War and fueled the most fabulous economic expansion in human history, including the

---

[1]**chimera** Something that is hoped or wished for but is impossible to actually achieve. [Editors' note.]

electricity-driven "New Economy." (Manufacturing and running computers consume 15 percent of U.S. electricity. Internet use alone accounts for half of the growth in demand for electricity.) So by 1990 proven reserves were . . . 17 billion barrels, not counting any in Alaska or Hawaii.

In 1975 proven reserves in the Persian Gulf were 74 billion barrels. In 1993 they were 663 billion, a ninefold increase. At the current rate of consumption, today's proven reserves would last 150 years. New discoveries will be made, some by vastly improved techniques of deep-water drilling. But environmental policies will define opportunities. The government estimates that beneath the U.S. outer continental shelf, which the government owns, there are at least 46 billion barrels of oil. But only 2 percent of the shelf has been leased for energy development.

Opponents of increased energy production usually argue for decreased consumption. But they flinch from conservation measures. A new $1 gasoline tax would dampen demand for gasoline, but it would stimulate demands for the heads of the tax increasers. After all, Americans get irritable when impersonal market forces add 25 cents to the cost of a gallon. Tougher fuel-efficiency requirements for vehicles would save a lot of energy. But who would save the legislators who passed those requirements? Beware the wrath of Americans who like to drive, and autoworkers who like to make cars that are large, heavy, and safer than the gasoline-sippers that environmentalists prefer.

Some environmentalism is a feel-good indulgence for an era 10 of energy abundance, which means an era of avoided choices. Or ignored choices—ignored because if acknowledged, they would not make the choosers feel good. Karl Zinsmeister, editor in chief of the *American Enterprise* magazine, imagines an oh-so-green environmentalist enjoying the most politically correct product on the planet—Ben & Jerry's ice cream. Made in a factory that depends on electricity-guzzling refrigeration, a gallon of ice cream requires four gallons of milk. While making that much milk, a cow produces eight gallons of manure, and flatulence with another eight gallons of methane, a potent "greenhouse" gas. And the cow consumes lots of water plus three pounds of grain and hay, which is produced with tractor fuel, chemical fertilizers, herbicides and insecticides, and is transported with truck or train fuel:

"So every time he digs into his Cherry Garcia, the conscientious environmentalist should visualize (in addition to world peace) a pile of grain, water, farm chemicals, and energy inputs much bigger than his ice cream bowl on one side of the table, and, on the other side of the table, a mound of manure eight times the size of his bowl, plus a balloon of methane that would barely fit under the dining room table."

Cherry Garcia. It's a choice. *Bon appétit.*   ■

George F. Will's strategies

Now let's look at Will's essay to see what techniques he uses to engage readers' interest and perhaps enable him to convince them—or at least make them think—that he is on to something. If you think some or all of his strategies are effective, consider adapting them for use in your own essays.

The title, "Being Green at Ben and Jerry's," does not at all prepare readers for an argument about drilling in the National Arctic Wildlife Refuge. But if you have read any of Will's other columns in *Newsweek,* you probably know that he is conservative and can guess that in this essay he'll poke some fun at the green folk—the environmentalists. Will can get away with using a title that isn't focused because he has a body of loyal readers who will read his pieces no matter what the topic is, but the rest of us have to give our readers some idea of our topic. In short, let your readers know early, perhaps in the title, where you'll be taking them.

The subtitle, "Some Environmental Policies Are Feel-Good Indulgences for an Era of Energy Abundance," perhaps added by the magazine's editor, suggests that the piece will concern energy. Moreover, the words "feel-good indulgences" signal to readers that Will believes the environmentalists are indulging themselves.

Paragraph 1 offers a striking comparison. Will wants his readers to believe that the area proposed for drilling is tiny, so he says that if they imagine the entire Arctic National Wildlife Refuge as a dinner table, the area proposed for drilling is the size of a dime. We think you'll agree that this opening seizes a reader's attention. Although some opponents to drilling in the ANWR have contested Will's analogy (saying the area would be much larger, perhaps comparable to the size of a dinner plate, or even a dinner plate broken in pieces, with roads and pipelines crossing between the fragments), the image is still highly effective. A dime is so small! And worth so little!

Another point about paragraph 1: Will's casual voice sounds like one you might hear in your own living room: "If you have an average-size dinner table," "The dime is larger," "at least as much oil." Your own essays need not adopt a highly formal style. Readers should think of you as serious but not solemn.

Will goes on to say that Senator John Kerry, an opponent of drilling and therefore on the side that Will opposes, dismisses the oil in the refuge as "a few drops." Will replies that it "could produce, for twenty-five years, at least as much oil as America currently imports from Saudi Arabia." Kerry's "a few drops" isn't literal, of course; he means that the oil is a drop in the bucket. But when one looks into the issue, one finds that estimates by responsible sources vary considerably—from 3.2 billion barrels to 11.5 billion barrels.

Paragraph 2 dismisses the Senate's debate ("almost comic . . . actually to buy farmers' votes").

Paragraph 3 offers statistics to make the point that "there is no energy crisis." Here, as in paragraph 1 (where he showed his awareness of Kerry's view), Will indicates that he's familiar with views other than his own. In arguing a case, it's important for a writer to let readers know that indeed there are other views—which the writer then shows are less substantial than the writer's own. Will is correct in saying that "per capita energy use is unchanged," but opponents might say, "Yes, per capita consumption hasn't increased; but given the population increase, the annual amount has vastly increased, which means that resources are being depleted and that pollution is increasing."

Paragraph 4 asserts again that there is no energy crisis, pokes fun at "full-time environmentalists" (perhaps even implying that such people ought to get respectable jobs), and ends with a bit of whimsy: These folks probably think we should go back to using windmills.

Paragraph 5, in support of the assertion that "Sometimes lofty environmentalism is a cover for crude politics," cites an authority (often an effective technique). Since readers aren't likely to recognize the name, Will also identifies him ("professor emeritus of philosophy at USC") and then offers further statistics. The paragraph begins by talking about "crude politics" and ends with this assertion: "Now power companies must import clean-burning coal, some from mines owned by Indonesia's Lippo Group, the heavy contributor to Clinton." In short, Will makes several strategic moves to suggest that at least some environmentalists' views are rooted in money and politics.

Paragraph 6 offers another statistic ("The United States has just 2.14 percent of the world's proven reserves of oil") and turns it against those who argue that therefore it's pointless to drill in Alaska.

In effect, Will is replying to people like Senator Kerry who say that the Arctic refuge provides only "a few drops of oil." The point, Will suggests, is not that it's impossible for the nation to achieve independence; rather, the point is that "domestic supplies can provide important insurance against uncertain foreign supplies."

Paragraph 7 begins smoothly with a transition, "Besides," and then offers additional statistics concerning the large amount of oil that the United States has held in proven reserves. For instance, by the end of World War II these reserves were enough to fuel "the most fabulous economic expansion in human history."

Paragraph 8 offers additional statistics, first about "proven reserves in the Persian Gulf" and then about an estimate—but only an estimate—of oil "beneath the U.S. outer continental shelf." We are not certain of Will's point here, but in any case the statistics suggest that he has done some homework.

Paragraph 9 summarizes the chief position (as Will sees it) of those on the other side of this issue: They "usually argue for decreased consumption," but they're afraid to argue for the sort of gasoline tax that might indeed decrease consumption because they know that many Americans want to drive large, heavy cars. Further, the larger, heavier cars that the environmentalists object to are in fact "safer than the gasoline-sippers that environmentalists prefer."

Paragraph 10 uses the term "feel-good indulgence," which also appears in the essay's subtitle; and now in the paragraph's third sentence we hear again of Ben and Jerry, whose names we haven't seen since reading the essay's title, "Being Green at Ben and Jerry's." Perhaps we've been wondering all this time why the title mentions Ben and Jerry. Surely most readers know that Ben and Jerry are associated with ice cream and therefore with cows and meadows, and probably many readers know that Ben and Jerry support environmentalism and other liberal causes. Drawing on an article by Karl Zinsmeister, editor of the *American Enterprise*, Will writes an extremely amusing paragraph in which he points out that the process of making ice cream "depends on electricity-guzzling refrigeration" and that the cows are essentially supported by fuel that transports fertilizers, herbicides, and insecticides. Further, in the course of producing the four gallons of milk required for one gallon of ice cream, the cows themselves—those darlings of the environmentalists—contribute "eight gallons of manure, and flatulence with another eight gallons of methane, a potent 'greenhouse' gas."

As we'll soon see in Will's next paragraph, the present paragraph is largely a lead-in for the quotation he gives in the next paragraph. He knows it isn't enough to give a quotation; a writer has to make use of it—by leading in to it, by commenting on it after inserting it, or both.

Paragraph 11 is entirely devoted to quoting Zinsmeister, who imagines an environmentalist digging into a dish of one of Ben and Jerry's most popular flavors, Cherry Garcia. We're invited to see the bowl of ice cream on one side of the table—here Will effectively evokes the table of paragraph 1—and a pile of manure on the other side, "plus a balloon of methane that would barely fit under the dining room table." This statement is vulgar, no doubt, but it's funny too. Will knows that humor as well as logic (and statistics and other evidence) can be among the key tools a writer uses in getting an audience to consider or accept an argument.

Paragraph 12 consists of three short sentences, adding up to less than a single line of type: "Cherry Garcia. It's a choice. *Bon appétit.*" None of the sentences mentions oil or the Arctic Refuge or statistics; therefore, this ending might seem irrelevant to the topic, but Will is very effectively saying, "Sure, you have a choice about drilling in the Arctic Refuge; any sensible person will choose the ice cream (drilling) rather than the manure and the gas (not drilling)."

Topics for Critical Thinking and Writing

1. What, if anything, makes George Will's essay interesting to you? What, if anything, makes it highly persuasive? How might it be made more persuasive?

2. In paragraph 10, Will clowns about the gas that cows emit, but apparently this gas, which contributes to global warming, is no laughing matter. The government of New Zealand, in an effort to reduce livestock emissions of methane and nitrous oxide, proposed a tax that would subsidize future research on the emissions. The tax would cost the average farmer $300 a year. Imagine that you're a New Zealand farmer. Write a letter to your representative, arguing for or against the tax.

3. Senator Barbara Boxer, campaigning against the proposal to drill in ANWR, spoke of the refuge as "God's gift to us" (*New York Times,* March 20, 2002). How strong an argument is this? Some opponents of the proposal have said that drilling in ANWR is as unthinkable as drilling in Yosemite or the Grand Canyon. Again,

how strong is this argument? Can you imagine circumstances in which you would support drilling in these places? Why, or why not? Do we have a moral duty to preserve certain unspoiled areas? Explain your response.

4. The Inupiat (Eskimo) who live in and near ANWR by a large majority favor drilling, seeing it as a source of jobs and a source of funding for schools, hospitals, and police. But the Ketchikan Indians, who speak of themselves as the "Caribou People," see drilling as a threat to the herds on which they depend for food and hides. How is it possible to balance the conflicting needs of these two groups?

5. Opponents of drilling in ANWR argue that over its lifetime of fifty years, the area would produce less than 1 percent of the fuel we need during the period and that therefore we shouldn't risk disturbing the area. Further, they argue that drilling in ANWR is an attempt at a quick fix to U.S. energy needs, whereas what the nation really needs are sustainable solutions, such as the development of renewable energy sources (e.g., wind and sun) and fuel-efficient automobiles. How convincing do you find these arguments? Explain your response.

6. Proponents of drilling include a large majority—something like 75 percent—of the people of Alaska, including its governor and its two senators. How much attention do their voices deserve?

7. Analyze the essay in terms of its use of *ethos, pathos,* and *logos.*

8. What sort of audience do you think Will is addressing? What values do his readers probably share? What makes you think so?

4

Visual Rhetoric: Thinking about Images as Arguments

A picture is worth a thousand words.

— PROVERB

"What is the use of a book," thought Alice, "without pictures or conversations?"

— LEWIS CARROLL

USES OF VISUAL IMAGES

Most visual materials that accompany written arguments serve one of several functions. One of the most common is to appeal to the reader's emotions (e.g., a photograph of a sad-eyed calf in a narrow pen can assist an argument against eating meat by inspiring sympathy for the animal). Pictures can also serve as visual evidence, offering proof that something occurred or appeared in a certain way at a certain moment. Pictures can help clarify numerical data (e.g., a graph showing five decades of law school enrollment by males and females). They can also add humor or satire to an essay. In this chapter, we concentrate on thinking critically about visual images. This means reading images in the same way we read print (or electronic) texts: by looking closely at them and discerning not only *what* they show but also *how* and *why* they convey a particular message, or argument.

When we discussed the **appeal to emotion** in Chapter 3 (p. 122), we quoted from Marc Antony's speech to the Roman populace in Shakespeare's play *Julius Caesar*. You'll recall that Antony stirred the mob by displaying Caesar's blood-stained mantle. He wasn't holding up a picture, but in a similar way he supplemented his words with visual material:

> Look, in this place ran Cassius' dagger through;
> See what a rent the envious Casca made;
> Through this, the well-belovèd Brutus stabbed. . . .

In courtrooms today, trial lawyers and prosecutors accomplish the same thing when doing the following:

- exhibiting photos of a bloody corpse, or
- holding up a murder weapon for jurors to see, or
- introducing victims as witnesses who sob while describing their ordeal.

Lawyers know that such visuals help make good arguments. Whether presented sincerely or gratuitously, visuals can have a significantly persuasive effect. Such appeals to emotion work on feelings, not logic. Think about the suit and tie that lawyers advise their male clients to wear: The attire helps make an argument to the jury about the defendant's character or credibility, even if he is actually lacking these qualities. Images, too, may be rationally connected to an argument (e.g., a gruesome image of a diseased lung in an anti-smoking ad makes a reasonable claim), but their immediate impact is more on the viewer's heart than the mind.

Like any kind of evidence, images make statements and support arguments. When Congress debated over whether to allow drilling in the Arctic National Wildlife Refuge (ANWR), both opponents and supporters made use of images:

- *Opponents* of drilling showed beautiful pictures of polar bears frolicking, wildflowers in bloom, and caribou on the move.
- *Proponents* of drilling showed bleak pictures of what they called "barren land" and "a frozen wasteland."

Both sides knew very well that images are powerfully persuasive, and they didn't hesitate to use them as supplements to words.

We invite you to think about the appropriateness of using such images in arguments. Was either side manipulating the "reality" of the ANWR? Or do images such as those described provide reasonable support for the ideas under consideration? Should argument be entirely a matter of reason, of logic (*logos*), without appeals to the emotions (*pathos*)? A statement that "the Arctic National Wildlife Refuge is a home for abundant wildlife, notably polar bears, caribou, and wildflowers" may not mean much until it is reinforced with breathtakingly beautiful images. Similarly, a statement that "most of the ANWR land is barren" may not mean much until it is corroborated by images of the vast bleakness. Each side selected a particular kind of image for a specific purpose—to support its position on drilling in the ANWR. Neither side was being dishonest, but both were appealing to emotions.

Types of Emotional Appeals

We began the preceding chapter by distinguishing between *argument*, which relies on reason (*logos*), and *persuasion*, which is a broad term that can include appeals to the emotions (*pathos*)—for example, an **appeal to pity**, such as an image of a sad-eyed calf. You might say, "Well, eating meat implies confining and killing animals," and regard the image as both reasonable and emotionally powerful. Or you might say, "Although it's emotionally powerful, this appeal to pity doesn't describe the condition of every meat animal. Some are treated humanely, slaughtered humanely, and eaten ethically." You might write a counterargument and include an image of free-range cattle on a farm (although in doing this, you too would be appealing to emotions).

The point is that images can be persuasive even if they don't make good arguments, in the same way threats of violence can be persuasive but do not make good arguments. The gangster Al Capone famously said, "You can get a lot more done with a kind word and a gun than with a kind word alone." Threats of violence appeal exclusively to the emotions—specifically, fear.

Advertisers commonly use the **appeal to fear** as a persuasive technique. While it is not a threat of violence, the appeal to fear is a threat of sorts. Showing a burglary, a car crash, embarrassing age spots, or a cockroach infestation can successfully convince consumers to buy a product—a home security system, a new car insurance policy, an age-defying skin cream, or a pesticide. Such images generate fear and anxiety at the same time that they offer the solution for it.

Appeal to self-interest is another persuasive tactic that writers can use. Consider these remarks, which use the word *interest* in the sense of "self-interest":

> Would you persuade, speak of Interest, not Reason.
> —Benjamin Franklin

> There are two levers for moving men—interest and fear.
> —Napoleon Bonaparte

Appeals to self-interest may be quite persuasive because they speak directly to what benefits you the most, not necessarily what benefits others in the community, society, or world. Such appeals are also common in advertising. "You can save bundles by shopping at Maxi-Mart," a commercial might claim, without making reference to sweatshop labor conditions, the negative impact of global commerce, or other troublesome aspects of what you see only as a great savings for yourself. You may be familiar with other types of emotional appeals in advertising that speak to the senses more than to the rational mind. Again, these kinds of appeals don't necessarily make good arguments for the products in question, but each can be highly persuasive — sometimes affecting us subconsciously. (The same applies to appeals in written arguments. This is why thinking critically about both words and images is so important.)

Here is a list of some additional kinds of appeals to emotion:

Sexual appeals (Example: showing a bikini-clad model standing near a product)

Bandwagon appeals (Example: showing crowds of people rushing to a sale)

Humor appeals (Example: showing a cartoon animal drinking X brand of beverage)

Celebrity appeals (Example: showing a famous person driving X brand of car)

Testimonial appeals (Example: showing a doctor giving X brand of vitamins to her kids)

Identity appeals (Example: showing a "good family" going to X restaurant)

Prejudice appeals (Example: showing a "loser" drinking X brand of beer)

Lifestyle appeals (Example: showing a jar of X brand of mustard on a silver platter)

Stereotype appeals (Example: showing a Latino person enjoying X brand of salsa)

Patriotic appeals (Example: showing X brand of mattress alongside an American flag)

EXERCISE

Watch the commercials that air during a television show, or examine the print advertisements in a popular magazine. Identify as many examples as possible of the types of appeals mentioned on the preceding pages. Is there a rational basis for any of the appeals you see? Are any appeals irrational even if they are effective? Why, or why not?

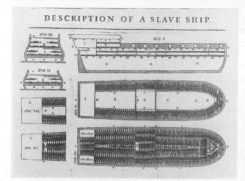

Images played an important role in the antislavery movement in the nineteenth century. On the top left is a diagram showing how human cargo was packed into a slave ship; it was distributed with Thomas Clarkson's *Essay on the Slavery and Commerce of the Human Species* (1804). On the top right is Frederick W. Mercer's photograph (April 2, 1863) of Gordon, a "badly lacerated" runaway slave. Images such as the slave ship and the runaway slave worked against slave owners' claims that slavery was a humane institution — claims that also were supported by illustrations, such as the woodcut at the bottom, titled *Attention Paid to a Poor Sick Negro,* from Josiah Priest's *In Defense of Slavery* (1843).

Top left: "Description of a Slave Ship, 1789 (print)/English School, (18th century)/WILBERFORCE HOUSE MUSEUM/© Wilberforce House, Hull City Museums and Art Galleries, UK/Bridgeman Images. *Top right:* Bettmann/Getty Images. *Bottom:* Josiah Priest's *In Defense of Slavery,* Rare Books and Manuscripts Department, Boston Public Library.

SEEING VERSUS LOOKING: READING ADVERTISEMENTS

Advertising is one of the most common forms of visual persuasion we encounter in everyday life. The influence of advertising in our culture is pervasive and subtle. Part of its power comes from our habit of internalizing the intended messages of words and images without thinking deeply about them. Once we begin decoding the ways in which advertisements are constructed—once we view them critically—we can understand how (or if) they work as arguments. We may then make better decisions about whether to buy particular products and what factors convinced us or failed to convince us.

To read an advertisement—or any image—critically, it helps to consider some basic rules from the field of **semiotics**, the study of signs and symbols. Fundamental to semiotic analysis is the idea that visual signs have shared meanings in a culture. If you approach a sink and see a red faucet and a blue faucet, you can be pretty sure which one will produce hot water and which one will produce cold. In a similar way, we almost subconsciously recognize the meanings of images in advertisements. Thus, one of the first strategies we can use in reading advertisements critically is **deconstructing** them, taking them apart to see what makes them work. It's helpful to remember that advertisements are enormously expensive to produce and disseminate, so nothing is left to chance. Teams of people typically scrutinize every part of an advertisement to ensure it communicates the intended message—although this doesn't imply that viewers must accept those messages. In fact, taking advertisements apart is the first step in being critical about them.

Taking apart an advertisement means examining each visual element. Consider the advertisement on the following page for Nike shoes featuring basketball star LeBron James. Already, you should see the celebrity appeal—an implicit claim that Nike shoes help make James a star player. The ad creates an association between the shoes and the sports champion. James's uniform number, 23, assists in this association by referencing another basketball legend (and Nike spokesperson), Michael Jordan. James is, in a way, presented as the progeny of Michael Jordan, as a new incarnation of a sports "god." WE ARE ALL WITNESSES, the text reads, drawing on language commonly used in religious settings to describe the second coming of Christ. James's arms are outstretched, Christ-like,

and seem to be illuminated by divine light from above. The uniform also references James's famous return to the Cleveland Cavaliers, his hometown team, after leaving the team abruptly to play four seasons with the Miami Heat. His "return" to Cleveland—his own second coming—the son of a sports god—and with the resonance of forgiveness, redemption, and salvation for Cleveland sports fans: All these associations work together to elevate James, Jordan, and Nike to exalted status. Of course, our description here is tongue-in-cheek. We're not gullible enough to believe this literally, and the ad's producers don't expect us to be; but they do hope that such an impression will be powerful enough to make us think of Nike the next time we shop for athletic shoes. If sports gods wear Nike, why shouldn't we?

This kind of analysis is possible when we recognize a difference between *seeing* and *looking*. **Seeing** is a physiological process involving light, the eye, and the brain. **Looking**, however, is a social process involving the mind. It suggests apprehending an image in terms of symbolic, metaphorical, and other social and cultural meanings. To do this, we must think beyond the *literal* meaning of an image or image element and consider its *figurative* meanings. If you look up *apple* in the dictionary, you'll find its literal, **denotative** meaning—a round fruit with thin red or green skin and a crisp flesh. But an apple also communicates figurative, **connotative** meanings. Connotative meanings are the cultural or emotional associations that an image suggests.

ABC/Photofest

The long-running ABC television series *Desperate Housewives*, which dramatized the furtive sex lives and exploits of suburban women, featured apples prominently in its advertisements.

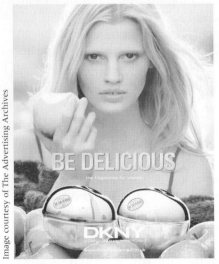

Image courtesy of The Advertising Archives

Image courtesy of The Advertising Archives

How does the DKNY advertisement use the symbolic, connotative meanings of the apple? In what ways does the advertisement for Bulova watches attempt to make an argument about the product?

The connotative meaning of an apple in Western culture dates back to the biblical story of the Garden of Eden, where Eve, tempted by a serpent, eats the fruit from the forbidden tree of knowledge and brings about the end of paradise on earth. Throughout Western culture, apples have come to represent knowledge and the pursuit of knowledge. Think of the ubiquitous Apple logo gracing so many mobile phones, tablets, and laptops: With its prominent bite, it symbolizes the way technology opens up new worlds of knowing. Sometimes, apples represent forbidden knowledge, temptation, or seduction—and biting into one suggests giving in to desires for new understandings and experiences. The story of Snow White offers just one example of an apple used as a symbol of temptation.

Let's look at two additional advertisements (pictured on p. 144), each of which relies almost entirely on images rather than words. The first, an ad for a TV comedy that made its debut in 2009, boldly displays the show's title and highlights the network name by setting it apart, but the most interesting words are in much smaller print:

Funny. On so many levels.

These words flatter the ad's readers, thus making them susceptible to the implicit message: "Look at this program." Why do we say the words are flattering? For three reasons:

- The small type size implies that the reader isn't someone whose attention can be caught only by headlines.
- The pun on "levels" (physical levels, and levels of humor) is a witty way of saying that the show offers not only the low comedy of physical actions but also the high comedy of witty talk—talk that, for instance, may involve puns.
- The two terse, incomplete sentences assume that the sophisticated reader doesn't need to have things explained at length.

The picture itself is attractive, showing what seems to be a wide variety of people (though not any faces or body types that in real life might cause viewers any uneasiness) posed in the style of a family portrait. Indeed, these wholesome figures, standing in affectionate poses, are all dressed in white (no real-life ketchup stains here) and are neatly framed—except for the patriarch, at the extreme right—by a pair of seated youngsters whose legs dangle down from the levels. The modern family, we're told, is large and varied (this one includes a gay son and his partner, and their adopted Vietnamese baby), smart and warm. Best of all, it is "Funny. On so many levels."

The second ad features just a single line of text: "No In-App Purchases." These words are set below the image of a shopping cart with a plus sign, which has come to be an almost universally recognized symbol for an electronic shopping cart. Both the text and the icon are textured and look a little rough at the edges, suggesting that they are made out of the very item they are advertising. After all, Play-Doh has been around since the 1930s; though the way children play has changed dramatically since then (most kids born now will grow up knowing what an "in-app purchase" is), by fashioning the electronic icon and text out of a nearly century-old product, the ad implies that just because a toy—or anything else—is new and high-tech, that does not make it inherently better than old-fashioned things. After all, the product being advertised has been around for nearly a century; how long will an app on a smartphone or tablet last until it is replaced with a newer version?

ABC/Modern Family

✓ A CHECKLIST FOR ANALYZING IMAGES (ESPECIALLY ADVERTISEMENTS)

☐ What is the overall effect of the design? Colorful and busy (suggesting activity)? Quiet and understated (e.g., chiefly white and grays, with lots of empty space)? Old-fashioned or cutting edge?

☐ What single aspect of the image immediately captures your attention? Its size? Its position on the page? The beauty of the image? The grotesqueness of the image? Its humor?

☐ Who is the audience for the image? Affluent young men? Housewives? Retired persons?

☐ What is the argument?

☐ Does the text make a rational appeal (*logos*)? ("Tests at a leading university prove that . . ."; "If you believe *X*, you should vote 'No' on this referendum" appeal to our sense of reason.)

☐ Does the image appeal to the emotions or to dearly held values (*pathos*)? (Images of starving children or maltreated animals appeal to our sense of pity; images of military valor may appeal to our patriotism; images of luxury may appeal to our envy; images of sexually attractive people may appeal to our desire to be like them; images of violence or of extraordinary ugliness — as in ads showing a human fetus being destroyed — may seek to shock us.)

☐ Does the image make an ethical appeal — that is, does it appeal to our character as a good human being (*ethos*)? (Ads by charitable organizations often appeal to our sense of decency, fairness, and pity; but ads that appeal to our sense of prudence — such as ads for insurance companies or investment houses — also make an ethical appeal).

☐ What is the relation of print to image? Does the image do most of the work, or does it serve to attract us and lead us on to read the text?

TOPICS FOR CRITICAL THINKING AND WRITING

1. Imagine that you work for a business—for instance, a vacation resort, a clothing manufacturer, or an automaker—that advertises in a publication such as *Time* or *Newsweek*. Design an advertisement

for the business: Describe the picture and write the text, and then, in an essay of 500 words, identify your target audience (college students? young couples about to buy their first home? retired persons?) and explain your purpose in choosing certain types of appeals (e.g., to reason, to the emotions, to the audience's sense of humor).

2. It is often said that colleges, like businesses, are selling a product. Examine a brochure or catalog that is sent to prospective college applicants, or locate your own college's view book, and analyze the kinds of appeals that some of the images make.

OTHER ASPECTS OF VISUAL APPEALS

As we saw with the uses of images relating to the Arctic National Wildlife Refuge, photographs can serve as evidence but have a peculiar relationship to the truth. We must never forget that images are constructed, selected, and used for specific purposes. When advertisers use images, they're trying to convince consumers to purchase a product or service. But when images serve as documentary evidence, we often assume they're showing the "truth" of the matter at hand. Our skepticism may be lower when we see an image in the newspaper or a magazine, assuming it captures a particular event or moment in time *as it really happened*. But historical images, images of events, news photographs, and other forms of visual evidence are not free from the potential for conscious or unconscious bias. Consider how liberal and conservative media sources portray the nation's president in images: One source may show him proud and smiling in bright light with the American flag behind him, while another might show him scowling in a darkened image suggestive of evil intent. Both are "real" images, but the framing, tinting, setting, and background can inspire significantly different responses in viewers.

As we saw with the image of LeBron James, certain postures, facial expressions, and settings can contribute to a photograph's interpretation. Martin Luther King Jr.'s great speech of August 28, 1963, "I Have a Dream," still reads very well on the page, but part of its immense appeal derives from its setting: King spoke to some 200,000 people in Washington, D.C., as he stood on the steps of the Lincoln Memorial. That setting, rich with associations of slavery and freedom, strongly assists King's argument. In fact, images of King delivering his speech are nearly inseparable from the very argument he was making. The visual aspects—the setting (the Lincoln Memorial with the Washington Monument and the Capitol in the distance) and King's gestures—are part of the speech's persuasive rhetoric.

Derrick Alridge, a historian, examined dozens of accounts of Martin Luther King Jr. in history books, and he found that images of King present him overwhelmingly as a messianic figure—standing before crowds, leading them, addressing them in postures reminiscent of a prophet. While King is an admirable figure, Alridge asserts, history books err by presenting him as more than human. Doing so ignores his personal struggles and failures and makes a myth out of the real man. This myth

Martin Luther King Jr. delivering his "I Have a Dream" speech on August 28, 1963, from the steps of the Lincoln Memorial.

Bettmann/Getty Images

Martin Luther King Jr. on "Chicken Bone Beach" in Atlantic City.

John Mosley/Courtesy Charles L. Blockson Afro American Collection suggests he was the epicenter of the civil rights movement, an effort that was actually conducted in different ways via different strategies on the part of many other figures whom King eclipsed. We may even get the idea that the entire civil rights movement began and ended with King alone. When he's presented as a holy prophet, it becomes easier to focus on his abstract messages about love, equality, and justice, and not on the specific policies and politics he advocated— his avowed socialist stances, for instance. While photographs of King seek to help us remember, they may actually portray him in a way that causes us to forget other things—for example, the fact that his approval rating among whites at the time of his death was lower than 30 percent, and among blacks lower than 50 percent.

Levels of Images

One helpful way of discerning the meanings of images by *looking* at them (see p. 141) is to utilize *seeing* first as a way to define what is plainly or literally present in them. You can begin by *seeing*—identifying the elements that are indisputably "there" in an image (the denotative level). Then you move on to *looking*— interpreting the meanings suggested by the elements that are present (the connotative level).

Semioticians distinguish between images' surface levels and deeper levels. The surface level is the **syntagmatic level**, and the deeper level is the **paradigmatic level**. The words *syntagmatic* and *paradigmatic* are related to the words *syntax* and *paradigm*.

Arguably, when we *see*, we pay attention only to the syntagmatic level. We notice the various elements included in an image. We *see* denotatively—that is, we observe just the explicit elements of the image. We aren't concerned with the meaning of the image's elements, but just with the fact that they're present.

When we *look*, we move to the paradigmatic level. That is, we speculate on the elements' deeper meanings—what they suggest figuratively, symbolically, or metaphorically in our cultural system. We may also consider the relationship of different elements to one another. When we do this, we look connotatively.

Syntagmatic analysis	**Paradigmatic analysis**
Seeing	Looking
Denotation	Connotation
Literal	Figurative
What is present	What it means
Understanding / Textual	Interpreting / Subtextual / Contextual

EXERCISE

Examine the images on this page. As you examine each one, do the following:

1. *See* the image. Perform a syntagmatic analysis thoroughly describing the image elements you observe. Write down as many elements as possible that you see.

2. *Look* at the image. Perform a paradigmatic analysis in which you take the elements you have observed and relate what they suggest by considering their figurative meanings, their meanings in relation to one another, and their meanings in the context of the images' production and consumption.

Margaret Bourke-White/Time & Life Pictures/Getty Images

Residents of Louisville, Kentucky, waiting in a bread line in 1937. A massive flood from January to February that year left nearly four hundred people dead and roughly one million people homeless across five states.

Adam Bettcher/Getty Images

Protestors rallying outside the office of Dr. Walter Palmer, a dentist from Bloomington, Minnesota. In July 2015, Palmer was accused of poaching a 13-year-old lion named Cecil that was living at Hwange National Park in Zimbabwe. Palmer reportedly paid $50,000 for the hunt and lured Cecil out of the sanctuary to shoot him.

The point here is that photographs promise a clear window into a past reality but are not unassailable guarantors of truth. In the digital age, it's remarkably easy to alter photographs, and we have become more suspicious of photographs as direct evidence of reality. Yet we still tend to trust certain sources more than others. To counteract this tendency, we can be more critical about images by asking three overarching questions about the contexts in which they are created, disseminated, and received. Within each question, other questions arise.

1. *Who produced the image?*   Who was the photographer? Under what circumstances was the picture taken? How is the subject of the image framed? What other visual information is included in the frame? What is emphasized and de-emphasized? What do you think is the image's intended effect?

2. *Who distributed the image?*   How widely has the image been distributed? Where has it been published (magazine, newspaper, blog, social media page)? What is the intended audience of the publication where the image appears? What purpose does the image serve? How does the image support the accompanying text? What alternative images exist?

3. *Who consumed the image?*   What type of audience is the likeliest viewer of the image? Are they likely to see it as negative or positive? Does the image inspire an emotional response? If so, what kind? What elements in the photograph are likely to generate certain kinds of responses?

A RULE FOR WRITERS If you think that pictures will help you to make the point you are arguing, include them with captions explaining their sources and relevance.

ACCOMMODATING, RESISTING, AND NEGOTIATING THE MEANING OF IMAGES

Most images are produced, selected, and published in order to have a specific effect on readers and viewers. This dominant meaning of an image supposes that the audience will react in a predictable way, usually based on the widespread **cultural codes** that operate within a society. Images of elegant women in designer dresses, rugged men driving pickup trucks, stodgy teachers, cutthroat CEOs, hipster computer programmers, and so on speak to generally accepted notions of what certain types of people are like. An image of a suburban couple in an automobile advertisement washing their new car subconsciously confirms and perpetuates a certain ideal of middle-class suburban life (a heterosexual couple, a well-trimmed lawn, a neatly painted house and picket fence—and a brand-new midsize sedan). An image of a teary-eyed young woman accepting a diamond ring from a handsome man will likely touch the viewer in a particular way, in part because of our society's cultural codes about the rituals of romantic love and marriage, gender roles, and the diamond ring as a sign of love and commitment.

These examples demonstrate that images can be constructed according to dominant connotations of gender, class, and racial, sexual, and political identity. When analyzing an image, ask yourself what cultural codes it endorses, what ideals it establishes as natural, what social norms or modes of everyday life it idealizes or assumes.

As image consumers, we often *accommodate* (i.e., passively accept) the cultural codes promoted in the media. For example, in the hypothetical advertisement featuring a wedding proposal, you might accept the producer's communicated ideals that men should propose to women, that women are emotional beings, and that diamond rings are the appropriate objects to represent love and commitment. When you **accommodate** cultural codes without understanding them critically, you allow the media that perpetuate these codes to interpret the world for you. That is, you accept their interpretations without questioning the social and cultural values implicit in their assumptions, many of which may actually run counter to your own or others' social and cultural values.

If you *resist* the cultural codes of an image, you actively criticize its message and meaning. Suppose you (1) question how the ad presents gender roles and marriage, (2) claim that it idealizes heterosexual marriage, and (3) point out that it confirms and extends traditional gender roles in which men are active and bold and women are passive and emotional. Moreover, you (4) argue that the diamond ring represents a misguided commodification of love because diamonds are kept deliberately scarce by large companies and, as such, are overvalued and overpriced; meanwhile, the ad prompts young couples to spend precious money at a time when their joint assets might be better saved, and because many diamonds come from third-world countries under essentially

slave labor conditions, the diamond is more a symbol of oppression than of love. If your analysis follows such paths, you **resist** the dominant message of the image in question. Sometimes, this is called an *oppositional reading*.

Negotiation, or a *negotiated reading*, the most useful mode of reading and viewing, involves a middle path— a process of revision that seeks to recognize and change the conditions that give rise to certain negative aspects of cultural codes. Negotiation implies a practical intervention into common viewing processes that help construct and maintain social conditions and relations. This intervention can be important when inequalities or stereotypes are perpetuated by cultural codes. A negotiated reading enables you to emphasize the ways in which individuals, social groups, and others relate to images and their dominant meanings, and how different personal and cultural perspectives can challenge those meanings. Without intervention there can be no revision, no positive social or cultural change. You **negotiate** cultural codes when:

- you understand the underlying messages of images and accept the general cultural implications of these codes, *but*
- you acknowledge that in some circumstances the general codes do not apply.

Using this scheme will help you analyze diverse kinds of images as well as develop more nuanced arguments about the messages those images convey.

EXERCISE

Examine the image above, which is an advertisement for Lego building blocks. Provide brief examples of how a viewer could accommodate, resist, or negotiate the images in the ad.

ARE SOME IMAGES NOT FIT TO BE SHOWN?

Images of suffering—either human or animal—can be immensely persuasive. In the nineteenth century, for instance, the antislavery movement made extremely effective use of images in its campaign. We reproduce two antislavery images earlier in this chapter, as well as a counterimage that sought to assure viewers that slavery is a beneficent system (p. 139). But are there some images not fit to print?

Until recently, many newspapers did not print pictures of lynched African Americans, hanged and burned and maimed. The reasons for not printing such images probably differed between South and North: Southern papers may have considered the images to be discreditable to whites, while northern papers may have deemed the images too revolting. Even today, when it's common-place for newspapers and television news to show pictures of dead victims of war, famine, or traffic accidents, one rarely sees bodies that are horribly maimed. (For traffic accidents, the body is usually covered, and we see only the smashed car.) The U.S. government has refused to release photographs showing the bodies of American soldiers killed in the war in Iraq, and it has been most reluctant to show pictures of dead Iraqi soldiers and civilians. Only after many Iraqis refused to believe that former Iraqi president Saddam Hussein's two sons had been killed did the U.S. government reluctantly release pictures showing the two men's blood-spattered faces—and some American newspapers and television programs refused to use the images.

There have been notable exceptions to this practice, such as Huynh Cong (Nick) Ut's 1972 photograph of children fleeing a napalm attack in Vietnam (below), which was widely reproduced in the United States and won the photographer a Pulitzer
Prize in 1973. It's
impossible to meas-
ure the influence of
this particular photo-
graph, but many
people believe that

Huynh Cong (Nick)
Ut, *The Terror of War:
Children on Route 1 near
Trang Bang*, 1972

AP Photo/Nick Ut

Eddie Adams, *Execution of Viet Cong Prisoner, Saigon,* 1968

AP Photo/Eddie Adams

it played a substantial role in increasing public pressure to end the Vietnam War. Another widely reproduced picture of horrifying violence is Eddie Adams's 1968 picture (above) of a South Vietnamese chief of police firing a pistol into the head of a Viet Cong prisoner.

The issue remains: Are some images unacceptable? For instance, although capital punishment—by methods including lethal injection, hanging, shooting, and electrocution—is legal in parts of the United States, every state in the Union prohibits the publication of pictures showing a criminal being executed.[1]

The most famous recent example of an image widely thought to be unprintable showed the murder of Daniel Pearl, a reporter for the *Wall Street Journal.* Pearl was captured and murdered in June 2002 by Islamic terrorists in Pakistan. His killers videotaped Pearl reading a statement denouncing American policy and then being decapitated. The video also shows a man's arm holding Pearl's head. The video ends with the killers making demands (such as the release of Muslim prisoners being held by the United States in Guantánamo Bay, Cuba) and asserting, "if our demands are not met, this scene will be repeated again and again."

The chief arguments against newspapers reproducing material from this video were as follows:

- The video and still images from it are unbearably gruesome.
- Showing the video would traumatize the Pearl family.
- The video is enemy propaganda.

Those who favored broadcasting the video on television and printing still images from it in newspapers offered these arguments:

- The photos would show the world what sort of enemy the United States is fighting.

[1]For more on this topic, see Wendy Lesser, *Pictures at an Execution* (1993).

Alexander Gardner, *Home of a Rebel Sharpshooter*, 1863. This photo illustrates the devastation wrought by the Battle of Gettysburg through focusing on a single dead soldier splayed out in a "sharpshooter's den."

- Newspapers have published pictures of other terrifying sights (notably, people leaping out of windows of the World Trade Center's Twin Towers on 9/11 and the space shuttle *Challenger* exploding in 1986).

- No one was worried about protecting the families of 9/11 or *Challenger* victims from seeing those traumatic images.

But is the comparison of the Daniel Pearl video to the photos of the Twin Towers and the *Challenger* valid? You may respond that individuals in the Twin Towers pictures aren't specifically identifiable and that the *Challenger* images, although horrifying, aren't as visually revolting as the picture of a severed head held up for view.

The *Boston Phoenix*, a weekly newspaper, published some images from the Pearl video and also put a link to the video (with a warning that the footage is "extremely graphic") on its Web site. The weekly's editor justified publication on the three grounds we list above. Pearl's wife, Mariane Pearl, was quoted in various newspapers as condemning the "heartless decision to air this despicable video." And a spokeswoman for the Pearl family, when asked for comment, referred reporters to a statement issued earlier, which said that broadcasters who show the video

> fall without shame into the terrorists' plan. . . . Danny believed that journalism was a tool to report the truth and foster understanding—not perpetuate propaganda and sensationalize tragedy. We had hoped that no part of this tape would ever see the light of day. . . . We urge all networks and news outlets to exercise responsibility and not aid the terrorists in spreading their message of hate and murder.[2]

Although some journalists expressed regret that Pearl's family was distressed, they insisted that journalists have a right to reproduce such material and that the images can serve the valuable purpose of shocking viewers into awareness.

Politics and Pictures

Consider, too, the controversy that erupted in 1991, during the Persian Gulf War, when the U.S. government decided that news media would not be allowed to photograph coffins returning with the bodies of military personnel killed during the war. In later years the policy was sometimes ignored, but in 2003 the George W. Bush administration decreed that there would be "no arrival ceremony for, or media coverage of, deceased military personnel returning [from Iraq or Afghanistan] . . . to the Dover (Delaware) base." The government enforced the policy strictly.

Members of the news media strongly protested, as did many others, chiefly on the basis of these arguments:

- The administration was trying to sanitize the war; that is, the government was depriving the public of important information—images—that showed the war's real cost.

- Grief for the deaths of military personnel is not a matter only for the families of the deceased. The sacrifices were made on behalf of the nation, and the nation should be allowed to grieve. Canada and Britain have no such ban; when military coffins are transported there, the public lines the streets to honor the fallen warriors. In fact, in Canada a portion of the highway near the Canadian base has been renamed "Highway of Heroes."

- The coffins at Dover Air Force base are not identified by name, so there is no issue about intruding on the privacy of grieving families.

[2]Quoted in the *Hartford Courant*, June 5, 2002, and reproduced on the Internet by the Freedom of Information Center, under the heading "Boston Paper Creates Controversy."

The Washington Post/Getty Images

The chief arguments in defense of the ban were as follows:

- Photographs violate the families' privacy.

- If the arrival of the coffins at Dover is publicized, some griev-ing families will think they should travel to Dover to be present when the bodies arrive. This may cause a financial hardship on the families.

- If the families give their consent, the press is *not* barred from individual graveside ceremonies at hometown burials. The ban extends only to the coffins' arrival at Dover Air Force Base.

In February 2009, President Obama changed the policy and permitted coverage of the transfer of bodily remains. In his Address to the Joint Session of Congress on February 24, 2009, he said, "For seven years we have been a nation at war. No longer will we hide its price." On February 27, Defense Secretary Robert M. Gates announced that the government ban was lifted and that families will decide whether to allow photographs and videos of the "digni-fied transfer process at Dover."

EXERCISE

In an argumentative essay of about 250 words—perhaps two or three paragraphs—give your view of the issue of permitting photos of military coffins. In an opening paragraph, you may want to both explain the issue and summarize the arguments that you reject. The second paragraph of a two-paragraph essay may present your reasons for rejecting those arguments. Additionally, you might devote a third paragraph to a more general reflection.

Topics for Critical Thinking and Writing

1. Marvin Kalb, a distinguished journalist, was quoted as saying that the public has a right to see the tape of Daniel Pearl's murder but that "common sense, decency, [and] humanity would encourage editors . . . to say 'no, it is not necessary to put this out.' There is no urgent demand on the part of the American people to see Daniel Pearl's death." What is your view?

2. In June 2006, two American soldiers were captured in Iraq. Later their bodies were found, dismembered and beheaded. Should newspapers have shown photographs of the mutilated bodies? Why, or why not? (In July 2006, insurgents in Iraq posted images on the Internet showing a soldier's severed head beside his body.)

Another issue concerning the appropriateness of showing certain images arose early in 2006. In September 2005, a Danish newspaper, accused of being afraid to show political cartoons that were hostile to Muslim terrorists, responded by publishing twelve cartoons. One cartoon showed the prophet Muhammad wearing a turban that looked like a bomb. The images at first didn't arouse much attention, but when they were reprinted in Norway in January 2006, they attracted worldwide attention and outraged Muslims, most of whom regard any depiction of Muhammad as blasphemous. Some Muslims in various Islamic nations burned Danish embassies and engaged in other acts of violence. Most non-Muslims agreed that the images were in bad taste; and apparently in deference to Islamic sensibilities (but possibly also out of fear of reprisals), very few Western newspapers reprinted the cartoons when they covered the news events. Most newspapers (including the *New York Times*) merely described the images. The editors of these papers believed that readers should be told the news, but that because the drawings were so offensive to some persons, they should be described rather than reprinted. A controversy then arose: Do readers of a newspaper deserve to *see* the evidence for themselves, or can a newspaper adequately fulfill its mission by offering only a verbal description? These questions arose again after the 2007 bombing of the French satirical newspaper

Charlie Hebdo, and then after another mass shooting at the same newspaper in 2015 that claimed the lives of twelve editors and staff members.

Persons who argued that the images should be reproduced in the media generally made these points:

- Newspapers should yield neither to the delicate sensibilities of some readers nor to threats of violence.

- Jews for the most part do not believe that God should be depicted (the prohibition against "graven images" appears in Exodus 20.3), but they raise no objections to such Christian images as Michelangelo's painting of God awakening Adam, depicted on the ceiling of the Sistine Chapel. Further, when Andres Serrano (a Christian) in 1989 exhibited a photograph of a small plastic crucifix submerged in urine, it outraged a wider public (several U.S. senators condemned it because the artist had received federal funds), but virtually all newspapers showed the image, and many even printed its title, *Piss Christ*. The subject was judged to be newsworthy, and the fact that some viewers would regard the image as blasphemous was not considered highly relevant.

- Our society values freedom of speech, and newspapers should not be intimidated. When certain pictures are a matter of news, readers should be able to see them.

In contrast, opposing voices made these points:

- Newspapers must recognize deep-seated religious beliefs. They should indeed report the news, but there is no reason to *show* images that some people regard as blasphemous. The images can be adequately *described* in words.

- The Jewish response to Christian images of God, and even the tolerant Christians' response to Serrano's image of the crucifix immersed in urine, are irrelevant to the issue of whether a Western newspaper should represent images of the prophet Muhammad. Virtually all Muslims regard depictions of Muhammad as blasphemous, and that's what counts.

- Despite all the Western talk about freedom of the press, the press does *not* reproduce all images that become matters of news. For instance, news items about the sale of child pornography do not include images of the pornographic photos.

EXERCISES: THINKING ABOUT IMAGES

1. Does the display of the Muhammad cartoons constitute an argument? If so, what is the conclusion, and what are the premises? If not, then what sort of statement, if any, does publishing these cartoons constitute?

2. Hugh Hewitt, an Evangelical Christian, offered a comparison to the cartoon of Muhammad wearing a bomblike turban. Suppose, he asked, an abortion clinic were bombed by someone claiming to be an Evangelical Christian. Would newspapers publish "a cartoon of Christ's crown of thorns transformed into sticks of TNT"? Do you think they would? If you were the editor of a newspaper, would you? Why, or why not?

3. One American newspaper, the *Boston Phoenix*, didn't publish any of the cartoons "out of fear of retaliation from the international brotherhood of radical and bloodthirsty Islamists who seek to impose their will on those who do not believe as they do. . . . We could not in good conscience place the men and women who work at the *Phoenix* and its related companies in physical jeopardy." Evaluate this position.

4. A week after the 2015 attack on *Charlie Hebdo*, and in response to media hesitancy to re-publish the offending images of Muhammad, the Index on Censorship and several other journalistic organizations called for all newspapers to publish them simultaneously and globally on January 8, 2015. "This unspeakable act of violence has challenged and assailed the entire press," said Lucie Morillon of Reporters Without Borders. "Journalism as a whole is in mourning. In the name of all those who have fallen in the defence of these fundamental values, we must continue *Charlie Hebdo*'s fight for the right to freedom of information." Evaluate this position.

WRITING ABOUT A POLITICAL CARTOON

Most editorial pages print political cartoons as well as editorials. Like the writers of editorials, cartoonists seek to persuade, but they rarely use words to *argue* a point. True, they may use a few words in speech balloons or in captions, but generally the drawing does most of the work. Because their aim usually is to convince the viewer that some person's action or proposal is ridiculous, cartoon-ists almost always **caricature** their subjects:

- They exaggerate the subject's distinctive features to the point at which . . .

- . . . the subject becomes grotesque and ridiculous—absurd, laughable, contemptible.

We agree that it's unfair to suggest that because, say, the politician who proposes such-and-such is short, fat, and bald, his proposal is ridiculous; but that's the way cartoonists work. Further, cartoonists are concerned with producing a striking image, not with exploring an issue, so they almost always oversimplify, implying that there really is no other sane view.

In the course of saying that (1) the figures in a cartoon are ridiculous and *therefore* their ideas are contemptible, and (2) there is only one side to the issue, cartoonists often use **symbolism**. Here's a list of common symbols:

- symbolic figures (e.g., the U.S. government as Uncle Sam)

- animals (e.g., the Democratic Party as donkey and the Republican Party as elephant)

- buildings (e.g., the White House as representing the nation's president)

- things (e.g., a bag with a dollar sign on it as representing a bribe)

For anyone brought up in U.S. culture, these symbols (like the human figures they represent) are obvious, and cartoonists assume that viewers will instantly recognize the symbols and figures, will get the joke, and will see the absurdity of whatever issue the car-toonist is seeking to demolish.

In writing about the argument presented in a cartoon, normally you will discuss the ways in which the cartoon makes its point. Caricature usually implies, "This is ridiculous, as you can plainly see by the absurdity of the figures depicted" or "What *X*'s proposal adds up to, despite its apparent complexity, is nothing more than. . . ." As we have said, this sort of persuasion, chiefly by ridicule, probably is unfair: An unattractive person certainly can offer a thoughtful polit-ical proposal, and almost always the issue is more complicated than the cartoonist indicates. But cartoons work largely by ridicule and the omission of counterarguments, and we shouldn't reject the possibility that the cartoonist has indeed highlighted the absurdity of the issue.

Walt Handelsman

✓ **A CHECKLIST FOR EVALUATING AN ANALYSIS OF POLITICAL CARTOONS**

☐ Is there a lead-in?

☐ Is there a brief but accurate description of the drawing?

☐ Is the source of the cartoon cited (perhaps with a comment by the cartoonist)?

☐ Is there a brief report of the event or issue that the cartoon is targeting, as well as an explanation of all the symbols?

☐ Is there a statement of the cartoonist's claim (thesis)?

☐ Is there an analysis of the evidence, if any, that the image offers in support of the claim?

☐ Is there an analysis of the ways in which the drawing's content and style help to convey the message?

☐ Is there adequate evaluation of the drawing's effectiveness?

☐ Is there adequate evaluation of the effectiveness of the text (caption or speech balloons) and of the fairness of the cartoon?

Your essay will likely include an *evaluation* of the cartoon. Indeed, the *thesis* underlying your analytic/argumentative essay may be that the cartoon is effective (persuasive) for such-and-such reasons but unfair for such-and-such other reasons.

In analyzing the cartoon—in determining the cartoonist's attitude—consider the following elements:

- the relative size of the figures in the image
- the quality of the lines (e.g., thin and spidery, or thick and seemingly aggressive)
- the amount of empty space in comparison with the amount of heavily inked space (a drawing with lots of inky areas conveys a more oppressive tone than a drawing that's largely open)
- the degree to which text is important, as well as its content and tone (is it witty, heavy-handed, or something else?)

Caution: If your instructor lets you choose a cartoon, be sure to select one with sufficient complexity to make the exercise worthwhile. (See also Thinking Critically: Analysis of a Political Cartoon.)

Let's look at an example. Jackson Smith wrote this essay in a composition course at Tufts University.

THINKING CRITICALLY ANALYSIS OF A POLITICAL CARTOON

Look at the cartoon on page 162. For each Type of Analysis section in the chart below, provide your own answer based on the cartoon. (Sample answers appear in the third column.)

Type of Analysis	Questions to Ask	Sample Answer	Your Answer
Context	*Who is the artist? Where and when was the cartoon published?*	"This cartoon by Walt Handelsman was originally published in *Newsday* on September 12, 2009. Handelsman, a Pulitzer Prize–winning cartoonist, drew this cartoon in response to recent breaches of political decorum."	

(continued)

THINKING CRITICALLY (*Continued*)

Type of Analysis	Questions to Ask	Sample Answer	Your Answer
Description	*What does the cartoon look like?*	"It depicts a group of Washington, D.C., tourists being driven past what the guide calls 'The Museum of Modern American Political Discourse,' a building in the shape of a giant toilet."	
Analysis	*How does the cartoon make its point? Is it effective?*	"The toilet as a symbol of the level of political discussion dominates the cartoon, effectively driving home the point that Americans are watching our leaders sink to new lows as they debate the future of our nation. By drawing the toilet on a scale similar to that of familiar monuments in Washington, Handelsman may be pointing out that today's politicians, rather than being remembered for great achievements like those of George Washington or Abraham Lincoln, will instead be remembered for their rudeness and aggression."	

Jackson Smith

Pledging Nothing? (Student Essay)

Gary Markstein's cartoon about the Pledge of Allegiance is one of dozens that can be retrieved by a search engine. It happens that every one of the cartoons that I retrieved mocked the courts for ruling that schools cannot require students to recite the Pledge of Allegiance in its present form, which includes the words "under God." I personally object to these words, so the cartoons certainly do not speak for me, but I'll try as impartially as possible to analyze the strength of Markstein's cartoon.

Markstein shows us, in the cartoon, four schoolchildren reciting the Pledge. Coming out of all four mouths is a speech balloon with the words, "One nation under nothing in particular." The children are facing a furled American flag, and to the right of the flag is a middle-aged female teacher, whose speech balloon is in the form of a cloud, indicating that she is *thinking* rather than saying the words, "God help us."

Certainly the image grabs us: little kids lined up reciting the Pledge of Allegiance, an American flag, a maternal-looking teacher, and, in fact, if one examines the cartoon closely, one sees an apple on the teacher's desk. It's almost a Norman Rockwell scene, except, of course, it is a cartoon, so the figures are all a bit grotesque—but, still, they are nice folks. What is *not* nice, Markstein says, is what these kids must recite, "One nation under nothing in particular." In fact, the cartoon is far from telling the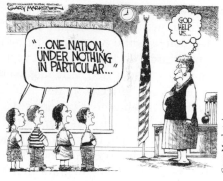

Gary Markstein

truth. Children who recite the Pledge without the words "under God" will still be saying that they are pledging allegiance to something quite specific—the United States:

> I pledge allegiance to the flag of the United States of America, and to the Republic for which it stands: one nation indivisible, with Liberty and Justice for all.

That's really quite a lot, very far from Markstein's "under nothing in particular." But no one, I suppose, expects fairness in a political cartoon—and of course this cartoon *is* political, because the issue of the Pledge has become a political football, with liberals on the whole wanting the words "under God" removed and conservatives on the whole wanting the words retained.

Let's now look at some of the subtleties of the cartoon. First, although, as I have said, cartoons present grotesque caricatures, the figures here are all affectionately presented. None of these figures is menacing. The teacher, with her spectacles and her rather dumpy figure, is clearly a benevolent figure, someone who in the eyes of the cartoonist rightly is disturbed about the fate of these little kids who are not allowed to say the words "under God." (Nothing, of course, prevents the children from speaking about God when they are not in the classroom. Those who believe in God can say grace at mealtime, can go to Sunday School, can go to church regularly, can pray before they go to bed, etc.) Markstein suggests that the absence of these words makes the entire Pledge meaningless ("under nothing in particular"), and in a master stroke he has conveyed this idea of impoverishment by showing a tightly furled flag, a flag that is presented as minimally as possible. After all, the flag could have been shown more fully, perhaps hanging from a pole that extended from a wall into the classroom, or the flag could have been displayed extended against a wall. Instead we get the narrowest of flags, something that is not much more than a furled umbrella, identifiable as the American flag by its stripes and a few stars in the upper third. Markstein thus cleverly suggests that with the loss of the words "under God," the flag itself is reduced to almost nothing.

Fair? No. Effective? Yes, and that's the job of a cartoonist. 5 Readers probably give cartoons no more than three or four seconds, and Markstein has made the most of those few seconds. The reader gets his point, and if the reader already holds this view, he or she probably says, "Hey, here's a great cartoon." I don't hold that view, but I am willing to grant that it is a pretty good cartoon, effectively making a point that I think is wrong-headed. ∎

VISUALS AS AIDS TO CLARITY: MAPS, GRAPHS, AND PIE CHARTS

Maps were part of the argument in the debate over drilling in the Arctic National Wildlife Refuge.

- Advocates of drilling argued that it would take place only in a tiny area. Their map showed Alaska, with an indication (in gray) of the much smaller part of Alaska that was the Refuge, and a further indication (cross-hatched) of what the advocates emphasized was a minuscule part of the Refuge.

- Opponents showed maps indicating the path of migrating caribou and the roads that would have to be constructed across the Refuge to get to the area where the drilling would take place.

Graphs, tables, and pie charts usually present quantitative data in visual form, helping writers to clarify dry statistical assertions. For instance, a line graph may illustrate how many immigrants came to the United States in each decade of the last century.

A bar graph (with bars running either horizontally or vertically) offers similar information. In the Coming to America graph, we can see at a glance that, say, the second bar on the lower left is almost double the length of the first, indicating that the number of immigrants almost doubled between 1850 and 1860.

A pie chart is a circle divided into wedges so that we can see, literally, how a whole comprises its parts. We can see, for instance, on page 168, that of an entire pie representing the regions of foreign-born U.S. immigrants, 36 percent were born in Central America and Mexico, 26 percent in Asia, 14 percent in Europe, and so on.

COMING TO AMERICA ...

Both the percentage and number of foreign-born people in the United States dropped during much of the twentieth century, but after 1970, the tide was turning again.

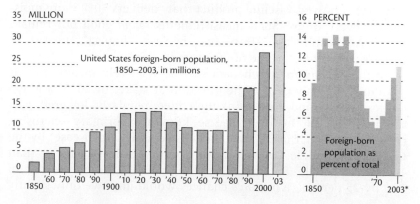

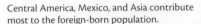

...FROM NEAR AND FAR

Central America, Mexico, and Asia contribute
most to the foreign-born population.

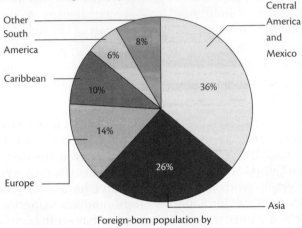

Foreign-born population by
region of birth, 2002

*Most recent estimate
Data from: United States Census Bureau

Because maps, charts, and graphs offer empirical data to support arguments, they communicate a high degree of reliability and
tend to be convincing. "Numbers don't lie," it is sometimes said, and
to some extent this is true. It's difficult to spin a fact like 1 + 1 = 2.
However, as Charles Seife notes in his book, *Proofiness*, numbers are
cold facts, but the measurements that numbers actually chart aren't
always so clear or free from bias and manipulation. Consider two
examples of advertising claims that Seife cites — one for a L'Oréal
mascara offering "twelve times more impact," and another for a
new and improved Vaseline product that "delivers 70% more moisture in every drop." Such measurements *sound* good but remain
relatively meaningless. (How was eyelash "impact" measured?
What is a percentage value of moisture?)

Another way in which data can be relatively meaningless is
by addressing only part of the question at stake. In 2013, a Mayo
Clinic study found that drinking coffee regularly lowered participants' risk of the liver disease known as primary sclerosing
cholangitis (PSC). But PSC is already listed as a "rare disease" by the
Centers for Disease Control and Prevention, affecting fewer than
1 in 2,000 people. So even if drinking coffee lowered the risk of
PSC by 25 percent, a person's chances would improve only slightly

---

✓ A CHECKLIST FOR CHARTS AND GRAPHS

☐ Is the source authoritative?

☐ Is the source cited?

☐ Will the chart or graph be intelligible to the intended audience?

☐ Is the caption, if any, clear and helpful?

---

from .0005 percent chance to .0004 percent chance—hardly a change at all, and hardly a rationale for drinking more coffee. Yet, statistical information showing a 25 percent reduction in PSC sounds significant, even more so when provided under a headline proclaiming "Drinking coffee helps prevent liver disease."

Consider other uses of numbers that Seife shows in his book to constitute "proofiness" (his title and word to describe the misuse of numbers as evidence):

- In 2006, George W. Bush declared No Child Left Behind a success in his State of the Union Address: "[B]ecause we acted," he said, "students are performing better in reading and math." (True, fourth to eighth graders showed improved scores, but other grade levels declined. In addition, fourth- to eighth-grade reading and math scores had been improving at an unchanged rate both before and after the NCLB legislation.)

- In 2000, the *New York Times* reported "Researchers Link Bad Debt to Bad Health" (the "dark side of the economic boom"). The researchers claimed that debt causes more illness, but in doing so they committed the correlation-causation fallacy: Just because two phenomena are correlated does not mean they are causally related. (Example: More people wear shorts in the summer and more people eat ice cream in the summer than during other seasons, but wearing shorts does not *cause* higher ice cream consumption.)

Finally, consider the following graph showing that eating Quaker Oats decreases cholesterol levels after just four weeks of daily servings. The bar graph suggests that cholesterol levels will plummet. But a careful look at the graph reveals that the vertical axis doesn't begin at zero. In this case, a relatively small change has been (mis)represented as much bigger than it actually is.

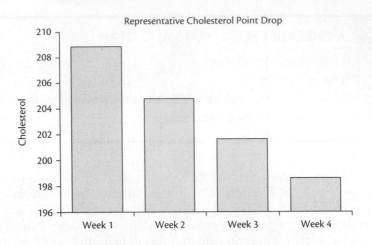

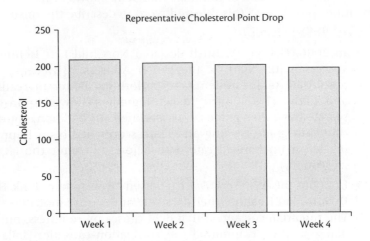

A more accurate representation of cholesterol levels after four weeks of eating Quaker Oats, using a graph that starts at zero, would look more like the second graph—showing essentially unchanged levels.

Following is another example showing unemployment rates during the Obama presidency. Note that here, too, the vertical axis doesn't start at zero, making the "rise" appear more dramatic than it actually was in reality.

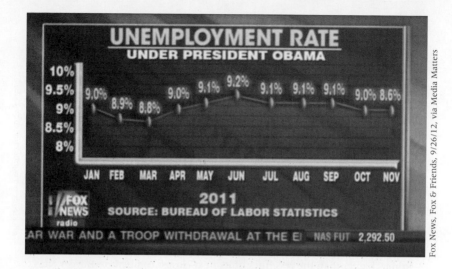

Fox News, Fox & Friends, 9/26/12, via Media Matters

USING VISUALS IN YOUR OWN PAPER

Every paper uses some degree of visual persuasion, merely in its appearance. Consider these elements of a paper's "look": title page; margins (ample, but not so wide that they indicate the writer's inability to produce a paper of the assigned length); double-spacing for the reader's convenience; headings and subheadings that indicate the progression of the argument; paragraphing; and so on. But you may also want to use visuals such as pictures, graphs, or pie charts. Keep a few guidelines in mind as you work with visuals, "writing" them into your own argument with as much care as you would read them in others' arguments:

- Consider your audience's needs and attitudes, and select the type of visuals—graphs, drawings, photographs—likely to be most persuasive to that audience.

- Consider the effect of color, composition, and placement within your document. Because images are most effective when they appear near the text that they supplement, do not group all images at the end of the paper.

Remember especially that images are almost never self-supporting or self-explanatory. They may be evidence for your argument

In this graph, McDonald's $41 billion in sales are shown to be about 3.5 times higher than the revenues of its next closest competitor, Burger King (at $11.3 billion), but the McDonald's logo graphic is about 13 times larger than Burger King's.

(e.g., Ut's photograph of napalm victims is *very* compelling evidence of suffering), but they aren't arguments themselves.

- Be sure to explain each visual that you use, integrating it into the verbal text that provides the logic and principal support behind your thesis.

- Be sure to cite the source of any visual that you paste into your argument.

Be alert to common ways in which graphs can be misleading:

- Vertical axis doesn't start at zero or skips numbers.

- Scale is given in very small units to make changes look big.

- Pie charts don't accurately divide on scale with percentages shown.

- Oversized graphics don't match the numbers they represent.

5

Writing an Analysis of an Argument

This is what we can all do to nourish and strengthen one another: listen to one another very hard, ask questions, too, send one another away to work again, and laugh in all the right places.

—NANCY MAIRS

I don't wait for moods. You accomplish nothing if you do that. Your mind must know it has got to get down to work.

—PEARL S. BUCK

Fear not those who argue but those who dodge.

—MARIE VON EBNER-ESCHENBACH

ANALYZING AN ARGUMENT

Examining the Author's Thesis

Most of your writing in other courses will require you to write an analysis of someone else's writing. In a course in political science you may have to analyze, say, an essay first published in *Foreign Affairs,* perhaps reprinted in your textbook, that argues against raising tariff barriers to foreign trade. Or a course in sociology may require you to analyze a report on the correlation between fatal accidents and drunk drivers under the age of twenty-one. Much of your writing, in short, will set forth reasoned responses to your reading as preparation for making an argument of your own.

Obviously, you must understand an essay before you can analyze it thoughtfully. You must read it several times—not just skim it—and (the hard part) you must think critically about it. Again, you'll find that your thinking is stimulated if you take notes and if you ask yourself questions about the material. Are there any Web sites or organizations dedicated to the material you are analyzing? If there are, visit some to see what others are saying about the material you are reviewing. Notes will help you to keep track of the writer's thoughts and also of your own responses to the writer's thesis. The writer probably *does* have a thesis, a claim, a point, and if so, you must try to locate it. Perhaps the thesis is explicitly stated in the title or in a sentence or two near the beginning of the essay or in a concluding paragraph, but perhaps you will have to infer it from the essay as a whole.

Notice that we said the writer *probably* has a thesis. Much of what you read will indeed be primarily an argument; the writer explicitly or implicitly is trying to support some thesis and to convince readers to agree with it. But some of what you read will be relatively neutral, with the argument just faintly discernible—or even with no argument at all. A work may, for instance, chiefly be a report: Here are the data, or here is what *X*, *Y*, and *Z* said; make of it what you will. A report might simply state how various ethnic groups voted in an election. In a report of this sort, of course, the writer hopes to persuade readers that the facts are correct, but no thesis is advanced—at least not explicitly or perhaps even consciously; the writer is not evidently arguing a point and trying to change readers' minds. Such a document differs greatly from an essay by a political analyst who presents similar findings to persuade a candidate to sacrifice the votes of one particular ethnic bloc and thereby get more votes from other blocs.

Examining the Author's Purpose

While reading an argument, try to form a clear idea of the author's **purpose**. Judging from the essay or the book, was the purpose to persuade, or was it to report? An analysis of a pure report (a work apparently without a thesis or argumentative angle) on ethnic voting will deal chiefly with the accuracy of the report. It will, for example, consider whether the sample poll was representative.

Much material that poses as a report really has a thesis built into it, consciously or unconsciously. The best evidence that the prose you are reading is argumentative is the presence of two kinds of key terms: transitions that imply the drawing of a conclusion (such as *therefore, because, for the reason that,* and *consequently*) and verbs that imply proof (such as *confirms, verifies, accounts for, implies, proves, disproves, is [in]consistent with, refutes,* and *it follows that*). Keep your eye out for such terms, and scrutinize their precise role whenever they appear. If the essay does not advance a thesis, think of one that it might support or some conventional belief that it might undermine. (See also Thinking Critically: Drawing Conclusions and Implying Proof on page 185.)

Examining the Author's Methods

If the essay advances a thesis, you will want to analyze the strategies or methods of argument that allegedly support the thesis.

- Does the writer quote authorities? Are these authorities competent in this field? Does the writer consider equally competent authorities who take a different view?

- Does the writer use statistics? If so, who compiled them, and are they appropriate to the point being argued? Can they be interpreted differently?

- Does the writer build the argument by using examples or analogies? Are they satisfactory?

- Are the writer's assumptions acceptable?

- Does the writer consider all relevant factors? Has he or she omitted some points that you think should be discussed? For instance, should the author recognize certain opposing positions and perhaps concede something to them?

- Does the writer seek to persuade by means of ridicule? If so, is the ridicule fair? Is it supported also by rational argument?

- Is the argument aimed at a particular audience?

In writing your analysis, you will want to tell readers something about the author's purpose and something about the author's **methods**. It is usually a good idea at the start of your analysis—if not in the first paragraph, then in the second or third—to let the reader know the purpose (and thesis, if there is one) of the work you are analyzing and then to summarize the work briefly.

Next, you will probably find it useful (readers will certainly find it helpful) to write out *your* thesis (your evaluation or judgment). You might say, for instance, that the essay is impressive but not conclusive, or is undermined by convincing contrary evidence, or relies too much on unsupported generalizations, or is wholly admirable. Remember, because your paper is itself an argument, it needs its own thesis.

And then, of course, comes the job of setting forth your analysis and the support for your thesis. There is no one way of going about this work. If, say, the author whose work you're analyzing gives four arguments (e.g., an appeal to common sense, the testimony of authorities, the evidence of comparisons, and an appeal to self-interest), you might want to do one of the following:

- Take up these four arguments in sequence.
- Discuss the simplest of the four, and then go on to the more difficult ones.
- Discuss the author's two arguments that you think are sound, and then turn to the two that you think are not sound (or perhaps the reverse).
- Apply one of these approaches, and then clinch your case by constructing a fifth argument that is absent from the work under scrutiny but is, in your view, highly important.

In short, the organization of your analysis may or may not follow the organization of the work you are analyzing.

Examining the Author's Persona

You will probably also want to analyze something a bit more elusive than the author's explicit arguments: the author's self-presentation. Does the author seek to persuade readers partly by presenting himself or herself as conscientious, friendly, self-effacing, authoritative, tentative, or in some other light? Most writers do two things:

- They present evidence.
- They present themselves (or, more precisely, they present the image of themselves that they wish us to behold).

In some persuasive writing this **persona** or **voice** or presentation of the self may be no less important than the presentation of evidence. In other cases, the persona may not much matter, but our point is that you should spend a little time looking at the author's self-presentation to consider if it's significant.

In establishing a persona, writers adopt various rhetorical strategies, ranging from the use of characteristic words to the use of a particular form of organization. For instance:

- The writer who speaks of an opponent's "gimmicks" instead of "strategy" probably is trying to downgrade the opponent and also to convey the self-image of a streetwise person.

- On a larger scale, consider the way in which evidence is presented and the kind of evidence that's offered. One writer may first bombard the reader with facts and then spend relatively little time drawing conclusions. Another may rely chiefly on generalizations, waiting until the end of the essay to bring the thesis home with a few details. Another may begin with a few facts and spend most of the space reflecting on these. One writer may seem professorial or pedantic, offering examples of an academic sort; another, whose examples are drawn from ordinary life, may seem like a regular guy.

All such devices deserve comment in your analysis.

The writer's persona, then, may color the thesis and help it develop in a distinctive way. If we accept the thesis, it is partly because the writer has won our goodwill by persuading us of his or her good character (*ethos*, in Aristotle's terms). Later we talk more about the appeal to the speaker's character—the so-called *ethical appeal*, but here we may say that good writers present themselves not as wise-guys, bullies, or pompous asses but as decent people whom the reader would like to invite to dinner.

The author of an essay may, for example, seem fair-minded and open-minded, treating the opposition with great courtesy and expressing interest in hearing other views. Such a tactic is itself a persuasive device. Another author may appear to rely on hard evidence such as statistics. This reliance on seemingly objective truths is itself a way of seeking to persuade—a rational way, to be sure, but a mode of persuasion nonetheless.

Especially in analyzing a work in which the author's persona and ideas are blended, you will want to spend some time commenting on the persona. Whether you discuss it near the beginning of your analysis or near the end will depend on how you want to construct your essay, and this decision will partly depend on the work you are analyzing. For example, if the author's persona is kept in the background and is thus relatively invisible, you may want to make that point fairly early to get it out of the way and then concentrate on more interesting matters. If, however, the persona is interesting—and perhaps seductive, whether because it seems so scrupulously objective or so engagingly subjective—you may want to hint at this quality early in your essay and then develop the point while you consider the arguments.

In short, the author's self-presentation usually matters. Recognize its effect, whether positive or negative.

Examining Persona and Intended Audience

A key element in understanding an argument lies in thinking about the intended audience—how the author perceives the audience and what strategies the author uses to connect to it. We have already said something about the creation of the author's persona. An author with a loyal following is, almost by definition, someone who in earlier writings has presented an engaging persona, a persona with a trustworthy *ethos*. A trusted author can sometimes cut corners and can perhaps adopt a colloquial tone that would be unacceptable in the writing of an unknown author.

Authors who want to win the assent of their audiences need to think about how they present information and how they present *themselves*. Consider how you prefer people to talk to you. What sorts of language do you find engaging? Much of course depends on the circumstances, notably the topic, the audience, and the place. A joke may be useful in an argument about whether the government should regulate junk food, but almost surely a joke will be inappropriate—will backfire, will alienate the audience—in an argument about abortion. The *way* an author addresses the reader (through an invented persona) can have a significant impact on the reader's perception of the author, which is to say perception of the author's *views*, the author's *argument*. A slip in tone or an error of fact, however small, may be enough for the audience to dismiss the author's argument. Understanding audience means thinking about all of the possible audiences who may come into contact with your writing or your message, and thinking about the consequences of what you write and where it is published.

You may recall a tweet by LeBron James, who formerly played basketball for the Cleveland Cavaliers but left to play for the Miami Heat. After James left the Cavaliers (and his home state of Ohio), the Los Angeles Lakers beat the Cavaliers by fifty-five points, and James tweeted: "Crazy. Karma is a b****. Gets you every time. It's not good to wish bad on anybody. God sees everything!" Cleveland fans not surprisingly perceived his tweet as a slap in the face. The broader audience, too, outside of Cleveland, perceived it as inappropriate. Though he has since returned to Cleveland and been

LeBron James, considering his audience while he was with the Miami Heat.

Layne Murdoch/Getty Images

largely forgiven by fans, LeBron James clearly did not think about his audience(s). To put it in rhetorical terms, LeBron James vastly diminished his *ethos.* Doubtless he wishes he could retract the tweet, but as the ancient Roman poet Horace said, *"Nescit vox missa reverti"* ("The word once spoken can never be recalled"), or, in plain proverbial English, "Think twice before you speak."

✓ A CHECKLIST FOR ANALYZING AN AUTHOR'S INTENDED AUDIENCE

☐ Where did the piece appear? Who published it? Why, in your view, might someone have found it worth publishing?

☐ In what technological format does this piece appear? Print journal? Online magazine? Blog? What does the technological format say about the piece or the author?

☐ Is the writing relatively informal — for instance, a tweet or a Facebook status update? Who is the intended audience? Are there other audiences who may also have an interest but whom the author has failed to consider? Why is this medium good or bad for the message?

☐ If *you* are the intended audience, what shared values do you have with the author?

☐ What strategies does the writer use to create a connection with the audience?

Consider Facebook status updates. Have you ever posted a status update and wished you could take it back only to find out it was too late? People you did not want to see it saw it before you could remove it. Have you ever tweeted or even texted something you wished you hadn't? When reading and writing more formal essays, it is equally important to think about who wrote what you are reading, and who will read what you are writing.

Summary

In the last few pages we have tried to persuade you that, in writing an analysis of a reading, you must do the following:

- Read and reread thoughtfully. Composing and keeping notes will help you to think about what you are reading.
- Be aware of the purpose of the material to which you are responding.

We have also tried to point out these facts:

- Most of the nonliterary material that you will read is designed to argue, to report, or to do both.
- Most of this material also presents the writer's personality, or voice, and this voice usually merits attention in an analysis. An essay on, say, nuclear war, in a journal devoted to political science, may include a voice that moves from an objective tone to a mildly ironic tone to a hortatory tone, and this voice is worth commenting on.

Possibly all this explanation is obvious. There is yet another point, equally obvious but often neglected by students who begin by writing an analysis and end up by writing only a summary, a shortened version of the work they have read: Although your essay is an analysis of someone else's writing, and you may have to include a summary of the work you are writing about, your essay is *your* essay, your analysis, not a mere summary. The thesis, the organization, and the tone are yours.

- Your thesis, for example, may be that although the author is convinced she has presented a strong case, her case is far from proved because . . .
- Your organization may be deeply indebted to the work you are analyzing, but it need not be. The author may have

begun with specific examples and then gone on to make generalizations and to draw conclusions, but you may begin with the conclusions.

- Your tone, similarly, may resemble your subject's (let's say the voice is courteous academic), but it will nevertheless have its own ring, its own tone of, say, urgency, caution, or coolness.

Most of the essays that we have included thus far are more or less in an academic style, and indeed several are by students and by professors. But argumentative writing is not limited to academicians—if it were, your college would not be requiring you to take a course in the subject. The following essay, in a breezy style, comes from a columnist who writes for the *New York Times*.

✓ A CHECKLIST FOR ANALYZING A TEXT

Have I considered all of the following matters?

☐ Who is the author? What stake might he or she have in writing this piece?

☐ Is the piece aimed at a particular audience? A neutral audience? Persons who are already sympathetic to the author's point of view? A hostile audience? What evidence enables me to identify the target audience?

☐ What is the author's thesis (argument, main point, claim)?

☐ What assumptions does the author make? Do I share them? If not, why not?

☐ Does the author ever confuse facts with beliefs or opinions?

☐ What appeals does the author make? To reason (*logos*), for instance, with statistics, the testimony of authorities, and personal experience? To the emotions (*pathos*), for instance, by an appeal to "our better nature" or to widely shared values? To our sense that the speaker is trustworthy (*ethos*)?

☐ How convincing is the evidence? Why do I think so?

☐ Are significant objections and counterevidence adequately discussed?

☐ How is the text organized, and is the organization effective? Are the title, the opening paragraphs, and the concluding paragraphs effective? In what ways?

(continued)

A CHECKLIST FOR ANALYZING A TEXT (Continued)

☐ If visual materials such as graphs, pie charts, or pictures are used, how persuasive are they? Do they make a logical appeal? (Charts and graphs presumably make a logical appeal.) Do they make an emotional appeal? An ethical appeal?

☐ What is the author's tone? Is it appropriate?

☐ To what extent has the author convinced me? Why?

AN ARGUMENT, ITS ELEMENTS, AND A STUDENT'S ANALYSIS OF THE ARGUMENT

Nicholas D. Kristof

Nicholas D. Kristof (b. 1959), a two-time Pulitzer Prize winner, grew up on a farm in Oregon. After graduating from Harvard, he was awarded a Rhodes scholarship to Oxford, where he studied law. In 1984 he joined the New York Times *as a correspondent, and since 2001 he has written as a columnist. The editorial that follows first appeared in the* New York Times *in 2005.*

For Environmental Balance, Pick Up a Rifle

Here's a quick quiz: Which large American mammal kills the most humans each year?

It's not the bear, which kills about two people a year in North America. Nor is it the wolf, which in modern times hasn't killed anyone in this country. It's not the cougar, which kills one person every year or two.

Rather, it's the deer. Unchecked by predators, deer populations are exploding in a way that is profoundly unnatural and that is destroying the ecosystem in many parts of the country. In a wilderness, there might be ten deer per square mile; in parts of New Jersey, there are up to 200 per square mile.

One result is ticks and Lyme disease, but deer also kill people more directly. A study for the insurance industry estimated that deer kill about 150 people a year in car crashes nationwide and cause $1 billion in damage. Granted, deer aren't stalking us, and they come out worse in these collisions—but it's still true that in a typical year, an American is less likely to be killed by Osama bin Laden than by Bambi.

If the symbol of the environment's being out of whack in the 5
1960s was the Cuyahoga River in Cleveland catching fire, one such
symbol today is deer congregating around what they think of as
salad bars and what we think of as suburbs.

So what do we do? Let's bring back hunting.

Now, you've probably just spilled your coffee. These days,
among the university-educated crowd in the cities, hunting is
viewed as barbaric.

The upshot is that towns in New York and New Jersey are
talking about using birth control to keep deer populations down.
(Liberals presumably support free condoms, while conservatives
back abstinence education.) Deer contraception hasn't been very
successful, though.

Meanwhile, the same population bomb has spread to bears.
A bear hunt has been scheduled for this week in New Jersey—
prompting outrage from some animal rights groups (there's also talk
of bear contraception: make love, not cubs).

As for deer, partly because hunting is perceived as brutal and 10
vaguely psychopathic, towns are taking out contracts on deer through
discreet private companies. Greenwich, Connecticut, budgeted
$47,000 this year to pay a company to shoot eighty deer from raised
platforms over four nights—as well as $8,000 for deer birth control.

Look, this is ridiculous.

We have an environmental imbalance caused in part by the
decline of hunting. Humans first wiped out certain predators—like
wolves and cougars—but then expanded their own role as predators to sustain a rough ecological balance. These days, though,
hunters are on the decline.

According to "Families Afield: An Initiative for the Future of
Hunting," a report by an alliance of shooting organizations, for every
hundred hunters who die or stop hunting, only sixty-nine hunters
take their place.

I was raised on *Bambi*—but also, as an Oregon farm boy, on
venison and elk meat. But deer are not pets, and dead deer are as
natural as live deer. To wring one's hands over them, perhaps after
polishing off a hamburger, is soggy sentimentality.

What's the alternative to hunting? Is it preferable that deer 15
die of disease and hunger? Or, as the editor of *Adirondack Explorer*
magazine suggested, do we introduce wolves into the burbs?

To their credit, many environmentalists agree that hunting can
be green. The New Jersey Audubon Society this year advocated
deer hunting as an ecological necessity.

There's another reason to encourage hunting: it connects people with the outdoors and creates a broader constituency for wilderness preservation. At a time when America's wilderness is being gobbled away for logging, mining, or oil drilling, that's a huge boon.

Granted, hunting isn't advisable in suburban backyards, and I don't expect many soccer moms to install gun racks in their minivans. But it's an abdication of environmental responsibility to eliminate other predators and then refuse to assume the job ourselves. In that case, the collisions with humans will simply get worse.

In October, for example, Wayne Goldsberry was sitting in a home in northwestern Arkansas when he heard glass breaking in the next room. It was a home invasion—by a buck.

Mr. Goldsberry, who is six feet one inch and weighs two hun-   20
dred pounds, wrestled with the intruder for forty minutes. Blood spattered the walls before he managed to break the buck's neck.

So it's time to reestablish a balance in the natural world—by accepting the idea that hunting is as natural as bird-watching.   ∎

Topics for Critical Thinking and Writing

1. What is Nicholas Kristof's chief thesis? (State it in one sentence.)

2. Does Kristof make any assumptions—tacit or explicit—with which you disagree? With which you agree? Write them down.

3. Is the slightly humorous tone of Kristof's essay inappropriate for a discussion of deliberately killing wild animals? Why, or why not?

4. If you are familiar with *Bambi*, does the story make any *argument* against killing deer, or does the story appeal only to our emotions?

5. Do you agree that "hunting is as natural as bird-watching" (para. 21)? In any case, do you think that an appeal to what is "natural" is a good argument for expanding the use of hunting?

6. To whom is Kristof talking? How do you know?

The Essay Analyzed

OK, time's up. Let's examine Kristof's essay with an eye to identifying those elements we mentioned earlier in this chapter (pp. 173–80) that deserve notice when examining *any* argument: the author's *thesis, purpose, methods, persona,* and *audience.* And while we're at it, let's also notice some other features of Kristof's essay that will help us appreciate its effects and evaluate it. We will thus

THINKING CRITICALLY DRAWING CONCLUSIONS AND IMPLYING PROOF

Look at Nicholas D. Kristof's essay on page 182. Provide two examples of sentences from Kristof's essay that use each type of conclusion or proof.

Indicator of Conclusion or Proof	Examples	Two Examples from Kristof's Essay
Transitions that imply the drawing of a conclusion	*therefore, because, for the reason that, consequently*	
Verbs that imply proof	*confirms, verifies, accounts for, implies, proves, disproves, is (in)consistent with, refutes, it follows that*	

be in a good position to write an evaluation or an argument that confirms, extends, or even rebuts Kristof's argument.

But first, a caution: Kristof's essay appeared in a newspaper where paragraphs are customarily very short, partly to allow for easy reading and partly because the columns are narrow and even short paragraphs may extend for an inch or two. If his essay were to appear in a book, doubtless the author would run many of the paragraphs together, making longer units. In analyzing a work, think about where it originally appeared. A blog, a print journal, an online magazine? Does the format in some measure influence the piece?

TITLE By combining "Environmental Balance" with "Rifle" — terms that don't seem to go together—Kristof starts off with a bang. He gives a hint of his *topic* (something about the environment) and of his thesis (some sort of way of introducing ecological balance). He also conveys something of his persona by introducing a rifle into the environment. He is, the title suggests, a no-nonsense, hard-hitting guy.

OPENING PARAGRAPHS Kristof immediately grabs hold of us ("Here's a quick quiz") and asks a simple question, but one that we probably have not thought much about: "Which large American mammal kills the most humans each year?" In paragraph 2 he tells us it is *not* the bear—the answer most readers probably come up with—nor is it the cougar. Not until paragraph 3 does Kristof give us the answer, the deer. But remember, Kristof is writing in a newspaper, where paragraphs customarily are very short. It takes us only a few seconds to get to the third paragraph and the answer.

THESIS What is the basic thesis Kristof is arguing? Somewhat unusually, Kristof does *not* announce it in its full form until paragraph 6 ("Let's bring back hunting"), but, again, his paragraphs are very short, and if the essay were published in a book, Kristof's first two paragraphs probably would be combined, as would the third and fourth.

PURPOSE Kristof's purpose is clear: He wants to *persuade* readers to adopt his view. This amounts to trying to persuade us that his thesis (stated above) is *true*. Kristof, however, does not show that his essay is argumentative or persuasive by using many of the key terms that normally mark argumentative prose. He doesn't call anything his *conclusion*, none of his statements is labeled *my premises*, and he doesn't connect clauses or sentences with *therefore* or *because*. Almost the only traces of the language of argument are "Granted" (para. 18) and "So" (i.e., *therefore*) in his final paragraph.

Despite the lack of argumentative language, the argumentative nature of his essay is clear. He has a thesis—one that will strike many readers as highly unusual—and he wants readers to accept it, so he must go on to *support* it; accordingly, after his introductory paragraphs, in which he calls attention to a problem and offers a solution (his thesis), he must offer evidence. And that is what much of the rest of the essay seeks to do.

METHODS Although Kristof will have to offer evidence, he begins by recognizing the folks on the other side, "the university-educated crowd in the cities, [for whom] hunting is viewed as barbaric" (para. 7). He goes on to spoof this "crowd" when, speaking of methods of keeping the deer population down, he says in paragraph 8, "Liberals presumably support free condoms, while conservatives back abstinence education." Ordinarily, it is a bad idea to make fun of persons who hold views other than your own—after all, they just may be on to something, they just might know something you don't know, and, in any case, impartial readers rarely want to align themselves with someone who mocks others. In the essay we are looking at, however, Kristof gets away with this smart-guy tone because he not only has loyal readers but also has written the entire essay in a highly informal or playful manner. Think again about paragraph 1, which begins "Here's a quick quiz." The informality is not only in the contraction (*Here's* versus *Here is*), but in the very idea of beginning by grabbing the readers and thrusting a quiz at them. The playfulness is evident throughout: For instance, immediately after Kristof announces his thesis, "Let's bring back hunting," he begins a new paragraph (7) with "Now, you've probably just spilled your coffee."

Kristof's methods of presenting evidence include providing ***statistics*** (paras. 3, 4, 10, and 13), giving ***examples*** (paras. 10, 19–20), and citing ***authorities*** (paras. 13 and 16).

PERSONA   Kristof presents himself as a confident, no-nonsense fellow, a persona that not many writers can get away with, but that probably is acceptable in a journalist who regularly writes a newspaper column. His readers know what to expect, and they read him with pleasure. But it would be inadvisable for an unknown writer to adopt this persona, unless perhaps he or she were writing for an audience that could be counted on to be friendly (in this instance, an audience of hunters). If this essay appeared in a hunting magazine, doubtless it would please and entertain its audience. It would not convert anybody, but conversion would not be its point if it appeared in a magazine read by hunters. In the *New York Times*, where the essay originally appeared, Kristof could count on a moderately sympathetic audience because he has a large number of faithful readers, but one can guess that many of these readers—chiefly city dwellers—read him for entertainment rather than for information about how they should actually behave.

By the way, when we speak of "faithful readers" we are in effect saying that the author has established good *ethos*, has convinced those readers that he or she is *worth* reading.

CLOSING PARAGRAPHS   The first two of the last three paragraphs report an episode (the home invasion by a buck) that Kristof presumably thinks is pretty conclusive evidence. The final paragraph begins with "So," strongly implying a logical conclusion to the essay.

Let's now turn to a student's analysis of Kristof's essay and then to our own analysis of the student's analysis. (We should say that the analysis of Kristof's essay that you have just read is partly indebted to the student's essay that you are about to read.)

Swinton 1

Betsy Swinton

Professor Knowles

English 101B

March 12, 2016

Tracking Kristof

Nicholas D. Kristof's "For Environmental Balance, Pick Up a Rifle" is an engaging piece of writing, but whether it is convincing is something I am not sure about. And I am not sure about it for two reasons: (1) I don't know much about the deer problem, and that's my fault; (2) I don't know much about the deer problem, and that's Kristof's fault. The first point needs no explanation, but let me explain the second.

Kristof is making an argument, offering a thesis: Deer are causing destruction, and the best way to reduce the destruction is to hunt deer. For all that I know, he may be correct both in his comment about what deer are doing and also in his comment about what must be done about deer. My ignorance of the situation is regrettable, but I don't think that I am the only reader from Chicago who doesn't know much about the deer problems in New Jersey, Connecticut, and Arkansas, the states that Kristof specifically mentions in connection with the deer problem. He announces his thesis early enough, in his sixth paragraph, and he is entertaining throughout his essay, but does he make a convincing case? To ask "Does he make a convincing case?" is to ask "Does he offer adequate evidence?" and "Does he show that his solution is better than other possible solutions?"

To take the first question: In a short essay Kristof can hardly give overwhelming evidence, but he does convince me that there is a problem. The most convincing evidence he gives appears in paragraph 16, where he says that the New Jersey Audubon Society "advocated deer hunting as an ecological necessity." I don't really know anything about the New Jersey Audubon Society, but I suppose that they are people with a deep interest in nature and in conservation, and if even such a group advocates deer hunting, there must be something to this solution.

I am even willing to accept his argument that, in this nation of meat-eaters, "to wring one's hands over them [dead deer], perhaps after polishing off a hamburger, is soggy senti-mentality" (para. 14). According to Kristof, the present alterna-tive to hunting deer is that we leave the deer to "die of disease and hunger" (para. 15). But what I am not convinced of is that there is no way to reduce the deer population other than by hunting. I don't think Kristof adequately explains why some sort of birth control is inadequate. In his eighth paragraph he makes a joke about controlling the birth of deer ("Liberals presumably support free condoms, while conservatives back abstinence education"), and the joke is funny, but it isn't an argument, it's just a joke. Why can't food containing some sort of sterilizing medicine be put out for the starving deer, food that will nourish them and yet make them unreproductive? In short, I don't think he has fairly informed his readers of alter-natives to his own positions, and because he fails to look at counterproposals, he weakens his own proposal.

Although Kristof occasionally uses a word or phrase that suggests argument, such as "Granted" (para. 18), "So" (final paragraph), and "There's another reason" (para. 17), he relies chiefly on forceful writing rather than on reasoning. And the second of his two reasons for hunting seems utterly unconvincing to me. His first, as we have seen, is that the deer population (and apparently the bear population) is out of control. His second (para. 17) is that hunting "connects people with the outdoors and creates a broader constituency for wilderness preservation." I am not a hunter and I have never been one. Perhaps that's my misfortune, but I don't think I am missing anything. And when I hear Kristof say, in his final sentence—the climactic place in his essay—that "hunting is as natural as bird-watching," I rub my eyes in disbelief. If he had me at least half-convinced by his statistics and his citation of the Audubon Society, he now loses me when he argues that hunting is "natural." One might as well say that war is natural, rape is natural, bribery is natural—all these terrible things occur, but we ought to deplore them and we ought to make every effort to see that they disappear.

In short, I think that Kristof has written an engaging essay, and he may well have an important idea, but I think that in his glib final paragraph, where he tells us that "hunting is as natural as bird-watching," he utterly loses the reader's confidence.

An Analysis of the Student's Analysis

Swinton's essay seems to us to be excellent, doubtless the product of a good deal of thoughtful revision. She does not cover every possible aspect of Kristof's essay—she concentrates on his reasoning and says very little about his style—but we think that given the limits of space (about 500 words), she does a good job. What makes this student's essay effective?

- The essay has a title ("Tracking Kristof") that is of at least a little interest; it picks up Kristof's point about hunting, and it gives a hint of what is to come.

- The author promptly identifies her subject (she names the writer and the title of his essay) early.

- Early in the essay she gives us a hint of where she will be going (in her first paragraph she tells us that Kristof's essay is "engaging . . . *but* . . .").

- She recognizes Kristof's audience at the start, and she suggests that he may not have given thought to this matter of the audience.

✓ A CHECKLIST FOR WRITING AN ANALYSIS OF AN ARGUMENT

Have I asked myself the following questions?

☐ Early in my essay have I accurately stated the writer's thesis (claim) and summarized his or her supporting reasons? Have I explained to my reader any disagreement about definitions of important terms?

☐ Have I, again fairly early in my essay, indicated where I will be taking my reader (i.e., have I indicated my general response to the essay I am analyzing)?

☐ Have I called attention to the strengths, if any, and the weaknesses, if any, of the essay?

☐ Have I commented not only on the *logos* (logic, reasoning) but also on the *ethos* (character of the writer, as presented in the essay)? For instance, has the author convinced me that he or she is well informed and is a person of goodwill? Or, in contrast, does the writer seem to be chiefly concerned with ridiculing those who hold a different view?

(continued)

A CHECKLIST FOR WRITING AN ANALYSIS OF AN ARGUMENT (*Continued*)

☐ If there is an appeal to *pathos* (emotion, originally meaning "pity for suffering," but now interpreted more broadly to include appeals to patriotism, humor, or loyalty to family, for example), is it acceptable? If not, why not?

☐ Have I used occasional brief quotations to let my reader hear the author's tone and to ensure fairness and accuracy?

☐ Is my analysis effectively organized?

☐ Have I taken account of the author's audience(s)?

☐ Does my essay, perhaps in the concluding paragraphs, indicate my agreement or disagreement with the writer but also my view of the essay as a piece of argumentative writing?

☐ Is my tone appropriate?

- She uses a few brief quotations, to give us a feel for Kristof's essay and to let us hear the evidence for itself, but she does not pad her essay with long quotations.

- She takes up all of Kristof's main points.

- She gives her essay a reasonable organization, letting us hear Kristof's thesis, letting us know the degree to which she accepts it, and finally letting us know her specific reservations about the essay.

- She concludes without the formality of "in conclusion"; "in short" nicely does the trick.

- Notice, finally, that she sticks closely to Kristof's essay. She does not go off on a tangent about the virtues of vegetarianism or the dreadful politics of the *New York Times*, the newspaper that published Kristof's essay. She was asked to analyze the essay, and she has done so.

EXERCISE

Take one of the essays not yet discussed in class or an essay assigned now by your instructor, and in an essay of 500 words analyze and evaluate it, guided by the checklists and examples we have provided.

6

Developing an Argument of Your Own

The difficult part in an argument is not to defend one's opinion but to know what it is.

—ANDRÉ MAUROIS

Imagine that you enter a parlor. You come late. When you arrive, others have long preceded you, and they are engaged in a heated discussion, a discussion too heated for them to pause and tell you exactly what it is about. In fact, the discussion had already begun long before any of them got there, so that no one present is qualified to retrace for you all the steps that had gone before. You listen for a while, until you decide that you have caught the tenor of the argument; then you put in your oar. Someone answers; you answer him; another comes to your defense; another aligns himself against you, to either the embarrassment or gratification of your opponent, depending upon the quality of your ally's assistance. However, the discussion is interminable. The hour grows late, you must depart. And you do depart, with the discussion still vigorously in progress.

—KENNETH BURKE

No greater misfortune could happen to anyone than that of developing a dislike for argument.

—PLATO

PLANNING, DRAFTING, AND REVISING AN ARGUMENT

First, hear the wisdom of Mark Twain: "When the Lord finished the world, He pronounced it good. That is what I said about my first work, too. But Time, I tell you, Time takes the confidence out of these incautious early opinions."

All of us, teachers and students, have our moments of confidence, but for the most part we know that it takes considerable effort to write clear, thoughtful, seemingly effortless prose. In a conversation we can cover ourselves with such expressions as "Well, I don't know, but I sort of think . . ." and we can always revise our position ("Oh, well, I didn't mean it that way"), but once we have handed in the final version of our writing, we are helpless. We are (putting it strongly) naked to our enemies.

Getting Ideas: Argument as an Instrument of Inquiry

In Chapter 1 we quoted Robert Frost, "To learn to write is to learn to have ideas," and we offered suggestions about generating ideas, a process traditionally called **invention**. A moment ago we said that we often improve our ideas when explaining them to someone else. Partly, of course, we're responding to questions or objections raised by our companion in the conversation. But partly we're responding to ourselves: Almost as soon as we hear what we have to say, we may find that it won't do, and if we're lucky, we may find a better idea surfacing. One of the best ways of getting ideas is to talk things over.

The process of talking things over usually begins with the text that you're reading: Your notes, your summary, and your annotations are a kind of dialogue between you and the author. You are also having a dialogue when you talk with friends about your topic. You are trying out and developing ideas. You're arguing, but not chiefly to persuade; rather, you're using argument in order to find the truth. Finally, after reading, taking notes, and talking, you may feel that you have some clear ideas and need only put them into writing. So you take up a sheet of blank paper, but then a paralyzing thought suddenly strikes: "I have ideas but just can't put them into words." The blank white page (or screen) stares back at you and you just can't seem to begin.

All writers, even professional ones, are familiar with this experience. Good writers know that waiting for inspiration is usually not the best strategy. You may be waiting a long time. The best thing to do is begin. Recall some of what we said in Chapter 1: *Writing is a way of thinking*. It's a way of *getting and developing ideas*. *Argument* is an instrument of inquiry as well as persuasion. It is an important part of *critical thinking*. It helps us clarify what we think. One reason we have trouble writing is our fear of putting ourselves on record, but another reason is our fear that we have no ideas worth putting down. However, by writing notes—or even free associations—and by writing a draft, no matter how weak, we can begin to think our way toward good ideas.

Three Brainstorming Strategies: Freewriting, Listing, and Diagramming

If you are facing an issue, debate, or topic and don't know what to write, this is likely because you don't yet know what you think. If, after talking about the topic with yourself (via your reading notes) and others, you are still unclear on what you think, try one of these three strategies:

Freewriting Write for five or six minutes, nonstop, without censoring what you produce. You may use what you write to improve your thinking. You may even dim your computer screen so you won't be tempted to look up and fiddle too soon with what you've just written. Once you have spent the time writing out your ideas, you can use what you've written to look further into the subject at hand.

Freewriting should be totally free. If you have some initial ideas, a good freewrite might look like this. (As a topic, let's imagine the writer below is thinking about how children's toys are constructed for different genders. The student is reflecting on the release of the Nerf Rebelle, a type of toy gun made specifically for girls.)

FREEWRITING: This year Nerf released a new toy made for girls, the Nerf Rebelle gun, an attempt the company made to offer toys for girls traditionally made for boys. This seems good—showing an effort toward equality between the sexes. Or is Nerf just trying to broaden its market and sell more toys (after all, boys are only half the population)? Or is it both? That could be my central question. But it is not like the gun makes no distinction between boys and girls. It is pink and purple and has feminine-looking designs on it. And with its "elle" ending the gun sounds small, cute, and girly. Does this toy represent true equality between the sexes, or does it just offer more in the way of feminine stereotypes? It shoots foam arrows, unlike the boys' version of the gun, which shoots bullets. This suggests Cupid, maybe—that is, the figure whose arrows inspire love—a stereotype that girls aren't saving the world but seeking love and marriage. Maybe it's also related to Katniss Everdeen from the *Hunger Games* movie. She carries a bow and arrow, too. Like a lot of female superheroes, Katniss is presented as both strong and sexy, powerful and vulnerable, masculine and feminine at the same time. What kind of messages does this send to young girls? Is it the same message suggested by the gun? Why do powerful women have to project traditional or stereotypical femininity at the same time? How does this work in other areas of life, like business and politics?

Notice that the writer here is jumping around, generating and exploring ideas while writing. Later she can return to the freewriting and begin organizing her ideas and observations. Notice that right in the middle of the freewriting she made a connection between the toy and the *Hunger Games* movie, and by extension to the larger culture in which forms of contemporary femininity can be found. This connection seems significant, and it may help the student to broaden her argument from a critique of the company's motives early on, to a more evidence-based piece about assumptions underlying certain trends in consumer and media culture. The point is that freewriting in this case led to new paths of inquiry and may have inspired further research into different kinds of toys and media.

Listing   Writing down keywords, just as you do when making a shopping list, is another way of generating ideas. When you make a shopping list, you write *ketchup,* and the act of writing it reminds you that you also need hamburger rolls—and *that* in turn reminds you that you also need tuna fish. Similarly, when preparing a list of ideas for a paper, just writing down one item will often generate another. Of course, when you look over the list, you'll probably drop some of these ideas—the dinner menu will change—but you'll be making progress. If you have a smartphone or tablet, use it to write down your thoughts. You can even e-mail these notes to yourself so you can access them later.

Here's an example of a student listing questions and making associations that could help him focus on a specific argument within a larger debate. The subject here is whether prostitution should be legalized.

LIST: Prostitutes — Law — How has the law traditionally policed sex? — What types of prostitutes exist? — What is prostitution? — Where is it already legal? — How does it work in places where it is legal? — Individual rights vs. public good? — Why shouldn't people be allowed to sell sex? — What are the "bad" effects of prostitution socially? — How many prostitutes are arrested every year? — Could prostitution be taxed? — Who suffers most from enforcement? — Who would suffer most if it were legal? — If it were legal, could its negative effects be better controlled? — Aren't "escort services" really prostitution rings for people with more money? — How is that dealt with? — Who goes into the "oldest business" and why?

Notice that the student doesn't really know the answers yet but is asking questions by free-associating and seeing what turns up as a productive line of analysis. The questions range from the definition of prostitution to its effects, and they might inspire the student to do some basic Internet research or even deeper research. Once you make a list, see if you can observe patterns or similarities among the items you listed, or if you invented a question worthy of its own thesis statement (e.g., "The enforcement of prostitution laws hurts X group unequally, and it uses a lot of public money that could better be used in other areas or toward regulating the trade rather than jailing people").

Diagramming   Sketching a visual representation of an essay is a kind of listing. Three methods of diagramming are especially common.

- *Clustering*   As we discuss on page 5, you can make an effective cluster by writing, in the middle of a sheet of paper, a word or phrase summarizing your topic (e.g., *fracking*; see diagram below), circling it, and then writing down and circling a related word (e.g., *energy independence*). Perhaps this

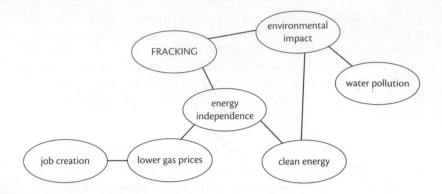

leads you to write *lower gas prices* and *clean energy*. You then circle these phrases and continue making connections. The next thing you think of is *environmental impact,* so you draw a line to *clean energy.* Then you think of *water pollution,* write it down and circle it, and draw another line to *environmental impact.* The next thing that occurs to you is *job creation,* so you write this down and circle it. You won't connect this to *clean energy,* but you might connect it to *lower gas prices* because both are generally positive economic effects. (If you can think of negative economic impacts on other industries or workers, write them down and circle them.) Keep going, jotting down ideas and making connections where possible, indicating relationships. Notice that you appear to be detailing and weighing the economic and environmental impacts of fracking. Whether you realized it or not, an argument is taking shape.

- *Branching*   Some writers find it useful to draw a tree, moving from the central topic to the main branches (chief ideas) and then to the twigs (aspects of the chief ideas).

- *Comparing in columns*   Draw a line down the middle of the page, and then set up two columns showing oppositions. For instance, if you are concerned with the environmental and economic impacts of fracking, you might head one column ENVIRONMENTAL and the other ECONOMIC. In the first column, you might write *water pollution, chemicals used,* and *other hazards?* In the second column, you might write *clean air, employment,* and *independence from unstable oil-producing countries.* You might go on to write, in the first column, *gas leaks* and *toxic waste,* and in the second, *cheaper fuel* and *cheaper electricity*—or whatever else relevant comes to mind.

All these methods can, of course, be executed with pen and paper, but you may also be able to use them on your computer depending on the capabilities of your software.

Whether you're using a computer or a pen, you put down some words and almost immediately see that they need improvement, not simply a little polishing but a substantial overhaul. You write, "Race should be counted in college admissions for two reasons," and as soon as you write those words, a third reason comes to mind. Or perhaps one of those "two reasons" no longer seems very good. As E. M. Forster said, "How can I know what I think till I see what I say?" We have to see what we say—we have to get something down on paper—before we realize that we need to make it better.

Writing, then, is really **rewriting**—that is, **revising**—and a revision is a *re-vision,* a second look. The essay that you submit— whether as hard copy or as a .doc file—should be clear and may appear to be effortlessly composed, but in all likelihood the clarity and apparent ease are the result of a struggle with yourself during which you refined your first thoughts. You begin by putting down ideas, perhaps in random order, but sooner or later comes the job of looking at them critically, developing what's useful in them and removing what isn't. If you follow this procedure you will be in the company of Picasso, who said that he "advanced by means of destruction." Any passages that you cut or destroy can be kept in another file in case you want to revisit those deletions later. Sometimes, you end up restoring them and developing what you discarded into a new essay with a new direction.

Whether you advance bit by bit (writing a sentence, revising it, writing the next, etc.) or whether you write an entire first draft and then revise it and revise it again and again is chiefly a matter of temperament. Probably most people combine both approaches, backing up occasionally but trying to get to the end fairly soon so that they can see rather quickly what they know, or think they know, and can then start the real work of thinking, of converting their initial ideas into something substantial.

Further Invention Strategies: Asking Good Questions

Asking Questions   Generating ideas, we said when talking about **topics** and **invention** strategies in Chapter 1 (p. 22) is mostly a matter of asking (and then thinking about) questions. In this book we include questions at the end of each argumentative essay, not to torment you but to help you think about the arguments—for instance, to turn your attention to especially important matters. If your instructor asks you to write an answer to one of these questions, you are lucky: Examining the question will stimulate your mind to work in a specific direction.

If your instructor doesn't assign a topic for an argumentative essay, you'll find that some ideas (possibly poor ones initially, but that doesn't matter because you'll soon revise) come to mind if you ask yourself questions. Begin determining where you stand on an issue (**stasis**) by asking the following five basic questions:

1. What is X?
2. What is the value of X?
3. What are the causes (or the consequences) of X?
4. What should (or ought or must) we do about X?
5. What is the evidence for my claims about X?

Let's spend a moment looking at each of these questions.

1. What is X?   We can hardly argue about the number of people sentenced to death in the United States in 2000—a glance at the appropriate government report will give the answer—but we can argue about whether capital punishment as administered in the United States is discriminatory. Does the evidence support the view that in the United States the death penalty is unfair? Similarly, we can ask whether a human fetus is a human being (in saying what something is, must we take account of its potentiality?), and even if we agree that a fetus is a human being, we can further ask whether it is a person. In *Roe v. Wade* the U.S. Supreme Court ruled that even the "viable" unborn human fetus is not a "person" as that term is used in the Fifth and Fourteenth Amendments. Here the question is this: Is the essential fact about the fetus that it is a person?

An argument of this sort makes a claim—that is, it takes a stand; but notice that it does not also have to argue for an action. Thus, it may argue that the death penalty is administered unfairly—that's a big enough issue—but it need not go on to argue that the death penalty should be abolished. After all, another possibility is that the death penalty should be administered fairly. The writer of the essay may be doing enough if he or she establishes the truth of the claim and leaves to others the possible responses.

2. What is the value of X?   College courses often call for literary judgments. No one can argue if you say you prefer the plays of Tennessee Williams to those of Arthur Miller. But academic papers are not mere declarations of preferences. As soon as you say that Williams is a better playwright than Miller, you have based your preference on implicit standards, and you must support your preference by giving evidence about the relative skill, insight, and accomplishments of both Williams and Miller. Your argument is an evaluation. The question now at issue is the merits of the two authors and the standards appropriate for making such an appraisal.

In short, an essay offering an evaluation normally has two purposes:

- to set forth an assessment
- to convince the reader that the assessment is reasonable

In writing an evaluation, you have to rely on criteria, and these will vary depending on your topic. For instance, in comparing the artistic merit of plays by Williams and by Miller, you may want to talk about the quality of the characterization, the importance of the theme, and so on. But if the topic is "Which playwright is more suitable to be taught in high school?" other criteria may be appropriate, such as these:

- the difficulty of the author's language
- the sexual content of some scenes
- the presence of obscene words

Alternatively, consider a nonliterary issue: On balance, are college fraternities and sororities good or bad? If good, how good? If bad, how bad? What criteria serve best in making our evaluation? Probably some or all of the following:

- testimony of authorities (e.g., persons who can offer first-hand testimony about the good or bad effects)
- inductive evidence (examples of good or bad effects)
- appeals to logic ("it follows, therefore, that . . .")
- appeals to emotion (e.g., an appeal to our sense of fairness)

3. What are the causes (or the consequences) of X? Why did the rate of auto theft increase during a specific period? If the death penalty is abolished, will that cause the rate of murder to increase? Problems such as these may be complex. The phenomena that people usually argue about—such as inflation, war, suicide, crime—have many causes, and it can be a mistake to speak of *the* cause of *X*. A writer in *Time* mentioned that the life expectancy of an average American male is about sixty-seven years, a figure that compares unfavorably with the life expectancy of males in Japan and Israel. The *Time* writer suggested that an important cause of the American male's relatively short life span is "the pressure to perform well in business." Perhaps. But the life expectancy of plumbers is no greater than that of managers and executives. Nutrition authority Jean Mayer, in an article in *Life*, attributed the relatively poor longevity of American males to a diet that is "rich in fat and poor in nutrients." Doubtless other authorities propose other causes, and in all likelihood no one cause entirely accounts for the phenomenon.

Consider a second example of discussions of causality, this one concerning the academic performance of girls in single-sex elementary schools, middle schools, and high schools. It is pretty much agreed (based on statistical evidence) that the graduates of these schools do better, as a group, than girls who graduate from coeducational schools. *Why* do girls in single-sex schools tend, as a group, to do better? What is the *cause*? The administrators of girls' schools usually attribute the success to the fact (we're putting the matter bluntly here) that young women flourish better in an atmosphere free from male intimidation: They allegedly gain confidence and become more expressive when they aren't threatened by the presence of males. This may be the answer, but skeptics have attributed the graduates' success to two other causes:

- Most single-sex schools require parents to pay tuition, and it is a documented fact that the children of well-to-do parents do better, academically, than the children of poor parents.

- Most single-sex schools are private schools, and they select students from a pool of candidates. Admissions officers select those candidates who seem to be academically promising—that is, students who have *already done well academically.*

In short, the girls who graduate from single-sex schools may owe their later academic success not to the schools' single-sex environment but to the fact that even at admission the students were academically stronger (again, we're speaking of a cohort, not of individuals) than the girls who attend coeducational schools.

The lesson? Be cautious in attributing a cause. There may be several causes.

The kinds of support that usually accompany claims of cause include the following:

- factual data, especially statistics
- analogies ("The Roman Empire declined because of X and Y"; "Our society exhibits X and Y; therefore . . .")
- inductive evidence

4. What should (or ought or must) we do about X? Must we always obey the law? Should the law allow eighteen-year-olds to drink alcohol? Should eighteen-year-olds be drafted to do one year of social service? Should pornography be censored? Should steroid use by athletes be banned? Ought there to be Good Samaritan laws, making it a legal duty for a stranger to intervene to save a person from death or great bodily harm, when one might do so with little or no risk to oneself? These questions involve conduct and policy; how we answer them will reveal our values and principles.

An essay answering questions of this sort usually has the following characteristics:

- It begins by explaining what the issue (the problem) is.
- Then it states why the reader should care about the issue.
- Next, it offers the proposed solution.
- Then it considers alternative solutions.
- Finally, it reaffirms the merit of the proposed solution, especially in light of the audience's interests and needs.

You'll recall that throughout this book we have spoken about devices that help a writer to generate ideas. If in drafting an essay concerned with policy you begin by writing down your thoughts on the five bulleted items listed above, you'll almost surely uncover ideas that you didn't know you had.

Support for claims of policy usually include the following:

- statistics
- appeals to common sense and to the reader's moral sense
- testimony of authorities

5. What is the evidence for my claims about X?   In commenting on the four previous topics, we have talked about the kinds of support that writers commonly offer. However, a few additional points are important.

Critical reading, writing, and thinking depend on identifying and evaluating the evidence for and against the claims one makes and encounters in the writings of others. It isn't enough to have an *opinion* or belief one way or the other; you need to be able to support your opinions—the bare fact of your sincere belief in what you say or write is not itself any *evidence* that what you believe is true.

What constitutes good reasons for opinions and adequate evidence for beliefs? The answer depends on the type of belief or opinion, assertion or hypothesis, claim or principle you want to assert. For example, there is good evidence that President John F. Kennedy was assassinated on November 22, 1963, because this is the date for his death reported in standard almanacs. You could further substantiate the date by checking the back issues of the *New York Times*. But a different kind of evidence is needed to support the proposition that the chemical composition of water is H_2O. And you would need still other kinds of evidence to support your beliefs about the likelihood of rain tomorrow, the probability that the Red Sox will win the pennant this year, the twelfth digit in the decimal expansion of pi, the average cumulative grades of graduating seniors over the past three years in your college, the relative merits of *Hamlet* and *Death of a Salesman*, and the moral dimensions of sexual harassment. None of these issues is merely a matter of opinion; yet about some of them, educated and informed people may disagree over the reasons, the evidence, and what they show. Sometimes, equally qualified experts examine the same evidence and draw different conclusions. Your job as a critical thinker is to be alert to the relevant reasons and evidence, as well as the basis of various conclusions, and to make the most of them as you present your views.

Again, an argument may answer two or more of our five basic questions. Someone who argues that pornography should (or should not) be censored will have to do the following:

- Mark out the territory of the discussion by defining pornography (our first question: What is X?).
- Examine the consequences of adopting the preferred policy (our third question).

- Perhaps argue about the value of that policy (our second question). Some people maintain that pornography produces crime, but others maintain that it provides a harmless outlet for impulses that otherwise might vent themselves in criminal behavior.

- Address the possible objection that censorship, however desirable on account of some of its consequences, may be unconstitutional and that even if censorship were constitutional, it would (or might) have undesirable side effects, such as repressing freedom of political opinion.

- Keep in mind our fifth question: What is the evidence for my claims?

Thinking about one or more of these questions may get you going. For instance, thinking about What is *X*? will require you to produce a definition; and as you do this, new ideas might arise. If a question seems relevant, it's a good idea to start writing—even just a fragmentary sentence. You'll probably find that one word leads to another and that ideas begin to appear. Even if these ideas seem weak as you write them, don't be discouraged; you will have put something on paper, and returning to these words, perhaps in five minutes or the next day, you'll probably find that some aren't at all bad and that others will stimulate you to better ones.

It may be useful to record your ideas in a special notebook or in a private digital notebook or document reserved for the purpose. Such a **journal** can be a valuable resource when it comes time to write your paper. Many students find it easier to focus their thoughts on writing if during the gestation period they've been jotting down relevant ideas on something more substantial than slips of paper or loose sheets. The very act of designating a traditional or digital notebook or document file as your journal for a course can be the first step in focusing your attention on the eventual need to write a paper.

Take advantage of the free tools at your disposal. Use the Internet and free Web tools, including RSS feeds, Google (Drive, sites, and others), Yahoo!, blogs, and wikis to organize your initial ideas and to solicit feedback. Talking with others can help, but sometimes there isn't time to chat. By using an RSS feed on a Web site that you think will provide good information on your topic (or a topic you're considering), you can receive notifications if the site has uploaded new material such as news links or op-eds. Posting a blog entry in a public space about your topic can also foster conversations about the topic and help you discover other opinions. Using the Internet to uncover and refine a topic is common practice, especially early in the research process.

If what we have just said doesn't sound convincing, and if you know from experience that you have trouble getting started with writing, don't despair. First aid is at hand in a sure-fire method that we will explain next.

The Thesis or Main Point

Let's assume that you are writing an argumentative essay—perhaps an evaluation of an argument in this book—and you have what seems to be a pretty good draft or at least a collection of notes that are the result of hard thinking. You really do have ideas now, and you want to present them effectively. How will you organize your essay? No one formula works best for every essayist and for every essay, but it is usually advisable to formulate a basic **thesis** (a claim, a central point, a chief position) and to state it early. Every essay that is any good, even a book-length one, has a thesis (a main point), which can be stated briefly—usually, in a sentence. Remember Coolidge's remark on the preacher's sermon on sin: "He was against it." Don't confuse the **topic** (sin) with the thesis (sin is bad). The thesis is the argumentative theme, the author's primary claim or contention, the proposition that the rest of the essay will explain and defend. Of course, the thesis may sound commonplace, but the book or essay or sermon ought to develop it in an interesting and convincing way.

Raising the Stakes of Your Thesis   Imagine walking across campus and coming upon a person ready to perform on a tightrope suspended between two buildings. He is wearing a glittering leotard and is eyeing up his challenge very seriously. Here's the thing, though: His tightrope is only *one foot off the ground*. Would you stop and watch him walk across it? Maybe, maybe not. Most people are likely to take a look and move on. If you did spend a few minutes watching, you wouldn't be very worried about the performer falling. If he lost his balance momentarily, you wouldn't gasp in horror. And if he walked across the tightrope masterfully, you might be somewhat impressed but not enraptured.

Now imagine the rope being a hundred feet off the ground. You and many others would almost certainly stop and witness the feat. The audience would likely be captivated, nervous about the performer potentially falling, "oohing" if he momentarily lost his balance, and cheering if he crossed the rope successfully.

Consider the tightrope as your thesis statement, the performer as writer, and the act of crossing as the argument. What we call "low-stakes" thesis statements are comparable to low tightropes: A low-stakes thesis statement itself may be interesting, but not much about it is vital to any particular audience. Low-stakes thesis statements lack a sense of importance or relevance. They may restate what is already widely known and accepted, or they may make a good point but not discuss any consequences. Some examples:

> Good nutrition and exercise can lead to a healthy life.
>
> Our education system focuses too much on standardized tests.
>
> Children's beauty pageants are exploitative.

Students can write well-organized, clear, and direct papers on these topics, but if the thesis is "low stakes" like these, then the performance would be similar to that of an expert walking across a tightrope *one foot off the ground*. The argument may be well executed, but few in the audience will be inspired by it.

However, if you raise the stakes by "raising the tightrope," you can compel readers to *want* to read and keep reading. There are several ways to raise the tightrope. First, *think about what is socially, culturally, or politically important* about your thesis statement and argument. Some writing instructors tell students to ask themselves "so what?" about the thesis, but this can be a vague directive. Here are some better questions: Why is your thesis important? What is the impact of your thesis on a particular group or demographic? What are the consequences of what you claim? What could happen if your position were *not* recognized? How can your argument benefit readers or compel them to action (by doing something or

Pornchai Kittiwongsakul/Getty Images

Kay Nietfeld/AFP/Getty Images

Tightropes, like these, can be raised to many different levels.

adopting a new belief)? What will readers *gain* by accepting your argument as convincing?

In formulating your thesis, keep in mind these points:

Different thesis statements may speak to different target audiences. An argument about changes in estate tax laws may not thrill all audiences, but for a defined group—accountants, lawyers, or the elderly, for instance—this may be quite controversial and highly relevant.

Not all audiences are equal—or equally interested in your thesis or argument. In this book, we generally select topics of broad importance. However, in a literature course, a film history course, or a political science course, you'll calibrate your thesis statements and arguments to an audience who is invested in those fields. In writing about the steep decline in bee populations, your argument might look quite different if you're speaking to ecologists as opposed to gardeners. (We will discuss audience in greater detail in the following section.)

Be wary of compare-and-contrast arguments. One of the most basic approaches to writing is to compare and contrast, a maneuver that produces a low-tightrope thesis. It normally looks like this: "X *and* Y *are similar in some ways and different in others.*" But if you think about it, *anything* can be compared and contrasted in this way, and doing so doesn't necessarily *tell* anything important. So, if you're writing a compare-and-contrast paper, make sure to include the reasons why it is important to compare and contrast these things. What benefit does the comparison yield? What significance does it have to some audience, some area of knowledge, some field of study?

✓ A CHECKLIST FOR A THESIS STATEMENT

Consider the following questions:

☐ Does the statement make an arguable assertion rather than (1) merely assert an unarguable fact, (2) merely announce a topic, or (3) declare an unarguable opinion or belief?

☐ Is the statement broad enough to cover the entire argument that I will be presenting, and is it narrow enough for me to cover the topic in the space allotted?

Imagining an Audience

Raising the tightrope of your thesis will also require you to imagine the *audience* you're addressing. The questions that you ask yourself in generating thoughts on a topic will primarily relate to the topic, but additional questions that consider the audience are always relevant:

- Who are my readers?
- What do they believe?
- What common ground do we share?
- What do I want my readers to believe?
- What do they need to know?
- Why should they care?

Let's think about these questions. The literal answer to the first probably is "my teacher," but (unless you receive instructions

THINKING CRITICALLY "WALKING THE TIGHTROPE"

Examine the low-stakes thesis statements provided below, and expand each one into a high-stakes thesis by including the importance of asserting it and by proposing a possible response. The first one has been done as an example.

Low-Stakes Thesis	High-Stakes Thesis
Good nutrition and exercise can lead to a healthy life.	One way to help solve the epidemic obesity problem in the United States is to remind consumers of a basic fact accepted by nearly all reputable health experts: Good nutrition and exercise can lead to a healthy life.
Every qualified American should vote.	
Spanking children is good/bad.	
Electric cars will reduce air pollution.	

to the contrary) you should not write specifically for your teacher. Instead, you should write for an audience that is, generally speaking, like your classmates. In short, your imagined audience is literate, intelligent, and moderately well informed, but its members don't know everything that you know, and they don't know your response to the problem being addressed. Your audience needs more information along those lines to make an intelligent decision about the issue.

For example, in writing about how children's toys shape the minds of young boys and girls differently, it may not be enough to simply say, "Toys are part of the gender socialization process." ("Sure they are," the audience might already agree.) However, if you raise the stakes, you have an opportunity to frame the questions that result from this observation: You frame the questions, lay out the issues, identify the problems, and note the complications that arise because of your basic thesis. You could point out that toys have a significant impact on the interests, identities, skills, and capabilities that children develop and carry into adulthood. Because toys are so significant, is it important to ask questions about whether they perpetuate gender-based stereotypes? Do toys help perpetuate social inequalities between the sexes? Most children think toys are "just fun," but they may be teaching kids to conform unthinkingly to the social expectations of their sex, to accept designated sex-based social roles, and to cultivate talents differently based on sex. Is this a good or a bad thing? Do toys facilitate growth, or do they have any limiting effects?

What audiences should be concerned with your topic? Maybe you're addressing the general public who buys toys for children at least some of the time. Maybe you're addressing parents who are raising young children. Maybe you're addressing consumer advocates, encouraging them to pressure toy manufacturers and retailers to produce more gender-neutral offerings. The point is that your essay should contain (and sustain) an assessment of the impact of your high-stakes thesis, and it should set out a clear course of action for a particular audience.

That said, if you know your audience well, you can argue for different courses of action that are most likely to be persuasive. You may not be very convincing if you argue to parents in general that they should never buy princess toys for their girls and avoid all Disney-themed toys. Perhaps you should argue simply that parents should be conscious of the gender messages that toys convey, offer their kids diverse toys, and talk to their children while playing with them about alternatives to the stereotypical messages that the toys convey. However, if you're writing for a magazine called *Radical Parenting* and your essay is titled "Buying Toys the Gender-Neutral Way," your audience and its expectations—therefore, your thesis and argument—may look far different. The bottom line is not just to know your audience but to define it.

The essays in this book are from many different sources with many different audiences. An essay from the *New York Times* addresses educated general readers; an essay from *Ms.* magazine targets readers sympathetic to feminism. An essay from *Commonweal*, a Roman Catholic publication for nonspecialists, is likely to differ in point of view or tone from one in *Time*, even though both articles may advance approximately the same position. The *Commonweal* article may, for example, effectively cite church fathers and distinguished Roman Catholic writers as authorities, whereas the *Time* article would probably cite few or none of these figures because a non-Catholic audience might be unfamiliar with them or, even if familiar, might be unimpressed by their views.

The tone as well as the gist of the argument is in some degree shaped by the audience. For instance, popular journals, such as *National Review* and *Ms.* Magazine, are more likely to use ridicule than are journals chiefly addressed to, say, an academic audience.

The Audience as Collaborator

If you imagine a particular audience and ask yourself what it does and doesn't need to be told, you will find that material comes to mind, just as when a friend asks you what a film you saw was about, who was in it, and how you liked it.

Your readers don't have to be told that Thomas Jefferson was an American statesman in the early years of this country's history, but they do have to be told that Elizabeth Cady Stanton was a late-nineteenth-century American feminist. Why? Because it's your hunch that your classmates never heard of her, or even if they have heard the name, they can't quite identify it. But what if your class has been assigned an essay by Stanton? In that case your imagined readers know Stanton's name and at least a little about her, so you don't have to identify her as an American of the nineteenth century. But you do still have to remind readers about relevant aspects of her essay, and you have to tell them about your responses to those aspects.

After all, even if the instructor has assigned an essay by Stanton, you cannot assume that your classmates know the essay inside out.

You can't say, "Stanton's third reason is also unconvincing," without reminding the reader, by means of a brief summary, of her third reason. Again:

- Think of your classmates—people like you—as your imagined readers.
- Be sure that your essay does not make unreasonable demands.

If you ask yourself,

- "What do my readers need to know?" and
- "What do I want them to believe?"

you will find some answers arising, and you will start writing.

We've said that you should imagine your audience as your classmates. But this isn't the whole truth. In a sense, your argument is addressed not simply to your classmates but to the world interested in ideas. Even if you can reasonably assume that your classmates have read only one work by Stanton, you can't begin your essay by writing, "Stanton's essay is deceptively easy." You have to name the work because it's possible that a reader is familiar with some other work by Stanton. And by precisely identifying your subject, you ease the reader into your essay.

Similarly, you won't open with a statement like this:

> The majority opinion in *Walker v. City of Birmingham* held that . . .

Rather, you'll write something like this:

> In *Walker v. City of Birmingham*, the U.S. Supreme Court ruled in 1966 that city authorities acted lawfully when they jailed Martin Luther King Jr. and other clergymen in 1963 for marching in Birmingham without a permit. Justice Potter Stewart delivered the majority opinion, which held that . . .

By the way, if you suffer from a writing block, the mere act of writing out such readily available facts will help you to get started. You'll find that writing a few words, perhaps merely copying the essay's title or an interesting quotation from the essay, will stimulate other thoughts that you didn't know you had.

Here, again, are the questions about audience. If you write on a computer, consider putting these questions into a file. For each assignment, copy the questions into the file you're working on, and then, as a way of generating ideas, *enter your responses, indented, under each question.*

1. Who are my readers?
2. What do they believe?
3. What common ground do we share?
4. What do I want my readers to believe?
5. What do they need to know?
6. Why should they care?

Thinking about your audience can help you get started; even more important, it can help you generate ideas. Our second and third questions about the audience ("What do they believe?" and "How much common ground do we share?") will usually help you get ideas flowing.

- Presumably, your imagined audience does not share your views, or at least does not fully share them. But why?
- How can these readers hold a position that to you seems unreasonable?

By putting yourself into your readers' shoes—and your essay will almost surely summarize the views that you're going to speak against—and by thinking about what your audience knows or thinks it knows, you will generate ideas. Spend time online reviewing Web sites dedicated to your topic. What do they have to say, and why do the authors hold these views?

Let's assume that you don't believe that people should be allowed to smoke in enclosed public places, but you know that some people hold a different view. Why do they hold it? Try to state their view *in a way that would be satisfactory to them.* Having done so, you may perceive that your conclusions and theirs differ because they're based on different premises—perhaps different ideas about human rights. Examine the opposition's premises carefully, and explain, first to yourself and ultimately to your readers, why you find some of those premises to be unacceptable.

Perhaps some facts are in dispute, such as whether exposure to tobacco is harmful to nonsmokers. The thing to do, then, is to check the facts. If you find that harm to nonsmokers has not been proved but you nevertheless believe that smoking should be prohibited in enclosed public places, of course you can't premise your argument on the wrongfulness of harming the innocent (in this

> **A RULE FOR WRITERS** If you wish to persuade, you have to begin by finding premises that you can share with your audience.

case, the nonsmokers). You'll have to develop arguments that take account of the facts.

Among the relevant facts there surely are some that your audience or your opponent will not dispute. The same is true of the values relevant to the discussion; both sides very likely believe in some of the same values (such as the principle mentioned above, that it is wrong to harm the innocent). These areas of shared agreement are crucial to effective persuasion in argument.

There are two good reasons for identifying and isolating the areas of agreement:

- There is no point in disputing facts or values on which you and your readers already agree.

- It usually helps to establish goodwill between yourself and your opponent when you can point to shared beliefs, assumptions, facts, and values.

In a few moments we will return to the need to share some of the opposition's ideas.

Recall that in composing college papers it's usually best to write for a general audience, an audience rather like your classmates but without the specific knowledge that they all share as students enrolled in one course. If the topic is smoking in public places, the audience presumably consists of smokers and nonsmokers. Thinking about our fifth question on page 209—"What do [readers] need to know?"—may prompt you to give statistics about the harmful effects of smoking. Or if you're arguing on behalf of smokers, it may prompt you to cite studies claiming that no evidence conclusively demonstrates that cigarette smoking is harmful to nonsmokers. If indeed you are writing for a general audience and you are not advancing a highly unfamiliar view, our second question ("What does the audience believe?") is less important here; but if the audience is specialized, such as an antismoking group, a group of restaurant owners who fear that antismoking regulations will interfere with their business, or a group of civil libertarians, an effective essay will have to address their special beliefs.

✓ A CHECKLIST FOR IMAGINING AN AUDIENCE

Have I asked myself the following questions?

☐ Who are my readers? How do I know?

☐ How much about the topic do they already know?

☐ Have I provided necessary background (including definitions of special terms) if the imagined readers probably are not especially familiar with the topic?

☐ Are these imagined readers likely to be neutral? Sympathetic? Hostile? Have I done enough online research to offer something useful to a hostile audience?

☐ If they're neutral, have I offered good reasons to persuade them? If they're sympathetic, have I done more than merely reaffirm their present beliefs? That is, have I perhaps enriched their views or encouraged them to act? If they're hostile, have I taken account of their positions, recognized their strengths but also called attention to their limitations, and offered a position that might persuade these hostile readers to modify their position?

In addressing their beliefs (let's assume that you don't share them—at least, not fully), you must try to establish some common ground. If you advocate requiring restaurants to provide nonsmoking areas, you should recognize the possibility that this arrangement will result in inconvenience for the proprietor. But perhaps (the good news) the restaurant will regain some lost customers or attract some new customers. This thought should prompt you to think of other kinds of evidence—perhaps testimony or statistics.

When you formulate a thesis and ask questions about it—such as who the readers are, what they believe, what they know, and what they need to know—you begin to get ideas about how to organize the material (or, at least, you realize that you'll have to work out some sort of organization). The thesis may be clear and simple, but the reasons (the argument) may take many pages. The thesis is the point; the argument sets forth the evidence that supports the thesis.

The Title

It's a good idea to announce the thesis in your essay's **title**. If you scan the table of contents of this book, you'll notice that a fair number of essayists use the title to let readers know, at least in a general way, what position they will advocate. Here are a few examples of titles that take a position:

Forgive Student Loans? Worst Idea Ever

Millennials Are Selfish and Entitled, and Helicopter Parents Are to Blame

The Draft Would Compel Us to Share the Sacrifice

True, these titles are not especially engaging, but the reader welcomes them because they give some information about the writer's thesis.

Some titles don't announce the thesis, but they do announce the topic:

Are We Slaves to Our Online Selves?

On Racist Speech

Should Governments Tax Unhealthy Foods and Drinks?

Although not clever or witty, the above titles are informative.

Some titles seek to attract attention or to stimulate the imagination:

A First Amendment Junkie

Why I Don't Spare "Spare Change"

Building Baby from the Genes Up

All of these are effective, but a word of caution is appropriate here. In seeking to engage your readers' attention, be careful not to sound like a wise guy. You want to engage the readers, not turn them off.

Finally, be prepared to rethink your title *after* completing the last draft of your paper. A title somewhat different from your working title may be an improvement because the finished paper may emphasize something entirely different from what you expected when you first gave it a title.

The Opening Paragraphs

Opening paragraphs are difficult to write, so don't worry about writing an effective opening when you're drafting. Just get some words down on paper and keep going. But when you revise your first draft, you should begin to think seriously about the effect of your opening.

A good introduction arouses readers' interest and prepares them for the rest of the paper. How? Opening paragraphs usually do at least one (and often all) of the following:

- attract readers' interest (often with a bold thesis statement or an interesting relevant statistic, quotation, or anecdote)
- prepare readers by giving some idea of the topic and often of the thesis
- give readers an idea of how the essay is organized
- define a key term

You may not wish to announce your thesis in the title, but if you don't announce it there, you should set it forth early in the argument, in the introductory paragraph or paragraphs. In an essay titled "Human Rights and Foreign Policy" (1982), U.S. ambassador to the United Nations Jeanne J. Kirkpatrick merely announces her topic (subject) as opposed to her thesis (point), but she hints at the thesis in her first paragraph, by deprecating President Jimmy Carter's policy:

> In this paper I deal with three broad subjects: first, the content and consequences of the Carter administration's human rights policy; second, the prerequisites of a more adequate theory of human rights; and third, some characteristics of a more successful human rights policy.

Alternatively, consider this opening paragraph from Peter Singer's "Animal Liberation":

> We are familiar with Black Liberation, Gay Liberation, and a variety of other movements. With Women's Liberation some thought we had come to the end of the road. Discrimination on the basis of sex, it has been said, is the last form of discrimination that is universally accepted and practiced without pretense, even in those liberal circles which have long prided themselves on their freedom from racial discrimination. But one should always be wary of talking of "the last remaining form of discrimination." If we have learned anything from the liberation movements, we should have learned how difficult it is to be aware of the ways in which we discriminate until they are forcefully pointed out to us. A liberation movement demands an expansion of our moral horizons, so that practices that were previously regarded as natural and inevitable are now seen as intolerable.

Although Singer's introductory paragraph nowhere mentions animal liberation, in conjunction with the essay's title it gives a good idea of what Singer is up to and where he is going. He knows that his audience will be skeptical, so he reminds them that in previous years many people were skeptical of reforms that are now taken for granted. He adopts a strategy used fairly often by writers who advance unconventional theses: Rather than beginning with a bold announcement of a thesis that may turn off some readers because it sounds offensive or absurd, Singer warms up his audience, gaining their interest by cautioning them politely that although they may at first be skeptical of animal liberation, if they stay with his essay they may come to feel that they have expanded their horizons.

Notice, too, that Singer begins by establishing common ground with his readers; he assumes, probably correctly, that they share his view that other forms of discrimination (now seen to be unjust) were once widely practiced and were assumed to be acceptable and natural. In this paragraph, then, Singer is not only showing himself to be fair-minded but is also letting readers know that he will advance a daring idea. His opening wins their attention and goodwill. A writer can hardly hope to do more. (Soon we'll talk a little more about winning the audience.)

Keep in mind the following points when writing introductory paragraphs:

- You may have to give background information that readers should keep in mind if they are to follow your essay.

- You may wish to define some terms that are unfamiliar or that you use in an unusual sense.

- If you're writing for an online publication (where your instructor or audience will encounter your argument on the Web), you might establish a context for your argument by linking to a news video that outlines the topic, or you might offer your thesis and then link to a news story that supports your claim. (Remember that using any videos, images, or links also requires a citation of some kind.) The beauty of publishing the piece in an online environment is that you can link directly to sources and use them more easily than if you were submitting a hard copy.

After announcing the topic, giving the necessary background, and stating your position (and perhaps the opposition's) in as engaging a manner as possible, you will do well to give the reader an idea of *how* you will proceed—that is, what the organization will

> **A RULE FOR WRITERS** In writing or revising introductory paragraphs, keep in mind this question: What do my readers need to know? Remember, your aim throughout is to write *reader-friendly* prose. Keeping the needs and interests of your audience constantly in mind will help you achieve this goal.

be. In other words, use the introduction to set up the organization of your essay. Your instructors may assign four- to six-page mini-research papers or ten- to fifteen-page research papers; if they assign an online venue, ask them about the approximate word count. No matter what the length, every paper needs to have a clear organization. The introduction is where you can accomplish three key things:

- hook your reader
- reveal your thesis and topic
- explain how you will organize your discussion of the topic— what you'll do first, second, third, and so on.

Look at Kirkpatrick's opening paragraph (p. 217) for an illustration. She tells her readers that she will address three subjects, and she names them. Her approach in the paragraph is concise, obvious, and effective.

Similarly, you may want to announce fairly early that there are, say, four common objections to your thesis and that you will take them up one by one, beginning with the weakest (or most widely held) and moving to the strongest (or least familiar), after which you will advance your own view in greater detail. Not every argument begins with refuting the other side, though many arguments do. The point to remember is that you usually ought to tell readers where you will be taking them and by what route. In effect, you give them an outline.

Organizing and Revising the Body of the Essay

We begin with a wise remark by a newspaper columnist, Robert Cromier: "The beautiful part of writing is that you don't have to get it right the first time—unlike, say, a brain surgeon."

In drafting an essay, you will of course begin with an organization that seems appropriate, but you may find, in rereading the draft, that some other organization is better. Here, for a start, is an organization that is common in argumentative essays:

1. Statement of the problem or issue
2. Statement of the structure of the essay (its organization)
3. Statement of alternative (but less adequate) solutions
4. Arguments in support of the proposed solution
5. Arguments answering possible objections
6. A summary, resolution, or conclusion

Let's look at each of these six steps.

1. Statement of the problem or issue   Whether the problem is stated briefly or at length depends on the nature of the problem and the writer's audience. If you haven't already defined unfamiliar terms or terms you use in a special way, now is the time to do so. In any case, it is advisable here to state the problem objectively (thereby gaining the reader's trust) and to indicate why the reader should care about the issue.

2. Statement of the structure of the essay   After stating the problem at the appropriate length, the writer often briefly indicates the structure of the rest of the essay. The structure used most frequently is suggested below, in points 3 and 4.

3. Statement of alternative (but less adequate) solutions   In addition to stating the alternatives fairly (letting readers know that you've done your homework), the writer conveys a willingness to recognize not only the integrity of opposing proposals but also the (partial) merit of at least some of the alternative solutions.

Our point in the previous sentence is important and worth amplifying. Because it is important to convey your goodwill—your sense of fairness—to the reader, it's advisable to show that you're familiar with the opposition and that you recognize the integrity of those who hold that view. You accomplish this by granting its merits as far as you can. (For more about this approach, see the essay by Carl R. Rogers on p. 394.)

The next stage, which constitutes most of the body of the essay, usually is this:

4. Arguments in support of the proposed solution   The evidence offered will depend on the nature of the problem. Relevant statistics, authorities, examples, or analogies may come to mind or be available. This is usually the longest part of the essay.

5. *Arguments answering possible objections*   These arguments may suggest the following:

  a. The proposal won't work (perhaps it is alleged to be too expensive, to make unrealistic demands on human nature, or to fail to reach the heart of the problem).

  b. The proposed solution will create problems greater than the problem under discussion. (A good example of a proposal that produced dreadful unexpected results is the law mandating a prison term for anyone over age eighteen in possession of an illegal drug. Heroin dealers then began to use children as runners, and cocaine importers followed the practice.)

6. *A summary, resolution, or conclusion*   Here the writer may seek to accommodate the opposition's views as far as possible but clearly suggest that the writer's own position makes good sense. A conclusion—the word comes from the Latin *claudere*, "to shut"—ought to provide a sense of closure, but it can be much more than a restatement of the writer's thesis. It can, for instance, make a quiet emotional appeal by suggesting that the issue is important and that the ball is now in the reader's court.

Of course, not every essay will follow this six-step pattern. But let's assume that in the introductory paragraphs you have sketched the topic (and have shown, or implied, that the reader doubtless is interested in it) and have fairly and courteously set forth the opposition's view, recognizing its merits ("I grant that," "admittedly," "it is true that") and indicating the degree to which you can share part of that view. You now want to set forth arguments explaining why you differ on some essentials.

In presenting your own position, you can begin with either your strongest or your weakest reasons. Each method of organization has advantages and disadvantages.

- If you begin with your strongest reason, the essay may seem to peter out.

- If you begin with your weakest reason, you build to a climax; but readers may not still be with you because they may have felt at the start that the essay was frivolous.

The solution to the latter possibility is to ensure that even your weakest argument demonstrates strength. You can, moreover, assure your readers that stronger points will soon follow and you offer this point first in order to show that you are aware of it and

Bill Watterson/Universal Uclick

that, slight though it is, it deserves some attention. The body of the essay, then, is devoted to arguing a position, which means offering not only supporting reasons but also refutations of possible objections to these reasons.

Doubtless you'll sometimes be uncertain, while drafting an essay, whether to present a given point before or after another point. When you write, and certainly when you revise, try to put yourself into the reader's shoes: Which point do you think the reader needs to know first? Which point *leads to* which further point? Your argument should not be a mere list of points; rather, it should clearly integrate one point with another in order to develop an idea. However, in all likelihood you won't have a strong sense of the best organization until you have written a draft and have reread it.

Checking Paragraphs   When you revise a draft, watch out for short paragraphs. Although a paragraph of only two or three sentences (like some in this chapter) may occasionally be helpful as a transition between complicated points, most short paragraphs are undeveloped paragraphs. Newspaper editors favor very short paragraphs because they can be read rapidly when printed in the narrow columns typical of newspapers. Many of the essays reprinted in this book originally were published in newspapers and, thus, consist of very short paragraphs, but they should *not* be regarded as models for your own writing.

A second note about paragraphs: Writers for online venues often "chunk" (i.e., they provide extra space for paragraph breaks)

> **A RULE FOR WRITERS** When you revise, make sure that your organization is clear to your readers.

rather than write a continuous flow. These writers chunk their text for several reasons, but chiefly because breaking up paragraphs and adding space between them makes some types of writing "scannable": The screen is easier to navigate because it isn't packed with text in a 12-point font. The breaks in paragraphs also allow the reader to see a complete paragraph without having to scroll.

Checking Transitions   Make sure, in revising, that the reader can move easily from the beginning of a paragraph to the end and from one paragraph to the next. Transitions help to signal the connections between units of the argument. For example ("For example" is a transition, indicating that an illustration will follow), they may illustrate, establish a sequence, connect logically, amplify, compare, contrast, summarize, or concede (see Thinking Critically: Using Transitions in Argument). Transitions serve as guideposts that enable the reader to move easily through your essay.

When writers revise an early draft, they chiefly do these tasks:

- They **unify** the essay by eliminating irrelevancies.
- They **organize** the essay by keeping in mind the imagined audience.
- They **clarify** the essay by fleshing out thin paragraphs, by ensuring that the transitions are adequate, and by making certain that generalizations are adequately supported by concrete details and examples.

We are not talking here about polish or elegance; we are talking about fundamental matters. Be especially careful not to abuse the logical connectives (*thus, as a result,* and so on). If you write several sentences followed by *therefore* or a similar word or phrase, be sure that what you write after the *therefore* really *does follow* from what has gone before. Logical connectives are not mere transitional devices that link disconnected bits of prose. They are supposed to mark a real movement of thought, which is the essence of an argument.

The Ending

What about concluding paragraphs, in which you summarize the main points and reaffirm your position?

If you can look back over your essay and add something that both enriches it and wraps it up, fine; but don't feel compelled to say, "Thus, in conclusion, I have argued *X, Y,* and *Z,* and I have refuted Jones." After all, *conclusion* can have two meanings: (1) ending, or finish, as the ending of a joke or a novel; or (2) judgment or decision reached after deliberation. Your essay should finish effectively (the first sense), but it need not announce a judgment (the second).

If the essay is fairly short, so that a reader can keep its general gist in mind, you may not need to restate your view. Just make

THINKING CRITICALLY USING TRANSITIONS IN ARGUMENT

Fill in examples of the types of transitions listed below, using topics of your choice. The first one has been done as an example.

Type of Transition	Type of Language Used	Example of Transition
Illustrate	*for example, for instance, consider this case*	"Many television crime dramas contain scenes of graphic violence. For example, in the episode of *Law and Order* titled . . ."
Establish a sequence	*a more important objection, a stronger example, the best reason*	
Connect logically	*thus, as a result, therefore, so, it follows*	
Amplify	*further, in addition to, moreover*	
Compare	*similarly, in a like manner, just as, analogously*	
Contrast	*on the one hand . . . on the other hand, in contrast, however, but*	
Summarize	*in short, briefly*	
Concede	*admittedly, granted, to be sure*	

> **A RULE FOR WRITERS** Emulate John Kenneth Galbraith, a distin-
> guished writer on economics. Galbraith said that in his fifth drafts
> he regularly introduced the note of spontaneity for which his writing
> was famous.

sure that you have covered the ground and that your last sentence
is a good one. Notice that the student essay printed later in this
chapter (p. 241) doesn't end with a formal conclusion, although it
ends conclusively, with a note of finality.

By "a note of finality" we do *not* mean a triumphant crowing.
It's far better to end with the suggestion that you hope you have by
now indicated why those who hold a different view may want to
modify it and accept yours.

If you study the essays in this book or the editorials and op-ed
pieces in a newspaper, you will notice that writers often provide a
sense of closure by using one of the following devices:

- a return to something stated in the introduction
- a glance at the wider implications of the issue (e.g., if smoking is restricted, other liberties are threatened)
- a hint toward unasked or answered questions that the audience might consider in light of the writer's argument
- a suggestion that the reader can take some specific action or
  do some further research (i.e., the ball is now in the reader's
  court)
- an anecdote that illustrates the thesis in an engaging way
- a brief summary (*Note:* This sort of ending may seem unnecessary and tedious if the paper is short and the summary
  merely repeats what the writer has already said.)

Two Uses of an Outline

The Outline as a Preliminary Guide   Some writers sketch an **outline** as soon as they think they know what they want to say, even
before writing a first draft. This procedure can be helpful in planning a tentative organization, but remember that in revising a draft
you'll likely generate some new ideas and have to modify the outline accordingly. A preliminary outline is chiefly useful as a means
of getting going, not as a guide to the final essay.

The Outline as a Way of Checking a Draft   Whether or not you use a preliminary outline, we strongly suggest that after writing what you hope is your last draft, you make an outline of it; there is no better way of finding out whether the essay is well organized.

Go through the draft, and write down the chief points in the order in which you make them. That is, prepare a table of contents — perhaps a phrase for each paragraph. Next, examine your notes to see what kind of sequence they reveal in your paper:

- Is the sequence reasonable? Can it be improved?
- Are any passages irrelevant?
- Does something important seem to be missing?

If no coherent structure or reasonable sequence clearly appears in the outline, then the full prose version of your argument probably doesn't have any either. Therefore, produce another draft by moving things around, adding or subtracting paragraphs — cutting and pasting them into a new sequence, with transitions as needed — and then make another outline to see if the sequence now is satisfactory.

You're probably familiar with the structure known as a **formal outline**. Major points are indicated by I, II, III; points within major points are indicated by A, B, C; divisions within A, B, C are indicated by 1, 2, 3; and so on. Thus:

I. Arguments for opening all Olympic sports to professionals
   A. Fairness
      1. Some Olympic sports are already open to professionals.
      2. Some athletes who really are not professionals are classified as professionals.
   B. Quality (achievements would be higher)

You may want to outline your draft according to this principle, or you might simply write a phrase for each paragraph and indent the subdivisions. But keep these points in mind:

- It is not enough for the parts to be ordered reasonably.
- The order must be made clear to the reader, usually by means of transitions such as *for instance, on the one hand . . . on the other hand, we can now turn to an opposing view,* and so on.

Here is another way of thinking about an outline. For each paragraph, write:

- what the paragraph *says*, and
- what the paragraph *does*.

An opening paragraph might be outlined thus:

- What the paragraph *says* is that the words "under God" in the Pledge of Allegiance should be omitted.
- What the paragraph *does* is, first, inform the reader of the thesis, and second, *provide some necessary background*—for instance, that the words were not in the original wording of the Pledge.

A dual outline of this sort will help you to see whether you have a final draft or a draft that needs refinement.

A Last Word about Outlines

Outlines may seem rigid to many writers, especially to those who compose online, where we're accustomed to cutting, copying, moving, and deleting as we draft. However, as mentioned earlier, an outline—whether you write it before drafting a single word or use it to evaluate the organization of something you've already written—is meant to be a guide rather than a straitjacket. Many writers who compose electronically find that the ability to keep banging out words—typing is so much easier than pushing a pen or pencil—and to cut and paste without actually reaching for scissors makes it easy to produce an essay that readers may find difficult to follow. (There is much truth in the proverb "Easy writing makes hard reading.") If you compose electronically, and especially if you continually add, delete, and move text around without a clear organizational goal in mind, be sure to read and outline your draft, and *then* examine the outline to see if indeed there is a reasonable organization.

Outlines are especially helpful for long essays, but even short ones benefit from a bit of advanced planning, a list of a few topics (drawn from notes already taken) that keep the writer moving in an orderly way. A longer work such as an honors or a master's thesis typically requires careful planning. An outline will be a great help in ensuring that you produce something that a reader can easily follow—but, of course, you may find as you write that the outline needs to be altered.

When readers reach the end of a piece of writing, they should feel that the writer has brought them to a decisive point and is not simply stopping abruptly and unexpectedly.

✓ A CHECKLIST FOR ORGANIZING AN ARGUMENT

☐ Does the introduction let the readers know where the author is taking them?

☐ Does the introduction state the problem or issue?

  ☐ Does it state the claim (the thesis)?

  ☐ Does it suggest the organization of the essay, thereby helping the reader to follow the argument?

☐ Do subsequent paragraphs support the claim?

  ☐ Do they offer evidence?

  ☐ Do they face objections to the claim and offer reasonable responses?

  ☐ Do they indicate why the author's claim is preferable?

  ☐ Do transitions (signposts such as *Furthermore, In contrast,* and *Consider as an example*) guide the reader through the argument?

☐ Does the essay end effectively, with a paragraph (at most, two paragraphs) bringing a note of closure — for instance, by indicating that the proposed solution is relatively simple? By admitting that although the proposed solution will be difficult to implement, it is certainly feasible? By reminding the reader of the urgency of the problem?

Tone and the Writer's Persona

Although this book is chiefly about argument in the sense of rational discourse—the presentation of reasons in support of a thesis or conclusion—the appeal to reason is only one form of persuasion. Another form is the appeal to emotion—to pity, for example. Aristotle saw, in addition to appeals to reason and to emotion, a third form of persuasion—the appeal to the speaker's character. He called it the **ethical appeal** (the Greek word for this kind of appeal is **ethos,** meaning "character"). The idea is that effective speakers convey the suggestion that they are

- informed,
- intelligent,
- fair minded (persons of goodwill), and
- honest.

Because they are perceived as trustworthy, their words inspire confidence in their listeners. It is a fact that when reading an argument we're often aware of the *person* or *voice* behind the words, and our assent to the argument depends partly on the extent to which we can share the speaker's assumptions and see the matter from his or her point of view—in short, the extent to which we can *identify* with the speaker.

How can a writer inspire the confidence that lets readers identify with him or her? First, the writer should possess the virtues Aristotle specified: intelligence or good sense, honesty, and benevolence or goodwill. As a Roman proverb puts it, "No one gives what he does not have." Still, possession of these qualities is not a guarantee that you will convey them in your writing. Like all other writers, you'll have to revise your drafts so that these qualities become apparent; stated more moderately, you'll have to revise so that nothing in the essay causes a reader to doubt your intelligence, honesty, and goodwill. A blunder in logic, a misleading quotation, a snide remark, even an error in spelling—all such slips can cause readers to withdraw their sympathy from the writer.

Of course, all good argumentative essays do not sound exactly alike; they do not all reveal the same speaker. Each writer develops his or her own voice, or (as literary critics and instructors call it) **persona**. In fact, one writer may have several voices or personae, depending on the topic and the audience. The president of the United States delivering an address on the State of the Union has one persona; when chatting with a reporter at his summer home, he has another. This change is not a matter of hypocrisy. Different circumstances call for different language. As a French writer put it, there is a time to speak of "Paris" and a time to speak of "the capital of the nation." When Abraham Lincoln spoke at Gettysburg, he didn't say "Eighty-seven years ago"; instead, he intoned "Four score and seven years ago." We might say that just as some occasions required him to be the folksy Honest Abe, the occasion of the dedication of hallowed ground at Gettysburg, where so many Civil War soldiers lost their lives, required him to be formal and solemn—thus, as president of the United States he appropriately

> **A RULE FOR WRITERS** Present yourself so that readers see you as knowledgeable, honest, open-minded, and interested in helping them to think about the significance of an issue.

used biblical language. Lincoln's election campaigns called for one persona, and the dedication of a military cemetery (an entirely different rhetorical situation) called for a different persona. For examples on how to vary tone, see Thinking Critically: Varying Tone.

When we talk about a writer's persona, we mean the way in which the writer presents his or her attitudes

- toward *the self,*
- toward *the audience,* and
- toward *the subject.*

Thus, if a writer says:

> I have thought long and hard about this subject, and I can say with assurance that . . .

we may feel that he is a self-satisfied egotist who probably is mouthing other people's opinions. Certainly he's mouthing clichés: "long and hard," "say with assurance."

Let's look at a subtler example of an utterance that reveals certain attitudes:

> President Nixon was hounded out of office by journalists.

The statement above conveys a respectful attitude toward Nixon ("President Nixon") and a hostile attitude toward the press (they are beasts, curs who "hounded" our elected leader). If the writer's attitudes were reversed, she might have said something like this:

> The press turned the searchlight on Tricky Dick's criminal shenanigans.

"Tricky Dick" and "criminal" are obvious enough, but notice that "shenanigans" also implies the writer's contempt for Nixon, and "turned the searchlight" suggests that the press is a source of illumination, a source of truth. The original version and the opposite version both say that the press was responsible for Nixon's resignation, but the original version ("President Nixon was hounded") conveys indignation toward journalists, whereas the revision conveys contempt for Nixon.

These two versions suggest two speakers who differ not only in their view of Nixon but also in their manner, including the seriousness with which they take themselves. Although the passage is very short, it seems to us that the first speaker conveys righteous indignation ("hounded"), whereas the second conveys amused contempt

THINKING CRITICALLY VARYING TONE

See the example of Abraham Lincoln's tone below. In the spaces provided, rewrite Lincoln's statement in wording that reflects qualities of other tones as indicated in the middle column.

Tone	Qualities of the Tone	Example
Abraham Lincoln	Invokes biblical rhetoric in an appeal to national unity	*Four score and seven years ago our fathers brought forth on this continent a new nation, conceived in liberty, and dedicated to the proposition that all men are created equal.*
More academic tone	Incorporates specific factual information and connects to overarching ideas	
More informal tone	Is accurate but simplified, forgoing much detail	
Too informal for most academic writing	Mischaracterizes or oversimplifies the thought process	

("shenanigans"). To our ears the tone, as well as the point, differs in the two versions.

We are talking now about **loaded words**, which convey the writer's attitude and, through their connotations, seek to win the reader to the writer's side. Compare the words in the left-hand column with those in the right:

freedom fighter	terrorist
pro-choice	pro-abortion
pro-life	antichoice
economic refugee	illegal alien
terrorist surveillance	domestic spying

The words in the left-hand column sound like good things; speakers who use them seek to establish themselves as virtuous people supporting worthy causes. The **connotations** (associations, overtones) of these pairs of words differ, even though the **denotations** (explicit meanings, dictionary definitions) are the same—just as the connotations of *mother* and *female parent* differ, although the denotations are the same. Similarly, although Lincoln's "four score and seven" and "eighty-seven" both denote "thirteen less than one hundred," they differ in connotation.

Tone is not only a matter of connotation (*hounded out of office* versus, let's say, *compelled to resign*, or *pro-choice* versus *pro-abortion*); it is also a matter of such things as the selection and type of examples. A writer who offers many examples, especially ones drawn from ordinary life, conveys a persona different from that of a writer who offers no examples or only an occasional invented instance. The first writer seems friendlier, more honest, more down-to-earth.

Last Words on Tone   On the whole, when writing an argument, it's advisable to be courteous and respectful of your topic, your audience, and people who hold views opposite to yours. It is rarely good for one's own intellectual development to regard as villains or fools persons who hold views different from one's own, especially if some of them are in the audience. Keep in mind the story of two strangers on a train who, striking up a conversation, found that both were clergymen, though of different faiths. Then one said to the other, "Well, why shouldn't we be friends? After all, we both serve God, you in your way and I in His."

Complacency is all right when telling a joke, but not when offering an argument:

- Recognize opposing views.
- Assume they are held in good faith.
- State them fairly. If you don't, you do a disservice not only to the opposition but also to your own position because the perceptive reader won't take you seriously.
- Be temperate in arguing your own position: "If I understand their view correctly . . ."; "It seems reasonable to conclude that . . ."; "Perhaps, then, we can agree that. . . ."
- Write calmly. If you become overly emotional, readers may interpret you as biased or unreasonable, and they may lose their confidence in you.

One way to practice thinking about tone and persona is to think about your professional e-mails. As a student, you probably send many e-mails to classmates and to your instructors or other offices on campus (e.g., the financial aid office, your academic advisor). As teachers, we are often surprised at how flippant and inattentive students are when e-mailing. How do you present yourself in your professional e-mails?

We, One, or I?

The use of *we* in the last sentence brings us to another point: Is it correct to use the first-person pronouns *I* and *we*? In this book, because three of us are writing, we often use *we* to mean the three authors. And we sometimes use *we* to mean the authors and the readers. This shifting use of one word can be troublesome, but we hope (clearly, the *we* here refers only to the authors) that we have avoided ambiguity. But can, or should, or must an individual use *we* instead of *I*? The short answer is no.

If you're simply speaking for yourself, use *I*. Attempts to avoid the first-person singular by saying things like "This writer thinks . . ." and "It is thought that . . ." and "One thinks that . . ." are far more irritating (and wordy) than the use of *I*. The so-called editorial *we* sounds as odd in a student's argument as the royal *we* does. (Mark Twain said that the only ones who can appropriately say *we* are kings, editors, and people with a tapeworm.) It's advisable to use *we* only when you are sure you're writing or speaking directly to an audience who holds membership in the same group, as in "We *students of* X *university* should . . ." or "We *the members of Theta Chi fraternity* need to. . . ." If the *we* you refer to has a referent, simply refer to what it means: Say "Americans are" rather than "We are," or "College students should" rather than "We should," or "Republicans need to" rather than "We need to."

Many students assume that using *one* will solve the problem of pronouns. But because one *one* leads to another, the sentence may end up sounding, as James Thurber once said, "like a trombone solo." It's best to admit that you are the author, and to use *I*. However, there is no need to preface every sentence with "I think." The reader knows that the essay is yours and that the opinions are yours; so use *I* when you must, but not needlessly. Do not write, "I think *X* movie is terrible"; simply say, "*X* movie is terrible." And do not add extra words that say more obvious things, like "*It is my idea that* the company needs a new mission statement." Just write, "*The company needs a new mission statement.*"

THINKING CRITICALLY ELIMINATING *WE, ONE,* AND *I*

Rewrite the following sentences to eliminate unnecessary uses of *I, we, one,* and other gratuitous statements of opinion.

Original Sentence	Rewritten Sentence
I think fracking is the best way to achieve energy independence and to create jobs.	Fracking is the best way to achieve energy independence and to create jobs.
In our country, we believe in equality and freedom.	
One should consider one's manners at formal dinner parties.	
In my opinion, the government should not regulate the sizes of sodas we can order.	
It is clearly the case that the new policy treats employees unfairly.	

Often you'll see *I* in journalistic writing and autobiographical writing—and in some argumentative writing, too—but in most argumentative writing it's best to state the facts and (when drawing reasonable conclusions from them) to keep yourself in the background. Why? The more you use *I* in an essay, the more your readers will attach *you* directly to the argument and may regard your position as personal rather than as relevant to themselves.

Avoiding Sexist Language

Courtesy as well as common sense requires that you respect your readers' feelings. Many people today find offensive the implicit sexism in the use of male pronouns to denote not only men but also women ("As the reader follows the argument, he will find . . ."). And sometimes the use of the male pronoun to denote all people is ridiculous ("An individual, no matter what his sex, . . .").

In most contexts there is no need to use gender-specific nouns or pronouns. One way to avoid using *he* when you mean any person is to use *he or she* (or *she or he*), but the result is sometimes cumbersome—although superior to the overly conspicuous *he/she* and *s/he*.

✓ A CHECKLIST FOR ATTENDING TO THE NEEDS
OF THE AUDIENCE

☐ Do I have a sense of what the audience probably knows about the issue?

☐ Do I have a sense of what the audience probably thinks about the issue?

☐ Have I stated the thesis clearly and sufficiently early in the essay?

☐ How much common ground do I probably share with the audience?

☐ Have I tried to establish common ground and then moved on to advance my position?

☐ Have I supported my arguments with sufficient details?

☐ Have I used appropriate language (e.g., defined terms that are likely to be unfamiliar)?

☐ Have I indicated why readers should care about the issue and should accept my views, or at least give them serious consideration?

☐ Is the organization clear?

☐ Have I used transitions where they are needed?

☐ If visual material (charts, graphs, pictures) will enhance my arguments, have I used them?

☐ Have I presented myself as a person who is fair, informed, and worth listening to? In short, have I conveyed a strong *ethos*?

Here are two simple ways to solve the problem:

- *Use the plural* ("As readers follow the argument, they will find . . .").

- *Recast the sentence* so that no pronoun is required ("Readers following the argument will find . . .").

Because *man* and *mankind* strike many readers as sexist when used in such expressions as "Man is a rational animal" and "Mankind has not yet solved this problem," consider using such words as *human being, person, people, humanity,* and *we.* (*Examples:* "Human beings are rational animals"; "We have not yet solved this problem.")

PEER REVIEW

Your instructor may suggest—or require—that you submit an early draft of your essay to a fellow student or small group of students for comment. Such a procedure benefits both author and readers: You get the responses of a reader, and the student-reader gets experience in thinking about the problems of developing an

---

 A CHECKLIST FOR PEER REVIEW OF A DRAFT OF AN ARGUMENT

Read through the draft quickly. Then read it again, with the following questions in mind. Remember: You are reading a draft, a work in progress. You're expected to offer suggestions, and you're expected to offer them courteously.

In a sentence, indicate the degree to which the draft shows promise of fulfilling the assignment.

☐ Is the writer's tone appropriate? Who is the audience?

☐ Looking at the essay as a whole, what thesis (main idea) is advanced?

☐ Are the needs of the audience kept in mind? For instance, do some words need to be defined? Is the evidence (e.g., the examples and the testimony of authorities) clear and effective?

☐ Can I accept the assumptions? If not, why not?

☐ Is any obvious evidence (or counterevidence) overlooked?

☐ Is the writer proposing a solution? If so,

    ☐ Are other equally attractive solutions adequately examined?

    ☐ Has the writer overlooked some unattractive effects of the proposed solution?

☐ Looking at each paragraph separately,

    ☐ What is the basic point?

    ☐ How does each paragraph relate to the essay's main idea or to the previous paragraph?

☐ Should some paragraphs be deleted? Be divided into two or more paragraphs? Be combined? Be moved elsewhere? (If you outline the essay by writing down the gist of each paragraph, you'll get help in answering these questions.)

☐ Is each sentence clearly related to the sentence that precedes and to the sentence that follows? If not, in a sentence or two indicate examples of good and bad transitions.

☐ Is each paragraph adequately developed? Are there sufficient details, perhaps brief supporting quotations from the text?

☐ Are the introductory and concluding paragraphs effective?

☐ What are the paper's chief strengths?

☐ Make at least two specific suggestions that you think will assist the author to improve the paper.

argument, especially such matters as the degree of detail that a writer needs to offer to a reader and the importance of keeping the organization evident to a reader.

Oral peer reviews allow for the give and take of discussion, but probably most students and most instructors find written peer reviews more helpful because reviewers think more carefully about their responses to the draft, and they help essayists to get beyond a knee-jerk response to criticism. Online reviews on a class Web site, through e-mail, or via another file-sharing service are especially helpful precisely because they are not face to face; the peer reviewer gets practice *writing*, and the essayist is not directly challenged. Sharing documents works well for peer review.

A STUDENT'S ESSAY, FROM ROUGH NOTES TO FINAL VERSION

While we were revising this textbook, we asked the students in one of our classes to write a short essay (500–750 words) on some ethical problem that concerned them. Because this assignment was the first writing assignment in the course, we explained that a good way to generate ideas is to ask oneself some questions, write down responses, question those responses, and write freely for ten minutes or so, not worrying about contradictions. We invited our students to hand in their initial notes along with the finished essay, so that we could get a sense of how they proceeded as writers. Not all of them chose to hand in their notes, but we were greatly encouraged by those who did. What encouraged us was the confirmation of an old belief—we call it a fact—that students will hand in a thoughtful essay if before preparing a final version they ask themselves *why* they think this or that, write down their responses, and are not afraid to change their minds as they proceed.

Here are the first notes of a student, Emily Andrews, who elected to write about whether to give money to street beggars. She simply put down ideas, one after the other.

Help the poor? Why do I (sometimes) do it?

I feel guilty, and think I should help them: poor, cold, hungry (but also some of them are thirsty for liquor, and will spend the money on liquor, not on food).

I also feel annoyed by them—most of them.

Where does the expression "the deserving poor" come from?

And "poor but honest"? Actually, that sounds odd. Wouldn't "rich but honest" make more sense?

Why don't they work? Fellow with red beard, always by bus stop in front of florist's shop, always wants a handout. He is a regular, there all day every day, so I guess he is in a way "reliable," so why doesn't he put the same time in on a job?

Or why don't they get help? Don't they know they need it? They *must* know they need it.

Maybe that guy with the beard is just a con artist. Maybe he makes more money by panhandling than he would by working, and it's a lot easier!

Kinds of poor—how to classify??
    drunks, druggies, etc.
    mentally ill (maybe drunks belong here, too)
    decent people who have had terrible luck

Why private charity?

Doesn't it make sense to say we (fortunate individuals) should give something—an occasional handout—to people who have had terrible luck? (I suppose some people might say there's no need for any of us to give anything—the government takes care of the truly needy—but I *do* believe in giving charity. A month ago a friend of the family passed away, and the woman's children suggested that people might want to make a donation in her name to a shelter for battered women. I know my parents made a donation.)

BUT how can I tell who is who, which are which? Which of these people asking for "spare change" really need (deserve???) help, and which are phonies? Impossible to tell.

Possibilities:

> Give to no one.
>
> Give to no one but make an annual donation, maybe to United Way.
>
> Give a dollar to each person who asks. This would probably not cost me even a dollar a day.
>
> Occasionally do without something—maybe a CD or a meal in a restaurant—and give the money I save to people who seem worthy.

WORTHY? What am I saying? How can I, or anyone, tell? The neat-looking guy who says he just lost his job may be a phony, and the dirty bum—probably a drunk—may desperately need food. (OK, so what if he spends the money on liquor instead of food? At least he'll get a little pleasure in life. No! It's not all right if he spends it on drink.)

Other possibilities:

> Do some volunteer work?
>
> To tell the truth, I don't want to put in the time. I don't feel *that* guilty.

So what's the problem?

Is it, How I can help the very poor (handouts, or through an organization)? or

How I can feel less guilty about being lucky enough to be able to go to college and to have a supportive family?

I can't quite bring myself to believe I should help every beggar who approaches, but I also can't bring myself to believe that I should do nothing, on the grounds that:

a. it's probably their fault
b. if they are deserving, they can get gov't help. No, I just can't believe that. Maybe some are too proud to look for government help, or don't know that they're entitled to it.

What to do?

On balance, it seems best to:

a. give to United Way
b. maybe also give to an occasional individual, if I happen to be moved, without worrying about whether he or she is "deserving" (since it's probably impossible to know)

A day after making these notes Emily reviewed them, added a few points, and then made a very brief selection from them to serve as an outline for her first draft:

Opening para.: "poor but honest"? Deserve "spare change"?

Charity: private or through organizations?

　　　　pros and cons

　　　　guy at bus

　　　　it wouldn't cost me much, but . . . better to give through organizations

Concluding para.: still feel guilty?

　　　　maybe mention guy at bus again?

After writing and revising a draft, Emily submitted her essay to a fellow student for peer review. She then revised her work in light of the peer's suggestions and her own further thinking.

On the next page we give the final essay. If after reading the final version you reread Emily's early notes, you'll notice that some of her notes never made it into the final version. But without the notes, the essay probably wouldn't have been as interesting as it is. When Emily made the notes, she wasn't so much putting down her ideas as *finding* ideas through the process of writing.

Andrews 1

Emily Andrews

Professor Barnet

English 102

January 15, 2016

Why I Don't Spare "Spare Change"

"Poor but honest." "The deserving poor." I don't know the origin of these quotations, but they always come to mind when I think of "the poor." But I also think of people who, perhaps through alcohol or drugs, have ruined not only their own lives but also the lives of others in order to indulge in their own pleasure. Perhaps alcoholism and drug addiction really are "diseases," as many people say, but my own feeling—based, of course, not on any serious study—is that most alcoholics and drug addicts can be classified with the "undeserving poor." And that is largely why I don't distribute spare change to panhandlers.

But surely among the street people there are also some who can rightly be called "deserving." Deserving of what? My spare change? Or simply the government's assistance? It happens that I have been brought up to believe that it is appropriate to make contributions to charity—let's say a shelter for battered women—but if I give some change to a panhandler, am I making a contribution to charity and thereby helping someone, or, on the contrary, am I perhaps simply encouraging someone not to get help? Or maybe even worse, am I supporting a con artist?

If one believes in the value of private charity, one can give either to needy individuals or to charitable organizations.

Andrews 2

In giving to a panhandler one may indeed be helping a person who badly needs help, but one cannot be certain that one is giving to a needy individual. In giving to an organization such as the United Way, in contrast, one can feel that one's money is likely to be used wisely. True, confronted by a beggar one may feel that *this* particular unfortunate individual needs help at *this* moment — a cup of coffee or a sandwich — and the need will not be met unless I put my hand in my pocket right now. But I have come to think that the beggars whom I encounter can get along without my spare change, and indeed perhaps they are actually better off for not having money to buy liquor or drugs.

It happens that in my neighborhood I encounter few panhandlers. There is one fellow who is always by the bus stop where I catch the bus to the college, and I never give him anything precisely because he is always there. He is such a regular that, I think, he ought to be able to hold a regular job. Putting him aside, I probably don't encounter more than three or four beggars in a week. (I'm not counting street musicians. These people seem quite able to work for a living. If they see their "work" as playing or singing, let persons who enjoy their performances pay them. I do not consider myself among their audience.) The truth of the matter is that since I meet so few beggars, I could give each one a dollar and hardly feel the loss. At most, I might go without seeing a movie some week. But I know nothing about these people, and it's my impression — admittedly based on almost no evidence — that they simply prefer begging to working. I am not generalizing about street people, and certainly I am not talking about street people in the big urban centers. I am talking only about the people whom I actually encounter.

That's why I usually do not give "spare change," and I don't think I will in the future. These people will get along without me. Someone else will come up with money for their coffee or their liquor, or, at worst, they will just have to do without. I will continue to contribute occasionally to a charitable organization, not simply (I hope) to salve my conscience but because I believe that these organizations actually do good work. But I will not attempt to be a mini-charitable organization, distributing (probably to the unworthy) spare change.

The Essay Analyzed

Finally, here are a few comments about the essay.

The title is informative, alerting the reader to the topic and the author's position. (By the way, the student told us that in her next-to-last draft, the title was "Is It Right to Spare 'Spare Change'?" This title, unlike the revision, introduces the topic but not the author's position.)

The opening paragraph holds a reader's interest, partly by alluding to the familiar phrase "the deserving poor" and partly by introducing the *un*familiar phrase "the *un*deserving poor." Notice, too, that this opening paragraph ends by clearly asserting the author's thesis. Writers need not always announce their thesis early, but it is usually advisable to do so.

Paragraph 2 begins by voicing what probably is the reader's somewhat uneasy—perhaps even negative—response to the first paragraph. That is, *the writer has a sense of her audience;* she knows how her reader feels, and she takes account of the feeling.

Paragraph 3 clearly sets forth the alternatives. A reader may disagree with the writer's attitude, but the alternatives seem to be stated fairly.

Paragraphs 4 and 5 are more personal than the earlier paragraphs. The writer, more or less having stated what she takes to be the facts, now is entitled to offer a highly personal response to them.

The final paragraph nicely wraps things up by means of the words "spare change," which go back to the title and to the end of the first paragraph. The reader thus experiences a sensation of completeness. The essayist, of course, hasn't solved the problem for all of us for all time, but she presents a thoughtful argument and ends the essay effectively.

EXERCISE

In a brief essay, state a claim and support it with evidence. Choose an issue in which you are genuinely interested and about which you already know something. You may want to interview a few experts and do some reading, but don't try to write a highly researched paper. Sample topics:

1. Students in laboratory courses should not be required to participate in the dissection of animals.

2. Washington, D.C., should be granted statehood.

3. In wartime, women should be subject to the military draft.

4. The annual Miss America contest is an insult to women.

5. The government should not offer financial support to the arts.

6. The chief fault of the curriculum in high school was . . .

7. No specific courses should be required in colleges or universities.

7

Using Sources

Research is formalized curiosity. It is poking and prying with a purpose.

— ZORA NEALE HURSTON

There is no way of exchanging information that does not involve an act of judgment.

— JACOB BRONOWSKI

For God's sake, stop researching for a while and begin to think.

— WALTER HAMILTON MOBERLY

A problem adequately stated is a problem on its way to being solved.

— R. BUCKMINSTER FULLER

I have yet to see any problem, however complicated, which, when you looked at it in the right way, did not become still more complicated.

—POUL ANDERSON

WHY USE SOURCES?

We have pointed out that one gets ideas by writing. In the exercise of writing a draft, ideas begin to form, and these ideas stimulate further ideas, especially when one questions—when one *thinks about*—what one has written. But of course in writing about complex, serious questions, nobody is expected to invent all the answers. On the contrary, a writer is expected to be familiar with the chief answers already produced by others and to make use of them through selective incorporation and criticism. In short,

246

writers are not expected to reinvent the wheel; rather, they are expected to make good use of it and perhaps round it off a bit or replace a defective spoke. In order to think out your own views in writing, you are expected to do some preliminary research into the views of others.

When you are trying to understand an issue, high-quality sources will inform you of the various approaches others have taken and will help you establish what the facts are. Once you are informed enough to take a position, the sources you present to your readers will inform and persuade them, just as expert witnesses are sometimes brought in to inform and persuade a jury.

Research isn't limited to the world of professors and scientists. In one way or another, everyone does research at some point. If you want to persuade your city council to increase the number of bicycle lanes on city streets, you could bolster your argument with statistics on how much money the city could save if more people rode their bikes to work. If you decide to open your own business, you would do plenty of market research to persuade the bank that you could repay a loan. Sources (whether published information or data you gather yourself through interviews, surveys, or observation) are not only useful for background information; well-chosen and carefully analyzed sources are evidence for your readers that you know what you're talking about and that your interpretation is sound.

In Chapters 5 and 6 we discussed *ethos* as an appeal that establishes credibility with readers. When you do competent research and thereby let your audience see that you have done your homework, it increases your *ethos*; your audience will trust you because they see that you are well informed, offering them not just your opinions but also an awareness of other opinions and of the relevant facts. Conducting thorough research not only helps you to develop your argument, but it also shows respect for your audience.

Research is often misconstrued as the practice of transcribing information. In fact, it's a process of asking questions and gathering information that helps you come to conclusions about an issue. By using the information you find as evidence, you can develop an effective argument. But don't spend too much time searching and then waiting until the last minute to start writing. As you begin your search, write down observations and questions. When you find a useful source, take notes on what you think it means in your own words. This way, you won't find yourself with a pile of printouts and books and no idea what to say about them. What you have to say will flow naturally out of the prewriting you've already done—and that prewriting will help guide your search.

The process of research isn't always straightforward and neat. It involves scanning what other people have said about a topic and seeing what kinds of questions have been raised. As you poke and pry, you will learn more about the issue, and that, in turn, will help you develop a question to focus your efforts. Once you have a central idea—a thesis—you can sharpen your search to seek out the evidence that will make your readers sit up and take notice.

Consider arguments about whether athletes should be permitted to take anabolic steroids, drugs that supposedly build up muscle, restore energy, and enhance aggressiveness. A thoughtful argument on this subject will have to take account of information that the writer can gather only by doing some research.

- Do steroids really have the effects commonly attributed to them?
- Are they dangerous?
- If they are dangerous, how dangerous are they?

After all, competitive sports are inherently dangerous, some of them highly so. Many boxers, mixed martial arts fighters, jockeys, and football players have suffered severe injury, even death, from competing. Does anyone believe that anabolic steroids are more dangerous than the contests themselves? Obviously, again, a respectable argument about steroids will have to show awareness of what is known about them.

Or consider this question:

Why did President Truman order that atomic bombs be dropped on Hiroshima and Nagasaki?

The most obvious answer is to end the war, but some historians believe he had a very different purpose. In their view, Japan's defeat was ensured before the bombs were dropped, and the Japanese were ready to surrender; the bombs were dropped not to save American (or Japanese) lives but to show Russia that the United States would not be pushed around. Scholars who hold this view, such as Gar Alperovitz in *Atomic Diplomacy* (1965), argue that Japanese civilians in Hiroshima and Nagasaki were incinerated not to save the lives of American soldiers who otherwise would have died in an invasion of Japan but to teach Stalin a lesson. Dropping the bombs, it is argued, marked not the end of the Pacific War but the beginning of the cold war.

One must ask: What evidence supports this argument or claim or thesis, which assumes that Truman could not have thought the bomb was needed to defeat the Japanese because the Japanese knew they were defeated and would soon surrender without a hard-fought defense that would cost hundreds of thousands of lives? What about the momentum that had built up to use the bomb? After all, years of effort and $2 billion had been expended to produce a weapon with the intention of using it to end the war against Germany. But Germany had been defeated without the use of the bomb. Meanwhile, the war in the Pacific continued unabated. If the argument we are considering is correct, all this background counted for little or nothing in Truman's decision, a decision purely diplomatic and coolly indifferent to human life. The task for the writer is to evaluate the evidence available and then to argue for or against the view that Truman's purpose in dropping the bomb was to impress the Soviet government.

A student writing on the topic will certainly want to consult the chief books on the subject (Alperovitz's, cited above, Martin Sherwin's *A World Destroyed* [1975], and John Toland's *The Rising Sun* [1970]) and perhaps reviews of them, especially the reviews in journals devoted to political science. (Reading a searching review of a serious scholarly book is a good way to identify quickly some of the book's main contributions and controversial claims.) Truman's letters and statements, and books and articles about Truman, are also clearly relevant, and doubtless important articles are to be found in recent issues of scholarly journals and electronic sources. In fact, even an essay on such a topic as whether Truman was morally justified in using the atomic bomb for *any* purpose will be a stronger essay if it is well informed about such matters as the estimated loss of life that an invasion would have cost, the international rules governing weapons, and Truman's own statements about the issue.

How does one go about finding the material needed to write a well-informed argument? We will provide help, but first we want to offer a few words about choosing a topic.

CHOOSING A TOPIC

We will be brief. If a topic is not assigned, choose one that

- interests you, and
- can be researched with reasonable thoroughness in the allotted time.

Topics such as censorship, the environment, and sexual harassment obviously impinge on our lives, and it may well be that one such topic is of especial interest to you. But the scope of these topics makes researching them potentially overwhelming. Type the word *censorship* into an **Internet** search engine, and you will be referred to millions of information sources.

This brings us to our second point—a manageable topic. Any of the previous topics would need to be narrowed substantially before you could begin searching in earnest. Similarly, a topic such as the causes of World War II can hardly be mastered in a few weeks or argued in a ten-page paper. It is simply too big.

You can, however, write a solid paper analyzing, evaluating, and arguing for or against General Eisenhower's views on atomic warfare. What were they, and when did he hold them? (In his books written in 1948 and 1963 Eisenhower says that he opposed the use of the bomb before Hiroshima and that he argued with Secretary of War Henry Stimson against dropping it, but what evidence supports these claims? Was Eisenhower attempting to rewrite history in his books?) Eisenhower's own writings and books and other information sources on Eisenhower will, of course, be the major sources for a paper on this topic, but you will also want to look at books and articles about Stimson and at publications that contain information about the views of other generals, so that, for instance, you can compare Eisenhower's view with Marshall's or MacArthur's.

Spend a little time exploring a topic to see if it will be interesting and manageable by taking one or more of these approaches:

- **Do a Web search on the topic.** Though you may not use any of the sites that turn up, you can quickly put your finger on the pulse of popular approaches to the issue by scanning the first page or two of results to see what issues are getting the most attention.

- **Plug the topic into one of the library's article databases.** Again, just by scanning titles you can get a sense of what questions are being raised.

- **Browse the library shelves where books on the topic are kept.** A quick check of the tables of contents of recently published books may give you ideas of how to narrow the topic.

- **Ask a librarian to show you where specialized reference books on your topic are found.** Instead of general encyclopedias, try sources like these:

CQ Researcher
Encyclopedia of Applied Ethics
Encyclopedia of Bioethics
Encyclopedia of Crime and Justice
Encyclopedia of Science, Technology, and Ethics

- **Talk to an expert.** Members of the faculty who specialize in the area of your topic might be able to spell out some of the most significant controversies around a topic and may point you toward key sources.

FINDING MATERIAL

What strategy you use for finding good sources will depend on your topic. Researching a current issue in politics or popular culture may involve reading recent newspaper articles, scanning information on government Web sites, and locating current statistics. Other topics may be best tackled by seeking out books and scholarly journal articles that are less timely but more in-depth and analytical. You may want to supplement library and Web sources with your own fieldwork by conducting surveys or interviews.

Critical thinking is crucial to every step of the research process. Whatever strategy you use, remember that you will want to find material that is authoritative, represents a balanced approach to the issues, and is persuasive. As you choose your sources, bear in mind they will be serving as your "expert witnesses" as you make a case to your audience. Their quality and credibility are crucial to your argument.

If you find what seems to be an excellent source, look at some of the sources that this author repeatedly cites.

Finding Quality Information Online

The Web is a valuable source of information for many topics and less helpful for others. In general, if you're looking for information on public policy, popular culture, current events, legal affairs, or any subject of interest to agencies of the federal or state government, the Web is likely to have useful material. If you're looking for literary criticism or scholarly analysis of historical or social issues, you will be better off using library databases, described later in this chapter.

To make good use of the Web, try these strategies:

- Use the most specific terms possible when using a general search engine; put phrases in quotes.

- Use the advanced search option to limit a search to a domain (e.g., *.gov* for government sites) or by date (such as Web sites updated in the past week or month).

- If you're not sure which sites might be good ones for research, try starting with one of the selective directories listed below instead of a general search engine.

- Consider which government agencies and organizations might be interested in your topic, and go directly to their Web sites.

- Follow "about" links to see who is behind a Web site and why they put the information on the Web. If there is no "about" link, delete everything after the first slash in the URL to go to the parent site to see if it provides information.

- Use clues in URLs to see where sites originate. For example, URLs containing *.k12* are hosted at elementary and secondary schools, so they may be intended for a young audience; those ending in *.gov* are government agencies, so they tend to provide official information.

- Always bear in mind that the sources you choose must be persuasive to your audience. Avoid sites that may be dismissed as unreliable or biased.

Some useful Web sites include the following:

Selective Web Site Directories
   ipl2 www.ipl.org
   Open Directory Project www.dmoz.org

Current News Sources
   Google News news.google.com
   Reuters www.reuters.com
   WikiNews en.wikinews.org/wiki/Main_Page
   World Newspapers www.world-newspapers.com
   World Press www.worldpress.org

Digital Primary Sources
   American Memory memory.loc.gov
   American Rhetoric www.americanrhetoric.com
   Avalon Project avalon.law.yale.edu

National Archives www.archives.gov
Smithsonian Source www.smithsoniansource.org

Government Information
   GPO Access gpo.gov/fdsys/
   Thomas (federal legislation) thomas.loc.gov
   U.S. Department of Labor www.dol.gov

Scholarly or Scientific Information
   CiteSeer citeseerx.ist.psu.edu
   Google Scholar scholar.google.com
   Microsoft Academic academic.microsoft.com/
   Taylor and Francis Open Access Journals www.tandfonline.com
      /page/openaccess

Statistical Information
   American FactFinder factfinder.census.gov
   Fedstats fedstats.sites.usa.gov/
   Pew Global Attitudes Project pewglobal.org
   U.S. Census Bureau www.census.gov
   U.S. Data and Statistics www.usa.gov/statistics
   United Nations Statistics Division unstats.un.org
   *U.S. Bureau of Labor Statistics Guide to U.S. and World Statistical
      Information* http://www.bls.gov/bls/other.htm

A WORD ABOUT WIKIPEDIA

Links to Wikipedia (http://www.wikipedia.org) often rise to the top of Web search results. This vast and decentralized site provides over a million articles on a wide variety of topics. However, anyone can contribute to the online encyclopedia, so the accuracy of articles varies, and in some cases, the coverage of a controversial issue is one-sided or disputed. Even when the articles are accurate, they provide only basic information. Wikipedia's founder, Jimmy Wales, cautions students against using it as a source, except for obtaining general background knowledge: "You're in college; don't cite the encyclopedia."[1] Still, Wikipedia often provides valuable bibliographies that will help you to get going.

---

[1]"Wikipedia Founder Discourages Academic Use of His Creation." *Chronicle of Higher Education: The Wired Campus,* 12 June 2006. chronicle.com/wiredcampus/article/1328
/wikipedia-founder-discourages-academic-use-of-his-creation

Finding Articles Using Library Databases

Your library has a wide range of general and specialized databases available through its Web site. Some databases provide references to articles (and perhaps abstracts or summaries) or may provide direct links to the entire text of articles. General and interdisciplinary databases include Academic Search Premier (produced by the EBSCOhost company) and Expanded Academic Index (from InfoTrac).

More specialized databases include PsycINFO (for psychology research) and ERIC (focused on topics in education). Others, such as JSTOR, are full-text digital archives of scholarly journals. You will likely have access to newspaper articles through LexisNexis or Proquest Newsstand, particularly useful for articles that are not available for free on the Web. Look at your library's Web site to see what your options are, or stop by the reference desk for a quick personalized tutorial.

When using databases, first think through your topic using the listing and diagramming techniques described on pages 196–98. List synonyms for your key search terms. As you search, look at words used in titles and descriptors for alternative ideas and make use of the "advanced search" option so that you can easily combine multiple terms. Rarely will you find exactly what you're looking for right away. Try different search terms and different ways to narrow your topic.

Most databases have an advanced search option that offers forms for combining multiple terms. In Figure 7.1, a search on "anabolic steroids" retrieved far too many articles. In this advanced search, three concepts are being combined in a search: anabolic steroids, legal aspects of their use, and use of them by athletes. Related terms are combined with the word "or": *law* or *legal*. The last letters of a word have been replaced with an asterisk so that any ending will be included in the search. *Athlet** will search for *athlete, athletes*, or *athletics*. Options on both sides of the list of articles retrieved offer opportunities to refine a search by date of publication or to restrict the results to only academic journals, magazines, or newspapers.

As with a Web search, you'll need to make critical choices about which articles are worth pursuing. In this example, the first article may not be useful because it concerns German law. The second and third look fairly current and potentially useful. Only the third has a full text link, but the others may be available in another

Figure 7.1   An Advanced Web Search

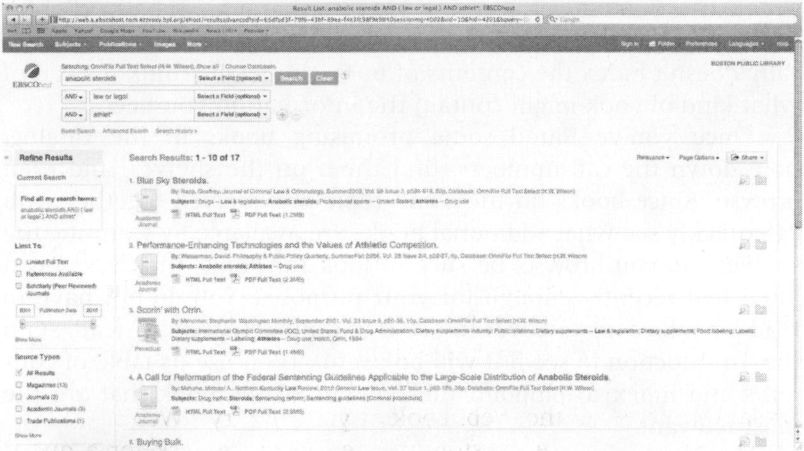

database. Many libraries have a program that will check other databases for you at the push of a button; in this case it's indicated by the "Find full text" button.

As you choose sources, keep track of them by selecting them. Then you can print off, save, or e-mail yourself the references you have selected. You may also have an option to export references to a citation management program such as RefWorks or EndNote. These programs allow you to create your own personal database of sources in which you can store your references and take notes. Later, when you're ready to create a bibliography, these programs will automatically format your references in MLA, APA, or another style. Ask a librarian if one of these programs is available to students on your campus.

Locating Books

The books that your library owns can be found through its online catalog. Typically, you can search by author or title or, if you don't have a specific book in mind, by keyword or subject. As with databases, think about different search terms to use, keeping an eye out for subject headings used for books that appear relevant. Take advantage of an "advanced search" option. You may, for example, be able to limit a search to books on a particular topic in English published within recent years. In addition to books, the catalog will also list DVDs, audio and video recordings, and other formats.

Unlike articles, books tend to cover broad topics, so be prepared to broaden your search terms. It may be that a book has a chapter or ten pages that are precisely what you need, but the catalog typically doesn't index the contents of books in detail. Think instead of what kind of book might contain the information you need.

Once you've found some promising books in the catalog, note down the call numbers, find them on the shelves, and then browse. Since books on the same topic are shelved together, you can quickly see what additional books are available by scanning the shelves. As you browse, be sure to look for books that have been published recently enough for your purposes. You do not have to read a book cover-to-cover to use it in your research. Instead, skim the introduction to see if it will be useful, then use its table of contents and index to pinpoint the sections of the book that are the most relevant.

If you are searching for a very specific name or phrase, you might try typing it into Google Book Search (books.google.com), which searches the contents of over seven million scanned books. Though it tends to retrieve too many results for most topics, and you may only be able to see a snippet of content, it can help you locate a particular quote or identify which books might include an unusual name or phrase. There is a "find in a library" link that will help you determine whether the books are available in your library.

INTERVIEWING PEERS AND LOCAL AUTHORITIES

You ought to try to consult experts—for instance, members of the faculty or other local authorities on art, business, law, and so forth. You can also consult interested laypersons. Remember, however, that experts have their biases and that "ordinary" people may have knowledge that experts lack. When interviewing experts, keep in mind Picasso's comment: "You mustn't always believe what I say. Questions tempt you to tell lies, particularly when there is no answer."

If you are interviewing your peers, you will probably want to make an effort to get a representative sample. Of course, even within a group not all members share a single view—many African Americans favor affirmative action, but not all do; some lawmakers support capital punishment, but again, many do not. Make an effort to talk to a range of people who might offer varied opinions. You may learn some unexpected things.

Here we will concentrate, however, on interviews with experts.

1. **Finding subjects for interviews** If you are looking for expert opinions, you may want to start with a faculty member on your campus. You may already know the instructor, or you may have to scan the catalog to see who teaches courses relevant to your topic. Department secretaries and college Web sites are good sources of information about the special interests of the faculty and also about lecturers who will be visiting the campus.

2. **Doing preliminary homework**   (a) In requesting the interview, make evident your interest in the topic and in the person. (If you know something about the person, you'll be able to indicate why you are asking.) (b) Request the interview, preferably in writing, a week in advance, and ask for ample time—probably half an hour to an hour. Indicate whether the material will be confidential, and (if you want to use a recorder) ask if you may record the interview. (c) If the person accepts the invitation, ask if he or she recommends any preliminary reading, and establish a time and a suitable place, preferably not the cafeteria during lunchtime.

3. **Preparing thoroughly**   (a) If your interviewee recommended any reading or has written on the topic, read the material. (b) Tentatively formulate some questions, keeping in mind that (unless you are simply gathering material for a survey of opinions) you want more than yes or no answers. Questions beginning with *Why* and *How* will usually require the interviewee to go beyond yes and no.

Even if your subject has consented to let you bring a recorder, be prepared to take notes on points that strike you as especially significant; without written notes, you will have nothing if the recorder has malfunctioned. Further, by taking occasional notes you will give the interviewee some time to think and perhaps to rephrase or to amplify a remark.

4. **Conducting the interview**   (a) Begin by engaging in brief conversation, without taking notes. If the interviewee has agreed to let you use a recorder, settle on the place where you will put it. (b) Come prepared with an opening question or two, but as the interview proceeds, don't hesitate to ask questions that you hadn't anticipated asking. (c) Near the end (you and your subject have probably agreed on the length of the interview) ask the subject if he or she wishes to add anything, perhaps by way of clarifying

some earlier comment. (d) Conclude by thanking the interviewee and by offering to provide a copy of the final version of your paper.

5. *Writing up the interview*   (a) As soon as possible—certainly, within twenty-four hours after the interview—review your notes and clarify them. At this stage, you can still remember the meaning of your abbreviated notes and shorthand devices (maybe you've been using *n* to stand for *nurses* in clinics where abortions are performed), but if you wait even a whole day you may be puzzled by your own notes. If you have recorded the interview, you may want to transcribe all of it—the laboriousness of this task is one good reason why many interviewers don't use recorders—and you may then want to scan the whole and mark the parts that now strike you as especially significant. If you have taken notes by hand, type them up, along with your own observations (e.g., "Jones was very tentative on this matter, but she said she was inclined to believe that . . ."). (b) Be especially careful to indicate which words are direct quotations. If in doubt, check with the interviewee.

EVALUATING YOUR SOURCES

Each step of the way, you will be making choices about your sources. As your research proceeds, from selecting promising items in a database search to browsing the book collection, you will want to use the techniques for previewing and skimming detailed on pages 45–47 in order to make your first selection. Ask yourself some basic questions:

- Is this source relevant?
- Is it current enough?
- Does the title and/or abstract suggest it will address an important aspect of my topic?
- Am I choosing sources that represent a range of ideas, not simply ones that support my opinion?
- Do I have a reason to believe that these sources are trustworthy?

Once you have collected a number of likely sources, you will want to do further filtering. Examine each one with these questions in mind:

- *Is this source credible? Does it include information about the author and his or her credentials that can help me decide whether to rely on it?* In the case of books, you might check a database for book reviews for a second opinion. In the case of Web sites, find out where the site came from and why it has been posted online. Don't use a Web source if you can't determine its authorship or purpose.

- *Will my audience find this source credible and persuasive?* Some publishers are more selective about which books they publish than others. University presses, for instance, have several experts read and comment on manuscripts before they decide which to publish. A story about U.S. politics from the *Washington Post*, whose writers conduct firsthand reporting in the nation's capital, carries more clout than a story from a small-circulation newspaper that is drawing its information from a wire service. A scholarly source may be more impressive than a magazine article.

- *Am I using the best evidence available?* Quoting directly from a government report may be more effective than quoting a news story that summarizes the report. Finding evidence that supports your claims in a president's speeches or letters is more persuasive than drawing your conclusions from a page or two of a history textbook.

- *Am I being fair to all sides?* Make sure you are prepared to address alternate perspectives, even if you ultimately take a position. Avoid sources that clearly promote an agenda in favor of ones that your audience will consider balanced and reliable.

- *Can I corroborate my key claims in more than one source?* Compare your sources to ensure that you aren't relying on facts that can't be confirmed. If you're having trouble confirming a source, check with a librarian.

- *Do I really need this source?* It's tempting to use all the books and articles you have found, but if two sources say essentially the same thing, choose the one that is likely to carry the most weight with your audience.

The information you will look for as you evaluate a Web source is often the same as what you need to record in a citation. You can streamline the process of creating a list of works cited by identifying these elements as you evaluate a source.

In Figure 7.2, the URL includes the ending *.gov*—meaning it is a government Web site, an official document that has been vetted. There is an "about" link that will explain the government agency's

Figure 7.2   A Page from a Government Web Site

① URL—Site has a .gov domain.

② Sponsor

③ Author

④ Link to homepage will explain that this institute is a government agency.

⑤ Web site name

⑥ Title of page

⑦ Scanning list will give an idea of whether source is reliable and useful.

mission. The date is found above the title of the page: "Revised March 2016." This appears to be a high-quality source of basic information on the issue.

The information you need to cite this report is also on the page; make sure you keep track of where you found the source and when, since Web sites can change. One way to do this is by creating an account at a social bookmarking site such as Delicious (delicious .com) or Diigo (diigo.com) where you can store and annotate Web sites.

Figure 7.3 shows how the information on a Web page might lead you to reject it as a source. Clearly, though this site purports to provide educational information, its primary purpose is to sell products. The graphics and text on the page emphasize the supposed benefits of these performance-enhancing drugs, promoting their use. The focus on performance enhancement and marketing rather than health sends up a red flag.

Figure 7.3   A Page from a Commercial Web Site

① This is a .com (commercial) site.

② The additional links provided in the user menu are suspect.

③ The information on the site promotes performance enhancement, not health.

④ Ads promote steroid use for cash prizes.

⑤ Steroids are for sale through the site.

TAKING NOTES

When it comes to taking notes, all researchers have their own habits that they swear by, and they can't imagine any other way of working. We still prefer to take notes on four-by-six-inch index cards, while others use a notebook or a computer for note taking. If you use a citation management program, such as RefWorks or EndNote, you can store your personal notes and commentary with the citations you have saved. Using the program's search function, you can easily pull together related notes and citations, or you can create project folders for your references so that you can easily review what you've collected.

Whatever method you use, the following techniques should help you maintain consistency and keep organized during the research process:

1. If you use a notebook or cards, write in ink (pencil gets smudgy), and write on only one side of the card or paper.

(Notes on the backs of cards tend to get lost, and writing on the back of paper will prevent you from later cutting up and rearranging your notes.) Consider using an online tool to keep up with your notes and ideas, for instance, a Google Doc, private blog, or wiki.

2. Summarize, for the most part, rather than quote at length.

3. Quote only passages in which the writing is especially effective or passages that are in some way crucial. These will be easy to access and use if kept in an online venue.

4. Make sure that all quotations are exact. Enclose quoted words within quotation marks, indicate omissions by ellipses (three spaced periods: . . .), and enclose within square brackets ([]) any insertions or other additions you make.

✓ A CHECKLIST FOR EVALUATING PRINT SOURCES

For Books:

☐ Is the book recent? If not, is the information I will be using from it likely or unlikely to change over time?

☐ What are the author's credentials?

☐ Is the book titled toward entertainment, or is it in-depth and even-handed?

☐ Is the book broad enough in its focus and written in a style I can understand?

☐ Does the book relate directly to my tentative thesis, or is it of only tangential interest?

☐ Do the arguments in the book seem sound, based on what I have learned about skillful critical reading and writing?

For Articles from Periodicals:

☐ Is the periodical recent?

☐ Is the author's name given? Does he or she seem a credible source?

☐ Does the article treat the topic superficially or in-depth? Does it take sides, or does it offer enough context so that I can make up my own mind?

☐ How directly does the article speak to my topic and tentative thesis?

☐ If the article is from a scholarly journal, am I sure I understand it?

5. *Never* copy a passage, changing an occasional word. *Either* copy it word for word, with punctuation intact, and enclose it within quotation marks, *or* summarize it drastically. If you copy a passage but change a word here and there, you may later make the mistake of using your note verbatim in your essay, and you will be guilty of plagiarism.

6. Give the page number of your source, whether you summarize or quote. If a quotation you have copied runs in the original from the bottom of page 210 to the top of page 211, in your notes put a diagonal line (/) after the last word on page 210, so that later, if in your paper you quote only the material from page 210, you will know that you must cite 210 and not 210–11.

✓ A CHECKLIST FOR EVALUATING ELECTRONIC SOURCES

An enormous amount of valuable material is available online — but so is an enormous amount of junk. True, there is also plenty of junk in books and journals, but most printed material has been subjected to a review process: Book publishers and editors of journals send manuscripts to specialized readers who evaluate them and recommend whether the material should or should not be published. Publishing online is quite different. Anyone can publish online with no review process: All that is needed is sufficient access to the Internet. Ask yourself:

☐ What person or organization produced the site (a commercial entity, a nonprofit entity, a student, an expert)? Check the electronic address to get a clue about the authorship. If there is a link to the author's homepage, check it out to learn about the author. Does the author have an affiliation with a respectable institution?

☐ What is the site's purpose? Is the site in effect an infomercial, or is it an attempt to contribute to a thoughtful discussion?

☐ Are the sources of information indicated and verifiable? If possible, check the sources.

☐ Is the site authoritative enough to use? (If it seems to contain review materials or class handouts, you probably don't want to take it too seriously.)

☐ When was the page made available? Is it out of date?

7. Indicate the source. The author's last name is enough if you have consulted only one work by the author; but if you consult more than one work by an author, you need further identification, such as both the author's name and a short title.

8. Add your own comments about the substance of what you are recording. Such comments as "but contrast with Sherwin" or "seems illogical" or "evidence?" will ensure that you are thinking as well as writing and will be of value when you come to transform your notes into a draft. Be sure, however, to enclose such notes within double diagonals (//), or to mark them in some other way, so that later you will know they are yours and not your source's. If you use a computer for note taking, you may wish to write your comments in italics or in a different font.

9. In a separate computer file or notebook page or on separate index cards, write a bibliographic entry for each source. The information in each entry will vary, depending on whether the source is a book, a periodical, an electronic document, and so forth. The kind of information (e.g., author and title) needed for each type of source can be found in the sections on MLA Format: The List of Works Cited (p. 288) or APA Format: The List of References (p. 302).

A NOTE ON PLAGIARIZING, PARAPHRASING, AND USING COMMON KNOWLEDGE

Plagiarism is the unacknowledged use of someone else's work. The word comes from a Latin word for "kidnapping," and plagiarism is indeed the stealing of something engendered by someone else. We won't deliver a sermon on the dishonesty (and folly) of plagiarism; we intend only to help you understand exactly what plagiarism is. The first thing to say is that plagiarism is not limited to the unacknowledged quotation of words.

A *paraphrase* is a sort of word-by-word or phrase-by-phrase translation of the author's language into your own language. Unlike a summary, then, a paraphrase is approximately as long as the original. Why would anyone paraphrase something? There are two good reasons:

- You may, as a reader, want to paraphrase a passage in order to make certain that you are thinking carefully about each word in the original.

- You may, as a writer, want to paraphrase a difficult passage in order to help your reader.

Paraphrase thus has its uses, but writers often use it unnecessarily, and students who overuse it may find themselves crossing the border into plagiarism. True, if you paraphrase you are using your own words, but

- you are also using someone else's ideas, and, equally important,
- you are using this other person's sequence of thoughts.

Even if you change every third word in your source, you are plagiarizing.

Here is an example of this sort of plagiarism, based on the previous sentence:

> Even if you alter every second or third word that your source gives, you still are plagiarizing.

Further, even if the writer of this paraphrase had cited a source after the paraphrase, he or she would still have been guilty of plagiarism. How, you may ask, can a writer who cites a source be guilty of plagiarism? Easy. Readers assume that only the gist of the idea is the source's and that the development of the idea—the way it is set forth—is the present writer's work. A paraphrase that runs to several sentences is in no significant way the writer's work: The writer is borrowing not only the idea but the shape of the presentation, the sentence structure. What the writer needs to do is to write something like this:

> Changing an occasional word does not free the writer from the obligation to cite a source.

And the source would still need to be cited, if the central idea were not a commonplace one.

We cannot overemphasize the point that even if you cite a source for your paraphrase you are nevertheless plagiarizing—unless you clearly indicate that the entire passage is a paraphrase of the source.

You are plagiarizing if, without giving credit, you use someone else's ideas—even if you put these ideas entirely into your own words. When you use another's ideas, you must indicate your indebtedness by saying something like "Alperovitz points out that . . ." or "Secretary of War Stimson, as Martin Sherwin notes, never expressed himself on this point." Alperovitz and Sherwin pointed out something that you had not thought of, and so you must give them credit if you want to use their findings.

Again, even if after a paraphrase you cite your source, you are plagiarizing. A reader assumes that the citation refers to information or an opinion, *not* to the presentation or development of the idea; and of course, in a paraphrase you are not presenting or developing the material in your own way.

Now consider this question: *Why* paraphrase? Often there is no good answer. Since a paraphrase is as long as the original, you may as well quote the original, if you think that a passage of that length is worth quoting. Probably it is *not* worth quoting in full; probably you should *not* paraphrase but rather should drastically *summarize* most of it, and perhaps quote a particularly effective phrase or two. As we explained on pages 62–64, the chief reason to paraphrase a passage is to clarify it—that is, to ensure that you and your readers understand a passage that—perhaps because it is badly written—is obscure.

Generally, what you should do is

- Take the idea and put it entirely into your own words, perhaps reducing a paragraph of a hundred words to a sentence of ten words, but you must still give credit for the idea.

- If you believe that the original hundred words are so perfectly put that they cannot be transformed without great loss, you'll have to quote them in full and cite your source. You may in this case want to tell the reader *why* you are quoting at such great length.

In short, chiefly you will quote or you will summarize, and only rarely will you paraphrase, but in all cases you will cite your source. There is no point in paraphrasing an author's hundred words into a hundred of your own. Either quote or summarize, but cite the source.

Keep in mind, too, that almost all generalizations about human nature, no matter how common and familiar (e.g., "males are innately more aggressive than females") are not indisputable facts; they are at best hypotheses on which people differ and therefore should either not be asserted at all or should be supported by some cited source or authority. Similarly, because nearly all statistics (whether on the intelligence of criminals or the accuracy of lie detectors) are the result of some particular research and may well have been superseded or challenged by other investigators, it

> ✓ **A CHECKLIST FOR AVOIDING PLAGIARISM**
>
> ☐ In my notes did I *always* put quoted material within quotation marks?
>
> ☐ In my notes did I summarize *in my own words* and give credit to the source for the idea?
>
> ☐ In my notes did I avoid paraphrasing, that is, did I avoid copying, keeping the structure of the source's sentences but using some of my own words? (Paraphrases of this sort, even with a footnote citing the source, are *not* acceptable, since the reader incorrectly assumes that the writing is essentially yours.)
>
> ☐ If in my paper I set forth a borrowed idea, do I give credit, even though the words and the structure of the sentences are entirely my own?
>
> ☐ If in my paper I quote directly, do I put the words within quotation marks and cite the source?
>
> ☐ Do I *not* cite material that can be considered common knowledge (material that can be found in numerous reference works, such as the date of a public figure's birth or the population of San Francisco or the fact that *Hamlet* is regarded as a great tragedy)?
>
> ☐ If I have the slightest doubt about whether I should or should not cite a source, have I taken the safe course and cited the source?

is advisable to cite a source for any statistics you use unless you are convinced they are indisputable, such as the number of registered voters in Memphis in 1988.

In contrast, there is something called **common knowledge,** and the sources for such information need not be cited. The term does not, however, mean exactly what it seems to. It is common knowledge, of course, that Ronald Reagan was an American president (so you don't cite a source when you make that statement), and under the conventional interpretation of this doctrine, it is also common knowledge that he was born in 1911. In fact, of course, few people other than Reagan's relatives know this date. Still, information that can be found in many places and that is indisputable belongs to all of us; therefore, a writer need not cite her source when she says that Reagan was born in 1911. Probably she checked a dictionary or an encyclopedia for the date, but the source doesn't matter. Dozens of sources will give exactly the same information, and in fact, no reader wants to be bothered with a citation on such a point.

Some students have a little trouble developing a sense of what is and what is not common knowledge. Although, as we have just said, readers don't want to hear about the sources for information that is indisputable and can be documented in many places, if you are in doubt about whether to cite a source, cite it. Better risk boring the reader a bit than risk being accused of plagiarism.

Your college or your class instructor probably has issued a statement concerning plagiarism. If there is such a statement, be sure to read it carefully.

COMPILING AN ANNOTATED BIBLIOGRAPHY

When several sources have been identified and gathered, many researchers prepare an annotated bibliography. This is a list providing all relevant bibliographic information (just as it will appear in your Works Cited list or References list) as well as a brief descriptive and evaluative summary of each source—perhaps one to three sentences. Your instructor may ask you to provide an annotated bibliography for your research project.

An annotated bibliography serves four main purposes:

- First, constructing such a document helps you to master the material contained in any given source. To find the heart of the argument presented in an article or book, to phrase it briefly, and to comment on it, you must understand it fully.

- Second, creating an annotated bibliography helps you to think about how each portion of your research fits into the whole of your project, how you will use it, and how it relates to your topic and thesis.

- Third, an annotated bibliography helps your readers: They can quickly see which items may be especially helpful in their own research.

- Fourth, in constructing an annotated bibliography at this early stage, you will get some hands-on practice at bibliographic format, thereby easing the job of creating your final bibliography (the Works Cited list or References list for your paper).

Following are two examples of entries for an annotated bibliography in MLA (Modern Language Association) format for a project on the effect of violence in the media. The first is for a book, the second for an article from a periodical. Notice that each entry does two things:

- It begins with a bibliographic entry—author (last name first), title, and so forth.
- Then it provides information about the content of the work under consideration, suggesting how each may be of use to the final research paper.

Clover, Carol J. *Men, Women, and Chain Saws: Gender in the Modern Horror Film*. Princeton UP, 1992. The author focuses on Hollywood horror movies of the 1970s and 1980s. She studies representations of women and girls in these movies and the responses of male viewers to female characters, suggesting that this relationship is more complex and less exploitative than the common wisdom claims.

Winerip, Michael. "Looking for an Eleven O'Clock Fix." *New York Times Magazine*, 11 Jan. 1998, pp. 30–40. The article focuses on the rising levels of violence on local television news and highlights a station in Orlando, Florida, that tried to reduce its depictions of violence and lost viewers as a result. Winerip suggests that people only claim to be against media violence, while their actions prove otherwise.

As you construct your annotated bibliography, consider posting your Word document in Google Drive for easy access and sharing.

Citation Generators　There are many citation generators available online. These generators allow you to enter the information about your source, and, with a click, they will create Works Cited entries in APA or MLA format. But just as you cannot trust spell- and grammar-checkers in Microsoft Word, you cannot trust these generators. You can use them to cite works, but if you do, be sure to double-check what they produce before submitting your essay. Always remember that responsible writers take care to cite their sources properly and that failure to do so puts you at risk for accusations of plagiarism.

WRITING THE PAPER

Organizing Your Notes

If you have read thoughtfully, taken careful (and, again, thought-ful) notes on your reading, and then (yet again) thought about these notes, you are well on the way to writing a good paper. You have, in fact, already written some of it in your notes. By now you should clearly have in mind the thesis you intend to argue. But you still have to organize the material, and, doubtless, even as you set about organizing it, you will find points that will require you to do some additional research and much additional thinking.

Divide your notes into clusters, each devoted to one theme or point (e.g., one cluster on the extent of use of steroids, another on evidence that steroids are harmful, yet another on arguments that even if harmful they should be permitted). If your notes are in a computer file, rearrange them into appropriate clusters. If you use index cards, simply sort them into packets. If you take notes in a notebook, either mark each note with a number or name indicating the cluster to which it belongs, or cut the notes apart and arrange them as you would cards. Put aside all notes that— however interesting—you now see are irrelevant to your paper.

Next, arrange the clusters or packets into a tentative sequence. In effect, you are preparing a **working outline.** At its simplest, say, you will give three arguments on behalf of *X* and then three counterarguments. (Or you might decide that it's better to alter-nate material from the two sets of three clusters each, following each argument with an objection. At this stage, you can't be sure of the organization you will finally use, but you can make a tentative decision.)

The First Draft

Draft the essay, without worrying much about an elegant opening paragraph. Just write some sort of adequate opening that states the topic and your thesis. When you revise the whole later, you can put some effort into developing an effective opening. (Most experienced writers find that the opening paragraph in the final version is almost the last thing they write.)

If your notes are on cards or notebook paper, carefully copy into the draft all quotations that you plan to use. If your notes are in a computer, you may simply cut and paste them from one file to another. Do keep in mind, however, that rewriting or retyping quotations will make you think carefully about them and may result in a more focused and thoughtful paper. (In the next section of this chapter we will talk briefly about leading into quotations and about the form of quotations.) Be sure to include citations in your drafts so that if you must check a reference later it will be easy to do so.

Later Drafts

Give the draft, and yourself, a rest—perhaps for a day or two—and then go back to it. Read it over, make necessary revisions, and then **outline** it. That is, on a sheet of paper chart the organization and development, perhaps by jotting down a sentence summarizing each paragraph or each group of closely related paragraphs. Your outline or map may now show you that the paper obviously suffers from poor organization. For instance, it may reveal that you neglected to respond to one argument or that you needlessly treated one point in two places. It may also help you to see that if you gave three arguments and then three counterarguments, you probably should instead have followed each argument with its rebuttal. However, if you alternated arguments and objections, it may now seem better to use two main groups—all the arguments and then all the criticisms.

No one formula is always right. Much will depend on the complexity of the material. If the arguments are highly complex, it is better to respond to them one by one than to expect a reader to hold three complex arguments in mind before you get around to responding. If, however, the arguments can be stated briefly and clearly, it is effective to state all three and then to go on to the responses. If you write on a computer, you will find it easy, even fun, to move passages of text around. Even so, you will probably want to print out a hard copy from time to time to review the structure of your paper. Allow enough time to produce several drafts.

A Few More Words about Organization

There is a difference between

- a paper that *has* an organization, and
- a paper that helpfully lets the reader know what the organization is.

You should write papers of the second sort, but (there is always a "but") take care not to belabor the obvious. Inexperienced writers sometimes either hide the organization so thoroughly that a reader cannot find it or they so ploddingly lay out the structure ("Eighth, I will show . . .") that the reader becomes impatient. Yet it is better to be overly explicit than to be obscure.

The ideal, of course, is the middle route. Make the overall strategy of your organization evident by occasional explicit signs at the beginning of a paragraph ("We have seen . . . ," "It is time to consider the objections . . . ," "By far the most important . . ."); elsewhere make certain that the implicit structure is evident to the reader. When rereading your draft, if you try to imagine that you are one of your classmates, you will probably be able to sense exactly where explicit signs are needed and where they are not needed. Better still, exchange drafts with a classmate in order to exchange (tactful) advice.

Another strategy for organizing an essay is to determine early on whether your approach uses **classification** or **division**. These two terms refer to the development of essays and to the function of individual paragraphs, so they may be used profitably together. **Classification** normally suggests surveying many items or aspects of an issue. You might be examining the various roles played by celebrities in international relations, or looking at many types of GMOs, or analyzing a range of characters in a novel. Classification suggests a collection of numerous things within the purview of your thesis. **Division**, in contrast, suggests looking at one thing very closely, and dividing it into parts—perhaps as a key example of your broader thesis. If you are using division, you might be examining the role of one celebrity in international relations (e.g., Bono), or looking at one particular GMO, or analyzing the role of one character within a novel. We can illustrate the difference in a hypothetical essay about the dangers of steroid use. If you're using classification, you might be looking at many different types of drugs and their uses in various sports by various athletes. You might be further pointing out the many effects of these substances and the controversies that surround each to support an overall thesis about the issue. If you're using division, you might be emphasizing a key drug, a key athlete, or a key case study to understand thoroughly its specific effects as representative of the whole.

Classification may be thought of as utilizing many *parts* to understand a *whole*. Division may be thought of as using a *whole* to understand many *parts*.

Choosing a Tentative Title

By now a couple of tentative titles for your essay should have crossed your mind. If possible, choose a title that is both interesting and informative. Consider these three titles:

Are Steroids Harmful?

The Fuss over Steroids

Steroids: A Dangerous Game

"Are Steroids Harmful?" is faintly interesting and lets the reader know the gist of the subject, but it gives no clue about the writer's thesis, the writer's contention or argument. "The Fuss over Steroids" is somewhat better, for it gives information about the writer's position. "Steroids: A Dangerous Game" is still better; it announces the subject ("steroids") and the thesis ("dangerous"), and it also displays a touch of wit because "game" glances at the world of athletics.

Don't try too hard, however; better a simple, direct, informative title than a strained, puzzling, or overly cute one. And remember to make sure that everything in your essay is relevant to your title. In fact, your title should help you to organize the essay and to delete irrelevant material.

The Final Draft

When at last you have a draft that is for the most part satisfactory, check to make sure that **transitions** from sentence to sentence and from paragraph to paragraph are clear ("Further evidence," "In contrast," "A weakness, however, is apparent"), and then worry about your opening and closing paragraphs. Your **opening paragraph** should be clear, interesting, and focused; if neither the title nor the first paragraph announces your thesis, the second paragraph probably should do so.

The **final paragraph** need not say, "In conclusion, I have shown that. . . ." It should effectively end the essay, but it need not summarize your conclusions. We have already offered a few words about final paragraphs (p. 79), but the best way to learn how to write such paragraphs is to study the endings of some of the essays in this book and to adopt the strategies that appeal to you.

Be sure that all indebtedness is properly acknowledged. We have talked about plagiarism; now we will turn to the business of introducing quotations effectively.

QUOTING FROM SOURCES

Incorporating Your Reading into Your Thinking: The Art and Science of Synthesis

At the beginning of Chapter 6 we quoted a passage by Kenneth Burke (1887–1993), a college dropout who became one of America's most important twentieth-century students of rhetoric. It is worth repeating:

> Imagine that you enter a parlor. You come late. When you arrive, others have long preceded you, and they are engaged in a heated discussion, a discussion too heated for them to pause and tell you exactly what it is about. In fact, the discussion had already begun long before any of them got there, so that no one present is qualified to retrace for you all the steps that had gone before. You listen for a while, until you decide that you have caught the tenor of the argument; then you put in your oar. Someone answers; you answer him; another comes to your defense; another aligns himself against you, to either the embarrassment or gratification of your opponent, depending upon the quality of your ally's assistance. However, the discussion is interminable. The hour grows late, you must depart. And you do depart, with the discussion still vigorously in progress.
>
> — *The Philosophy of Literary Form* (Baton Rouge: Louisiana State University Press, 1941), 110–11.

Why do we quote this passage? Because it is your turn to join the unending conversation.

During the process of reading, and afterward, you will want to listen, think, say to yourself something like this:

- "No, no, I see things very differently; it seems to me that . . ." or
- "Yes, of course, but on one large issue I think I differ," or
- "Yes, sure, I agree, but I would go further and add . . ." or
- "Yes, I agree with your conclusion, but I hold this conclusion for reasons very different from the ones that you offer."

During your composition courses at least (and we think during your entire life), you will be reading or listening and will sometimes want to put in your oar—you will sometimes want to respond in writing, for example in the form of a Letter to the Editor or in a memo at your place of employment. In the course of your response you almost surely will have to summarize the idea or ideas you are responding to, so that your readers will understand the context of your remarks. These ideas may not come from a single source; you may be responding to several sources. For instance, you may be responding to a report and also to some comments that the report evoked. In any case, you will state these ideas briefly and fairly and will then set forth your thoughtful responses, thereby giving the reader a statement that you hope represents an advance in the argument, even if only a tiny one. That is, you will **synthesize** sources, combining existing material into something new, drawing nourishment from what has already been said (giving credit, of course), and converting it into something new—a view that you think is worth considering.

Let's pause for a moment and consider this word *synthesis*. You probably are familiar with *photosynthesis*, the chemical process in green plants that produces carbohydrates from carbon dioxide and hydrogen. Synthesis, again, combines pre-existing elements and produces something new. In our use of the word *synthesis*, even a view that you utterly reject becomes a part of your new creation *because it helped to stimulate you to formulate your view*; without the idea that you reject, you might not have developed the view that you now hold. Consider the words of Francis Bacon, Shakespeare's contemporary:

> Some books are to be tasted, others to be swallowed, and some few to be chewed and digested.

Your instructor will expect you to digest your sources—this doesn't mean you need to accept them but only that you need to read them thoughtfully—and that, so to speak, you make them your own thoughts by refining them. Your readers will expect you to tell them *what you make out of your sources*, which means that you will go beyond writing a summary and will synthesize the material into your own contribution. *Your* view is what is wanted, and readers expect this view to be thoughtful—not mere summary and not mere tweeting.

A RULE FOR WRITERS In your final draft *you must give credit to all of your sources*. Let the reader know whether you are quoting (in this case, you will use quotation marks around all material directly quoted), or whether you are summarizing (you will explicitly say so), or whether you are paraphrasing (again, you will explicitly say so).

The Use and Abuse of Quotations

When is it necessary, or appropriate, to quote? Sometimes, the reader must see the exact words of your source; the gist won't do. If you are arguing that Z's definition of *rights* is too inclusive, your readers have to know exactly how Z defined *rights*. Your brief summary of the definition may be unfair to Z; in fact, you want to convince your readers that you're being fair, and so you quote Z's definition, word for word. Moreover, if the passage is only a sentence or two long, or even if it runs to a paragraph, it may be so compactly stated that it defies summary. And to attempt to paraphrase it—substituting *natural* for *inalienable,* and so forth—saves no space and only introduces imprecision. There is nothing to do but to quote it, word for word.

Second, you may want to quote a passage that could be summarized but that is so effectively stated that you want the readers to have the pleasure of reading the original. Of course, readers won't give you credit for writing these words, but they will appreciate your taste and your effort to make especially pleasant the business of reading your paper.

In short, use (but don't overuse) quotations. Speaking roughly, quotations

- should occupy no more than 10 to 15 percent of your paper, and
- they may occupy much less.

Most of your paper should set forth your ideas, not other people's ideas.

How to Quote

LONG AND SHORT QUOTATIONS **Long quotations** (more than four lines of typed prose or three or more lines of poetry) are set off from the text. To set off material, start on a new line, indent one-half inch from the left margin, and type the quotation double-spaced. Do not enclose quotations within quotation marks if you are setting them off.

Short quotations are treated differently. They are embedded within the text; they are enclosed within quotation marks, but otherwise they do not stand out.

All quotations, whether set off or embedded, must be exact. If you omit any words, you must indicate the ellipsis by substituting three spaced periods for the omission; if you insert any words or punctuation, you must indicate the addition by enclosing it within square brackets, not to be confused with parentheses.

Original   The Montgomery bus boycott not only brought national attention to the discriminatory practices of the South, but elevated a twenty-six-year-old preacher to exalted status in the civil rights movement.

Quotation in   "The Montgomery bus boycott . . . elevated
student paper   [King] to exalted status in the civil rights movement."

LEADING INTO A QUOTATION   Now for a less mechanical matter: the way in which a quotation is introduced. To say that it is "introduced" implies that one leads into it, though on rare occasions a quotation appears without an introduction, perhaps immediately after the title. Normally one leads into a quotation by giving any one or more of the following (*warning*: using them all at once can get unwieldy and produce awkward sentences):

- the *name of the author* and (no less important) the author's expertise or authority
- an indication of *the source of the quotation, by title and/or year*
- *clues signaling the content of the quotation and the purpose* it serves in the present essay

For example:

William James provides a clear answer to Huxley when he says that ". . ."

Psychologist William James provides a clear answer to Huxley when he says that ". . ."

In *The Will to Believe* (1897), psychologist William James *provides a clear answer* to Huxley when he says that ". . ."

Any of these work, especially because William James is quite well known. When you're quoting from a lesser-known author, it becomes more important to identify his or her expertise and perhaps the source, as in "Biographer Theodora Bosanquet, author of *Henry James at Work* (1982), subtly criticized Huxley's vague ideas on religion by writing '. . .'."

Note that in all of the above samples, the writer uses the lead-in to signal to readers the general tone of the quotation to follow. The writer uses "a clear answer" to signal that what's coming is, in fact, clear. The writer uses "subtly criticized" and "vague" to indicate that the following words by Bosanquet will be critical and will point out a shortcoming in Huxley's ideas. In this way, the writer anticipates and controls the meaning of the quotation for the reader. If the writer believed otherwise, the lead-ins might have run thus:

> William James attempts to answer Huxley, but his response does not really meet the difficulty Huxley calls attention to. James writes, ". . ."

or thus:

> Biographer Theodora Bosanquet, author of *Henry James at Work* (1982), unjustly criticized Huxley's complex notion of religion by writing ". . ."

In this last example, clearly the words "unjustly criticized" imply that the essayist wants the reader to interpret the quotation as an unjust criticism. Similarly, Huxley's idea is presented as "complex," not vague.

SIGNAL PHRASES Think of your writing as a conversation between you and your sources. As in conversation, you want to be able to move smoothly between different, sometimes contrary, points of view. You also want to be able to set your thoughts apart from those of your sources. Signal phrases make it easy for readers to know where your information came from and why it's trustworthy by pointing to key facts about the source:

> *According to* psychologist Stephen Ceci . . .

> A report published by the U.S. Bureau of Justice Statistics *concludes* . . .

> Feminist philosopher Sandra Harding *argues* . . .

THINKING CRITICALLY USING SIGNAL PHRASES

In the space provided, rewrite each signal phrase using a different structure. The first has been done as an example. Use different verbs to introduce each source.

Original Signal Phrase	Revised Signal Phrase
According to political economist Robert Reich . . .	. . . claims Robert Reich.
The National Health Council reports . . .	
The *Harvard Law Review* claims . . .	
As science essayist Jennifer Ackerman suggests . . .	

To avoid repetitiveness, vary your sentence structure:

> . . . *claims* Stephen Ceci.

> . . . *according to* a report published by the U.S. Bureau of Statistics.

Some useful verbs to introduce sources include the following:

acknowledges	disputes
argues	observes
believes	points out
claims	recommends
contends	reports
denies	suggests

Note that papers written using MLA style refer to sources in the present tense (*acknowledge, argue, believe*). Papers written in APA style use the past tense (*acknowledged, argued, believed*).

LEADING OUT OF A QUOTATION   You might think of providing quotations as a three-stage process that includes the **lead-in**, the **quotation** itself, and the **lead-out**. The lead-out gives you a chance to interpret the quoted material, further controlling the intended meaning, telling the reader what is most important. In the lead-out, you have a chance to reflect upon the quotation and to shift back toward your own ideas and analysis. Consider this three-stage process applied in the following two ways:

> In his first book, *A World Restored* (1954), future Secretary of Defense Henry Kissinger wrote the famous axiom "History is the memory of states." It is the collective story of an entire people, displayed in public museums and libraries, taught in schools, and passed on from generation to generation.

> In his first book, *A World Restored* (1954), Nixon's former Secretary of Defense Henry Kissinger wrote glibly, "History is the memory of states." By asserting that history is largely the product of self-interested propaganda, Kissinger's words suggest that the past is maintained and controlled by whatever groups happen to hold power.

Note the three-step process, and note especially how the two examples convey different meanings of Kissinger's famous phrase. In the lead-in to the first sample, Kissinger's "future" role suggests hope. It signals a figure whose influence is growing. By using *famous* and *axiom*, the author presents the quotation as "true" or even timeless. In the lead-out, the role of the state in preserving history is optimistic and idealistic.

In the second sample, "former" is used in the lead-in, suggesting Kissinger's later association with the ousted president. Readers are told that Kissinger "wrote glibly" even before they are told what he wrote, so readers may tend to read the quoted words that way. In the lead-out, the state becomes a more nefarious source of history-keeping, one not interested in accommodating marginal voices or alternative perspectives, or remembering events inconvenient to its authority or righteousness.

Again, we hope you can see in these examples how the three-step process facilitates a writer's control over the meanings of quotations. Returning to our earlier example, if after reading something by Huxley the writer had merely stated that "William James says . . . ," readers wouldn't know whether they were getting confirmation, refutation, or something else. The essayist would have put a needless burden on the readers. Generally speaking, the more difficult the quotation, the more important is the introductory or

> **A RULE FOR WRITERS** In introducing a quotation, it is usually advisable to signal the reader *why* you are using the quotation by means of a lead-in consisting of a verb or a verb and adverb, such as *claims*, or *convincingly shows*, or *admits*.

explanatory lead-in, but even the simplest quotation profits from some sort of brief lead-in, such as "James reaffirms this point when he says. . . ."

DOCUMENTATION

In the course of your essay, you will probably quote or summarize material derived from a source. You must give credit, and although there is no one form of documentation to which all scholarly fields subscribe, you will probably be asked to use one of two. One, established by the Modern Language Association (MLA), is used chiefly in the humanities; the other, established by the American Psychological Association (APA), is used chiefly in the social sciences.

We include two papers that use sources. "An Argument for Corporate Responsibility" (p. 308) uses the MLA format. "The Role of Spirituality and Religion in Mental Health" (p. 317) follows the APA format. (You may notice that various styles are illustrated in other selections we have included.)

In some online venues you can link directly to your sources. If your assignment is to write a blog or some other online text, linking helps the reader to look at a note or citation or the direct source quickly and easily. For example, in describing or referencing a scene in a movie, you can link to reviews of the movie, or to a YouTube of the trailer, or to the exact scene that you're discussing. These kinds of links can help your audience get a clearer sense of your point. When formatting such a link in your text, make sure the link opens in a new window so that readers won't lose their place in your original text. In a blog, linking to sources usually is easy and helpful.

A Note on Footnotes (and Endnotes)

Before we discuss these two formats, a few words about footnotes are in order. Before the MLA and the APA developed their rules of style, citations commonly appeared in footnotes. Although today footnotes are not so frequently used to give citations, they still may be useful for another purpose. (The MLA suggests endnotes rather than footnotes, but most readers seem to think that, in fact, footnotes are preferable to endnotes. After all, who wants to keep shifting from a page of text to a page of notes at the rear?) If you want to include some material that may seem intrusive in the body of the paper, you may relegate it to a footnote: For example, you might translate a quotation given in a foreign language, or you might demote from text to footnote a paragraph explaining why you aren't taking account of such-and-such a point. By putting the matter in a footnote you signal to the reader that it is dispensable; it's relevant but not essential, something extra that you are, so to speak, tossing in. Don't make a habit of writing this sort of note, but there are times when it is appropriate to do so.

MLA Format: Citations within the Text

Brief citations within the body of the essay give credit, in a highly abbreviated way, to the sources for material you quote, summarize, or make use of in any other way. These *in-text citations* are made clear by a list of sources, titled Works Cited, appended to the essay. Thus, in your essay you may say something like this:

> Commenting on the relative costs of capital punishment and life imprisonment, Ernest van den Haag says that he doubts "that capital punishment really is more expensive" (33).

The **citation,** the number 33 in parentheses, means that the quoted words come from page 33 of a source (listed in the Works Cited) written by van den Haag. Without a Works Cited, a reader would have no way of knowing that you are quoting from page 33 of an article that appeared in the February 8, 1985, issue of the *National Review.*

Usually, the parenthetic citation appears at the end of a sentence, as in the example just given, but it can appear elsewhere; its position will depend chiefly on your ear, your eye, and the context. You might, for example, write the sentence thus:

> Ernest van den Haag doubts that "capital punishment really is more expensive" than life imprisonment (33), but other writers have presented figures that contradict him.

Five points must be made about these examples:

1. ***Quotation marks*** The closing quotation mark appears after the last word of the quotation, *not* after the parenthetic citation. Since the citation is not part of the quotation, the citation is not included within the quotation marks.

2. ***Omission of words (ellipsis)*** If you are quoting a complete sentence or only a phrase, as in the examples given, you do not need to indicate (by three spaced periods) that you are omitting material before or after the quotation. But if for some reason you want to omit an interior part of the quotation, you must indicate the omission by inserting an *ellipsis,* the three spaced dots. To take a simple example, if you omit the word "really" from van den Haag's phrase, you must alert the reader to the omission:

> Ernest van den Haag doubts that "capital punishment . . . is more
> expensive" than life imprisonment (33).

Suppose you're quoting a sentence but wish to omit material from the end of the sentence. Suppose, also, that the quotation forms the end of your sentence. Write a lead-in phrase, quote what you need from the source, then type the ellipses for the omission, close the quotation, give the parenthetic citation, and finally type a fourth period to indicate the end of your sentence.

Here's an example. Suppose you want to quote the first part of a sentence that runs, "We could insist that the cost of capital punishment be reduced so as to diminish the differences." Your sentence would incorporate the desired extract as follows:

> Van den Haag says, "We could insist that the cost of capital
> punishment be reduced . . ." (33).

3. ***Punctuation with parenthetic citations*** In the preceding examples, the punctuation (a period or a comma in the examples) *follows* the citation. If, however, the quotation ends with a question mark, include the question mark *within* the quotation, since it is part of the quotation, and put a period *after* the citation:

> Van den Haag asks, "Isn't it better — more just and more useful —
> that criminals, if they do not have the certainty of punishment, at
> least run the risk of suffering it?" (33).

But if the question mark is your own and not in the source, put it after the citation, thus:

> What answer can be given to van den Haag's doubt that "capital punishment really is more expensive" (33)?

4. *Two or more works by an author*   If your list of Works Cited includes two or more works by an author, you cannot, in your essay, simply cite a page number because the reader will not know which of the works you are referring to. You must give additional information. You can give it in your lead-in, thus:

> In "New Arguments against Capital Punishment," van den Haag expresses doubt that "capital punishment really is more expensive" than life imprisonment (33).

Or you can give the title, in a shortened form, within the citation:

> Van den Haag expresses doubt that "capital punishment really is more expensive" than life imprisonment ("New Arguments" 33).

5. *Citing even when you do not quote*   Even if you don't quote a source directly, but use its point in a paraphrase or a summary, you will give a citation:

> Van den Haag thinks that life imprisonment costs more than capital punishment (33).

Note that in all of the previous examples, the author's name is given in the text (rather than within the parenthetic citation). But there are several other ways of giving the citation, and we shall look at them now. (We've already seen, in the example given under paragraph 4, that the title and the page number can appear within the citation.)

AUTHOR AND PAGE NUMBER IN PARENTHESES

> It has been argued that life imprisonment is more costly than capital punishment (van den Haag 33).

AUTHOR, TITLE, AND PAGE NUMBER IN PARENTHESES

We have seen that if the Works Cited list includes two or more works by an author, you will have to give the title of the work on which you are drawing, either in your lead-in phrase or within the parenthetic citation. Similarly, if you're citing someone who is listed more than once in the Works Cited, and for some reason you don't mention the name of the author or the work in your lead-in, you must add the information in the citation:

> Doubt has been expressed that capital punishment is as costly as life imprisonment (van den Haag, "New Arguments" 33).

A GOVERNMENT DOCUMENT OR A WORK OF CORPORATE AUTHORSHIP

Treat the issuing body as the author. Thus, you will write something like this:

> The Commission on Food Control, in *Food Resources Today*, concludes that there is no danger (37-38).

A WORK BY TWO AUTHORS

If a work is by *two authors,* give the names of both authors, either in the parenthetic citation (the first example below) or in a lead-in (the second example below):

> There is not a single example of the phenomenon (Christakis and Fowler 293).

> Christakis and Fowler insist there is not a single example of the phenomenon (293).

A WORK BY MORE THAN TWO AUTHORS

If there are *more than two authors,* give the last name of the first author, followed by *et al.* (an abbreviation for *et alii,* Latin for "and others"), thus:

> Gittleman et al. argue (43) that . . .

or

> On average, the cost is even higher (Gittleman et al. 43).

PARENTHETIC CITATION OF AN INDIRECT SOURCE (CITATION OF MATERIAL THAT ITSELF WAS QUOTED OR SUMMARIZED IN YOUR SOURCE)

Suppose you're reading a book by Jones in which she quotes Smith and you wish to use Smith's material. Your citation must refer the reader to Jones—the source you're using—but of course, you cannot attribute the words to Jones. You will have to make it clear that you are quoting Smith, and so after a lead-in phrase like "Smith says," followed by the quotation, you will give a parenthetic citation along these lines:

(qtd. in Jones 324-25).

PARENTHETIC CITATION OF TWO OR MORE WORKS

The costs are simply too high (Smith 301; Jones 28).

Notice that a semicolon, followed by a space, separates the two sources.

A WORK IN MORE THAN ONE VOLUME

This is a bit tricky. If you have used only one volume, in the Works Cited you will specify the volume, and so in the parenthetic in-text citation you won't need to specify the volume. All you need to include in the citation is a page number, as illustrated by most of the examples that we have given.

If you have used more than one volume, the parenthetic citation will have to specify the volume as well as the page, thus:

Jackson points out that fewer than 150 people fit this description (2: 351).

The reference is to page 351 in volume 2 of a work by Jackson.

If, however, you are citing not a page but an entire volume— let's say volume 2—your parenthetic citation will look like this:

Jackson exhaustively studies this problem (vol. 2).

or

Jackson (vol. 2) exhaustively studies this problem.

Notice the following points:

- In citing a volume and page, the volume number, like the page number, is given in arabic (not roman) numerals, even if the original used roman numerals to indicate the volume number.
- The volume number is followed by a colon, then a space, then the page number.
- If you cite a volume number without a page number, as in the last example quoted, the abbreviation is *vol.* Otherwise, do *not* use such abbreviations as *vol.* and *p.* and *pg.*

AN ANONYMOUS WORK

For an anonymous work, give the title in your lead-in, or give it in a shortened form in your parenthetic citation:

A Prisoner's View of Killing includes a poll taken of the inmates on death row (32).

or

A poll is available (*Prisoner's View* 32).

AN INTERVIEW

Probably you won't need a parenthetic citation because you'll say something like

Vivian Berger, in an interview, said . . .

or

According to Vivian Berger, in an interview . . .

and when your reader turns to the Works Cited, he or she will see that Berger is listed, along with the date of the interview. But if you don't mention the source's name in the lead-in, you'll have to give it in the parentheses, thus:

Contrary to popular belief, the death penalty is not reserved for serial killers and depraved murderers (Berger).

AN ELECTRONIC SOURCE

Electronic sources, such as Web sites, are generally not divided into pages. Therefore, the in-text citation for such sources cites only the author's name (or, if a work is anonymous, the title):

According to the Web site for the American Civil Liberties Union . . .

If the source does use pages or breaks down further into paragraphs or screens, insert the appropriate identifier or abbreviation (*p.* or *pp.* for page or pages; *par.* or *pars.* for paragraph or paragraphs; *screen* or *screens*) before the relevant number:

The growth of day care has been called "a crime against poster-ity" by a spokesman for the Institute for the American Family (Terwilliger, screens 1-2).

MLA Format: The List of Works Cited

As the previous pages explain, parenthetic documentation consists of references that become clear when the reader consults the list titled Works Cited at the end of an essay.

The list of Works Cited begins on its own page and continues the pagination of the essay: If the last page of text is 10, then the Works Cited begins on page 11. Type the page number in the upper right corner, a half inch from the top of the sheet and flush with the right margin. Next, type the heading Works Cited (*not* enclosed within quotation marks and not italic), centered, one inch from the top, and then double-space and type the first entry.

Here are some general guidelines.

FORM ON THE PAGE

- Begin each entry flush with the left margin, but if an entry runs to more than one line, indent a half inch for each succeeding line of the entry. This is known as a hanging indent, and most word processing programs can achieve this effect easily.
- Double-space each entry, and double-space between entries.
- Italicize titles of works published independently (which the MLA also calls *containers*; see page 289), such as books, pamphlets, and journals. Enclose within quotation marks a work

not published independently—for instance, an article in a journal or a short story.

- If you are citing a book that includes the title of another book, italicize the main title, but do *not* italicize the title mentioned. Example:

  A Study of Mill's On Liberty

- In the sample entries below, pay attention to the use of commas, colons, and the space after punctuation.

ALPHABETICAL ORDER

- Arrange the list alphabetically by author, with the author's last name first.
- For information about anonymous works, works with more than one author, and two or more works by one author, see below.

Here is more detailed advice.

THE AUTHOR'S NAME

Notice that the last name is given first, but otherwise the name is given as on the title page. Do not substitute initials for names written out on the title page.

If your list includes two or more works by an author, do not repeat the author's name for the second title; instead represent it by three hyphens followed by a period. The sequence of the works is determined by the alphabetical order of the titles. Thus, Smith's book titled *Poverty* would be listed ahead of her book *Welfare*. See the example on page 291, listing two works by Roger Brown.

Anonymous works are listed under the first word of the title or the second word if the first is *A, An,* or *The* or a foreign equivalent. We discuss books by more than one author, government documents, and works of corporate authorship on pages 291–92.

CONTAINERS AND PUBLICATION INFORMATION

When a source being documented comes from a larger source, the larger source is considered a *container*, because it contains the smaller source you are citing. For example, a container might be an anthology, a periodical, a Web site, a television program, a database, or an online archive. The context of a source will help you determine what counts as a container.

In Works Cited lists, the title of a container is listed after the period following the author's name. The container title is generally italicized and followed by a comma, since the information that follows describes the container. (More on this below.) Disregard any unusual typography, such as the use of all capital letters or the use of an ampersand (&) for *and*. Italicize the container title (and subtitle, if applicable; separate them by a colon), but do not italicize the period that concludes this part of the entry.

- Capitalize the first word and the last word of the title.

- Capitalize all nouns, pronouns, verbs, adjectives, adverbs, and subordinating conjunctions (e.g., *although, if, because*).

- Do not capitalize (unless it's the first or last word of the title or the first word of the subtitle) articles (e.g., *a, an, the*), prepositions (e.g., *in, on, toward, under*), coordinating conjunctions (e.g., *and, but, or, for*), or the *to* in infinitives.

When citing a source within a container, the title of the source should be the first element following the author's name. The source title should be set within quotation marks with a period inside the closing quotation mark. The title of the container is then listed, followed by a comma, with additional information—including publication information, dates, and page ranges—about the container set off by commas.

> Boyle, T. C. "Achates McNeil." *After the Plague: Stories*, Viking
> Penguin, 2001, pp. 82-101.

This example cites a story, "Achates McNeil," from an anthology—or container—called *After the Plague: Stories*. The anthology was published by Viking Penguin in 2001, and the story appears on pages 82 through 101.

Note that the full name of the publisher is listed. Always include the full names of publishers, except for terms such as "Inc." and "Company." Retain terms such as "Books" and "Publisher." The only exception is university presses, which are abbreviated thus: *Yale UP, U of Chicago P, State U of New York P*.

SAMPLE ENTRIES   Here are some examples illustrating the points we have covered thus far:

Brown, Roger. *Social Psychology*. Free Press, 1965.

- - - . *Words and Things*. Free Press, 1958.

Haidt, Jonathan. "The Uses of Adversity." *The Happiness Hypothesis: Finding Modern Truth in Ancient Wisdom*, Basic Books, 2006, pp. 135-154.

Hartman, Chester. *The Transformation of San Francisco*. Rowman and Littlefield Publishers, 1984.

Kellerman, Barbara. *The Political Presidency: Practice of Leadership from Kennedy through Reagan*. Oxford UP, 1984.

These examples provide general guidelines for the kind of information you need to include in your Works Cited list. On the following pages, you will find more specific information for listing different kinds of sources.

A BOOK BY MORE THAN ONE AUTHOR

The book is alphabetized under the last name of the first author named on the title page. If there are *two authors*, the name of the second author is given in the normal order, *first name first, after the first author's name*.

Gilbert, Sandra M., and Susan Gubar. *The Madwoman in the Attic: The Woman Writer and the Nineteenth-Century Literary Imagination*. Yale UP, 1979.

Notice, again, that although the first author's name is given *last name first*, the second author's name is given in the normal order, first name first. Notice, too, that a comma is added after the first name of the first author, separating the authors.

If there are *more than two authors*, give the name only of the first, followed by a comma, and then add *et al.* (Latin for "and others").

Zumeta, William, et al. *Financing American Higher Education in the Era of Globalization*. Harvard Education Press, 2012.

GOVERNMENT DOCUMENTS

If the writer is not known, treat the government and the agency as the author. Most federal documents are issued by the Government Printing Office (abbreviated to *GPO*) in Washington, D.C.

United States, Office of Technology Assessment. *Computerized Manufacturing Automation: Employment, Education, and the Workplace.*
GPO, 1984.

WORKS OF CORPORATE AUTHORSHIP

Begin the citation with the corporate author, even if the same
body is also the publisher, as in the first example:

American Psychiatric Association. *Psychiatric Glossary.* American
Psychiatric Association, 1984.

Human Rights Watch. *World Report of 2015: Events of 2014.* Seven
Stories Press, 2015.

A REPRINT (E.G., A PAPERBACK VERSION OF AN OLDER CLOTHBOUND BOOK)

After the title, give the date of original publication (it can usually be found on the reverse of the title page of the reprint you are
using), then a period, and then the publisher and date of the edition you are using. The example indicates that de Mille's book was
originally published in 1951 and that the student is using the 2015
reprint with an introduction by Joan Acocella.

de Mille, Agnes. *Dance to the Piper.* 1951. Introduction by Joan
Acocella, New York Review Books, 2015.

A BOOK IN SEVERAL VOLUMES

If you have used more than one volume, in a citation within
your essay you will (as explained on p. 286) indicate a reference to,
say, page 250 of volume 3 thus: (3: 250).

If, however, you have used only one volume of the set—let's
say volume 3—in your entry in the Works Cited, specify which
volume you used, as in the next example:

Friedel, Frank. *Franklin D. Roosevelt.* Vol. 3, Little Brown, 1973. 4 vols.

With such an entry in the Works Cited, the parenthetic citation
within your essay would be to the page only, not to the volume and
page, because a reader who consults the Works Cited will understand that you used only volume 3. In the Works Cited, you may

specify volume 3 and not give the total number of volumes, or you may add the total number of volumes, as in the preceding example.

BOOK WITH MORE THAN ONE PUBLISHER

If a book is listed as having been published by two or more publishers, separate the publishers with a slash, and include a space before and after the slash.

Hornby, Nick. *About a Boy*. Riverhead / Penguin Putnam, 1998.

A BOOK WITH AN AUTHOR AND AN EDITOR

Kant, Immanuel. *The Philosophy of Kant: Immanuel Kant's Moral and Political Writings*. Edited by Carl J. Friedrich, Modern Library, 1949.

If you are making use of the editor's introduction or other editorial material rather than the author's work, list the book under the name of the editor rather than of the author, as shown below under An Introduction, Foreword, or Afterword.

A REVISED EDITION OF A BOOK

Arendt, Hannah. *Eichmann in Jerusalem*. Revised and enlarged ed., Viking, 1965.

Honour, Hugh, and John Fleming. *The Visual Arts: A History*. 7th ed., Laurence King Publishing, 2013.

A TRANSLATED BOOK

Ullmann, Regina. *The Country Road: Stories*. Translated by Kurt Beals, New Directions Publishing, 2015.

AN INTRODUCTION, FOREWORD, OR AFTERWORD

Dunham, Lena. Foreword. *The Liars' Club*, by Mary Karr, Penguin Classics, 2015, pp. xi-xiii.

Usually, an introduction or comparable material is listed under the name of the author of the book (here Karr) rather than under the name of the writer of the foreword (here Dunham), but if you are referring to the apparatus rather than to the book itself, use the form just given. The words *Introduction, Preface, Foreword,* and *Afterword* are neither enclosed within quotation marks nor italicized.

A BOOK WITH AN EDITOR BUT NO AUTHOR

Let's assume that you have used a book of essays written by various people but collected by an editor (or editors), whose name(s) appears on the collection.

> Horner, Avril, and Anne Rowe, editors. *Living on Paper: Letters from*
> *Iris Murdoch*. Princeton UP, 2016.

A WORK WITHIN A VOLUME OF WORKS BY ONE AUTHOR

The following entry indicates that a short work by Susan Sontag, an essay called "The Aesthetics of Silence," appears in a book by Sontag titled *Styles of Radical Will*. Notice that the inclusive page numbers of the short work are cited, not merely page numbers that you may happen to refer to but the page numbers of the entire piece.

> Sontag, Susan. "The Aesthetics of Silence." *Styles of Radical Will*,
> Farrar, Straus, and Giroux, 1969, pp. 3-34.

A BOOK REVIEW

Here is an example, citing Walton's review of Mitchell's book. Walton's review was published in a journal: *The New York Review of Books*.

> Walton, James. "Noble, Embattled Souls." Review of *The Bone*
> *Clocks and Slade House*, by David Mitchell. *The New York Review*
> *of Books*, 3 Dec. 2015, pp. 55-58.

In this case, Walton's review has a title ("Noble, Embattled Souls") that appears between the period following the reviewer's name and *Review*.

If a review is anonymous, list it under the first word of the title, or under the second word if the first is *A, An,* or *The*. If an anonymous review has no title, begin the entry with *Review of,* and then give the title of the work reviewed; alphabetize the entry under the title of the work reviewed.

AN ARTICLE OR ESSAY IN A COLLECTION

A book may consist of a collection (edited by one or more persons) of new essays by several authors. Here is a reference to one essay in such a book. (The essay by Sayrafiezadeh occupies pages 3 to 29 in a collection edited by Marcus.)

> Sayrafiezadeh, Saïd. "Paranoia." *New American Stories*, edited by
> Ben Marcus, Vintage Books, 2015, pp. 3-29.

MULTIPLE WORKS FROM THE SAME COLLECTION

You may find that you need to cite multiple sources from within a single container, such as several essays from the same edited anthology. In these cases, provide an entry for the entire anthology (the entry for Marcus below) and a shortened entry for each selection. Alphabetize the entries by authors' or editors' last names.

> Eisenberg, Deborah. "Some Other, Better Otto." Marcus, pp. 94-136.

> Marcus, Ben, editor. *New American Stories*. Vintage Books, 2015.

> Sayrafiezadeh, Saïd. "Paranoia." Marcus, pp. 3-29.

BOOK WITH A TITLE IN ITS TITLE

If the book title contains a title that is normally italicized, do not italicize the title within the book title. If the book title contains a title normally placed in quotation marks, retain the quotation marks and italicize the entire title.

> Masur, Louis P. *Runaway Dream:* Born to Run *and Bruce Springsteen's*
> *American Vision*. Bloomsbury, 2009.

> Lethem, Jonathan. *"Lucky Alan" and Other Stories*. Doubleday, 2015.

BOOK IN A SERIES

After the publication information, list the series name as it appears on the title page.

> Denham, A. E., editor. *Plato on Art and Beauty*. Palgrave Macmillan,
> 2012. Philosophers in Depth.

AN ARTICLE IN A REFERENCE WORK (INCLUDING A WIKI)

For a *signed* article, begin with the author's last name. (If the article is signed with initials, check elsewhere in the volume for a list of abbreviations, which will inform you who the initials stand for, and use the following form.) Provide the name of the article, the publication title, edition number (if applicable), the publisher, and the copyright year.

> Robinson, Lisa Clayton. "Harlem Writers Guild." *Africana: The Encyclopedia of the African and African American Experience.* 2nd ed., Oxford UP, 2005.

For an unsigned article, begin with the title of the article:

> "Ball's in Your Court, The." *The American Heritage Dictionary of Idioms.* 2nd ed., Houghton Mifflin Harcourt, 2013.

For an online reference work, such as a wiki, include the author name and article name followed by the name of the Web site, the date of publication or the most recent update, and the URL (without *http://* before it).

> Durante, Amy M. "Finn Mac Cumhail." *Encyclopedia Mythica*, 17 Apr. 2011, www.pantheon.org/articles/f/finn_mac_cumhail.html.

> "House Music." *Wikipedia*, 16 Nov. 2015, en.wikipedia.org/wiki /House_music.

A TELEVISION OR RADIO PROGRAM

Be sure to include the title of the episode or segment (in quotation marks), the title of the show (italicized), the producer or director of the show, the network, and the date of the airing. Other information, such as performers, narrator, and so forth, may be included if pertinent.

> "Fast Times at West Philly High." *Frontline*, produced by Debbie Morton, PBS, 17 July 2012.

> "Federal Role in Support of Autism." *Washington Journal*, narrated by Robb Harleston, C-SPAN, 1 Dec. 2012.

AN ARTICLE IN A SCHOLARLY JOURNAL

The title of the article is enclosed within quotation marks, and the title of the journal is italicized.

Some journals are paginated consecutively; the pagination of the second issue begins where the first issue leaves off. Other journals begin each issue with page 1.

> Matchie, Thomas. "Law versus Love in The Round House." *Midwest Quarterly*, vol. 56, no. 4, Summer 2015, pp. 353-64.

Matchie's article occupies pages 353 to 364 in volume 56, which was published in 2015. When available, give the issue number as well. (If the journal is, for instance, a quarterly, there will be four page *1*'s each year, so the issue number must be given.)

AN ARTICLE IN A WEEKLY, BIWEEKLY, MONTHLY, OR BIMONTHLY PUBLICATION

Do not include volume or issue numbers, even if given.

> Thompson, Mark. "Sending Women to War: The Pentagon Nears a Historic Decision on Equality at the Front Lines." *Time*, 14 Dec. 2015, pp. 53-55.

AN ARTICLE IN A NEWSPAPER

Because a newspaper usually consists of several sections, a section number or a capital letter may precede the page number. The example indicates that an article appears on page 1 of section C.

> Bray, Hiawatha. "As Toys Get Smarter, Privacy Issues Emerge." *The Boston Globe*, 10 Dec. 2015, p. C1.

AN UNSIGNED EDITORIAL

> "The Religious Tyranny Amendment." *New York Times,* 15 Mar. 1998, p. 16. Editorial.

A LETTER TO THE EDITOR

> Lasken, Douglas. *New York Times*. 15 Mar. 1998, p. 16. Letter.

A PUBLISHED OR BROADCAST INTERVIEW

Give the name of the interview subject and the interviewer, followed by the relevant publication or broadcast information, in the following format:

Weddington, Sarah. "Sarah Weddington: Still Arguing for *Roe*." Interview by Michele Kort, *Ms.*, Winter 2013, pp. 32-35.

Tempkin, Ann, and Anne Umland. Interview by Charlie Rose. *Charlie Rose: The Week*, PBS, 9 Oct. 2015.

AN INTERVIEW YOU CONDUCT

Akufo, Dautey. Personal interview, 11 Apr. 2016.

A PERSONAL OR PROFESSIONAL WEB SITE

Include the following elements, separated by periods: the name of the person who created the site (omit if not given, as in Figure 7.4), site title (italicized), name of any sponsoring institution or organization; date of electronic publication or of the latest update (if given; if not, provide the date you accessed the site at the end of the citation); and the URL (without *http://*).

Legal Guide for Bloggers. Electronic Frontier Foundation, www.eff .org/issues/bloggers/legal. Accessed 5 Apr. 2016.

AN ARTICLE IN AN ONLINE PERIODICAL

Give the same information as you would for a print article, plus the URL. (See Figure 7.5.)

Acocella, Joan. "In the Blood: Why Do Vampires Still Thrill?" *New Yorker*, 16 March 2009. www.newyorker.com/magazine/2009/03 /16/in-the-blood.

A POSTING TO AN ONLINE DISCUSSION LIST

The citation includes the author's name, the subject line of the posting, the name of the forum, the host of the forum, the date the material was posted, and the URL.

Figure 7.4 Citing a Blog

① URL

② Sponsor of Web site

③ No author given; start citation with the title.

④ No date of publication given; include date of access in citation.

Robin, Griffith. "Write for the Reading Teacher." *Developing Digital*
    Literacies, NCTE, 23 Oct. 2015, ncte.connectedcommunity.org
    /communities/community-home/digestviewer/viewthread
    ?GroupId=1693&MID=24520&tab=digestviewer&CommunityKey
    =628d2ad6-8277-4042-a376-2b370ddceabf.

A FACEBOOK POST OR COMMENT

Include the name of the Facebook page on which the post appeared, the name of the post (or the post on which the comment appears), the name of the site, the date, and the URL of the post or comment.

Figure 7.5 Citing an Online Magazine

① URL

② Title of periodical

③ Title of article

④ Subtitle of article

⑤ Author

⑥ Publication date. If the article doesn't have a publication date, include the date you accessed it.

> Bedford English. "Stacey Cochran Explores Reflective Writing in the Classroom and as a Writer: http://ow.ly/YkjVB." *Facebook*, 15 Feb. 2016, www.facebook.com/BedfordEnglish /posts/10153415001259607.

AN E-MAIL MESSAGE

Include the name of the sender, the title of the message, the name of the recipient, and the date of the message.

> Thornbrugh, Caitlin. "Coates Lecture." Received by Rita Anderson, 20 Oct. 2015.

A TEXT MESSAGE

Include the name of the sender, the title of the message, the name of the recipient, and the date of the message.

Naqvi, Sahin. Message to the author, 18 Nov. 2015.

TWITTER POST (TWEET)

Include the handle of the poster, the content of the Tweet (enclosed in quotation marks), the name of the site, the date and time of the post, and the URL.

Curiosity Rover. "Can you see me waving? How to spot #Mars in the night
   sky: https://youtu.be/hv8hVvJlcJQ." *Twitter*, 5 Nov. 2015, 11:00
   a.m., twitter.com/marscuriosity/status/672859022911889408.

A DATABASE SOURCE

Treat material obtained from a database like other printed material, but at the end of the entry add (if available) the title of the database (italicized), and a permalink or DOI (digital object identifier) if the source has one. If a source does not, then include a URL (without the protocol, such as *http://*).

Coles, Kimberly Anne. "The Matter of Belief in John Donne's Holy
   Sonnets." *Renaissance Quarterly*, vol. 68, no. 3, Fall 2015,
   pp. 899-931. JSTOR, doi:10.1086/683855.

Macari, Anne Marie. "Lyric Impulse in a Time of Extinction." *American
   Poetry Review*, vol. 44, no. 4, July/Aug. 2015, pp. 11-14.
   General OneFile, go.galegroup.com/.

Caution: Although we have covered many kinds of sources, it's entirely possible that you will come across a source that doesn't fit any of the categories that we have discussed. For greater explanations of these matters, covering the proper way to cite all sorts of troublesome and unbelievable (but real) sources, see the *MLA Handbook,* Eighth Edition (Modern Language Association of America, 2016).

APA Format: Citations within the Text

Your paper will conclude with a separate page headed References, on which you list all of your sources. If the last page of your essay is numbered 10, number the first page of the References 11.

The APA style emphasizes the date of publication; the date appears not only in the list of references at the end of the paper but also in the paper itself, when you give a brief parenthetic citation of a source that you have quoted or summarized or in any other way used. Here is an example:

Statistics are readily available (Smith, 1989, p. 20).

The title of Smith's book or article will be given at the end of your paper in the list titled References. We discuss the form of the material listed in the References after we look at some typical citations within the text of a student's essay.

A SUMMARY OF AN ENTIRE WORK

Smith (1988) holds the same view.

or

Similar views are held widely (Smith, 1988; Jones & Metz, 1990).

A REFERENCE TO A PAGE OR TO PAGES

Smith (1988) argues that "the death penalty is a lottery, and blacks usually are the losers" (p. 17).

A REFERENCE TO AN AUTHOR WHO HAS MORE THAN ONE WORK IN THE LIST OF REFERENCES

If in the References you list two or more works that an author published in the same year, the works are listed in alphabetical order, by the first letter of the title. The first work is labeled *a,* the second *b,* and so on. Here is a reference to the second work that Smith published in 1989:

Florida presents "a fair example" of how the death penalty is administered (Smith, 1989b, p. 18).

APA Format: The List of References

Your brief parenthetic citations are made clear when the reader consults the list you give in the References. Type this list on a separate page, continuing the pagination of your essay.

AN OVERVIEW   Here are some general guidelines.

FORM ON THE PAGE

- Begin each entry flush with the left margin, but if an entry runs to more than one line, indent five spaces for each succeeding line of the entry.
- Double-space each entry, and double-space between entries.

ALPHABETICAL ORDER

- Arrange the list alphabetically by author.
- Give the author's last name first and then the initial of the first name and of the middle name (if any).
- If there is more than one author, name all of the authors up to seven, again inverting the name (last name first) and giving only initials for first and middle names. (But do not invert the editor's name when the entry begins with the name of an author who has written an article in an edited book.) When there are two or more authors, use an ampersand (&) before the name of the last author. Example (here, of an article in the tenth volume of a journal called *Developmental Psychology*):

Drabman, R. S., & Thomas, M. H. (1974). Does media violence increase children's tolerance of real-life aggression? *Developmental Psychology, 10*, 418-421.

- For eight or more authors, list the first six followed by three ellipsis dots and then the last author. If you list more than one work by an author, do so in the order of publication, the earliest first. If two works by an author were published in the same year, give them in alphabetical order by the first letter of the title, disregarding *A, An,* or *The,* and their foreign equivalent. Designate the first work as *a,* the second as *b*. Repeat the author's name at the start of each entry.

Donnerstein, E. (1980a). Aggressive erotica and violence against women. *Journal of Personality and Social Psychology, 39*, 269-277.

Donnerstein, E. (1980b). Pornography and violence against women. *Annals of the New York Academy of Sciences, 347*, 227-288.

Donnerstein, E. (1983). Erotica and human aggression. In R. Green
& E. Donnerstein (Eds.), *Aggression: Theoretical and empirical
reviews* (pp. 87-103). New York, NY: Academic Press.

FORM OF TITLE

- In references to books, capitalize only the first letter of the
  first word of the title (and of the subtitle, if any) and capitalize proper nouns. Italicize the complete title (but not the
  period at the end).

- In references to articles in periodicals or in edited books, capitalize only the first letter of the first word of the article's title
  (and subtitle, if any) and all proper nouns. Do not put the
  title within quotation marks or italicize it. Type a period after
  the title of the article. For the title of the journal and the volume and page numbers, see the next instruction.

- In references to periodicals, give the volume number in arabic numerals, and italicize it. Do *not* use *vol.* before the number, and do not use *p.* or *pg.* before the page numbers.

SAMPLE REFERENCES   Here are some samples to follow.

A BOOK BY ONE AUTHOR

Pavlov, I. P. (1927). *Conditioned reflexes* (G. V. Anrep, Trans.). London,
England: Oxford University Press.

A BOOK BY MORE THAN ONE AUTHOR

Belenky, M. F., Clinchy, B. M., Goldberger, N. R., & Torule, J. M.
(1986). *Women's ways of knowing: The development of self,
voice, and mind.* New York, NY: Basic Books.

A COLLECTION OF ESSAYS

Christ, C. P., & Plaskow, J. (Eds.). (1979). *Woman-spirit rising:
A feminist reader in religion.* New York, NY: Harper & Row.

A WORK IN A COLLECTION OF ESSAYS

Fiorenza, E. (1979). Women in the early Christian movement. In
C. P. Christ & J. Plaskow (Eds.), *Woman-spirit rising: A feminist
reader in religion* (pp. 84-92). New York, NY: Harper & Row.

GOVERNMENT DOCUMENTS

If the writer is not known, treat the government and the agency as the author. Most federal documents are issued by the U.S. Government Printing Office in Washington, D.C. If a document number has been assigned, insert that number in parentheses between the title and the following period.

> United States Congress. Office of Technology Assessment. (1984). *Computerized manufacturing automation: Employment, education, and the workplace.* Washington, DC: U.S. Government Printing Office.

AN ARTICLE IN A JOURNAL WITH CONTINUOUS PAGINATION

> Tversky, A., & Kahneman, D. (1981). The framing of decisions and the psychology of choice. *Science, 211,* 453-458.

AN ARTICLE IN A JOURNAL THAT PAGINATES EACH ISSUE SEPARATELY

> Foot, R. J. (1988-89). Nuclear coercion and the ending of the Korean conflict. *International Security, 13*(4), 92-112.

The reference informs us that the article appeared in issue number 4 of volume 13.

AN ARTICLE FROM A MONTHLY OR WEEKLY MAGAZINE

> Greenwald, J. (1989, February 27). Gimme shelter. *Time, 133,* 50-51.
> Maran, S. P. (1988, April). In our backyard, a star explodes. *Smithsonian, 19,* 46-57.

AN ARTICLE IN A NEWSPAPER

> Connell, R. (1989, February 6). Career concerns at heart of 1980s campus protests. *Los Angeles Times,* pp. 1, 3.

(*Note:* If no author is given, simply begin with the title followed by the date in parentheses.)

✓ A CHECKLIST FOR CRITICAL PAPERS USING SOURCES

Ask yourself the following questions:

☐ Are all borrowed words and ideas credited, including those from Internet sources?

☐ Are all summaries and paraphrases acknowledged as such?

☐ Are quotations and summaries not too long?

☐ Are quotations accurate? Are omissions of words indicated by three spaced periods? Are additions of words enclosed within square brackets?

☐ Are quotations provided with helpful lead-ins?

☐ Is documentation in proper form?

And, of course, you will also ask yourself the questions that you would ask of a paper that did not use sources, such as:

☐ Is the topic sufficiently narrowed?

☐ Is the thesis (to be advanced or refuted) stated early and clearly, perhaps even in the title?

☐ Is the audience kept in mind? Are opposing views stated fairly and as sympathetically as possible? Are controversial terms defined?

☐ Are assumptions likely to be shared by readers? If not, are they argued rather than merely asserted?

☐ Is the focus clear (evaluation, recommendation of policy)?

☐ Is evidence (examples, testimony, statistics) adequate and sound?

☐ Are inferences valid?

☐ Is the organization clear (effective opening, coherent sequence of arguments, unpretentious ending)?

☐ Is all worthy opposition faced?

☐ Is the tone appropriate?

☐ Has the paper been carefully proofread?

☐ Is the title effective?

☐ Is the introduction effective?

☐ Is the structure reader-friendly?

☐ Is the ending effective?

A BOOK REVIEW

Daniels, N. (1984). Understanding physician power [Review of the book *The social transformation of American medicine*]. *Philosophy and Public Affairs, 13,* 347-356.

Daniels is the reviewer, not the author of the book. The book under review is called *The Social Transformation of American Medicine,* but the review, published in volume 13 of *Philosophy and Public Affairs,* had its own title, "Understanding Physician Power."

If the review does not have a title, retain the square brackets, and use the material within as the title. Proceed as in the example just given.

A WEB SITE

American Psychological Association. (1995). Lesbian and gay parenting. Retrieved June 12, 2000, from http://www.apa.org/pi /parent.html

AN ARTICLE IN AN ONLINE PERIODICAL

Carpenter, S. (2000, October). Biology and social environments jointly influence gender development. *Monitor on Psychology 31*(9). Retrieved from http://www.apa.org/monitor/

For a full account of the APA method of dealing with all sorts of unusual citations, see the sixth edition (2010) of the APA manual, *Publication Manual of the American Psychological Association.*

AN ANNOTATED STUDENT RESEARCH PAPER IN MLA FORMAT

The following argument makes good use of sources. Early in the semester the students were asked to choose one topic from a list of ten and to write a documented argument of 750 to 1,250 words (three to five pages of double-spaced typing). The completed paper was due two weeks after the topics were distributed. The assignment, a prelude to working on a research paper of 2,500 to 3,000 words, was in part designed to give students practice in finding and in using sources. Citations are given in the MLA form.

Lesley Timmerman

Professor Jennifer Wilson

English 102

15 August 2016

Title is
focused and
announces
the thesis.

An Argument for Corporate Responsibility

Opponents of corporate social responsibility (CSR)

argue that a company's sole duty is to generate profits.

According to them, by acting for the public good, corpora-

tions are neglecting their primary obligation to make money.

However, as people are becoming more and more conscious

Double-space
between the
title and first
paragraph—
and through-
out the essay.

of corporate impacts on society and the environment, sep-

arating profits from company practices and ethics does not

make sense. Employees want to work for institutions that

share their values, and consumers want to buy products from

companies that are making an impact and improving people's

lives. Furthermore, businesses exist in an interdependent

world where the health of the environment and the well-being

Brief
statement of
one side of the
issue.

of society really do matter. For these reasons, corporations

have to take responsibility for their actions, beyond making

money for shareholders. For their own benefit as well as the

public's, companies must strive to be socially responsible.

Summary of
the opposing
view.

In his article "The Case against Corporate Social

Responsibility," *Wall Street Journal* writer Aneel Karnani

argues that CSR will never be able to solve the world's prob-

lems. Thinking it can, Karnani says, is a dangerous illusion.

He recommends that instead of expecting corporate managers

to act in the public interest, we should rely on philanthropy

Timmerman 2

and government regulation. Karnani maintains that "Managers who sacrifice profit for the common good [. . .] are in effect imposing a tax on their shareholders and arbitrarily deciding how that money should be spent." In other words, according to Karnani, corporations should not be determining what constitutes socially responsible behavior; individual donors and the government should. Certainly, individuals should continue to make charitable gifts, and governments should maintain laws and regulations to protect the public interest. However, Karnani's reasoning for why corporations should be exempt from social responsibility is flawed. With very few exceptions, corporations' socially responsible actions are not arbitrary and do not sacrifice long-term profits.

In fact, corporations have already proven that they can contribute profitably and meaningfully to solving significant global problems by integrating CSR into their standard practices and long-term visions. Rather than focusing on shareholders' short-term profits, many companies have begun measuring their success by "profit, planet and people" — what is known as the "triple bottom line." Businesses operating under this principle consider their environmental and social impacts, as well as their financial impacts, and make responsible and compassionate decisions. For example, such businesses use resources efficiently, create healthy products, choose suppliers who share their ethics, and improve economic opportunities for people in the communities they serve. By doing so, companies often save money. They also

Lead-in to quotation.

1" margin on each side and at bottom.

Essayist's response to the quotation.

Author concisely states her position.

Transitions ("For example," "also") alert readers to where the writer is taking them.

contribute to the sustainability of life on earth and ensure the sustainability of their own businesses. In their book *The Triple Bottom Line: How Today's Best-Run Companies Are Achieving Economic, Social, and Environmental Success*, coauthors Savitz and Weber demonstrate that corporations need to become sustainable, in all ways. They argue that "the only way to succeed in today's interdependent world is to embrace sustainability" (xi). The authors go on to show that, for the vast majority of companies, a broad commitment to sustainability enhances profitability (Savitz and Weber 39).

For example, PepsiCo has been able to meet the financial expectations of its shareholders while demonstrating its commitment to the triple bottom line. In addition to donating over $16 million to help victims of natural disasters, Pepsi has woven concerns for people and for the planet into its company practices and culture (Bejou 4). For instance, because of a recent water shortage in an area of India where Pepsi runs a plant, the company began a project to build community wells (Savitz and Weber 160). Though Pepsi did not cause the water shortage nor was its manufacturing threatened by it, "Pepsi realizes that the well-being of the community is part of the company's responsibility" (Savitz and Weber 161). Ultimately, Pepsi chose to look beyond the goal of maximizing short-term profits. By doing so, the company improved its relationship with this Indian community, improved people's daily lives and opportunities, and improved its own reputation. In other words, Pepsi

Timmerman 4

embraced CSR and ensured a more sustainable future for everyone involved.

Another example of a wide-reaching company that is working toward greater sustainability on all fronts is Walmart. The corporation has issued a CSR policy that includes three ambitious goals: "to be fully supplied by renewable energy, to create zero waste and to sell products that sustain people and the environment" ("From Fringe to Mainstream"). As Dr. Doug Guthrie, dean of George Washington University's School of Business, noted in a recent lecture, if a company as powerful as Walmart were to succeed in these goals, the impact would be huge. To illustrate Walmart's potential influence, Dr. Guthrie pointed out that the corporation's exports from China to the United States are equal to Mexico's total exports to the United States. In committing to CSR, the company's leaders are acknowledging how much their power depends on the earth's natural resources, as well as the communities who produce, distribute, sell, and purchase Walmart's products. The company is also well aware that achieving its goals will "ultimately save the company a great deal of money" ("From Fringe to Mainstream"). For good reason, Walmart, like other companies around the world, is choosing to act in *everyone's* best interest.

Recent research on employees' and consumers' social consciousness offers companies further reason to take corporate responsibility seriously. For example, studies show that workers care about making a difference (Meister). In many

Author now introduces statistical evidence that, if introduced earlier, might have turned the reader off.

cases, workers would even take a pay cut to work for a more responsible, sustainable company. In fact, 45% of workers said they would take a 15% reduction in pay "for a job that makes a social or environmental impact" (Meister). Even more said they would take a 15% cut in pay to work for a company with values that match their own (Meister). The numbers are most significant among Millennials (those born between, approximately, 1980 and the early 2000s). Fully 80% of Millennials said they "wanted to work for a company that cares about how it impacts and contributes to society," and over half said they would not work for an "irresponsible company" (Meister). Given this more socially conscious generation, companies are going to find it harder and harder to ignore CSR. To recruit and retain employees, employers will need to earn the admiration, respect, and loyalty of their workers by becoming "good corporate citizen[s]" (qtd. in "From Fringe to Mainstream").

Similarly, studies clearly show that CSR matters to today's consumers. According to an independent report, 80% of Americans say they would switch brands to support a social cause (Cone Communications 6). Fully 88% say they approve of companies' using social or environmental issues in their marketing (Cone Communications 5). And 83% say they "wish more of the products, services and retailers would support causes" (Cone Communications 5). Other independent surveys corroborate these results, confirming that today's customers, especially Millennials, care about more than just price ("From Fringe to Mainstream"). Furthermore, plenty of companies

Timmerman 6

have seen what happens when they assume that consumers do not care about CSR. For example, in 1997, when Nike customers discovered that their shoes were manufactured by child laborers in Indonesia, the company took a huge financial hit (Guthrie). Today, Information Age customers are even more likely to educate themselves about companies' labor practices and environmental records. Smart corporations will listen to consumer preferences, provide transparency, and commit to integrating CSR into their long-term business plans.

> Author argues that it is in the *companies'* interest to be socially responsible.

    In this increasingly interdependent world, the case against CSR is becoming more and more difficult to defend. Exempting corporations and relying on government to be the world's conscience does not make good social, environmental, or economic sense. Contributors to a recent article in the online journal *Knowledge@Wharton,* published by the Wharton School of Business, agree. Professor Eric Orts maintains that "it is an outmoded view to say that one must rely only on the government and regulation to police business responsibilities. What we need is re-conception of what the purpose of business is" (qtd. in "From Fringe to Mainstream"). The question is, what should the purpose of a business be in today's world? Professor of Business Administration David Bejou of Elizabeth City State University has a thoughtful and sensible answer to that question. He writes,

> Author's lead-in to the quotation guides the reader's response to the quotation.

    . . . it is clear that the sole purpose of a business
    is not merely that of generating profits for its

owners. Instead, because compassion provides the
necessary equilibrium between a company's purpose and the needs of its communities, it should
be the new philosophy of business. (Bejou 1)

As Bejou implies, the days of allowing corporations to act in
their own financial self-interest with little or no regard for
their effects on others are over. None of us can afford such a
narrow view of business. The world is far too interconnected.
A seemingly small corporate decision — to buy coffee beans
directly from local growers or to install solar panels — can
affect the lives and livelihoods of many people and determine the environmental health of whole regions. A business,
just like a government or an individual, therefore has an
ethical responsibility to act with compassion for the public
good.

Upbeat
ending.
   Fortunately, corporations have many incentives to
act responsibly. Customer loyalty, employee satisfaction,
overall cost-saving, and long-term viability are just some of
the advantages businesses can expect to gain by embracing
comprehensive CSR policies. Meanwhile, companies have very
little to lose by embracing a socially conscious view. These
days, compassion is profitable. Corporations would be wise
to recognize the enormous power, opportunity, and responsibility they have to effect positive change.

Timmerman 8

Works Cited

Bejou, David. "Compassion as the New Philosophy of Business." *Journal of Relationship Marketing*, vol. 10, no. 1, Apr. 2011, pp. 1-6. *Taylor and Francis*, doi:10 .1080/15332667.2011.550098.

Cone Communications. 2010 *Cone Cause Evolution Study*. Cone, 2010, www.conecomm.com/research -blog/2010-cause-evolution-study.

"From Fringe to Mainstream: Companies Integrate CSR Initiatives into Everyday Business." *Knowledge@ Wharton*, 23 May 2012, knowledge.wharton.upenn .edu/article/from-fringe-to-mainstream-companies -integrate-csr-initiatives-into-everyday-business/.

Guthrie, Doug. "Corporate Social Responsibility: A State Department Approach." *Promoting a Comprehensive Approach to Corporate Social Responsibility (CSR)*, George P. Shultz National Foreign Affairs Training Center, 22 May 2012. *YouTube*, 23 Aug. 2013, www.youtube.com/watch?v=99cJMe6wERc.

Karnani, Aneel. "The Case against Corporate Social Responsibility." *Wall Street Journal*, 14 June 2012, www.wsj.com/articles/SB100014240527487033380004 575230112664504890.

Meister, Jeanne. "Corporate Social Responsibility: A Lever for Employee Attraction & Engagement." *Forbes*, 7 June 2012, www.forbes.com/sites/jeannemeister/2012/06/07 /corporate-social-responsibility-a-lever-for-employee -attraction-engagement/#6125425a7511.

Savitz, Andrew W., with Karl Weber. *The Triple Bottom Line: How Today's Best-Run Companies Are Achieving Economic, Social, and Environmental Success*, Jossey-Bass, 2006.

Alphabetical by author's last name.

Hanging indent ½".

An article on a blog without a known author.

A clip from YouTube.

AN ANNOTATED STUDENT RESEARCH PAPER IN APA FORMAT

The following paper is an example of a student paper that uses APA format.

Running Head: RELIGION IN MENTAL HEALTH   1

The Role of Spirituality and Religion

in Mental Health

Laura DeVeau

English 102

Professor Gardner

April 12, 2016

The APA-style cover page gives title, author, and course information.

Short form of
title and page
number as
running head.

The Role of Spirituality and Religion

in Mental Health

It has been called "a vestige of the childhood of mankind," "the feeling of something true, total and absolute," "an

Citation of
multiple
works from
references.

otherworldly answer as regards the meaning of life" (Jones,
1991, p. 1; Amaro, 1998; Kristeva, 1987, p. 27). It has been
compared to medicine, described as a psychological cure for
mental illness, and also referred to as the cause of a dangerous
fanaticism. With so many differing opinions on the impact of
religion in people's lives, where would one begin a search for the
truth? Who has the answer: Christians, humanists, objectivists,
atheists, psychoanalysts, Buddhists, philosophers, cults? This
was my dilemma at the advent of my research into how religion
and spirituality affect the mental health of society as a whole.

In this paper, I explore the claims, widely accepted
by professionals in the field of psychology, that religious and
spiritual practices have a negative impact on mental health.
In addition, though, I cannot help but reflect on how this

Acknowledg-
ment of
opposing
viewpoints.

exploration has changed my beliefs as well. Religion is such
a personal experience that one cannot be dispassionate in
reporting it. One can, however, subject the evidence provided
by those who have studied the issue to critical scrutiny.
Having done so, I find myself in disagreement with those
who claim religious feelings are incompatible with sound
mental health. There is a nearly limitless number of beliefs
regarding spirituality. Some are organized and involve rituals
like mass or worship. Many are centered around the existence

RELIGION IN MENTAL HEALTH   3

of a higher being, while others focus on the self. I have
attempted to uncover the perfect set of values that lead to a
better lifestyle, but my research has pointed me in an entirely
different direction, where no single belief seems to be adequate but where spiritual belief in general should be valued
more highly than it is currently in mental health circles.

Thesis explicitly introduced.

I grew up in a moderately devout Catholic family.
Like many young people raised in a household where one
religion is practiced by both parents, it never occurred to me
to question those beliefs. I went through a spiritual cycle,
which I believe much of Western society also experiences. I
attended religious services because I had to. I possessed a
blind, unquestioning acceptance of what I was being taught
because the adults I trusted said it was so. Like many adoles-
cents and young adults, though, I stopped going to church
when I was old enough to decide because I thought I had
better things to do. At this stage, we reach a point when we
begin searching for a meaning to our existence. For some,
this search is brought on by a major crisis or a feeling of
emptiness in their daily lives, while for others it is simply a
part of growing up. This is where we begin to make personal
choices, but with the barrage of options, where do we turn?

Beginning with the holistic health movement in the
eighties, there has been a mass shift from traditional religions
to less structured spiritual practices such as meditation, yoga,
the Cabala, and mysticism (Beyerman, 1989). They venture
beyond the realm of conventional dogmatism and into the

Author and date cited for summary or paraphrase.

RELIGION IN MENTAL HEALTH   4

new wave of spirituality. Many of these practices are based on
the notion that health of the mind and spirit equals health of
the body. Associated with this movement is a proliferation of
retreats offering a chance to get in touch with the beauty and
silence of nature and seminars where we can take "a break
from our everyday environment where our brains are bustling
and our bodies are exhausting themselves" ("Psychological
benefits," 1999). A major concept of the spiritual new wave
is that it focuses inward toward the individual psyche, rather
than outward toward another being like a god. Practitioners
do not deny the existence of this being, but they believe
that to fully love another, we must first understand ourselves.
Many find this a preferable alternative to religions where the
individual is seen as a walking dispenser of sin who is very
fortunate to have a forgiving creator. It is also a relief from
the scare tactics like damnation used by traditional religions
to make people behave. Many, therefore, praise the potential
psychological benefits of such spirituality.

    While I believe strongly in the benefits of the new
wave, I am not willing to do away with structured religion, for
I find that it also has its benefits. Without the existence of
churches and temples, it would be harder to expose the public
to values beneficial to mental stability. It is much more difficult
to hand a child a copy of the Cabala and say "Read this, and
then get back to me on it" than it is to bring a child to a service where the ideas are represented with concrete examples.
My religious upbringing presented me with a set of useful

Anonymous source cited by title and date.

Clear transition refers to previous paragraph.

RELIGION IN MENTAL HEALTH   5

morals and values, and it does the same for millions of others
who are brought up in this manner. Many people, including
some followers of the new wave, are bitter toward Christianity
because of events in history like the Crusades, the Inquisition,
the Salem witch trials, and countless other horrific acts supposedly committed in the name of God. But these events were
based not on biblical teachings but on pure human greed and
lust for power. We should not reject the benevolent possibilities of organized religion on the basis of historical atrocities
any more than we should abandon public education because a
few teachers are known to mistreat children.

Another factor contributing to the reluctance concerning religion is the existence of cults that seduce people into
following their extreme teachings. The victims are often at
vulnerable times in their lives, and the leaders are usually very
charming, charismatic, and sometimes also psychotic or otherwise mentally unstable. Many argue that if we acknowledge
these groups as dangerous cults, then we must do the same
for traditional religions such as Christianity and Islam, which
are likewise founded on the teachings of charismatic leaders.
Again, though, critics are too quick to conflate all religious
and spiritual practice; we must distinguish between those who
pray and attend services and those who commit group suicide
because they think that aliens are coming to take over the
world. Cults have provided many psychologists, who are eager
to discount religion as a factor in improving mental health, with
an easy target. Ellis (1993), the founder of rational-emotive

When the
author's
name appears
in text, only
the date
is cited in
parentheses.

therapy, cites many extreme examples of religious commitment, such as cults and antiabortion killings, to show that commitment is hazardous to one's sanity. Anomalies like these should not be used to speak of religion as a whole, though. Religion is clearly the least of these people's mental problems.

Besides Ellis, there are many others in the field of psychology who do not recognize religion as a potential aid for improving the condition of the psyche. Actually, fewer than 45% of the members of the American Psychiatric Association even believe in God. The general American public has more than twice that percentage of religious devotees (Larson, 1998). Going back to the days of Freud, many psychologists have held atheist views. The father of psychoanalysis himself called religion a "universal obsessional neurosis." Psychologists have long rejected research that demonstrates the benefits of spirituality by saying that this research is biased. They claim that such studies are out to prove that religion helps because the researchers are religious people who need to justify their beliefs.

While this may be true in some instances, there is also some quite empirical research available to support the claims of those who promote religion and spirituality. The *Journal for the Scientific Study of Religion* has conducted many studies examining the effects of religion on individuals and groups. In one example, the relationship between religious coping methods and positive recovery after major stressful events was observed. The results indicated not only that spirituality was not harmful to the mind but that "the

RELIGION IN MENTAL HEALTH   7

positive religious coping pattern was tied to benevolent outcomes, including fewer symptoms of psychological distress,
[and] reports of psychological and spiritual growth as a result
of the stressor" (Pargament, Smith, Koening, and Perez,
1998, p. 721). Clearly, the benefits of piety can, in fact, be
examined empirically, and in some cases the results point to
a positive correlation between religion and mental health.

     But let us get away from statistics and studies. If
religion is both useless and dangerous, as so many psychologists claim, we must ask why it has remained so vital a part
of humanity for so long. Even if it can be reduced to a mere
coping method that humans use to justify their existence and
explain incomprehensible events, is it futile? I would suggest
that this alone represents a clear benefit to society. Should
religion, if it cannot be proven as "true," be eliminated and
life be based on scientific fact alone? Surely many would find
this a pointless existence. With all the conflicting knowledge I
have gained about spirituality during my personal journey and
my research, one idea is clear. It is not the depth of devotion,
the time of life when one turns to religion, or even the particular combination of beliefs one chooses to adopt that will
improve the quality of life. There is no right or wrong answer
when it comes to self-fulfillment. It is whatever works for the
individual, even if that means holding no religious or spiritual
beliefs at all. But clearly there *are* benefits to be gained, at
least for some individuals, and mental health professionals
need to begin acknowledging this fact in their daily practice.

Marginal notes:

Bracketed word in quotation not in original source.

Author, date, and page number are cited for a direct quotation.

Conclusion restates and strengthens thesis.

RELIGION IN MENTAL HEALTH   8

References
begin on a
new page.

|

An online
source.

|

A book.

|

An article or
a chapter in a
book.

|

An article in a
journal.

|

Anonymous
source
alphabetized
by title.

|

References

Amaro, J. (1998). Psychology, psychoanalysis and religious

faith. *Nielsen's psychology of religion pages*. Retrieved

March 17, 2016, from http://www.psywww.com

/psyrelig/amaro.html

Beyerman A. K. (1989). *The holistic health movement*.

Tuscaloosa, AL: Alabama University Press.

Ellis, A. (1993). Dogmatic devotion doesn't help, it hurts.

In B. Slife (Ed.), *Taking sides: Clashing views on

controversial psychological issues* (pp. 297-301).

New York, NY: Scribner.

Jones, J. W. (1991). *Contemporary psychoanalysis and religion:

Transference and transcendence*. New Haven, CT: Yale

University Press.

Kristeva, J. (1987). *In the beginning was love: Psychoanalysis

and faith*. New York, NY: Columbia University Press.

Larson, D. (1998). Does religious commitment improve mental

health? In B. Slife (Ed.), *Taking sides: Clashing views

on controversial psychological issues* (pp. 292-296).

New York, NY: Scribner.

Pargament, K. I., Smith, B. W., Koening, H. G., & Perez, L.

(1998). Patterns of positive and negative religious

coping with major life stressors. *Journal for the

Scientific Study of Religion, 37*, 710-724.

"Psychological benefits." (1999). *Walking the labyrinth*.

Retrieved April 3, 2016, from http://www.labyrinthway

.com/html/benefits.html

PART TWO

FURTHER VIEWS
on ARGUMENT

8

A Philosopher's View: The Toulmin Model

All my ideas hold together, but I cannot elaborate them all at once.

— JEAN-JACQUES ROUSSEAU

Clarity has been said to be not enough. But perhaps it will be time to go into that when we are within measurable distance of achieving clarity on some matter.

— J. L. AUSTIN

[Philosophy is] a peculiarly stubborn effort to think clearly.

— WILLIAM JAMES

Philosophy is like trying to open a safe with a combination lock: Each little adjustment of the dials seems to achieve nothing, only when everything is in place does the door open.

—LUDWIG WITTGENSTEIN

In Chapter 3, we explained the contrast between making *deductive* and *inductive* arguments, the two main methods people use to reason. Either:

- we make explicit something concealed in what we already accept (**deduction**), or
- we use what we have observed as a basis for asserting or proposing something new (**induction**).

These two types of reasoning share some structural features, as we also noticed. Both deductive and inductive reasoning seek to establish a **thesis** (or conclusion) by offering **reasons** for accepting the conclusion. Thus, every argument contains both a thesis and one or more supportive reasons.

After a little scrutiny, we can in fact point to several features shared by all arguments, whether deductive or inductive, good or bad. We use the vocabulary popularized by Stephen Toulmin, Richard Rieke, and Allan Janik in their book *An Introduction to Reasoning* (1979; second edition 1984) to explore the various elements of argument. Once these elements are understood, it is possible to analyze an argument using their approach and their vocabulary in what has come to be known as "The Toulmin Method."

THE CLAIM

Every argument has a purpose, goal, or aim—namely, to establish a **claim** (*conclusion* or *thesis*). Suppose you are arguing in favor of equal rights for women. You might state your thesis or claim as follows:

> Men and women ought to have equal rights.

A more precise formulation of the claim might be this:

> Men and women ought to have equal legal rights.

A still more precise formulation might be this:

> Equal legal rights for men and women ought to be protected by our Constitution.

The third version of this claim states what the controversy in the 1970s over the Equal Rights Amendment was all about. (Both houses of Congress passed it in 1972, but the number of state legislatures that needed to ratify it before the Amendment could be added to the Constitution failed to do so before Congress's mandated deadline of June 30, 1982.)

In other words, the *claim* being made in an argument is the whole point of making the argument in the first place. Consequently, when you read or analyze someone else's argument, the first questions you should ask are these:

- What is the argument intended to prove or establish?
- *What claim is it making?*
- Has this claim been clearly and precisely formulated, so that it unambiguously asserts what its advocate wants it to assert?

GROUNDS

Once we have the argument's purpose or point clearly in mind and thus know what the arguer is aiming to establish, then we can look for the evidence, reasons, support—in short, for the **grounds**—on which that claim is based. In a *deductive* argument, these grounds are the premises from which the claim is deduced; in an *inductive* argument, the grounds are the evidence—which could be based on a sample, an observation, or an experiment—that makes the claim plausible or probable.

Not every kind of claim can be supported by every kind of ground, and, conversely, not every kind of ground gives equally good support for every kind of claim. Suppose, for instance, that I claim half the students in the classroom are women. I can establish the *grounds* for this claim in any of several ways. For example:

1. I can count all the women and all the men. Suppose the total equals fifty. If the number of women is twenty-five and the number of men is twenty-five, I have vindicated my claim.
2. I can count a sample of ten students—perhaps the first ten to walk into the classroom—and find that in the sample five of the students are women. I thus have inductive—plausible but not conclusive—grounds for my claim.
3. I can point out that the students in the college divide equally into men and women and then claim that this class is a representative sample of the whole college.

Clearly, ground 1 is stronger than ground 2, and 2 is much stronger than 3.

Up to this point, we have merely restated points about premises and conclusions that were covered in Chapter 3. We want now to consider four additional features of arguments.

WARRANTS

Once we have the claim or the point of an argument fixed in mind and have isolated the evidence or reasons offered in its support, the next question to ask is this:

Exactly how do the reasons offered in support of the conclusion work? In other words, what kind of guarantee—**warrant**—is provided to demonstrate that the reasons proffered actually do support the claim or lead to the conclusion? (A *warrant* in this context is like the *warranty* you get when you buy something.)

In ordinary and straightforward *deductive* arguments, warrants take different forms. In the simplest cases, we can point to the way in which the *meanings* of the key terms are really equivalent. Thus, if John is taller than Bill, then Bill must be shorter than John. We know this because we know what "is shorter than" and "is taller than" mean. If *A* is taller than *B*, it must be the case that *B* is shorter than *A*; those are the meanings of the phrases being used here. Of course, everyone involved does have to know the language well enough to understand the relationship between "is taller than" and "is shorter than." The *warrant* in this case is the common understanding of what those two phrases mean.

In other cases, we may need to be more resourceful. A reliable tactic is to think up a simple *parallel argument*, an argument exactly parallel in form and structure to the argument we are trying to defend. If the two arguments really do have the same form and structure, and we are ready to accept the simpler one, then we can point out that the more complex argument must be accepted—because the two arguments have exactly the same structure. For example, if we want to argue that it is reasonable for FedEx to charge more for its delivery services than the U.S. Postal Service (USPS) does, we could point out that since it seems entirely reasonable to pay higher costs for special services from the USPS such as overnight delivery promised by a certain time (depending on factors such as location), then it is reasonable to pay even higher fees for similar overnight delivery by FedEx because that service includes sending someone to pick up what you want delivered.

In simple *inductive* arguments, we are likely to point to the way in which observations or sets of data constitute a *representative sample* of a whole population, even if not every member of the sample is strictly in evidence. For instance, when scattered information is plotted on a graph, the trend line does not have to touch each (or even any) of the data points as long as they are scattered above and below the line in roughly equal numbers in pairs that are roughly equidistant from the trend line. We can defend this projection on the grounds that it takes all of the points into account in the least complicated way. In such a case, the warrant is this combination of *inclusiveness* and *simplicity*.

Establishing the warrants for our reasoning—that is, explaining why our grounds really do support our claims—can quickly become a highly technical and exacting procedure that goes far beyond the aims of this book. Even so, developing a "feel" for why reasons or grounds are or are not relevant to what they are alleged to support is important. "That's just my view" is *not* a convincing warrant for any argument. Even without formal training, however, one can sense that something is wrong with many bad arguments. Here is one example: British professor C. E. M. Joad found himself standing on a station platform, annoyed because he had just missed his train. Then another train, making an unscheduled stop, pulled up to the platform in front of him. Joad decided to jump aboard, only to hear the conductor say, "I'm afraid you'll have to get off, Sir. This train doesn't stop here." "In that case," replied the professor, "don't worry. I'm not on it."

BACKING

A really solid argument may need even further support, especially if what we're arguing is complicated. *Warrants*, remember, explain the way our *grounds* support our *claims*. The next task, however, is to be able to show that we can back up what we have claimed by showing that the reasons we have given for a claim are good reasons. To establish that kind of further support for an argument is to provide **backing.**

What is appropriate backing for one kind of argument might be quite inappropriate for another kind of argument. For example, the kinds of reasons relevant to support an amendment to the Constitution are completely different from the kinds appropriate to settle the question of what caused the defeat of Napoleon's invasion of Russia in 1812. Arguments for the amendment might be rooted in an appeal to fairness, whereas arguments about the military defeat might be rooted in letters and other documents in French and Russian archives. The *canons* (established conventions) of good argument in two such dramatically different cases have to do with the means that scholarly communities in law and history, respectively, have developed over the years to support, defend, challenge, and undermine a given kind of argument.

Another way of stating this point is to recognize that once you have given reasons for a claim, you are then likely to be challenged to explain why your reasons are good reasons—why, that is, anyone should believe your reasons rather than regard them skeptically. They have to be the right kinds of reasons, given the field you are arguing about. Why (to give a simple example) should we accept the testimony of Dr. X when Dr. Y, equally renowned, supports the opposite side? What more do we need to know before "expert testimony" is appropriately invoked? For a different kind of case: When and why is it safe to rest a prediction on a small though admittedly carefully selected sample? And still another: Why is it legitimate to argue that (1) if I dream I am the king of France, then I must exist, whereas it is illegitimate to argue that (2) if I dream I am the king of France, then the king of France must exist?

To answer challenges of these sorts is to back up one's reasons, to give them legitimate *backing*. No argument is any better than its backing.

MODAL QUALIFIERS

As we have seen, all arguments are made up of assertions or propositions that can be sorted into four categories:

- the *claim* (conclusion, thesis to be established)
- the *grounds* (explicit reasons advanced)
- the *warrant* (guarantee, evidence, or principle that legitimates the ground by connecting it to the claim)
- the *backing* (relevant support, implicit assumptions)

All of the kinds of propositions that emerge when we assert something in an argument have what philosophers call a **modality**. This means that propositions generally indicate—explicitly or tacitly—the *character* and *scope* of what is believed to be their likely truth.

Character has to do with the nature of the claim being made, the extent of an argument's presumed reach. Both making and evaluating arguments require being clear about whether they are *necessary, probable, plausible,* or *possible.* Consider, for example, a claim that it is to the advantage of a college to have a racially diverse student body. Is that *necessarily* or only *probably* true? What about an argument that a runner who easily wins a 100-meter race should also be able to win at 200 meters? Is this *plausible*—or only *possible*? Indicating the *character* with which an assertion is advanced is crucial to any argument for or against it. Furthermore, if there is more than one reason for making a claim, and all of those reasons are *good*, it is still possible that one of those good reasons may be *better* than the others. If so, the better reason should be stressed.

Indicating the *scope* of an assertion is equally crucial to how an argument plays out. *Scope* entails such considerations as whether the proposition is thought to be true *always* or just *sometimes*. Further, is the claim being made supposed to apply in *all* instances or just in *some*? Assertions are usually clearer, as well as more likely to be true, if they are explicitly *quantified* and *qualified*. Suppose, for example, that you are arguing against smoking, and the ground for your claim is this:

Heavy smokers cut short their life span.

In this case, there are three obvious alternative quantifications to choose among: *All* smokers cut short their life span, *most* do, or only *some* do. Until the assertion is quantified in one of these ways, we really don't know what is being asserted—and so we don't know what degree and kind of evidence or counterevidence is relevant. Other quantifiers include *few, rarely, often, sometimes, perhaps, usually, more or less, regularly, occasionally*.

Scope also has to do with the fact that empirical generalizations are typically *contingent* on various factors. Indicating such contingencies clearly is an important way to protect a generalization against obvious counterexamples. Thus, consider this empirical generalization:

Students do best on final examinations if they study hard for them.

Are we really to believe that students who cram ("study hard" in that concentrated sense) for an exam will do better than those who do the work diligently throughout the whole course ("study hard" in that broader sense) and therefore do not need to cram for the final? Probably not; what is really meant is that *all other things being equal* (in Latin, *ceteris paribus*), concentrated study just before an exam will yield good results. Alluding in this way to the contingencies—the things that might derail the argument—shows that the writer is aware of possible exceptions and is conceding them from the start.

In sum, sensitivity to both character and (especially) scope—paying attention to the role played by quantifiers, qualifiers, and contingencies and making sure you use appropriate ones for each of your assertions—will strengthen your arguments enormously. Not least of the benefits is that you will reduce the peculiar vulnerabilities of an argument that is undermined by exaggeration and other misguided generalizations.

REBUTTALS

Very few arguments of any interest are beyond dispute, conclusively knockdown affairs. Only very rarely is the claim of an argument so rigidly tied to its grounds, warrants, and backing—and with its quantifiers and qualifiers argued in so precise a manner—that it proves its conclusion beyond any possibility of doubt. On the contrary, most arguments have many counterarguments, and sometimes one of these counterarguments is more convincing than the original argument.

Suppose someone has taken a sample that appears to be random: An interviewer on your campus accosts the first ten students she encounters, and seven of them are fraternity or sorority members. She is now ready to argue that seven-tenths of enrolled students belong to Greek organizations.

You believe, however, that the Greeks are in the minority; you point out that she happens to have conducted her interview around the corner from the Panhellenic Society's office just off Sorority Row. Her random sample is anything but random. The ball is now back in her court as you await her response to your rebuttal.

As this example illustrates, it is safe to say that we do not understand our own arguments very well until we have tried to get a grip on the places in which they are vulnerable to criticism, counterattack, or refutation. We have already, in Chapter 3, quoted Edmund Burke—but the passage is worth repeating: "He that wrestles with us strengthens our nerves, and sharpens our skill. Our antagonist is our helper."

To be sure, in everyday conversation we may not enjoy being in the company of people who interrupt to ask what are our grounds, warrants, backing, and so forth. The poet T. S. Eliot amusingly characterized himself as such a person:

How Unpleasant to Meet Mr. Eliot!

How unpleasant to meet Mr. Eliot!
With his features of clerical cut.
And his brow so grim
And his mouth so prim
And his conversation, so nicely
Restricted to What Precisely

And If and Perhaps and But . . .
How unpleasant to meet Mr. Eliot!
(Whether his mouth be open or
shut.)

Still, if we wish to make serious
progress in thinking and arguing
about significant issues, cultivating
alertness to possible weak spots in
arguments—our own arguments as
well as those of others—and incorporating thoughtful responses to
anticipated criticisms will always be
helpful.

Would you want to argue with
Mr. Eliot?

THINKING CRITICALLY CONSTRUCTING A TOULMIN ARGUMENT

Choose a topic or issue that interests you. In the spaces provided,
supply a sentence or two for each step of a Toulmin argument about
your topic.

Step of Toulmin Argument	Question this Step Addresses	Your Sentence(s)
Claim	*What is your argument?*	
Grounds	*What is your evidence?*	
Warrant	*What reasoning connects your evidence to your argument?*	
Backing	*Why should the reader agree with your grounds?*	
Rebuttal	*What are the objections to this argument?*	
Qualifier	*What are the limits of your argument?*	

PUTTING THE TOULMIN METHOD TO WORK:

Responding to an Argument

Let's take a look at another argument—it happens to be on why buying directly from farmers near you won't save the planet—and see how the Toulmin method can be applied. The checklist on page 338 can help you focus your thoughts as you read.

James E. McWilliams

James E. McWilliams (b. 1968), the author of Just Food, *is an associate professor of history at Texas State University. This piece first appeared in* Forbes Magazine *on August 3, 2009.*

The Locavore Myth: Why Buying from Nearby Farmers Won't Save the Planet

Buy local, shrink the distance food travels, save the planet. The locavore movement has captured a lot of fans. To their credit, they are highlighting the problems with industrialized food. But a lot of them are making a big mistake. By focusing on transportation, they overlook other energy-hogging factors in food production.

Take lamb. A 2006 academic study (funded by the New Zealand government) discovered that it made more environmental sense for a Londoner to buy lamb shipped from New Zealand than to buy lamb raised in the U.K. This finding is counterintuitive—if you're only counting food miles. But New Zealand lamb is raised on pastures with a small carbon footprint, whereas most English lamb is produced under intensive factory-like conditions with a big carbon footprint. This disparity overwhelms domestic lamb's advantage in transportation energy.

New Zealand lamb is not exceptional. Take a close look at water usage, fertilizer types, processing methods, and packaging techniques and you discover that factors other than shipping far outweigh the energy it takes to transport food. One analysis, by Rich Pirog of the Leopold Center for Sustainable Agriculture, showed that transportation accounts for only 11 percent of food's carbon footprint. A fourth of the energy required to produce food is expended in the consumer's kitchen. Still more energy is consumed per meal in a restaurant, since restaurants throw away most of their leftovers.

Locavores argue that buying local food supports an area's farmers and, in turn, strengthens the community. Fair enough. Left unacknowledged, however, is the fact that it also hurts farmers in other parts of the world. The U.K. buys most of its green beans from Kenya. While it's true that the beans almost always arrive in airplanes—the form of transportation that consumes the most energy—it's also true that a campaign to shame English consumers with small airplane stickers affixed to flown-in produce threatens the livelihood of 1.5 million sub-Saharan farmers.

Another chink in the locavores' armor involves the way food miles are calculated. To choose a locally grown apple over an apple trucked in from across the country might seem easy. But this decision ignores economies of scale. To take an extreme example, a shipper sending a truck with 2,000 apples over 2,000 miles would consume the same amount of fuel per apple as a local farmer who takes a pickup 50 miles to sell 50 apples at his stall at the green market. The critical measure here is not food miles but apples per gallon.

The one big problem with thinking beyond food miles is that it's hard to get the information you need. Ethically concerned consumers know very little about processing practices, water availability, packaging waste, and fertilizer application. This is an opportunity for watchdog groups. They should make life-cycle carbon counts available to shoppers.

Until our food system becomes more transparent, there is one thing you can do to shrink the carbon footprint of your dinner: Take the meat off your plate. No matter how you slice it, it takes more energy to bring meat, as opposed to plants, to the table. It takes 6 pounds of grain to make a pound of chicken and 10 to 16 pounds to make a pound of beef. That difference translates into big differences in inputs. It requires 2,400 liters of water to make a burger and only 13 liters to grow a tomato. A majority of the water in the American West goes toward the production of pigs, chickens, and cattle.

The average American eats 273 pounds of meat a year. Give up red meat once a week and you'll save as much energy as if the only food miles in your diet were the distance to the nearest truck farmer.

If you want to make a statement, ride your bike to the farmer's market. If you want to reduce greenhouse gases, become a vegetarian.

■

✓ A CHECKLIST FOR USING THE TOULMIN METHOD

Have I asked the following questions?

☐ What claim does the argument make?

☐ What grounds are offered for the claim?

☐ What warrants the inferences from the grounds to the claim?

☐ What backing supports the claim?

☐ With what modalities are the claim and grounds asserted?

☐ To what rebuttals are the claim, grounds, and backing vulnerable?

THINKING WITH TOULMIN'S METHOD

Remember to make use of the checklist above as you work to find the claim(s), grounds, and warrant(s) that McWilliams puts forward in this short essay.

- First and foremost, what **claim** is the author making? Is it in his title? The opening sentence? Or is it buried in the first paragraph?

McWilliams really gives away his game in his title, even though he opens the essay itself in a way that might make the reader think he is about to launch into a defense of the locavore movement. He even goes out of his way to praise its members ("To their credit . . ."). The signal that his claim really appears already in the title and that he is *not* going to defend the locavore movement is the way he begins the fourth sentence. Notice that although you may have been told that starting a sentence with *But* isn't the best way to write, McWilliams here does so to good effect. Not only does he dramatically counter what he said just prior to that; he also sets up the final sentence of the paragraph, which turns out to be crucial. In this way, he draws sharp attention to his *claim*. How would you state his claim?

- Second, what are the **grounds,** the evidence or reasons, that the author advances in support of his claim?

As it turns out, McWilliams spells out only one example as evidence for his claim. What is it? Is it convincing? Should he have provided more evidence or reasons at this point? It turns out that he does have other grounds to offer—but he mentions them only later. What are those other pieces of evidence?

- Third, what **warrants** does McWilliams offer to show why we should accept his grounds? What authority does he cite? How effective and convincing is this way of trying to get us to accept the grounds he offered in support of his claim?

The essence of the Toulmin method lies in these three elements: the claim(s), the grounds, and the warrant(s). If you have extracted these from McWilliams's essay, you are well on the way to being able to identify the argument he is putting forward. So far, so good. Further probing, however—looking for the other three elements of the Toulmin method (the backing, the modal qualifiers and quantifiers, and the rebuttal)—is essential before you are in a position to actually evaluate the argument. So let's go on.

- Fourth, what **backing** does McWilliams provide? What reasons does he give that might persuade us to accept his argument? Look for what he claimed came out of the analysis that was his basic warrant. He certainly seems to be using factual information—but what if you challenged him? Has he provided adequate reasons for us to believe him? What could he (or would he have to) be able to tell us if we challenged him with questions like "How do you know . . . ?" or "Why do you believe . . . ?" In other words, has he provided adequate backing? Or does he want us to just accept his statement of the facts?

- Fifth, does McWilliams use **modal qualifiers**? Can you find phrases like "in most cases" or "generally it is true that . . ."? Or does he write so boldly—with little in the way of qualifiers or quantifiers—that readers are left uncertain about whether to accept his position? Where might he have effectively used qualifiers?

- Finally, does McWilliams use **rebuttals,** the reasons given in anticipation of someone rejecting the author's claim, or conceding the claim but rejecting the grounds? Does McWilliams anticipate rejections and prepare rebuttals? Does he offer anything to forestall criticisms? If so, what is it that he does? If not, what could or should he have done?

Just how good an argument has McWilliams made? Is he convincing? If you identified weak points in his argument, what are they? Can you help strengthen the argument? If so, how?

9

A Logician's View: Deduction, Induction, Fallacies

Logic is the anatomy of thought.

—JOHN LOCKE

Logic takes care of itself; all we have to do is to look and see how it does it.

—LUDWIG WITTGENSTEIN

In Chapter 3 we introduced the terms *deduction, induction,* and *fallacy.* Here we discuss them in greater detail.

DEDUCTION

The basic aim of deductive reasoning is to start with some assumption or premise and extract from it a conclusion—a logical consequence—that is concealed but implicit in it. Thus, taking the simplest case, if I assert as a premise

1a. Nuclear power poses more risks of harm to the environment than fossil fuels.

then it is a matter of simple deduction to infer the conclusion that

1b. Fossil fuels pose fewer risks of harm to the environment than nuclear power.

Anyone who understands English would grant that 1b follows 1a—or equivalently, that 1b can be validly deduced from 1a—because whatever two objects, A and B, you choose, if A does *more things than B*, then B must do *fewer things than A*.

Thus, in this and all other cases of valid deductive reasoning, we can say not only that we are entitled to *infer* the conclusion from the premise—in this case, infer 1b from 1a—but that the premise *implies* the conclusion. Remember, too, the conclusion (1b) that fossil fuels pose fewer risks than nuclear power—inferred or deduced from the statement (1a) that nuclear power poses more risks—does not depend on the truth of the statement that nuclear power poses more risks. If the speaker (falsely) asserts that nuclear power poses more risks, then the hearer validly (i.e., logically) concludes that fossil fuels pose fewer risks. Thus, 1b follows from 1a whether or not 1a is true; consequently, if 1a is true, then so is 1b; but if 1a is false, then 1b must be false also.

Let's take another example—more interesting but comparably simple:

2a. President Truman was underrated by his critics.

Given 2a, a claim amply verified by events of the 1950s, one is entitled to infer that

2b. His critics underrated President Truman.

On what basis can we argue that 2a implies 2b? The two propositions are equivalent because a rule of English grammar assures us that we can convert the position of subject and predicate phrases in a sentence by shifting from the passive to the active voice (or vice versa) without any change in the conditions that make the proposition true (or false).

Both pairs of examples illustrate that in deductive reasoning, our aim is to transform, reformulate, or restate in our conclusion some (or, as in the two examples above, all) of the information contained in our premises.

Remember, even though a proposition or statement follows from a previous proposition or statement, the statements need not be true. We can see why if we consider another example. Suppose someone asserts or claims that

3a. The Gettysburg Address is longer than the Declaration of Independence.

As every student of American history knows, 3a is false. But false or not, we can validly deduce from it that

3b. The Declaration of Independence is shorter than the Gettysburg Address.

This inference is valid (even though the conclusion is untrue) because the conclusion follows logically (more precisely, deductively) from 3a: In English, as we know, the meaning of "*A* is shorter than *B*," which appears in 3b, is simply the converse of "*B* is longer than *A*," which appears in 3a.

The deductive relation between 3a and 3b reminds us again that the idea of validity, which is so crucial to deduction, is not the same as the idea of truth. False propositions have implications—logical consequences—too, just as true propositions do.

In the three pairs of examples so far, what can we point to as the warrant for our claims? Well, look at the reasoning in each case; the arguments rely on rules of ordinary English, on the accepted meanings of words like *on*, *under*, and *underrated*.

In many cases, of course, the deductive inference or pattern of reasoning is much more complex than that which we have seen in the examples so far. When we introduced the idea of deduction in Chapter 3, we gave as our primary example the *syllogism*. Here is another example:

4. Texas is larger than California; California is larger than Arizona; therefore, Texas is larger than Arizona.

The conclusion in this syllogism can be derived from the two premises; that is, anyone who asserts the two premises is committed to accepting the conclusion as well, whether or not one thinks of it.

Notice again that the *truth* of the conclusion is not established merely by validity of the inference. The conclusion in this syllogism happens to be true. And the premises of this syllogism imply the conclusion. But the argument establishes the conclusion only because both of the premises on which the conclusion depends are true. Even a Californian admits that Texas is larger than California, which in turn is larger than Arizona. In other words, argument 4 is a *sound* argument because (as we explained in Chapter 3) it is valid and all its premises are true. All—and only—arguments that *prove* their conclusions have these two traits.

How might we present the warrant for the argument in 4? Short of a crash course in formal logic, either of two strategies might suffice. One is to argue from the fact that the validity of the inference depends on the meaning of a key concept, *being larger than*. This concept has the property of *transitivity,* a property that many concepts share (e.g., *is equal to, is to the right of, is smarter than*—all are transitive concepts). Consequently, whatever *A, B,* and *C* are, if *A* is larger than *B,* and *B* is larger than *C,* then *A* will be larger than *C.* The final step is to substitute "Texas," "California," and "Arizona" for *A, B,* and *C,* respectively.

A second strategy, less abstract and more graphic, is to think of representing Texas, California, and Arizona by nested circles. Thus, the first premise in argument 4 would look like this:

The second premise would look like this:

The conclusion would look like this:

We can see that this conclusion follows from the premises because it amounts to nothing more than what one gets by superimposing the two premises on each other. Thus, the whole argument can be represented like this:

$$\left(\text{TX} \; \overline{\text{CA}}\right) \; + \; \left(\text{CA} \; \overline{\text{AZ}}\right) \; = \; \left(\text{TX} \; \overline{\text{AZ}}\right)$$

The so-called middle term in the argument—California—disappears from the conclusion; its role is confined to be the link between the other two terms, Texas and Arizona, in the premises. (This is an adaptation of the technique used in elementary formal logic known as Venn diagrams.) In this manner one can give graphic display to the important fact that the conclusion follows from the premises because one can literally *see* the conclusion represented by nothing more than a representation of the premises.

Both of these strategies bring out the fact that validity of deductive inference is a purely *formal* property of argument. Each strategy abstracts the form from the content of the propositions involved to show how the concepts in the premises are related to the concepts in the conclusion.

For the sake of illustration, here is another syllogistic argument with the same logical features as argument 4. (A nice exercise is to restate argument 5 using diagrams in the manner of argument 4.)

5. African American slaves were treated worse than white indentured servants. Indentured white servants were treated worse than free white labor. Therefore, African American slaves were treated worse than free white labor.

Not all deductive reasoning occurs in syllogisms, however, or at least not in syllogisms like the ones in 4 and 5. (The term *syllogism* is sometimes used to refer to any deductive argument of any form, provided only that it has two premises.) In fact, syllogisms such as 4 are not the commonest form of our deductive reasoning at all. Nor are they the simplest (and, of course, not the most complex). For an argument that is even simpler, consider this:

6. If a youth is an African American slave, he is probably treated worse than a youth in indentured service. This youth is an African American slave. Therefore, he is probably treated worse than if he had been an indentured servant.

Here the pattern of reasoning has the form: If *A*, then *B*; *A*; therefore, *B*. Notice that the content of the assertions represented by *A* and *B* don't matter; any set of expressions having the same form or structure will do equally well, including assertions built out of meaningless terms, as in this example:

7. If the slithy toves, then the gyres gimble. The slithy toves. Therefore, the gyres gimble.

Argument 7 has the form: If *A*, then *B*; *A*; therefore *B*. As a piece of deductive inference it is every bit as good as argument 6. Unlike 6, however, 7 is of no interest to us because none of its assertions make any sense (unless you're a reader of Lewis Carroll's "Jabberwocky," and even then the sense of 7 is doubtful). You cannot, in short, use a valid deductive argument to prove anything unless the premises and the conclusion are *true,* but they can't be true unless they *mean* something in the first place.

This parallel between arguments 6 and 7 shows once again that deductive validity in an argument rests on the *form* or structure of the argument, and not on its content or meaning. If all one can say about an argument is that it is valid—that is, its conclusion follows from the premises—one has not given a sufficient reason for accepting the argument's conclusion. It has been said that the devil can quote scripture; similarly, an argument can be deductively valid and of no further interest or value whatever because valid (but false) conclusions can be drawn from false or even meaningless assumptions. For example:

8. New York's Metropolitan Museum of Art has the finest collection of abstract impressionist paintings in the world. The finest collection of abstract impressionist paintings includes dozens of canvases by Winslow Homer. Therefore, the Metropolitan Museum of Art has dozens of paintings by Winslow Homer.

Here the conclusion follows validly from the premises, even though all three propositions are false. Nevertheless, although validity by itself is not enough, it is a necessary condition of any deductive argument that purports to establish its conclusion.

Now let's consider another argument with the same form as 8, only more interesting:

9. If President Truman knew the Japanese were about to surrender, then it was immoral of him to order that atom bombs be dropped on Hiroshima and Nagasaki. Truman knew the Japanese were about to surrender. Therefore, it was immoral of him to order dropping those bombs.

As in the two previous examples, anyone who assents to the premises in argument 9 must assent to the conclusion; the form of arguments 8 and 9 is identical. But do the premises of argument 9 *prove* the conclusion? That depends on whether both premises are true. Well, are they? This turns on a number of considerations, and it is worthwhile pausing to examine this argument closely to illustrate the kinds of things that are involved in answering this question.

Let's begin by examining the second (minor) premise. Its truth is controversial even to this day. Autobiography, memoranda, other documentary evidence—all are needed to assemble the evidence to back up the grounds for the thesis or claim made in the conclusion of this valid argument. Evaluating this material effectively will probably involve not only further deductions but inductive reasoning as well.

Now consider the first (major) premise in argument 9. Its truth doesn't depend on what history shows but on the moral principles one accepts. The major premise has the form of a hypothetical proposition ("if . . . then . . .") and asserts a connection between two very different kinds of things. The antecedent of the hypothetical (the clause following "if") mentions facts about Truman's *knowledge,* and the consequent of the hypothetical (the clause following "then") mentions facts about the *morality* of his conduct in light of such knowledge. The major premise as a whole can thus be seen as expressing *a principle of moral responsibility.*

Such principles can, of course, be controversial. In this case, for instance, is the principle peculiarly relevant to the knowledge and conduct of a president of the United States? Probably not; it is far more likely that this principle is merely a special case of a more general proposition about anyone's moral responsibility. (After all, we know a great deal more about the conditions of our own moral responsibility than we do about those of high government officials.) We might express this more general principle in this way: If we have knowledge that would make our violent conduct unnecessary, then we are immoral if we deliberately act violently anyway. Thus, accepting this general principle can serve as a basis for defending the major premise of argument 9.

We have examined this argument in some detail because it illustrates the kinds of considerations needed to test not only whether a given argument is valid but also whether its premises are true—that is, whether its premises really prove the conclusion.

The great value of the form of argument known as hypothetical syllogism, exemplified by arguments 6 and 7, is that the structure of the argument is so simple and so universally applicable in reasoning that it is often both easy and worthwhile to formulate one's claims so that they can be grounded by an argument of this sort.

Before leaving the subject of deductive inference, let's consider three other forms of argument, each of which can be found in actual use elsewhere in the readings in this volume. The simplest of these is **disjunctive syllogism,** so called because its major premise is a **disjunction.** For example:

10. Either censorship of television shows is overdue, or our society is indifferent to the education of its youth. Our society

is not indifferent to the education of its youth. Therefore, censorship of television is overdue.

Notice, by the way, that the validity of an argument, as in this case, does not turn on pedantic repetition of every word or phrase as the argument moves along; nonessential elements can be dropped, or equivalent expressions substituted for variety without adverse effect on the reasoning. Thus, in conversation or in writing, the argument in 10 might actually be presented like this:

11. Either censorship of television is overdue, or our society is indifferent to the education of its youth. But, of course, we aren't indifferent; it's censorship that's overdue.

The key feature of disjunctive syllogism, as example 11 suggests, is that the conclusion is whichever of the disjuncts is left over after the others have been negated in the minor premise. Thus, we could easily have a very complex disjunctive syllogism, with a dozen disjuncts in the major premise, and seven of them denied in the minor premise, leaving a conclusion of the remaining five. Usually, however, a disjunctive argument is formulated in this manner: Assert a disjunction with two or more disjuncts in the major premise; then *deny all but one* in the minor premise; and infer validly the remaining disjunct as the conclusion. That was the form of argument 11.

Another type of argument, especially favored by orators and rhetoricians, is the **dilemma.** Ordinarily, we use the term *dilemma* in the sense of an awkward predicament, as when we say, "His dilemma was that he didn't have enough money to pay the waiter." But when logicians refer to a dilemma, they mean a forced choice between two or more equally unattractive alternatives. For example, the predicament faced by the U.S. government in 2014 in deciding how to deal with the growth of the Islamic State in Syria can be posed as a dilemma. Two major choices emerged. The United States could ally itself with the Syrian government, or it could support rebel groups inside Syria who fight against ISIS. The dilemma is that the Syrian government, a dictatorship under Bashar al-Assad, has attempted to crush political reform movements in Syria, and it actively supports groups the United States deems terrorist organizations, such as Hamas and Hezbollah. Also, some important U.S. allies such as Saudi Arabia oppose the al-Assad regime. On the other hand, if the United States were to support resistance groups within Syria, it would open itself up to charges that it was funding and arming groups hostile to the al-Assad regime, making them vulnerable to attack from the Syrian government and angering Syrian allies such as Russia, which may well be called upon to support strikes against the United States. The dilemma might be phrased as such:

12. If the United States supports the Syrian government, it would also be supporting a dictatorship that has been linked to terrorism and crimes against humanity, and that furthermore is an enemy of some of our closest Middle Eastern allies. If the United States supports rebel groups within Syria, it may be subject to attack by the al-Assad regime, extending the Syrian civil war and inviting potentially dangerous conflict with Russia. Either the United States supports a dictatorship, or it supports internal resistance groups. In either case, unattractive consequences follow.

Notice first the structure of the argument: two conditional propositions asserted as premises, followed by another premise that states a **necessary truth**. (The premise, "Either we support the Libyan dictatorship, or we support the Libyan rebels," is a disjunction; since its two alternatives are exhaustive, one of the two alternatives must be true. Such a statement is often called analytically true, or a *tautology*.) No doubt the conclusion of this dilemma follows from its premises.

But does the argument prove, as it purports to do, that whatever the U.S. government does, it will suffer "unattractive consequences"? It is customary to speak of "the horns of the dilemma," as though the challenge posed by the dilemma were like a bull ready to gore us no matter which direction we turn. But if the two conditional premises failed to exhaust the possibilities, then we can escape from the dilemma by going "between the horns," that is, by finding a third alternative. If (as in this case) that isn't possible, we can still ask whether both of the main premises are true. (In this argument, it should be clear that neither of the main premises spells out all or even most of the consequences that could be foreseen.) Even so, in cases where both of these conditional premises are true, it may be that the consequences of one alternative are nowhere nearly so bad as those of the other. If that is true, but our reasoning stops before evaluating that fact, we may be guilty of failing to distinguish between the greater and the lesser of two admitted evils. The logic of the dilemma itself cannot decide this choice for us. Instead, we must bring to bear empirical inquiry and imagination to the evaluation of the grounds of the dilemma itself.

Writers commonly use the term *dilemma* without explicitly formulating the dilemma to which they refer, leaving it for the readers to do. And sometimes, what is called a dilemma really isn't one. (Remember the dog's tail? Calling it a leg doesn't make it a leg.) As an example, consider the plight of Sophie in William Styron's novel, *Sophie's Choice*. The scene is Birkenau, the main Nazi extermination camp during World War II. Among the thousands arriving at the prison gates are Sophie and her two children, Jan and Eva. On the train platform a Nazi SS medical officer confronts them. He will decide which are the lucky ones; they will live to work in the camp. The rest will go to their death in the gas chambers. When Sophie insists she is Polish but not Jewish, the officer says she may choose one of her children to be saved. Which of the two should she save? On what basis ought Sophie resolve her dilemma? It looks as if she has only two alternatives, each of which presents an agonizing outcome. Or is there a third way out?

Finally, one of the most powerful and dramatic forms of argument is **reductio ad absurdum** (from the Latin, meaning "reduction to absurdity"). The idea of a reductio argument is to disprove a proposition by showing the absurdity of its inevitable conclusion. It is used, of course, to refute your opponent's position and prove your own. For example, in Plato's *Republic,* Socrates asks an old gentleman, Cephalus, to define right conduct. Cephalus says that it consists of paying your debts and keeping your word. Socrates rejects this answer by showing that it leads to a contradiction. He argues that Cephalus cannot have given the correct answer because if we believe that he did, we will quickly encounter contradictions; in some cases, when you keep your word you will nonetheless be doing the wrong thing. For suppose, says Socrates, that you borrowed a weapon from a man, promising to return it when he asks for it. One day he comes to your door, demanding his weapon and swearing angrily that he intends to murder a neighbor. Keeping your word under those circumstances would be absurd, Socrates implies, and the reader of the dialogue is left to infer that Cephalus's definition, which led to this result, has been refuted.

Let's take a closer look at another example. Suppose you are opposed to any form of gun control, whereas I am in favor of gun control. I might try to refute your position by attacking it with a reductio argument. To do that, I start out by assuming the very opposite of what I believe or favor; instead, I try to establish a contradiction that results from following out the consequences of this initial assumption. My argument might look like this:

13. Let's assume your position—namely, that there ought to be no legal restrictions of any kind on the sale and ownership

of guns. That means that you'd permit having every neighborhood hardware store sell pistols and rifles to whoever
walks in the door. But that's not all. You apparently also
would permit selling machine guns to children, antitank
weapons to lunatics, small-bore cannons to the nearsighted,
as well as guns and ammunition to anyone with a criminal
record. But this is utterly preposterous. No one could favor
such a dangerous policy. So the only question worth debat-
ing is what kind of gun control is necessary.

Now in this example, my reductio of your position on gun
control is not based on claiming to show that you have strictly
contradicted yourself, for there is no purely logical contradiction
in opposing all forms of gun control. Instead, what I have tried
to do is to show that there is a contradiction between what you
profess—no gun controls at all—and what you probably really
believe, if only you'll stop to think about it—which is that no luna-
tic should be allowed to buy a loaded machine gun.

My refutation of your position rests on whether I succeed in
establishing an inconsistency among your own beliefs. If it turns
out that you really believe lunatics should be free to purchase guns
and ammunition, then my attempted refutation fails.

In explaining reductio ad absurdum, we have had to rely
on another idea fundamental to logic, that of **contradiction,** or
inconsistency. (We used this idea, remember, to define validity in
Chapter 3. A deductive argument is valid if and only if the process of affirming the premises and denying the conclusion results
in a contradiction.) The opposite of contradiction is **consistency,**
a notion of hardly less importance to good reasoning than validity. These concepts deserve a few words of further explanation and
illustration. Consider this pair of assertions:

14. Abortion is homicide.
15. Racism is unfair.

No one would plausibly claim that we can infer or deduce 15 from
14, or, for that matter, 14 from 15. This almost goes without saying because there is no evident connection between these two
assertions. They are unrelated assertions; logically speaking, they
are *independent* of each other. In such cases the two assertions are
mutually *consistent;* that is, both could be true—or both could be
false. But now consider another proposition:

16. Euthanasia is not murder.

Could a person assert 14 (*Abortion is homicide*) and also assert 16 (*Euthanasia is not murder*) and be consistent? This question is equivalent to asking whether one could assert the **conjunction** of these two propositions—namely:

17. Abortion is homicide, and euthanasia is not murder.

It's not so easy to say whether 17 is consistent or inconsistent. The kinds of moral scruples that might lead a person to assert one of these conjuncts (i.e., one of the two initial propositions, *Abortion is homicide* and *Euthanasia is not murder*) might lead to the belief that the other one must be false and thus to the conclusion that 17 is inconsistent. (Notice that if 14 were the assertion that *Abortion is murder*, instead of *Abortion is homicide*, the problem of asserting consistently both 14 and 16 would be more acute.) Yet if we think again, we might imagine someone being convinced that there is no inconsistency in asserting that *Abortion is homicide*, say, and that *Euthanasia is not murder*, or even the reverse. (For instance, suppose you believed that the unborn deserve a chance to live and that putting terminally ill persons to death in a painless manner and with their consent confers a benefit on them.)

Let us generalize: We can say of any set of propositions that they are *consistent* if and only if *all could be true together*. (Notice that it follows from this definition that propositions mutually imply each other, as do *Seabiscuit was America's fastest racehorse* and *America's fastest racehorse was Seabiscuit*.) Remember that, once again, the truth of the assertions in question doesn't matter. Two propositions can be consistent or not, quite apart from whether they are true. Not so with falsehood: It follows from our definition of consistency that an *inconsistent* proposition must be *false*. (We have relied on this idea in explaining how a reductio ad absurdum argument works.)

Assertions or claims that are not consistent can take either of two forms. Suppose you assert proposition 14, that abortion is homicide, early in an essay you are writing, but later you assert that

18. Abortion is harmless.

You have now asserted a position on abortion that is strictly contrary to the one with which you began—contrary in the sense that both assertions 14 and 18 cannot be true. It is simply not true that if an abortion involves killing a human being (which is what *homicide* strictly means), then it causes no one any harm (killing a person always causes harm—even if it is excusable, justifiable, not wrong, the best thing to do in the circumstances, and so on). Notice that although 14 and 18 cannot both be true, they *can* both be false. In fact, many people who are perplexed about the morality of abortion believe precisely this. They concede that abortion does harm the fetus, so 18 must be false; but they also believe that abortion doesn't kill a person, so 14 must also be false.

Let's consider another, simpler case. If you describe the glass as half empty and I describe it as half full, both of us can be right; the two assertions are consistent, even though they sound vaguely incompatible. (This is the reason that disputing over whether the glass is half full or half empty has become the popular paradigm of a futile, purely *verbal disagreement*.) But if I describe the glass as half empty whereas you insist that it is two-thirds empty, then we have a real disagreement; your description and mine are strictly contrary, in that both cannot be true—although both *can* be false. (Both are false if the glass is only one-quarter full.)

This, by the way, enables us to define the difference between a pair of **contradictory** propositions and a pair of **contrary** propositions. Two propositions are contrary if and only if both cannot be true (though both can be false); two propositions are contradictory if and only if they are such that if one is true the other must be false, and vice versa. Thus, if Jack says that Alice Walker's *The Color Purple* is a better novel than Mark Twain's *Huckleberry Finn*, and Jill says, "No, *Huckleberry Finn* is better than *The Color Purple*," she is contradicting Jack. If what either one of them says is true, then what the other says must be false.

A more subtle case of contradiction arises when two or more of one's own beliefs implicitly contradict each other. We may find ourselves saying "Travel is broadening," and saying an hour later "People don't really change." Just beneath the surface of these two beliefs lies a self-contradiction: How can travel broaden us unless it influences—and changes—our beliefs, values, and outlook? But if we can't really change ourselves, then traveling to new places won't change us, either. (Indeed, there is a Roman saying to the effect that travelers change the skies above them, not their hearts.) "Travel is broadening" and "People don't change" collide with each other; something has to give.

Our point, of course, is not that you must never say today something that contradicts something you said yesterday. Far from it; if you think you were mistaken yesterday, of course you will take a different position today. But what you want to avoid is what George Orwell called *doublethink* in his novel *1984*: "*Doublethink* means the power of holding two contradictory beliefs in one's mind simultaneously, and accepting them both."

Genuine contradiction, and not merely contrary assertion, is the situation we should expect to find in some disputes. Someone advances a thesis—such as the assertion in 14, *Abortion is homicide*— and someone else flatly contradicts it by the simple expedient of negating it, thus:

19. Abortion is not homicide.

If we can trust public opinion polls, many of us are not sure whether to agree with 14 or with 19. But we should agree that whichever is true, *both* cannot be true, and *both* cannot be false. The two assertions, between them, exclude all other possibilities; they pose a forced choice for our belief. (Again, we have met this idea, too, in a reductio ad absurdum.)

Now it is one thing for Jack and Jill in a dispute or argument to contradict each other. It is quite another matter for Jack to contradict himself. One wants (or should want) to avoid self-contradiction because of the embarrassing position that results: Once I have contradicted myself, what are others to believe I really believe? What, indeed, *do* I believe, for that matter?

It may be, as Emerson observed, that a "foolish consistency is the hobgoblin of little minds"—that is, it may be shortsighted to purchase a consistency in one's beliefs at the expense of flying in the face of common sense. But making an effort to avoid a foolish inconsistency is the hallmark of serious thinking.

While we're speaking of inconsistency, let's spend a moment on **paradox.** The word refers to two different things:

- an assertion that is essentially self-contradictory and therefore cannot be true
- a seemingly contradictory assertion that nevertheless may be true

An example of the first might be "Evaluations concerning quality in literature are all a matter of personal judgment, but Shakespeare is the world's greatest writer." It is hard to make any sense out of this assertion. Contrast it with a paradox of the second sort, a *seeming* contradiction that may make sense, such as "The longest way around is the shortest way home," or "Work is more fun than fun," or "The best way to find happiness is not to look for it." Here we have assertions that are striking because as soon as we hear them we realize that although they seem inconsistent and self-defeating, they contain (or may contain) profound truths. Paradoxes of this second sort are especially common in religious texts, where they may imply a mysterious reality concealed by a world of contradictory appearances. Examples are "Some who are last shall be first, and some who are first shall be last" (Jesus, quoted in Luke 13:30), and "Death, thou shalt die" (the poet John Donne, alluding to the idea that the person who has faith in Jesus dies to this world but lives eternally). If you use the word *paradox* in your own writing—for instance, to characterize an argument that you're reading—be sure that the reader will understand in which sense you're using the word. (And, of course, you won't want to write paradoxes of the first, self-contradictory sort.)

INDUCTION

Deduction involves logical thinking that applies to absolutely any assertion or claim—because every possible statement, true or false, has deductive logical consequences. Induction is relevant to one kind of assertion only; namely, to **empirical** or *factual* claims. Other kinds of assertions (such as definitions, mathematical equations, and moral or legal norms) simply are not the product of inductive reasoning and cannot serve as a basis for further inductive thinking.

And so, in studying the methods of induction, we are exploring tactics and strategies useful in gathering and then using **evidence**—empirical, observational, experimental—in support of a belief as its ground. Modern scientific knowledge is the product of these methods, and they differ somewhat from one science to another because they depend on the theories and technology appropriate to each of the sciences. Here all we can do is discuss generally the more abstract features common to inductive inquiry generally. For fuller details, you must eventually consult a physicist, chemist, geologist, or their colleagues and counterparts in other scientific fields.

Observation and Inference

Let's begin with a simple example. Suppose we have evidence (actually we don't, but that won't matter for our purposes) in support of the claim that

1. In a sample of 500 smokers, 230 persons observed have cardiovascular disease.

The basis for asserting 1—the evidence or ground—would be, presumably, straightforward physical examination of the 500 persons in the sample, one by one.

With this claim in hand, we can think of the purpose and methods of induction as pointing in two opposite directions: toward establishing the basis or ground of the very empirical proposition with which we start (in this example, the observation stated in 1) or toward understanding what that observation indicates or suggests as a more general, inclusive, or fundamental fact of nature.

In each case, we start from something we *do* know (or take for granted and treat as a sound starting point)—some fact of nature, perhaps a striking or commonplace event that we have observed and recorded—and then go on to something we do *not* fully know and perhaps cannot directly observe. In example 1, only the second of these two orientations is of any interest, so let's concentrate exclusively on it. Let's also generously treat as a *method* of induction any regular pattern or style of nondeductive reasoning that we could use to support a claim such as that in 1.

Anyone truly interested in the observed fact that *230 of 500 smokers have cardiovascular disease* is likely to start speculating about, and thus be interested in finding out, whether any or all of several other propositions are also true. For example, one might wonder whether

2. *All* smokers have cardiovascular disease or will develop it during their lifetimes.

This claim is a straightforward generalization of the original observation as reported in claim 1. When we think inductively about the linkage between 1 and 2, we are reasoning from an observed sample (some smokers—i.e., 230 of the 500 *observed*) to the entire membership of a more inclusive class (*all* smokers, whether observed or not). The fundamental question raised by reasoning from the narrower claim 1 to the broader claim 2 is whether we have any ground for believing that what is true of *some* members of a class is true of them *all*. So the difference between 1 and 2 is that of *quantity* or scope.

We can also think inductively about the *relation* between the factors mentioned in 1. Having observed data as reported in 1, we may be tempted to assert a different and more profound kind of claim:

3. Smoking *causes* cardiovascular disease.

Here our interest is not merely in generalizing from a sample to a whole class; it is the far more important one of *explaining* the observation with which we began in claim 1. Certainly, the preferred, even if not the only, mode of explanation for a natural phenomenon is a *causal* explanation. In proposition 3, we propose to explain the presence of one phenomenon (cardiovascular disease) by the prior occurrence of an independent phenomenon (smoking). The observation reported in 1 is now serving as evidence or support for this new conjecture stated in 3.

Our original claim in 1 asserted no causal relation between anything and anything else; whatever the cause of cardiovascular disease may be, that cause is not observed, mentioned, or assumed in assertion 1. Similarly, the observation asserted in claim 1 is consistent with many explanations. For example, the explanation of 1 might not be 3, but some other, undetected, carcinogenic factor unrelated to smoking—for instance, exposure to high levels of radon. The question one now faces is what can be added to 1, or teased out of it, to produce an adequate ground for claiming 3. (We shall return to this example for closer scrutiny.)

But there is a third way to go beyond 1. Instead of a straightforward generalization, as we had in 2, or a pronouncement on the cause of a phenomenon, as in 3, we might have a more complex and cautious further claim in mind, such as this:

4. Smoking is a factor in the causation of cardiovascular disease in some persons.

This proposition, like 3, advances a claim about causation. But 4 is obviously a weaker claim than 3. That is, other observations, theories, or evidence that would require us to reject 3 might be consistent with 4; evidence that would support 4 could easily fail to be enough to support 3. Consequently, it is even possible that 4 is true although 3 is false, because 4 allows for other (unmentioned) factors in the causation of cardiovascular disease (e.g., genetic or dietary factors) that may not be found in all smokers.

Propositions 2, 3, and 4 differ from proposition 1 in an important respect. We began by assuming that 1 states an empirical fact based on direct observation, whereas these others do not. Instead, they state empirical *hypotheses* or conjectures—tentative generalizations not fully confirmed—each of which goes beyond the observed facts asserted in 1. Each of 2, 3, and 4 can be regarded as an *inductive inference* from 1. We can also say that 2, 3, and 4 are hypotheses relative to 1, even if they are not relative to some other starting point (such as all the information that scientists today really have about smoking and cardiovascular disease).

Probability

Another way of formulating the last point is to say that whereas proposition 1, a statement of observed fact (*230 out of 500 smokers have cardiovascular disease*), has a **probability** of 1.0—that is, it is absolutely certain—the probability of each of the hypotheses stated in 2, 3, and 4, *relative* to 1, is smaller than 1.0. (We need not worry here about how much smaller than 1.0 the probabilities are, nor about how to calculate these probabilities precisely.) Relative to some starting point other than 1, however, the probability of the same three hypotheses might be quite different. Of course, it still wouldn't be 1.0, absolute certainty. But it takes only a moment's reflection to realize that no matter what the probability of 2 or 3 or 4 may be relative to 1, those probabilities in each case will be quite different relative to different information, such as this:

5. Ten persons observed in a sample of 500 smokers have cardiovascular disease.

The idea that a *given proposition can have different probabilities* relative to different bases is fundamental to all inductive reasoning. The following example makes a convincing illustration. Suppose we want to consider the probability of this proposition being true:

6. Susanne Smith will live to be eighty.

Taken as an abstract question of fact, we cannot even guess what the probability is with any assurance. But we can do better than guess; we can in fact even calculate the answer, if we get some further information. Thus, suppose we are told that

7. Susanne Smith is seventy-nine.

Our original question then becomes one of determining the probability that 6 is true given 7; that is, relative to the evidence contained in proposition 7. No doubt, if Susanne Smith really is seventy-nine, then the probability that she will live to be eighty is greater than if we know only that

8. Susanne Smith is more than nine years old.

Obviously, a lot can happen to Susanne in the seventy years between nine and seventy-nine that isn't very likely to happen in the one year between seventy-nine and eighty. And so, proposition 6 is more probable relative to proposition 7 than it is relative to proposition 8.

Let's suppose for the sake of the argument that the following is true:

9. Ninety percent of women alive at age seventy-nine live to be eighty.

Given this additional information, and the information that Susanne is seventy-nine, we now have a basis for answering our original question about proposition 6 with some precision. But suppose, in addition to 8, we are also told that

10. Susanne Smith is suffering from inoperable cancer.

and also that

11. The survival rate for women suffering from inoperable cancer is 0.6 years (i.e., the average life span for women after a diagnosis of inoperable cancer is about seven months).

With this new information, the probability that 6 will be true drops significantly, all because we can now estimate the probability in relation to a new body of evidence.

The probability of an event, thus, is not a fixed number but one that varies because it is always relative to some evidence—and given different evidence, one and the same event can have different probabilities. In other words, the probability of any event is always relative to how much is known (assumed, believed), and because different persons may know different things about a given event, or the same person may know different things at different times, one and the same event can have two or more probabilities. This conclusion is not a paradox but a logical consequence of the concept of what it is for an event to have (i.e., to be assigned) a probability.

If we shift to the *calculation* of probabilities, we find that generally there are two ways to calculate them. One way to proceed is by the method of **a priori** or **equal probabilities**—that is, by reference to the relevant possibilities taken abstractly and apart from any other information. Thus, in an election contest with only two candidates, Smith and Jones, each of the candidates has a fifty-fifty chance of winning (whereas in a three-candidate race, each candidate would have one chance in three of winning). Therefore, the probability that Smith will win is 0.5, and the probability that Jones will win is also 0.5. (The sum of the probabilities of all possible independent outcomes must always equal 1.0, which is obvious enough if you think about it.)

But in politics the probabilities are not reasonably calculated so abstractly. We know that many empirical factors affect the outcome of an election and that a calculation of probabilities in ignorance of those factors is likely to be drastically misleading. In our example of the two-candidate election, suppose Smith has strong party support and is the incumbent, whereas Jones represents a party long out of power and is further handicapped by being relatively unknown. No one who knows anything about electoral politics would give Jones the same chance of winning as Smith. The two events are not equiprobable in relation to all the information available.

Moreover, a given event can have more than one probability. This happens whenever we calculate a probability by relying on different bodies of data that report how often the event in question has been observed to happen. Probabilities calculated in this way are **relative frequencies.** Our earlier hypothetical example of

S. Harris/Cartoonstock

Susanne Smith provides an illustration. If she is a smoker and we have observed that 100 out of a random set of 500 smokers have cardiovascular disease, we have a basis for claiming that she has a probability of 100 in 500, or 0.2 (one-fifth), of having this disease. However, if other data have shown that 250 out of 500 women smokers ages eighty or older have cardiovascular disease, we have a basis for believing that there is a probability of 250 in 500, or 0.5 (one-half), that she has this disease. Notice that in both calculations we assume that Susanne Smith is not among the persons we have examined. In both cases we infer the probability of her having this disease from observing its frequency in populations that exclude her.

Both methods of calculating probabilities are legitimate; in each case the calculation is relative to observed circumstances. But as the examples show, it is most reasonable to have recourse to the method of equiprobabilities only when few or no other factors affecting possible outcomes are known.

Mill's Methods

Now let's return to our earlier discussion of smoking and cardiovascular disease and consider in greater detail the question of a causal connection between the two phenomena. We began thus:

1. In a sample of 500 smokers, 230 persons observed have cardiovascular disease.

We regarded 1 as an observed fact, though in truth, of course, it is mere supposition. Our question now is how we might augment this information so as to strengthen our confidence that

3. Smoking *causes* cardiovascular disease.

or at least that

4. Smoking is a factor in the causation of cardiovascular disease in some persons.

Suppose further examination showed that

12. In the sample of 230 smokers with cardiovascular disease, no other suspected factor (such as genetic predisposition, lack of physical exercise, age over fifty) was also observed.

Such an observation would encourage us to believe that 3 or 4 is true. Why? Because we're inclined to believe also that no matter what the cause of a phenomenon is, it must *always* be present when its effect is present. Thus, the inference from 1 to 3 or 4 is supported by 12, using **Mill's Method of Agreement,** named after the British philosopher, John Stuart Mill (1806–1873), who first formulated it. It's called a method of agreement because of the way in which the inference relies on *agreement* among the observed phenomena where a presumed cause is thought to be *present.*

Let's now suppose that in our search for evidence to support 3 or 4 we conduct additional research and discover that

13. In a sample of 500 nonsmokers, selected to be representative of both sexes, different ages, dietary habits, exercise patterns, and so on, none is observed to have cardiovascular disease.

This observation would further encourage us to believe that we had obtained significant additional confirmation of 3 or 4. Why? Because we now know that factors present (such as male sex, lack of exercise, family history of cardiovascular disease) in cases where the effect is absent (no cardiovascular disease observed) cannot be the cause. This is an example of **Mill's Method of Difference,** so called because the cause or causal factor of an effect must be *different* from whatever factors are present when the effect is *absent.*

Suppose now that, increasingly confident we've found the cause of cardiovascular disease, we study our first sample of 230 smokers ill with the disease, and we discover this:

14. Those who smoke two or more packs of cigarettes daily for ten or more years have cardiovascular disease either much younger or much more severely than those who smoke less.

This is an application of **Mill's Method of Concomitant Variation,** perhaps the most convincing of the three methods. Here we deal not merely with the presence of the conjectured cause (smoking) or the absence of the effect we are studying (cardiovascular disease), as we were previously, but with the more interesting and subtler matter of the *degree and regularity of the correlation* of the supposed cause and effect. According to the observations reported in 14, it strongly appears that the more we have of the "cause" (smoking), the sooner or the more intense the onset of the "effect" (cardiovascular disease).

Notice, however, what happens to our confirmation of 3 and 4 if, instead of the observation reported in 14, we had discovered that

15. In a representative sample of 500 nonsmokers, cardiovascular disease was observed in 34 cases.

(We won't pause here to explain what makes a sample more or less representative of a population, although the representativeness of samples is vital to all statistical reasoning.) Such an observation would lead us almost immediately to suspect some other or additional causal factor: Smoking might indeed be *a* factor in causing cardiovascular disease, but it can hardly be *the* cause because (using Mill's Method of Difference) we cannot have the effect, as we do in the observed sample reported in 15, unless we also have the cause.

An observation such as the one in 15, however, is likely to lead us to think our hypothesis that *smoking causes cardiovascular disease* has been disconfirmed. But we have a fallback position ready — we can still defend a weaker hypothesis; namely, 4: *Smoking is a factor in the causation of cardiovascular disease in some persons.* Even if 3 stumbles over the evidence in 15, 4 does not. It is still quite possible that smoking is a factor in causing this disease, even if it isn't the *only* factor — and if it is, then 4 is true.

Confirmation, Mechanism, and Theory

Notice that in the discussion so far, we have spoken of the *confirmation* of a hypothesis, such as our causal claim in 4, but not of its *verification*. (Similarly, we have imagined very different evidence, such as that stated in 15, leading us to speak of the *dis*confirmation of 3, though not of its *falsi*fication.) Confirmation (getting some evidence for) is weaker than verification (getting sufficient evidence to regard as true), and our (imaginary) evidence so far in favor of 4 falls well short of conclusive support. Further research — the study of more representative or much larger samples, for example — might yield very different observations. It might lead us to conclude that although initial research had confirmed our hypothesis about smoking as the cause of cardiovascular disease, the additional information obtained subsequently disconfirmed the hypothesis. For most interesting hypotheses, both in detective stories and in modern science, there is both confirming and disconfirming evidence simultaneously. The challenge is to evaluate the hypothesis by considering such conflicting evidence.

As long as we confine our observations to *correlations* of the sort reported in our several (imaginary) observations, such as proposition 1, *230 smokers in a group of 500 have cardiovascular disease*, or 12, *230 smokers with the disease share no other suspected factors*, such as lack of exercise, any defense of a *causal* hypothesis such as claim 3, *Smoking causes cardiovascular disease*, or claim 4, *Smoking is a factor in causing the disease*, is not likely to convince the skeptic or lead those with beliefs alternative to 3 and 4 to abandon them and agree with us. Why is that? It is because a causal hypothesis without any account of the *underlying mechanism* by means of which the (alleged) cause produces the effect will seem superficial. Only when we can specify in detail *how* the (alleged) cause produces the effect will the causal hypothesis be convincing.

In other cases, in which no mechanism can be found, we seek instead to embed the causal hypothesis in a larger *theory,* one that rules out as incompatible any causal hypothesis except the favored one. (That is, we appeal to the test of consistency and thereby bring deductive reasoning to bear on our problem.) Thus, perhaps we cannot specify any mechanism—any underlying structure that generates a regular sequence of events, one of which is the effect we are studying—to explain why, for example, the gravitational mass of a body causes it to attract other bodies. But we can embed this claim in a larger context of physical theory that rules out as inconsistent any alternative causal explanation. To do that convincingly in regard to any given causal hypothesis, as this example suggests, requires detailed knowledge of the current state of the relevant body of scientific theory—something far beyond our need to consider in further detail here.

FALLACIES

The straight road on which sound reasoning proceeds gives little latitude for cruising about. Irrationality, carelessness, passionate attachment to one's unexamined beliefs, and the sheer complexity of some issues occasionally spoil the reasoning of even the best of us. Although in this book we reprint many varied voices and arguments, we hope we've reprinted no readings that exhibit the most flagrant errors or commit the graver abuses against the canons of good reasoning. Nevertheless, an inventory of those abuses and their close examination can be an instructive (as well as an amusing) exercise—instructive because the diagnosis and repair of error help to fix more clearly the principles of sound reasoning on which such remedial labors depend; amusing because we are so constituted that our perception of the nonsense of others can stimulate our minds, warm our hearts, and give us comforting feelings of superiority.

The discussion that follows, then, is a quick tour through the twisting lanes, mudflats, forests, and quicksands of the faults that one sometimes encounters in reading arguments that stray from the highway of clear thinking.

Fallacies of Ambiguity

AMBIGUITY   Near the center of the town of Concord, Massachusetts, is an empty field with a sign reading "Old Calf Pasture." Hmm. A pasture in former times in which calves grazed? A pasture now in use for old calves? An erstwhile pasture for old calves? These alternative readings arise because of **ambiguity**; brevity in the sign has produced a group of words that give rise to more than one possible interpretation, confusing the reader and (presumably) frustrating the sign writer's intentions.

Consider a more complex example. Suppose someone asserts *People have equal rights* and also *Everyone has a right to property.* Many people believe both these claims, but their combination involves an ambiguity. According to one interpretation, the two claims entail that everyone has an *equal right* to property. (That is, you and I each have an equal right to whatever property we have.) But the two claims can also be interpreted to mean that everyone has a *right to equal property.* (That is, whatever property you have a right to, I have a right to the same, or at least equivalent, property.) The latter interpretation is revolutionary, whereas the former is not. Arguments over equal rights often involve this ambiguity.

DIVISION   In the Bible, we read that the apostles of Jesus were twelve and that Matthew was an apostle. Does it follow that Matthew was twelve years old? No. To argue in this way from a property of a group to a property of a member of that group is to commit the **fallacy of division.** The example of the apostles may not be a very tempting instance of this error; here is a classic version that is a bit more interesting: If it is true that the average American family has 1.8 children, does it follow that your brother and sister-in-law are likely to have 1.8 children? If you think it does, you have committed the fallacy of division.

COMPOSITION   Could an all-star team of professional basketball players beat the Boston Celtics in their heyday—say, the team of 1985–1986? Perhaps in one game or two, but probably not in seven out of a dozen games in a row. As students of the game know, teamwork is an indispensable part of outstanding performance, and the 1985–1986 Celtics were famous for their self-sacrificing style of play.

The **fallacy of composition** can be convincingly illustrated, therefore, in this argument: *A team of five NBA all-stars is the best team in basketball if each of the five players is the best at his position.* The fallacy is called composition because the reasoning commits the error of arguing from the true premise that each member of a group has a certain property to the not necessarily true conclusion that the group (the composition) itself has the property. (That is, because *A* is the best player at forward, *B* is the best center, and so on, therefore, the team of *A, B, . . .* is the best team.)

EQUIVOCATION   In a delightful passage in Lewis Carroll's *Through the Looking-Glass,* the king asks his messenger, "Who did you pass on the road?" and the messenger replies, "Nobody." This prompts the king to observe, "Of course, Nobody walks slower than you," provoking the messenger's sullen response: "I do my best. I'm sure nobody walks much faster than I do." At this the king remarks with surprise, "He can't do that or else he'd have been here first!" (This, by the way, is the classic predecessor of the famous comic dialogue "Who's on First?" between the comedians Bud Abbott and Lou Costello.) The king and the messenger are equivocating on the term *nobody.* The messenger uses it in the normal way as an indefinite pronoun equivalent to "not anyone." But the king uses the word as though it were a proper noun, *Nobody,* the rather odd name of some person. No wonder the king and the messenger talk right past each other.

Equivocation (from the Latin for "equal voice"—i.e., giving utterance to two meanings at the same time in one word or phrase) can ruin otherwise good reasoning, as in this example: *Euthanasia is a good death; one dies a good death when one dies peacefully in old age; therefore, euthanasia is dying peacefully in old age.* The etymology of *euthanasia* is literally "a good death," so the first premise is true. And the second premise is certainly plausible. But the conclusion of this syllogism is false. Euthanasia cannot be defined as a peaceful death in one's old age, for two reasons. First, euthanasia requires the intervention of another person who kills someone (or lets the person die); second, even a very young person can be euthanized. The problem arises because "a good death" works in the second premise in a manner that does not apply to euthanasia. Both meanings of "a good death" are legitimate, but when used together, they constitute an equivocation that spoils the argument.

The fallacy of equivocation takes us from the discussion of confusions in individual claims or grounds to the more troublesome fallacies that infect the linkages between the claims we make and the grounds (or reasons) for them. These are the fallacies that occur in statements that, following the vocabulary of the Toulmin method, are called the *warrant* of reasoning. Each fallacy is an example of reasoning that involves a **non sequitur** (Latin for "It does not follow"). That is, the *claim* (the conclusion) does not follow from the *grounds* (the premises).

For a start, here is an obvious non sequitur: "He went to the movies on three consecutive nights, so he must love movies." Why doesn't the claim ("He must love movies") follow from the grounds ("He went to the movies on three consecutive nights")? Perhaps the person was just fulfilling an assignment in a film course (maybe he even hated movies so much that he had postponed three assignments to see films and now had to see them all in quick succession), or maybe he went with a girlfriend who was a movie buff, or maybe . . . —well, there are any number of other possible reasons.

Fallacies of Presumption

DISTORTING THE FACTS   Facts can be distorted either intentionally (to deceive or mislead) or unintentionally, and in either case usually (but not invariably) to the benefit of whoever is doing the distortion. Consider this not entirely hypothetical case. A pharmaceutical company spends millions of dollars to develop a new drug that will help pregnant women avoid spontaneous abortion. The company reports its findings, but it doesn't also report that its researchers have learned of a serious downside for this drug in many cases, resulting in deformed limbs in the neonate. Had the company informed the public of this fact, the drug would not have been certified for use.

Here is another case. Half a century ago the surgeon general reported that smoking cigarettes increased the likelihood that smokers would eventually suffer from lung cancer. The cigarette manufacturers vigorously protested that the surgeon general relied on inconclusive research and was badly misleading the public about the health risks of smoking. It later turned out that the tobacco companies knew that smoking increased the risk of lung cancer—a fact established by the company's own laboratories but concealed from the public. Today, thanks to public access to all the facts, it is commonplace knowledge that inhaled smoke—including secondhand smoke—is a risk factor for many illnesses.

POST HOC, ERGO PROPTER HOC   One of the most tempting errors in reasoning is to ground a claim about causation on an observed temporal sequence; that is, to argue "after this, therefore because of this" (which is what the phrase *post hoc, ergo propter hoc* means in Latin). Nearly forty years ago, when the medical community first announced that smoking tobacco caused lung cancer, advocates for the tobacco industry replied that doctors were guilty of this fallacy.

These industry advocates argued that medical researchers had merely noticed that in some people, lung cancer developed *after* considerable smoking, indeed, years after; but (they insisted) this correlation was not at all the same as a causal relation between smoking and lung cancer. True enough. The claim that *A causes B* is not the same as the claim that *B comes after A*. After all, it was possible that smokers as a group had some other common trait and that this factor was the true cause of their cancer.

As the long controversy over the truth about the causation of lung cancer shows, to avoid the appearance of fallacious *post hoc* reasoning one needs to find some way to link the observed phenomena (the correlation between smoking and the onset of lung cancer). This step requires some further theory and preferably some experimental evidence for the exact sequence or physical mechanism, in full detail, of how ingestion of tobacco smoke is a crucial factor—and is not merely an accidental or happenstance prior event—in the subsequent development of the cancer.

MANY QUESTIONS   The old saw, "When did you stop beating your wife?" illustrates the **fallacy of many questions.** This question, as one can readily see, is unanswerable unless all three of its implicit presuppositions are true. The questioner presupposes that (1) the addressee has or had a wife, (2) he has beaten her, and (3) he has stopped beating her. If any of these presuppositions is false, then the question is pointless; it cannot be answered strictly and simply with a date or time.

HASTY GENERALIZATION   From a logical point of view, **hasty generalization** is the precipitous move from true assertions about *one* or a *few* instances to dubious or even false assertions about *all*. For example, while it may be true that the only native Hungarians you personally know do not speak English very well, that is no basis for asserting that all Hungarians do not speak English very well. Or if the clothes you recently ordered online turn out not to fit very well, it doesn't follow that *all* online clothes turn out to be too large or too small. A hasty generalization usually lies behind a **stereotype**—that is, a person or event treated as typical of a whole class. Thus, in 1914, after the German invasion of Belgium, during which the invaders committed numerous atrocities, the German troops were quickly stereotyped by the Allies as brutal savages who skewered helpless babies on their bayonets.

THE SLIPPERY SLOPE   One of the most familiar arguments against any type of government regulation is that if it is allowed, then it will be just the first step down the path that leads to ruinous interference, overregulation, and totalitarian control. Fairly often we encounter this mode of argument in the public debates over handgun control, the censorship of pornography, and physician-assisted suicide. The argument is called the **slippery slope argument** (or the **wedge argument**, from the way people use the thin end of a wedge to split solid things apart; it is also called, rather colorfully, "letting the camel's nose under the tent"). The fallacy here is in implying that the first step necessarily leads to the second, and so on down the slope to disaster, when in fact there is no necessary slide from the first step to the second. (Would handgun registration lead to a police state? Well, it hasn't in Switzerland.) Sometimes, the argument takes the form of claiming that a seemingly innocent or even attractive principle that is being applied in a given case (censorship of pornography, to avoid promoting sexual violence) requires one for the sake of consistency to apply the same principle in other cases, only with absurd and catastrophic results (censorship of everything in print, to avoid hurting anyone's feelings).

Here's an extreme example of this fallacy in action:

> Automobiles cause more deaths than handguns do. If you oppose handguns on the ground that doing so would save lives of the innocent, you'll soon find yourself wanting to outlaw the automobile.

Does opposition to handguns have this consequence? Not necessarily. Most people accept without dispute the right of society to regulate the operation of motor vehicles by requiring drivers to have a license, a greater restriction than many states impose on gun ownership. Besides, a gun is a lethal weapon designed to kill, whereas an automobile or truck is a vehicle designed for transportation. Private ownership and use in both cases entail risks of death to the innocent. But there is no inconsistency in a society's refusal to tolerate this risk in the case of guns and its willingness to do so in the case of automobiles.

Closely related to the slippery slope is what lawyers call a **parade of horrors,** an array of examples of terrible consequences that will or might follow if we travel down a certain path. A good example appears in Justice William Brennan's opinion for the Supreme Court in *Texas v. Johnson* (1989), regarding a Texas law against burning the American flag in political protest. If this law is allowed to stand, Brennan suggests, we may next find laws against burning the presidential seal, state flags, and the Constitution.

FALSE ANALOGY   Argument by analogy, as we point out in Chapter 3 and as many of the selections in this book show, is a familiar and even indispensable mode of argument. But it can be treacherous because it runs the risk of the **fallacy of false analogy.** Unfortunately, we have no simple or foolproof way of distinguishing between the useful, legitimate analogies and the others. The key question to ask yourself is this: Do the two things put into analogy differ in any essential and relevant respect, or are they different only in unimportant and irrelevant aspects?

In a famous example from his discussion in support of suicide, philosopher David Hume rhetorically asked: "It would be no crime in me to divert the Nile or Danube from its course, were I able to effect such purposes. Where then is the crime of turning a few ounces of blood from their natural channel?" This is a striking analogy, except that it rests on a false assumption. No one has the right to divert the Nile or the Danube or any other major international watercourse; it would be a catastrophic crime to do so without the full consent of people living in the region, their government, and so forth. Therefore, arguing by analogy, one might well say that no one has the right to take his or her own life, either. Thus, Hume's own analogy can be used to argue against his thesis that suicide is no crime. But let's ignore the way in which his example can be turned against him. The analogy is a terrible one in any case. Isn't it obvious that the Nile, regardless of its exact course, would continue to nourish Egypt and the Sudan, whereas the blood flowing out of someone's veins will soon leave that person dead? The fact that the blood is the same blood, whether in a person's body or in a pool on the floor (just as the water of the Nile is the same body of water no matter what path it follows to the sea) is, of course, irrelevant to the question of whether one has the right to commit suicide.

Let's look at a more complex example. During the 1960s, when the United States was convulsed over the purpose and scope of its military involvement in Southeast Asia, advocates of more vigorous U.S. military participation appealed to the so-called domino effect, supposedly inspired by a passing remark from President Eisenhower in the 1950s. The analogy refers to the way in which a row of standing dominoes will collapse, one after the other, if the first one is pushed. If Vietnam turns Communist, according to this analogy, so too will its neighbors, Laos and Cambodia, followed by Thailand and then Burma, until the whole region is as communist as China to the north. The domino analogy (or metaphor) provided, no doubt, a vivid illustration and effectively portrayed the worry of many anti-Communists. But did it really shed any light on the likely pattern of political and military developments in the region? The history of events there during the 1970s and 1980s did not bear out the domino analogy.

STRAW MAN   It is often tempting to reframe or report your opponent's thesis to make it easier to attack and perhaps refute it. If you do this in the course of an argument, you are creating a straw man, a thing of no substance that's easily blown away. The straw man you've constructed is usually a radically conservative or extremely liberal thesis, which few if any would want to defend. That's why it is easier to refute than the view your opponent actually holds. "So you defend the death penalty—and all the horrible things done in its name. No one in his right mind would hold such a view." It's highly unlikely that your opponent supports *everything* that has been done in the name of capital punishment—crucifixion and beheading, for example, or execution of the children of the guilty offender.

SPECIAL PLEADING   We all have our favorites—relatives, friends, and neighbors—and we're all too likely to show that favoritism in unacceptable ways. How about this: "Yes, I know Billy hit Sally first, but he's my son. He's a good boy, and I know he must have had a good reason." Or this: "True, she's late for work again—the third time this week!—but her uncle's my friend, and it will be embarrassing to me if she's fired, so we'll just ignore it." Special pleading inevitably leads to unmerited advantages.

BEGGING THE QUESTION   The argument over whether the death penalty is a deterrent illustrates another fallacy. From the fact that you live in a death-penalty state and were not murdered yesterday, we cannot infer that the death penalty was a deterrent. Yet it is tempting to make this inference, perhaps because—all unaware—we are relying on the **fallacy of begging the question.** If someone tacitly assumes from the start that the death penalty is an effective deterrent, then the fact that you weren't murdered yesterday certainly looks like evidence for the truth of that assumption. But it isn't, so long as there are competing but unexamined alternative explanations, as in this case. (The fallacy is called "begging the question," *petitio principii* in Latin, because the conclusion of the argument is hidden among its assumptions—and so the conclusion, not surprisingly, follows from the premises.)

Of course, the fact that you weren't murdered is *consistent* with the claim that the death penalty is an effective deterrent, just as someone else's being murdered is also consistent with that claim (because an effective deterrent need not be a *perfect* deterrent). In general, from the fact that two propositions are consistent with each other, we cannot infer that either is evidence for the other.

Note: The term "begging the question" is often wrongly used to mean "raises the question," as in "His action of burning the flag begs the question, What drove him to do such a thing?"

FALSE DICHOTOMY   Sometimes, oversimplification takes a more complex form, in which contrary possibilities are wrongly presented as though they were exhaustive and exclusive. "Either we get tough with drug users, or we must surrender and legalize all drugs." Really? What about doing neither and instead offering education and counseling, detoxification programs, and incentives to "Say no"? A favorite of debaters, **either/or reasoning** always runs the risk of ignoring a third (or fourth) possibility. Some disjunctions are indeed exhaustive: "Either we get tough with drug users, or we do not." This proposition, though vague (what does "get tough" really mean?), is a tautology; it cannot be false, and there is no third alternative. But most disjunctions do not express a pair of *contradictory* alternatives: They offer only a pair of *contrary* alternatives, and mere contraries do not exhaust the possibilities (recall our discussion of contraries versus contradictories on pp. 352–53).

A writer would be guilty of creating a **false dichotomy** if, for example, in an argument in favor of flogging his entire discussion was built on the relative superiority of whipping over imprisonment, as though there was no alternative punishment worth considering.

But of course, there is—notably, community service (especially for white-collar offenders, juveniles, and many first offenders).

OVERSIMPLIFICATION   "Poverty causes crime," "Taxation is unfair," "Truth is stranger than fiction"—these are examples of generalizations that exaggerate and therefore oversimplify the truth. Poverty as such can't be the sole cause of crime because many poor people do not break the law. Some taxes may be unfairly high, others unfairly low—but there is no reason to believe that *every* tax is unfair to all those who have to pay it. Some true stories do amaze us as much or more than some fictional stories, but the reverse is true, too. (In the language of the Toulmin method, **oversimplification** is the result of a failure to use suitable modal qualifiers in formulating one's claims or grounds or backing.)

RED HERRING   The fallacy of **red herring,** less colorfully named irrelevant thesis, occurs when one tries to distract one's audience by invoking a consideration that is irrelevant to the topic under discussion. (This fallacy probably gets its name from the fact that a rotten herring, or a cured herring, which is reddish, will throw pursuing hounds off the right track.) Consider this case: Some critics, seeking to defend our government's refusal to sign the Kyoto accords to reduce global warming, argue that signing is supported mainly by left-leaning scientists. This argument supposedly shows that global warming—if there is such a thing—is not a serious, urgent issue. But claiming that the supporters of these accords are left-inclined is a red herring, an irrelevant thesis. By raising doubts about the political views of the advocates of signing, critics distract attention from the scientific question (Is there global warming?) and also from the separate political question (Ought the U.S. government sign the accords?). The refusal of a government to sign the accords doesn't show there is no such thing as global warming. And even if all the advocates of signing were left-leaning (they aren't), this fact (if it were a fact, but it isn't) would not show that worries about global warming are exaggerated.

Fallacies of Relevance

TU QUOQUE   The Romans had a word for it: *Tu quoque* means "you, too." Consider this: "You're a fine one, trying to persuade me to give up smoking when you indulge yourself with a pipe and a cigar from time to time. Maybe I should quit, but then so should you. As things stand now, however, it's hypocritical of you to complain about my smoking when you persist in the same habit." The fallacy is this: The merit of a person's argument has nothing to do with the person's character or behavior. Here the assertion that smoking is bad for one's health is *not* weakened by the fact that a smoker offers the argument.

THE GENETIC FALLACY   A member of the family of fallacies that includes poisoning the well and ad hominem (see below) is the-**genetic fallacy.** Here the error takes the form of arguing against a claim by pointing out that its origin (genesis) is tainted or that it was invented by someone deserving our contempt. Thus, one might attack the ideas of the Declaration of Independence by pointing out that its principal author, Thomas Jefferson, was a slaveholder. Assuming that it is not anachronistic and inappropriate to criticize a public figure of two centuries ago for practicing slavery, and conceding that slavery is morally outrageous, it is nonetheless fallacious to attack the ideas or even the sincerity of the Declaration by attempting to impeach the credentials of its author. Jefferson's moral faults do not by themselves falsify, make improbable, or constitute counterevidence to the truth or other merits of the claims made in his writings. At most, one's faults cast doubt on one's integrity or sincerity if one makes claims at odds with one's practice.

The genetic fallacy can take other forms less closely allied to ad hominem argument. For example, an opponent of the death penalty might argue this:

> Capital punishment arose in barbarous times; but we claim to be civilized; therefore, we should discard this relic of the past.

Such reasoning shouldn't be persuasive because the question of the death penalty for our society must be decided by the degree to which it serves our purposes—justice and defense against crime, presumably—to which its historic origins are irrelevant. The practices of beer- and wine-making are as old as human civilization, but their origin in antiquity is no reason to outlaw them in our time. The curious circumstances in which something originates usually play no role in its validity. Anyone who would argue that nothing good could possibly come from molds and fungi is refuted by Sir Alexander Fleming's discovery of penicillin in 1928.

POISONING THE WELL   During the 1970s some critics of the Equal Rights Amendment (ERA) argued against it by pointing out that

Marx and Engels, in their *Communist Manifesto*, favored equality of women and men—and therefore the ERA was immoral, undesirable, and perhaps even a Communist plot. This kind of reasoning is an attempt to **poison the well**; that is, an attempt to shift attention from the merits of the argument—the validity of the reasoning, the truth of the claims—to the source or origin of the argument. Such criticism deflects attention from the real issue; namely, whether the view in question is true and what the quality of evidence is in its support. The mere fact that Marx (or Hitler, for that matter) believed something does not show that the belief is false or immoral; just because some scoundrel believes the world is round, that is no reason for you to believe it is flat.

APPEAL TO IGNORANCE   In the controversy over the death penalty, the issues of deterrence and executing the innocent are bound to be raised. Because no one knows how many innocent persons have been convicted for murder and wrongfully executed, it is tempting for abolitionists to argue that the death penalty is too risky. It is equally tempting for proponents of the death penalty to argue that since no one knows how many people have been deterred from murder by the threat of execution, we abolish it at society's peril.

Each of these arguments suffers from the same flaw: the **fallacy of appeal to ignorance**. Each argument invites the audience to draw an inference from a premise that is unquestionably true—but what is that premise? It asserts that there is something "we don't know." But what we *don't* know cannot be *evidence* for (or against) anything. Our ignorance is no reason for believing anything, except perhaps that we ought to undertake an appropriate investigation in order to replace our ignorance with reliable information.

AD HOMINEM   Closely allied to poisoning the well is another fallacy, **ad hominem** argument (from the Latin for "against the person"). A critic can easily yield to the temptation to attack an argument or theory by trying to impeach or undercut the credentials of its advocates.

Example: Jones is arguing that prayer should not be permitted in public schools, and Smith responds by pointing out that Jones has twice been convicted of assaulting members of the clergy. Jones's behavior doubtless is reprehensible, but the issue is not Jones, it is prayer in school, and what must be scrutinized is Jones's argument, not his police record or his character.

APPEAL TO AUTHORITY   The example of Jefferson that we gave to illustrate the genetic fallacy can be turned around to illustrate another fallacy. One might easily imagine someone from the South in 1860 defending the slave-owning society of that day by appealing to the fact that no less a person than Jefferson—a brilliant public figure, thinker, and leader by any measure—owned slaves. Or today one might defend capital punishment on the ground that Abraham Lincoln, surely one of the nation's greatest presidents, signed many death warrants during the Civil War, authorizing the execution of Union soldiers. No doubt the esteem in which such figures as Jefferson and Lincoln are deservedly held amounts to impressive endorsement for whatever acts and practices, policies, and institutions, they supported. But the **authority** of these figures in itself is not evidence for the truth of their views, so their authority cannot be a reason for anyone to agree with them. Obviously, Jefferson and Lincoln themselves could not support their beliefs by pointing to the fact that they held them. Because their own authority is no reason for them to believe what they believe, it is no reason for anyone else, either.

Sometimes, the appeal to authority is fallacious because the authoritative person is not an expert on the issue in dispute. The fact that a high-energy physicist has won the Nobel Prize is no reason for attaching any special weight to her views on the causes of cancer, the reduction of traffic accidents, or the legalization of marijuana. However, one would be well advised to attend to her views on the advisability of ballistic missile-defense systems, for there may be a connection between the kind of research for which she received the prize and the defense research projects.

All of us depend heavily on the knowledge of various experts and authorities, so we tend to respect their views. Conversely, we should resist the temptation to accord their views on diverse subjects the same respect that we grant them in the area of their expertise.

APPEAL TO FEAR   The Romans called this fallacy *ad baculum*, "resorting to violence" (*baculum* means "stick" or "club"). Trying to persuade people to agree with you by threatening them with painful consequences is obviously an appeal that no rational person would contemplate. The violence need not be physical; if you threaten someone with the loss of a job, for instance, you are still using a stick. Violence or the threat of harmful consequences in the course of an argument is beyond reason and always shows the haste or impatience of those who appeal to it. It is also an indication that the argument on its merits would be unpersuasive, inconclusive, or worse. President Teddy Roosevelt's epigrammatic doctrine for the kind of foreign policy he favored—"Speak softly but carry a big stick"—illustrates an attempt to have it both ways: an appeal to reason for starters but a recourse to coercion, or the threat of coercion, as a backup if needed.

Finally, we add two fallacies, not easily embraced by Engels's three categories that have served us well thus far (ambiguity, erroneous presumption, and irrelevance): death by a thousand qualifications and protecting the hypothesis.

DEATH BY A THOUSAND QUALIFICATIONS   In a letter of recommendation sent in support of an applicant for a job on your newspaper, you find this sentence: "Young Smith was the best student I've ever taught in an English course." Pretty strong endorsement, you think, except that you don't know, because you haven't been told, that the letter writer is a very junior faculty member, has been teaching for only two years, is an instructor in the history department, taught a section of freshman English as a courtesy for a sick colleague, and had only eight students enrolled in the course. Thanks to these implicit qualifications, the letter writer did not lie or exaggerate in his praise; but the effect of his sentence on you, the unwitting reader, is quite misleading. The explicit claim in the letter, and its impact on you, is quite different from the tacitly qualified claim in the mind of the writer.

Death by a thousand qualifications gets its name from the ancient torture of death by a thousand small cuts. Thus, a bold assertion can be virtually killed, its true content reduced to nothing, bit by bit, as all the appropriate or necessary qualifications are added to it. Consider another example. Suppose you hear a politician describing another country (let's call it Ruritania so as not to offend anyone) as a "democracy"—except it turns out that Ruritania doesn't have regular elections, lacks a written constitution, has no independent judiciary, prohibits religious worship except of the state-designated deity, and so forth. So what remains of the original claim that Ruritania is a democracy is little or nothing. The qualifications have taken all the content out of the original description.

PROTECTING THE HYPOTHESIS   In Chapter 3, we contrasted *reasoning* and *rationalization* (or the finding of bad reasons for what one intends to believe anyway). Rationalization can take subtle forms, as the following example indicates. Suppose you're standing with a friend on the shore or on a pier, and you watch as a ship heads out to sea. As it reaches the horizon, it slowly disappears—first the hull, then the upper decks, and finally the tip of the mast. Because the ship (you both assume) isn't sinking, it occurs to you that this sequence of observations provides evidence that the earth's surface is curved. Nonsense, says your companion. Light waves sag, or bend down, over distances of a few miles, and so a flat surface (such as the ocean) can intercept them. Hence, the ship, which appears to be going "over" the horizon, really isn't: It's just moving steadily farther and farther away in a straight line. Your friend, you discover to your amazement, is a card-carrying member of the Flat Earth Society (yes, there really is such an organization). Now most of us would regard the idea that light rays bend down in the manner required by the Flat Earther's argument as a rationalization whose sole purpose is to protect the flat-earth doctrine against counterevidence. We would be convinced it was a rationalization, and not a very good one at that, if the Flat Earther held to it despite a patient and thorough explanation from a physicist that showed modern optical theory to be quite incompatible with the view that light waves sag.

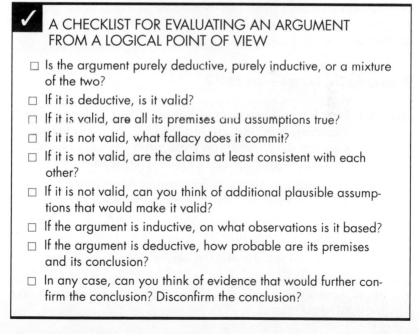

✓ A CHECKLIST FOR EVALUATING AN ARGUMENT
FROM A LOGICAL POINT OF VIEW

☐ Is the argument purely deductive, purely inductive, or a mixture of the two?

☐ If it is deductive, is it valid?

☐ If it is valid, are all its premises and assumptions true?

☐ If it is not valid, what fallacy does it commit?

☐ If it is not valid, are the claims at least consistent with each other?

☐ If it is not valid, can you think of additional plausible assumptions that would make it valid?

☐ If the argument is inductive, on what observations is it based?

☐ If the argument is deductive, how probable are its premises and its conclusion?

☐ In any case, can you think of evidence that would further confirm the conclusion? Disconfirm the conclusion?

This example illustrates two important points about the *backing* of arguments. First, it is always possible to protect a hypothesis by abandoning adjacent or connected hypotheses; this is the tactic our Flat Earth friend has used. This maneuver is possible, however, only because—and this is the second point—whenever we test a hypothesis, we do so by taking for granted (usually, quite unconsciously) many other hypotheses as well. So the evidence for the hypothesis we think we are confirming is impossible to separate entirely from the adequacy of the connected hypotheses. As long as we have no reason to doubt that light rays travel in straight lines (at least over distances of a few miles), our Flat Earth friend's argument is unconvincing. But once that hypothesis is itself put in doubt, the idea that seemed at first to be a pathetic rationalization takes on an even more troublesome character.

There are, then, not one but two fallacies exposed by this example. The first and perhaps graver one is in rigging your hypothesis so that *no matter what* observations are brought against it, you will count nothing as falsifying it. The second and subtler one is in thinking that as you test one hypothesis, all of your other background beliefs are left safely to one side, immaculate and uninvolved. On the contrary, our beliefs form a corporate structure, intertwined and connected to one another with great complexity, and no one of them can ever be singled out for unique and isolated application, confirmation, or disconfirmation to the world around us.

Exercise: Fallacies—or Not?

Here, for diversion and practice, are some fallacies in action. Some of these statements, however, are not fallacies. Can you tell which is which? Can you detect *what* has gone wrong in the cases where something has gone wrong? Please explain your reasoning.

1. Abortion is murder—and it doesn't matter whether we're talking about killing a human embryo or a human fetus.

2. Euthanasia is not a good thing, it's murder—and it doesn't matter how painful one's dying may be.

3. Never loan a tool to a friend. I did once and never got it back.

4. If the neighbors don't like our loud music, that's just too bad. After all, we have a right to listen to the music we like when and where we want to play it.

5. The Good Samaritan in the Bible was pretty foolish; he was taking grave risks with no benefits for him in sight.

6. "Shoot first and ask questions afterward" is a good epigram for the kind of foreign policy we need.

7. "You can fool some of the people all of the time, and you can fool all the people some of the time, but you can't fool all the people all of the time." That's what Abraham Lincoln said, and he was right.

8. It doesn't matter whether Shakespeare wrote the plays attributed to him. What matters is whether the plays are any good.

9. The Golden Gate Bridge in San Francisco ought to be closed down. After all, just look at all the suicides that have occurred there.

10. Reparations for African Americans are way overdue; it's just another version of the reparations eventually paid to the Japanese Americans who were wrongly interned in 1942 during World War II.

11. Animals don't have rights any more than do trees or stones. They don't have desires, either. What they have are feelings and needs.

12. The average American family is said to have 2.1 children. This is absurd—did you ever meet 2.1 children?

13. My marriage was a failure, which just proves my point: Don't ever get married in the first place.

14. The Red Queen in *Alice in Wonderland* was right: Verdict first, evidence later.

15. Not until astronauts sailed through space around the moon and could see its back side for themselves did we have adequate reason to believe that the moon even had a back side.

16. If you start out with a bottle of beer a day and then go on to a glass or two of wine on the weekends, you're well on your way to becoming a hopeless drunk.

17. Two Indians are sitting on a fence. The small Indian is the son of the big Indian, but the big Indian is not the small Indian's father. How is that possible?

18. If you toss a coin five times and each time it comes up heads, is it more likely than not that on the sixth throw you'll come up heads again—or is it more likely that you'll come up tails? Or is neither more likely?

19. Going to church on a regular basis is bad for your health. Instead of sitting in a pew for an hour each Sunday, you'd be better off taking an hour's brisk walk.

20. You can't trust anything he says. When he was young, he was an avid Communist.

21. Since 9/11 we've tried and convicted few terrorists, so our defense systems must be working.

22. We can trust the White House in its press releases because it's a reliable source of information.

23. Intelligent design must be true because the theory of evolution can't explain how life began.

24. Andreas Serrano's notorious photograph called *Piss Christ* (1989), showing a small plastic crucifix submerged in a glass of urine, never should have been put on public display, let alone financed by public funds.

25. Doubting Thomas was right—you need more than somebody's say-so to support a claim of resurrection.

26. You are a professional baseball player and you have a good-luck charm. When you wear it, the team wins. When you don't wear it, the team loses. What do you infer?

27. Resolve the following dilemma: When it rains, you can't fix the hole in the roof. When it's not raining, there is no need to mend the roof. Conclusion: Leave the roof as it is.

28. You are at the beach, and you watch a ship steaming toward the horizon. Bit by bit it disappears from view—first the masts, then the upper deck, then the main deck, then the stern, and then it's gone. Why would it be wrong to infer that the ship is sinking?

29. How can it be true that "it's the exception that proves the rule"? If anything, isn't it the exception that *dis*proves the rule?

30. How come herbivores don't eat herbs?

31. In the 1930s it was commonplace to see ads announcing "More Doctors Smoke Camels." What do you make of such an ad?

32. Suppose the only way you could save five innocent people was by killing one of them. Would you do it? Suppose the only way you could save one innocent person was by killing five others. Would you do it?

Max Shulman

Having read about proper and improper arguments, you are now well equipped to read a short story on the topic.

Max Shulman (1919–1988) began his career as a writer when he was a journalism student at the University of Minnesota. Later he wrote humorous novels, stories, and plays. One of his novels, Barefoot Boy

with Cheek *(1943), was made into a musical, and another,* Rally Round
the Flag, Boys! *(1957), was made into a film starring Paul Newman and
Joanne Woodward.* The Tender Trap *(1954), a play he wrote with Robert
Paul Smith, still retains its popularity with theater groups.*

   *"Love Is a Fallacy" was first published in 1951, when demeaning ster-
eotypes about women and minorities were widely accepted in the marketplace as well as the home. Thus, jokes about domineering mothers-in-law
or about dumb blondes routinely met with no objection.*

Love Is a Fallacy

Cool was I and logical. Keen, calculating, perspicacious, acute,
and astute—I was all of these. My brain was as powerful as a
dynamo, as precise as a chemist's scales, as penetrating as a scalpel.
And—think of it!—I was only eighteen.

It is not often that one so young has such a giant intellect. Take,
for example, Petey Bellows, my roommate at the university. Same
age, same background, but dumb as an ox. A nice enough fellow,
you understand, but nothing upstairs. Emotional type. Unstable.
Impressionable. Worst of all, a faddist. Fads, I submit, are the very
negation of reason. To be swept up in every new craze that comes
along, to surrender yourself to idiocy just because everybody else is
doing it—this, to me, is the acme of mindlessness. Not, however, to
Petey.

One afternoon I found Petey lying on his bed with an expression of such distress on his face that I immediately diagnosed
appendicitis. "Don't move," I said. "Don't take a laxative. I'll call a
doctor."

"Raccoon," he mumbled thickly.

"Raccoon?" I said, pausing in my flight.   5

"I want a raccoon coat," he wailed.

I perceived that his trouble was not physical, but mental. "Why
do you want a raccoon coat?"

"I should have known it," he cried, pounding his temples.
"I should have known they'd come back when the Charleston
came back. Like a fool I spent all my money for textbooks, and now
I can't get a raccoon coat."

"Can you mean," I said incredulously, "that people are actually
wearing raccoon coats again?"

"All the Big Men on Campus are wearing them. Where've you   10
been?"

"In the library," I said, naming a place not frequented by Big
Men on Campus.

He leaped from the bed and paced the room. "I've got to have a raccoon coat," he said passionately. "I've got to!"

"Petey, why? Look at it rationally. Raccoon coats are unsanitary. They shed. They smell bad. They weigh too much. They're unsightly. They——"

"You don't understand," he interrupted impatiently. "It's the thing to do. Don't you want to be in the swim?"

"No," I said truthfully.   15

"Well, I do," he declared. "I'd give anything for a raccoon coat. Anything!"

My brain, that precision instrument, slipped into high gear. "Anything?" I asked, looking at him narrowly.

"Anything," he affirmed in ringing tones.

I stroked my chin thoughtfully. It so happened that I knew where to get my hands on a raccoon coat. My father had had one in his undergraduate days; it lay now in a trunk in the attic back home. It also happened that Petey had something I wanted. He didn't *have* it exactly, but at least he had first rights on it. I refer to his girl, Polly Espy.

I had long coveted Polly Espy. Let me emphasize that my desire 20 for this young woman was not emotional in nature. She was, to be sure, a girl who excited the emotions, but I was not one to let my heart rule my head. I wanted Polly for a shrewdly calculated, entirely cerebral reason.

I was a freshman in law school. In a few years I would be out in practice. I was well aware of the importance of the right kind of wife in furthering a lawyer's career. The successful lawyers I had observed were, almost without exception, married to beautiful, gracious, intelligent women. With one omission, Polly fitted these specifications perfectly.

Beautiful she was. She was not yet of pin-up proportions, but I felt sure that time would supply the lack. She already had the makings.

Gracious she was. By gracious I mean full of graces. She had an erectness of carriage, an ease of bearing, a poise that clearly indicated the best of breeding. At table her manners were exquisite. I had seen her at the Kozy Kampus Korner eating the specialty of the house—a sandwich that contained scraps of pot roast, gravy, chopped nuts, and a dipper of sauerkraut—without even getting her fingers moist.

Intelligent she was not. In fact, she veered in the opposite direction. But I believed that under my guidance she would smarten up.

At any rate, it was worth a try. It is, after all, easier to make a beautiful dumb girl smart than to make an ugly smart girl beautiful.

"Petey," I said, "are you in love with Polly Espy?"   25

"I think she's a keen kid," he replied, "but I don't know if you'd call it love. Why?"

"Do you," I asked, "have any kind of formal arrangement with her? I mean are you going steady or anything like that?"

"No. We see each other quite a bit, but we both have other dates. Why?"

"Is there," I asked, "any other man for whom she has a particular fondness?"

"Not that I know of. Why?"   30

I nodded with satisfaction. "In other words, if you were out of the picture, the field would be open. Is that right?"

"I guess so. What are you getting at?"

"Nothing, nothing," I said innocently, and took my suitcase out of the closet.

"Where you going?" asked Petey.

"Home for the weekend." I threw a few things into the bag.   35

"Listen," he said, clutching my arm eagerly, "while you're home, you couldn't get some money from your old man, could you, and lend it to me so I can buy a raccoon coat?"

"I may do better than that," I said with a mysterious wink and closed my bag and left.

"Look," I said to Petey when I got back Monday morning. I threw open the suitcase and revealed the huge, hairy, gamy object that my father had worn in his Stutz Bearcat in 1925.

"Holy Toledo!" said Petey reverently. He plunged his hands into the raccoon coat and then his face. "Holy Toledo!" he repeated fifteen or twenty times.

"Would you like it?" I asked.   40

"Oh yes!" he cried, clutching the greasy pelt to him. Then a canny look came into his eyes. "What do you want for it?"

"Your girl," I said, mincing no words.

"Polly?" he said in a horrified whisper. "You want Polly?"

"That's right."

He flung the coat from him. "Never," he said stoutly.   45

I shrugged. "Okay. If you don't want to be in the swim, I guess it's your business."

I sat down in a chair and pretended to read a book, but out of the corner of my eye I kept watching Petey. He was a torn man.

First he looked at the coat with the expression of a waif at a bakery window. Then he turned away and set his jaw resolutely. Then he looked back at the coat, with even more longing in his face. Then he turned away, but with not so much resolution this time. Back and forth his head swiveled, desire waxing, resolution waning. Finally he didn't turn away at all; he just stood and stared with mad lust at the coat.

"It isn't as though I was in love with Polly," he said thickly. "Or going steady or anything like that."

"That's right," I murmured.

"What's Polly to me, or me to Polly?"   50

"Not a thing," said I.

"It's just been a casual kick—just a few laughs, that's all."

"Try on the coat," said I.

He complied. The coat bunched high over his ears and dropped all the way down to his shoe tops. He looked like a mound of dead raccoons. "Fits fine," he said happily.

I rose from my chair. "Is it a deal?" I asked, extending my hand.   55

He swallowed. "It's a deal," he said and shook my hand.

I had my first date with Polly the following evening. This was in the nature of a survey; I wanted to find out just how much work I had to do to get her mind up to the standard I required. I took her first to dinner. "Gee, that was a delish dinner," she said as we left the restaurant. Then I took her to a movie. "Gee, that was a marvy movie," she said as we left the theater. And then I took her home. "Gee, I had a sensaysh time," she said as she bade me good night.

I went back to my room with a heavy heart. I had gravely underestimated the size of my task. This girl's lack of information was terrifying. Nor would it be enough merely to supply her with information. First she had to be taught to *think*. This loomed as a project of no small dimensions, and at first I was tempted to give her back to Petey. But then I got to thinking about her abundant physical charms and about the way she entered a room and the way she handled a knife and fork, and I decided to make an effort.

I went about it, as in all things, systematically. I gave her a course in logic. It happened that I, as a law student, was taking a course in logic myself, so I had all the facts at my fingertips. "Polly," I said to her when I picked her up on our next date, "tonight we are going over to the Knoll and talk."

"Oo, terrif," she replied. One thing I will say for this girl: You   60 would go far to find another so agreeable.

We went to the Knoll, the campus trysting place, and we sat down under an old oak, and she looked at me expectantly: "What are we going to talk about?" she asked.

"Logic."

She thought this over for a minute and decided she liked it. "Magnif," she said.

"Logic," I said, clearing my throat, "is the science of thinking. Before we can think correctly, we must first learn to recognize the common fallacies of logic. These we will take up tonight."

"Wow-dow!" she cried, clapping her hands delightedly.   65

I winced, but went bravely on. "First let us examine the fallacy called Dicto Simpliciter."

"By all means," she urged, batting her lashes eagerly.

"Dicto Simpliciter means an argument based on an unqualified generalization. For example: Exercise is good. Therefore everybody should exercise."

"I agree," said Polly earnestly. "I mean exercise is wonderful. I mean it builds the body and everything."

"Polly," I said gently, "the argument is a fallacy. *Exercise is good* 70 is an unqualified generalization. For instance, if you have heart disease, exercise is bad, not good. Many people are ordered by their doctors *not* to exercise. You must *qualify* the generalization. You must say exercise is *usually* good, or exercise is good *for most people*. Otherwise you have committed a Dicto Simpliciter. Do you see?"

"No," she confessed. "But this is marvy. Do more! Do more!"

"It will be better if you stop tugging at my sleeve," I told her, and when she desisted, I continued. "Next we take up a fallacy called Hasty Generalization. Listen carefully: You can't speak French. I can't speak French. Petcy Bellows can't speak French. I must therefore conclude that nobody at the University of Minnesota can speak French."

"Really?" said Polly, amazed. "*Nobody?*"

I hid my exasperation. "Polly, it's a fallacy. The generalization is reached too hastily. There are too few instances to support such a conclusion."

"Know any more fallacies?" she asked breathlessly. "This is 75 more fun than dancing even."

I fought off a wave of despair. I was getting nowhere with this girl, absolutely nowhere. Still, I am nothing if not persistent. I continued. "Next comes Post Hoc. Listen to this: Let's not take Bill on our picnic. Every time we take him out with us, it rains."

"I know somebody just like that," she exclaimed. "A girl back home—Eula Becker, her name is. It never fails. Every single time we take her on a picnic—"

"Polly," I said sharply, "it's a fallacy. Eula Becker doesn't *cause* the rain. She has no connection with the rain. You are guilty of Post Hoc if you blame Eula Becker."

"I'll never do it again," she promised contritely. "Are you mad at me?"

I sighed. "No, Polly, I'm not mad." 80

"Then tell me some more fallacies."

"All right. Let's try Contradictory Premises."

"Yes, let's," she chirped, blinking her eyes happily.

I frowned, but plunged ahead. "Here's an example of Contradictory Premises: If God can do anything, can He make a stone so heavy that He won't be able to lift it?"

"Of course," she replied promptly. 85

"But if He can do anything, He can lift the stone," I pointed out.

"Yeah," she said thoughtfully. "Well, then I guess He can't make the stone."

"But He can do anything," I reminded her.

She scratched her pretty, empty head. "I'm all confused," she admitted.

"Of course you are. Because when the premises of an argu- 90 ment contradict each other, there can be no argument. If there is an irresistible force, there can be no immovable object. If there is an immovable object, there can be no irresistible force. Get it?"

"Tell me some more of this keen stuff," she said eagerly.

I consulted my watch. "I think we'd better call it a night. I'll take you home now, and you go over all the things you've learned. We'll have another session tomorrow night."

I deposited her at the girls' dormitory, where she assured me that she had had a perfectly terrif evening, and I went glumly home to my room. Petey lay snoring in his bed, the raccoon coat huddled like a great hairy beast at his feet. For a moment I considered waking him and telling him that he could have his girl back. It seemed clear that my project was doomed to failure. The girl simply had a logic-proof head.

But then I reconsidered. I had wasted one evening; I might as well waste another. Who knew? Maybe somewhere in the extinct crater of her mind a few embers still smoldered. Maybe somehow I could fan them into flame. Admittedly it was not a prospect fraught with hope, but I decided to give it one more try.

Seated under the oak the next evening I said, "Our first fallacy 95
tonight is called Ad Misericordiam."

She quivered with delight.

"Listen closely," I said. "A man applies for a job. When the boss
asks him what his qualifications are, he replies that he has a wife
and six children at home, the wife is a helpless cripple, the children
have nothing to eat, no clothes to wear, no shoes on their feet, there
are no beds in the house, no coal in the cellar, and winter is coming."

A tear rolled down each of Polly's pink cheeks. "Oh, this is
awful, awful," she sobbed.

"Yes, it's awful," I agreed, "but it's no argument. The man
never answered the boss's question about his qualifications. Instead
he appealed to the boss's sympathy. He committed the fallacy of Ad
Misericordiam. Do you understand?"

"Have you got a handkerchief?" she blubbered.   100

I handed her a handkerchief and tried to keep from screaming
while she wiped her eyes. "Next," I said in a carefully controlled
tone, "we will discuss False Analogy. Here is an example: Students
should be allowed to look at their textbooks during examinations.
After all, surgeons have X rays to guide them during an operation,
lawyers have briefs to guide them during a trial, carpenters have
blueprints to guide them when they are building a house. Why,
then, shouldn't students be allowed to look at their textbooks during an examination?"

"There now," she said enthusiastically, "is the most marvy idea
I've heard in years."

"Polly," I said testily, "the argument is all wrong. Doctors, lawyers, and carpenters aren't taking a test to see how much they have
learned, but students are. The situations are altogether different,
and you can't make an analogy between them."

"I still think it's a good idea," said Polly.

"Nuts," I muttered. Doggedly I pressed on. "Next we'll try 105
Hypothesis Contrary to Fact."

"Sounds yummy," was Polly's reaction.

"Listen: If Madame Curie had not happened to leave a photo-
graphic plate in a drawer with a chunk of pitchblende, the world
today would not know about radium."

"True, true," said Polly, nodding her head. "Did you see the
movie? Oh, it just knocked me out. That Walter Pidgeon is so
dreamy. I mean he fractures me."

"If you can forget Mr. Pidgeon for a moment," I said coldly,
"I would like to point out that the statement is a fallacy. Maybe

Madame Curie would have discovered radium at some later date. Maybe somebody else would have discovered it. Maybe any number of things would have happened. You can't start with a hypothesis that is not true and then draw any supportable conclusions from it."

"They ought to put Walter Pidgeon in more pictures," said 110 Polly. "I hardly ever see him any more."

One more chance, I decided. But just one more. There is a limit to what flesh and blood can bear. "The next fallacy is called Poisoning the Well."

"How cute!" she gurgled.

"Two men are having a debate. The first one gets up and says, 'My opponent is a notorious liar. You can't believe a word that he is going to say.' . . . Now, Polly, think. Think hard. What's wrong?"

I watched her closely as she knit her creamy brow in concentration. Suddenly a glimmer of intelligence—the first I had seen—came into her eyes. "It's not fair," she said with indignation. "It's not a bit fair. What chance has the second man got if the first man calls him a liar before he even begins talking?"

"Right!" I cried exultantly. "One hundred percent right. It's 115 not fair. The first man has *poisoned the well* before anybody could drink from it. He has hamstrung his opponent before he could even start. . . . Polly, I'm proud of you."

"Pshaw," she murmured, blushing with pleasure.

"You see, my dear, these things aren't so hard. All you have to do is concentrate. Think—examine—evaluate. Come now, let's review everything we have learned."

"Fire away," she said with an airy wave of her hand.

Heartened by the knowledge that Polly was not altogether a cretin, I began a long, patient review of all I had told her. Over and over and over again I cited instances, pointed out flaws, kept hammering away without letup. It was like digging a tunnel. At first everything was work, sweat, and darkness. I had no idea when I would reach the light, or even *if* I would. But I persisted. I pounded and clawed and scraped, and finally I was rewarded. I saw a chink of light. And then the chink got bigger and the sun came pouring in and all was bright.

Five grueling nights this took, but it was worth it. I had made 120 a logician out of Polly; I had taught her to think. My job was done. She was worthy of me at last. She was a fit wife for me, a proper hostess for my many mansions, a suitable mother for my well-heeled children.

It must not be thought that I was without love for this girl.
Quite the contrary. Just as Pygmalion loved the perfect woman he
had fashioned, so I loved mine. I decided to acquaint her with my
feelings at our very next meeting. The time had come to change
our relationship from academic to romantic.

"Polly," I said when next we sat beneath our oak, "tonight we
will not discuss fallacies."

"Aw, gee," she said, disappointed.

"My dear," I said, favoring her with a smile, "we have now
spent five evenings together. We have gotten along splendidly. It is
clear that we are well matched."

"Hasty Generalization," said Polly brightly.   125

"I beg your pardon," said I.

"Hasty Generalization," she repeated. "How can you say that
we are well matched on the basis of only five dates?"

I chuckled with amusement. The dear child had learned her
lessons well. "My dear," I said, patting her hand in a tolerant manner, "five dates is plenty. After all, you don't have to eat a whole
cake to know that it's good."

"False Analogy," said Polly promptly. "I'm not a cake. I'm a girl."

I chuckled with somewhat less amusement. The dear child had 130
learned her lesson perhaps too well. I decided to change tactics.
Obviously the best approach was a simple, strong, direct declaration of love. I paused for a moment while my massive brain chose
the proper words. Then I began:

"Polly, I love you. You are the whole world to me, and the
moon and the stars and the constellations of outer space. Please,
my darling, say that you will go steady with me, for if you will not,
life will be meaningless. I will languish. I will refuse my meals. I
will wander the face of the earth, a shambling, hollow-eyed hulk."

There, I thought, folding my arms, that ought to do it.

"Ad Misericordiam," said Polly.

I ground my teeth. I was not Pygmalion; I was Frankenstein,
and my monster had me by the throat. Frantically I fought back the
tide of panic surging through me. At all costs I had to keep cool.

"Well, Polly," I said, forcing a smile, "you certainly have learned 135
your fallacies."

"You're darn right," she said with a vigorous nod.

"And who taught them to you, Polly?"

"You did."

"That's right. So you do owe me something, don't you, my
dear? If I hadn't come along you never would have learned about
fallacies."

"Hypothesis Contrary to Fact," she said instantly.   140

I dashed perspiration from my brow. "Polly," I croaked, "you mustn't take all these things so literally. I mean this is just classroom stuff. You know that the things you learn in school don't have anything to do with life."

"Dicto Simpliciter," she said, wagging her finger at me playfully.

That did it. I leaped to my feet, bellowing like a bull. "Will you or will you not go steady with me?"

"I will not," she replied.

"Why not?" I demanded.   145

"Because this afternoon I promised Petey Bellows that I would go steady with him."

I reeled back, overcome with the infamy of it. After he promised, after he made a deal, after he shook my hand! "That rat!" I shrieked, kicking up great chunks of turf. "You can't go with him, Polly. He's a liar. He's a cheat. He's a rat."

"Poisoning the Well," said Polly, "and stop shouting. I think shouting must be a fallacy too."

With an immense effort of will, I modulated my voice. "All right," I said. "You're a logician. Let's look at this thing logically. How could you choose Petey Bellows over me? Look at me—a brilliant student, a tremendous intellectual, a man with an assured future. Look at Petey—a knothead, a jitterbug, a guy who'll never know where his next meal is coming from. Can you give me one logical reason why you should go steady with Petey Bellows?"

"I certainly can," declared Polly. "He's got a raccoon coat."   ∎ 150

Topic for Critical Thinking and Writing

After you have finished reading "Love Is a Fallacy," you may want to write an argumentative essay of 500 to 750 words on one of the following topics: (1) the story, rightly understood, is not antiwoman; (2) if the story is antiwoman, it is equally antiman; (3) the story is antiwoman but nevertheless belongs in this book; or (4) the story is antiwoman and does not belong in the book.

A Psychologist's View: Rogerian Argument

Real communication occurs . . . when we listen with understanding.

— CARL ROGERS

The first duty of a wise advocate is to convince his opponents that he understands their arguments, and sympathizes with their just feelings.

— SAMUEL TAYLOR COLERIDGE

ROGERIAN ARGUMENT: AN INTRODUCTION

Carl R. Rogers (1902–1987), perhaps best known for his book entitled *On Becoming a Person* (1961), was a psychotherapist, not a teacher of writing. This short essay by Rogers (on pp. 394–400) has, however, exerted much influence on instructors who teach argument. Written in the 1950s, this essay reflects the political climate of the cold war between the United States and the Soviet Union, which dominated headlines for more than forty years (1947–1989). Several of Rogers's examples of bias and frustrated communication allude to the tensions of that era.

On the surface, many arguments seem to show *A* arguing with *B*, presumably seeking to change *B*'s mind; but *A*'s argument is really directed not to *B* but to *C*. This attempt to persuade a nonparticipant is evident in the courtroom, where neither the prosecutor (*A*) nor the defense lawyer (*B*) is really trying to convince the opponent.

Michael Rougier/Getty Images

Carl R. Rogers leading a panel discussion in 1966.

Rather, both are trying to convince a third party, the jury (*C*). Prosecutors don't care whether they convince defense lawyers; they don't even mind infuriating defense lawyers because their only real goal is to convince the jury. Similarly, the writer of a letter to a newspaper, taking issue with an editorial, doesn't expect to change the paper's policy. Rather, the writer hopes to convince a third party, the reader of the newspaper.

But suppose *A* really does want to bring *B* around to *A*'s point of view. Suppose Mary really wants to persuade the teacher to allow her little lamb to stay in the classroom. Rogers points out that when we engage in an argument, if we feel our integrity or our identity is threatened, we will stiffen our position. (The teacher may feel that his or her dignity is compromised by the presence of the lamb and will scarcely attend to Mary's argument.) The sense of threat may be so great that we are unable to consider the alternative views being offered, and we therefore remain unpersuaded. Threatened, we may defend ourselves rather than our argument, and little communication will take place. Of course, a third party might say that we or our opponent presented the more convincing case, but we, and perhaps the opponent, have scarcely listened to each other, and so the two of us remain apart.

Rogers suggests, therefore, that a writer who wishes to communicate with someone (as opposed to convincing a third party) needs to reduce the threat. In a sense, the participants in the argument need to become partners rather than adversaries. Rogers writes, "Mutual communication tends to be pointed toward solving a problem rather than toward attacking a person or group." Thus, in an essay on whether schools should test students for use of drugs, the writer need not—and probably should not—see the issue as black or white, as *either / or*. Such an essay might indicate that testing is undesirable because it may have bad effects, *but in some circumstances* it may be acceptable. This qualification does not mean that one must compromise. Thus, the essayist might argue that the potential danger to liberty is so great that no circumstances justify testing students for drugs. But even such an essayist should recognize the merit (however limited) of the opposition and should grant that the position being advanced itself entails great difficulties and dangers.

A writer who wishes to reduce the psychological threat to the opposition and thus facilitate partnership in the study of some issue can do several things:

- show sympathetic understanding of the opposing argument
- recognize what is valid in it
- recognize and demonstrate that those who take the other side are nonetheless persons of goodwill

Advocates of Rogerian argument are likely to contrast it with Aristotelian argument, saying that the style of argument associated with Aristotle (384–322 B.C., Greek philosopher and rhetorician) has these two characteristics:

- It is adversarial, seeking to refute other views.
- It sees the listener as wrong, as someone who now must be overwhelmed by evidence.

In contrast to the confrontational Aristotelian style, which allegedly seeks to present an airtight case that compels belief, Rogerian argument (it is said) has the following characteristics:

- It is nonconfrontational, collegial, and friendly.
- It respects other views and allows for multiple truths.
- It seeks to achieve some degree of assent rather than convince utterly.

Thus, in the first part of an argumentative essay, a writer who takes Rogers seriously will usually

1. state the problem,
2. give the opponent's position, and
3. grant whatever validity the writer finds in that position — for instance, will recognize the circumstances in which the position would indeed be acceptable.

Next, the writer will, if possible,

4. attempt to show how the opposing position will be improved if the writer's own position is accepted.

Sometimes, of course, the differing positions may be so far apart that no reconciliation can be proposed, in which case the writer will probably seek to show how the problem can best be solved by adopting the writer's own position. We have discussed these matters in Chapter 6, but not from the point of view of a psychotherapist, and so we reprint Rogers's essay here. (This essay was orginally presented on October 11, 1951, at Northwestern University's Centennial Conference on Communications.)

Carl R. Rogers

Communication: Its Blocking and Its Facilitation

It may seem curious that a person whose whole professional effort is devoted to psychotherapy should be interested in problems of communication. What relationship is there between providing therapeutic help to individuals with emotional maladjustments and the concern of this conference with obstacles to communication? Actually the relationship is very close indeed. The whole task of psychotherapy is the task of dealing with a failure in communication. The emotionally maladjusted person, the "neurotic," is in difficulty first because communication within himself has broken down, and second because as a result of this his communication with others has been damaged. If this sounds somewhat strange, then let me put it in other terms. In the "neurotic" individual, parts of himself which have been termed unconscious, or repressed, or denied to awareness, become blocked off so that they no longer communicate themselves to the conscious or managing part of himself. As long as this is true, there are distortions in the way he communicates himself to others, and so he suffers both within himself, and in his interpersonal relations. The task of psychotherapy is to help the person achieve, through a special relationship with a therapist, good communication within himself. Once this is achieved he can communicate more freely and more effectively with others. We may say then that psychotherapy is good communication, within and between men. We may also turn that statement around and it will still be true. Good communication, free communication, within or between men, is always therapeutic.

It is, then, from a background of experience with communication in counseling and psychotherapy that I want to present here two ideas. I wish to state what I believe is one of the major factors in blocking or impeding communication, and then I wish to present what in our experience has proven to be a very important way to improving or facilitating communication.

I would like to propose, as an hypothesis for consideration, that the major barrier to mutual interpersonal communication is our very natural tendency to judge, to evaluate, to approve or disapprove, the statement of the person, or the other group. Let me illustrate my meaning with some very simple examples. As you leave the meeting tonight, one of the statements you are likely to hear is, "I didn't like that man's talk." Now what do you respond? Almost invariably your reply will be either approval or disapproval of the attitude expressed. Either you respond, "I didn't either. I thought it was terrible," or else you tend to reply, "Oh, I thought it was really good." In other words, your primary reaction is to evaluate what has just been said to you, to evaluate it from *your* point of view, your own frame of reference.

Or take another example. Suppose I say with some feeling, "I think the Republicans are behaving in ways that show a lot of good sound sense these days," what is the response that arises in your mind as you listen? The overwhelming likelihood is that it will be evaluative. You will find yourself agreeing, or disagreeing, or making some judgment about me such as "He must be a conservative," or "He seems solid in his thinking." Or let us take an illustration from the international scene. Russia says vehemently, "The treaty with Japan is a war plot on the part of the United States." We rise as one person to say "That's a lie!"

This last illustration brings in another element connected 5 with my hypothesis. Although the tendency to make evaluations is common in almost all interchange of language, it is very much heightened in those situations where feelings and emotions are deeply involved. So the stronger our feelings, the more likely it is that there will be no mutual element in the communication. There will be just two ideas, two feelings, two judgments, missing each other in psychological space. I'm sure you recognize this from your own experience. When you have not been emotionally involved yourself, and have listened to a heated discussion, you often go away thinking, "Well, they actually weren't talking about the same thing." And they were not. Each was making a judgment, an evaluation, from his own frame of reference. There was really nothing which could be called communication in any genuine sense.

This tendency to react to any emotionally meaningful statement by forming an evaluation of it from our own point of view, is, I repeat, the major barrier to interpersonal communication.

But is there any way of solving this problem, of avoiding this barrier? I feel that we are making exciting progress toward this goal and I would like to present it as simply as I can. Real communication occurs, and this evaluative tendency is avoided, when we listen with understanding. What does that mean? It means *to see the expressed idea and attitude from the other person's point of view, to sense how it feels to him, to achieve his frame of reference in regard to the thing he is talking about.*

Stated so briefly, this may sound absurdly simple, but it is not. It is an approach which we have found extremely potent in the field of psychotherapy. It is the most effective agent we know for altering the basic personality structure of an individual, and improving his relationships and his communications with others. If I can listen to what he can tell me, if I can understand how it seems to him, if I can see its personal meaning for him, if I can sense the emotional flavor which it has for him, then I will be releasing potent forces of change in him. If I can really understand how he hates his father, or hates the university, or hates communists—if I can catch the flavor of his fear of insanity, or his fear of atom bombs, or of Russia—it will be of the greatest help to him in altering those very hatreds and fears, and in establishing realistic and harmonious relationships with the very people and situations toward which he has felt hatred and fear. We know from our research that such empathic understanding—understanding *with* a person, not *about* him—is such an effective approach that it can bring about major changes in personality.

Some of you may be feeling that you listen well to people, and that you have never seen such results. The chances are very great indeed that your listening has not been of the type I have described. Fortunately I can suggest a little laboratory experiment which you can try to test the quality of your understanding. The next time you get into an argument with your wife, or your friend, or with a small group of friends, just stop the discussion for a moment and for an experiment, institute this rule. "Each person can speak up for himself only *after* he has first restated the ideas and feelings of the previous speaker accurately, and to that speaker's satisfaction." You see what this would mean. It would simply mean that before presenting your own point of view, it would be necessary for you to really achieve the other speaker's frame of reference—to understand his thoughts and feelings so well that you could summarize them for him. Sounds simple, doesn't it? But if you try it you will discover it one of the most difficult things you have ever tried to do. However, once you have been able to see the other's point of view, your own comments will have to be drastically revised. You will also find the emotion going out of the discussion, the differences being reduced, and those differences which remain being of a rational and understandable sort.

Can you imagine what this kind of an approach would mean if it were projected into larger areas? What would happen to a labor-management dispute if it was conducted in such a way that labor, without necessarily agreeing, could accurately state management's point of view in a way that management could accept; and management, without approving labor's stand, could state labor's case in a way that labor agreed was accurate? It would mean that real communication was established, and one could practically guarantee that some reasonable solution would be reached.

If then this way of approach is an effective avenue to good 10 communication and good relationships, as I am quite sure you will agree if you try the experiment I have mentioned, why is it not more widely tried and used? I will try to list the difficulties which keep it from being utilized.

In the first place it takes courage, a quality which is not too widespread. I am indebted to Dr. S. I. Hayakawa, the semanticist, for pointing out that to carry on psychotherapy in this fashion is to take a very real risk, and that courage is required. If you really understand another person in this way, if you are willing to enter his private world and see the way life appears to him, without any attempt to make evaluative judgments, you run the risk of being changed yourself. You might see it his way, you might find yourself influenced in your attitudes or your personality. This risk of being changed is one of the most frightening prospects most of us can face. If I enter, as fully as I am able, into the private world of a neurotic or psychotic individual, isn't there a risk that I might become lost in that world? Most of us are afraid to take that risk. Or if we had a Russian communist speaker here tonight, or Senator Joe McCarthy, how many of us would dare to try to see the world from each of these points of view? The great majority of us could not *listen*; we would find ourselves compelled to *evaluate*, because listening would seem too dangerous. So the first requirement is courage, and we do not always have it.

But there is a second obstacle. It is just when emotions are strongest that it is most difficult to achieve the frame of reference of the other person or group. Yet it is the time the attitude is most needed, if communication is to be established. We have not found this to be an insuperable obstacle in our experience in psychotherapy. A third party, who is able to lay aside his own feelings and evaluations, can assist greatly by listening with understanding to each person or group and clarifying the views and attitudes each holds. We have found this very effective in small groups in which contradictory or antagonistic attitudes exist. When the parties to a dispute realize that they are being understood, that someone sees how the situation seems to them, the statements grow less exaggerated and less defensive, and it is no longer necessary to maintain the attitude, "I am 100 percent right and you are 100 percent wrong." The influence of such an understanding catalyst in the group permits the members to come closer and closer to the objective truth involved in the relationship. In this way mutual communication is established and some type of agreement becomes much more possible. So we may say that though heightened emotions make it much more difficult to understand *with* an opponent, our experience makes it clear that a neutral, understanding, catalyst type of leader or therapist can overcome this obstacle in a small group.

This last phrase, however, suggests another obstacle to utilizing the approach I have described. Thus far all our experience has been with small face-to-face groups—groups exhibiting industrial tensions, religious tensions, racial tensions, and therapy groups in which many personal tensions are present. In these small groups our experience, confirmed by a limited amount of research, shows that this basic approach leads to improved communication, to greater acceptance of others and by others, and to attitudes which are more positive and more problem-solving in nature. There is a decrease in defensiveness, in exaggerated statements, in evaluative and critical behavior. But these findings are from small groups. What about trying to achieve understanding between larger groups that are geographically remote? Or between face-to-face groups who are not speaking for themselves, but simply as representatives of others, like the delegates at Kaesong?[1] Frankly we do not know the answers to these questions. I believe the situation might be put this way. As social scientists we have a tentative

---

[1]**the delegates at Kaesong** Representatives of North and South Korea met at the border town of Kaesong to arrange terms for an armistice to hostilities during the Korean War (1950–1953). [All notes are the editors'.]

test-tube solution of the problem of breakdown in communication. But to confirm the validity of this test-tube solution, and to adapt it to the enormous problems of communication breakdown between classes, groups, and nations, would involve additional funds, much more research, and creative thinking of a high order.

Even with our present limited knowledge we can see some steps which might be taken, even in large groups, to increase the amount of listening *with*, and to decrease the amount of evaluation *about*. To be imaginative for a moment, let us suppose that a therapeutically oriented international group went to the Russian leaders and said, "We want to achieve a genuine understanding of your views and even more important, of your attitudes and feelings, toward the United States. We will summarize and resummarize the views and feelings if necessary, until you agree that our description represents the situation as it seems to you." Then suppose they did the same thing with the leaders in our own country. If they then gave the widest possible distribution to these two views, with the feelings clearly described but not expressed in name-calling, might not the effect be very great? It would not guarantee the type of understanding I have been describing, but it would make it much more possible. We can understand the feelings of a person who hates us much more readily when his attitudes are accurately described to us by a neutral third party, than we can when he is shaking his fist at us.

But even to describe such a first step is to suggest another 15 obstacle to this approach of understanding. Our civilization does not yet have enough faith in the social sciences to utilize their findings. The opposite is true of the physical sciences. During the war[2] when a test-tube solution was found to the problem of synthetic rubber, millions of dollars and an army of talent was turned loose on the problem of using that finding. If synthetic rubber could be made in milligrams, it could and would be made in the thousands of tons. And it was. But in the social science realm, if a way is found of facilitating communication and mutual understanding in small groups, there is no guarantee that the finding will be utilized. It may be a generation or more before the money and the brains will be turned loose to exploit that finding.

In closing, I would like to summarize this small-scale solution to the problem of barriers in communication, and to point out certain of its characteristics.

[2]**the war** World War II.

I have said that our research and experience to date would make it appear that breakdowns in communication, and the evaluative tendency which is the major barrier to communication, can be avoided. The solution is provided by creating a situation in which each of the different parties come to understand the other from the *other's* point of view. This has been achieved, in practice, even when feelings run high, by the influence of a person who is willing to understand each point of view empathically, and who thus acts as a catalyst to precipitate further understanding.

This procedure has important characteristics. It can be initiated by one party, without waiting for the other to be ready. It can even be initiated by a neutral third person, providing he can gain a minimum of cooperation from one of the parties.

This procedure can deal with the insincerities, the defensive exaggerations, the lies, the "false fronts" which characterize almost every failure in communication. These defensive distortions drop away with astonishing speed as people find that the only intent is to understand, not judge.

This approach leads steadily and rapidly toward the discovery 20 of the truth, toward a realistic appraisal of the objective barriers to communication. The dropping of some defensiveness by one party leads to further dropping of defensiveness by the other party, and truth is thus approached.

This procedure gradually achieves mutual communication. Mutual communication tends to be pointed toward solving a problem rather than toward attacking a person or group. It leads to a situation in which I see how the problem appears to you, as well as to me, and you see how it appears to me, as well as to you. Thus accurately and realistically defined, the problem is almost certain to yield to intelligent attack, or if it is in part insoluble, it will be comfortably accepted as such.

This then appears to be a test-tube solution to the breakdown of communication as it occurs in small groups. Can we take this small-scale answer, investigate it further, refine it; develop it and apply it to the tragic and well-nigh fatal failures of communication which threaten the very existence of our modern world? It seems to me that this is a possibility and a challenge which we should explore.   ∎

✓ A CHECKLIST FOR ANALYZING ROGERIAN ARGUMENT

☐ Have I stated the problem and indicated that a dialogue is possible?

☐ Have I stated at least one other point of view in a way that would satisfy its proponents?

☐ Have I been courteous to those who hold views other than mine?

☐ Have I enlarged my own understanding to the extent that I can grant validity, at least in some circumstances, to at least some aspects of other positions?

☐ Have I stated my position and indicated the contexts in which I believe it is valid?

☐ Have I pointed out the ground that we share?

☐ Have I shown how other positions will be strengthened by accepting some aspects of my position?

Edward O. Wilson

Edward O. Wilson, born in Birmingham, Alabama, in 1929, is an emeritus professor of evolutionary biology at Harvard University. A distinguished writer as well as a researcher and teacher, Wilson has twice won the Pulitzer Prize for General Non-Fiction. We reprint a piece first published in 2006 in Wilson's book The Creation: An Appeal to Save Life on Earth.

Letter to a Southern Baptist Minister

Dear Pastor:

We have not met, yet I feel I know you well enough to call you friend. First of all, we grew up in the same faith. As a boy I too answered the altar call; I went under the water. Although I no longer belong to that faith, I am confident that if we met and spoke privately of our deepest beliefs, it would be in a spirit of mutual respect and good will. I know we share many precepts of moral behavior. Perhaps it also matters that we are both Americans and, insofar as it might still affect civility and good manners, we are both Southerners.

I write to you now for your counsel and help. Of course, in doing so, I see no way to avoid the fundamental differences in our respective worldviews. You are a literalist interpreter of Christian Holy Scripture. You reject the conclusion of science that mankind evolved from lower forms. You believe that each person's soul is immortal, making this planet a way station to a second, eternal life. Salvation is assured those who are redeemed in Christ.

I am a secular humanist. I think existence is what we make of it as individuals. There is no guarantee of life after death, and heaven and hell are what we create for ourselves, on this planet. There is no other home. Humanity originated here by evolution from lower forms over millions of years. And yes, I will speak plain, our ancestors were apelike animals. The human species has adapted physically and mentally to life on Earth and no place else. Ethics is the code of behavior we share on the basis of reason, law, honor, and an inborn sense of decency, even as some ascribe it to God's will.

For you, the glory of an unseen divinity; for me, the glory of the universe revealed at last. For you, the belief in God made flesh to save mankind; for me, the belief in Promethean[1] fire seized to set men free. You have found your final truth; I am still searching. I may be wrong, you may be wrong. We may both be partly right.

Does this difference in worldview separate us in all things? It 5 does not. You and I and every other human being strive for the same imperatives of security, freedom of choice, personal dignity, and a cause to believe in that is larger than ourselves.

Let us see, then, if we can, and you are willing, to meet on the near side of metaphysics in order to deal with the real world we share. I put it this way because you have the power to help solve a great problem about which I care deeply. I hope you have the same concern. I suggest that we set aside our differences in order to save the Creation. The defense of living Nature is a universal value. It doesn't rise from, nor does it promote, any religious or ideological dogma. Rather, it serves without discrimination the interests of all humanity.

Pastor, we need your help. The Creation—living Nature—is in deep trouble. Scientists estimate that if habitat conversion and other destructive human activities continue at their present rates, half the species of plants and animals on Earth could be either gone

---

[1]**Promethean** In Greek mythology, Prometheus was a Titan who looked after mankind, going so far as to steal fire from Mount Olympus to give it to humans. [Editors' note.]

or at least fated for early extinction by the end of the century. A full quarter will drop to this level during the next half century as a result of climate change alone. The ongoing extinction rate is calculated in the most conservative estimates to be about a hundred times above that prevailing before humans appeared on Earth, and it is expected to rise to at least a thousand times greater or more in the next few decades. If this rise continues unabated, the cost to humanity, in wealth, environmental security, and quality of life, will be catastrophic.

Surely we can agree that each species, however inconspicuous and humble it may seem to us at this moment, is a masterpiece of biology, and well worth saving. Each species possesses a unique combination of genetic traits that fits it more or less precisely to a particular part of the environment. Prudence alone dictates that we act quickly to prevent the extinction of species and, with it, the pauperization of Earth's ecosystems—hence of the Creation.

You may well ask at this point, Why me? Because religion and science are the two most powerful forces in the world today, including especially the United States. If religion and science could be united on the common ground of biological conservation, the problem would soon be solved. If there is any moral precept shared by people of all beliefs, it is that we owe ourselves and future generations a beautiful, rich, and healthful environment.

I am puzzled that so many religious leaders, who spiritually 10 represent a large majority of people around the world, have hesitated to make protection of the Creation an important part of their magisterium.[2] Do they believe that human-centered ethics and preparation for the afterlife are the only things that matter? Even more perplexing is the widespread conviction among Christians that the Second Coming is imminent, and that therefore the condition of the planet is of little consequence. Sixty percent of Americans, according to a 2004 poll, believe that the prophecies of the book of Revelation are accurate. Many of these, numbering in the millions, think the End of Time will occur within the life span of those now living. Jesus will return to Earth, and those redeemed by Christian faith will be transported bodily to heaven, while those left behind will struggle through severe hard times and, when they die, suffer eternal damnation. The condemned will remain in hell, like those already consigned in the generations before them, for a trillion trillion years, enough for the universe to expand to its own,

---

[2]**magisterium** The official teaching of the Roman Catholic Church. [Editors' note.]

entropic death, time enough for countless universes like it afterward to be born, expand, and likewise die away. And that is just the beginning of how long condemned souls will suffer in hell—all for a mistake they made in choice of religion during the infinitesimally small time they inhabited Earth.

For those who believe this form of Christianity, the fate of 10 million other life forms indeed does not matter. This and other similar doctrines are not gospels of hope and compassion. They are gospels of cruelty and despair. They were not born of the heart of Christianity. Pastor, tell me I am wrong!

However you will respond, let me here venture an alternative ethic. The great challenge of the twenty-first century is to raise people everywhere to a decent standard of living while preserving as much of the rest of life as possible. Science has provided this part of the argument for the ethic: the more we learn about the biosphere, the more complex and beautiful it turns out to be. Knowledge of it is a magic well: the more you draw from it, the more there is to draw. Earth, and especially the razor-thin film of life enveloping it, is our home, our wellspring, our physical and much of our spiritual sustenance.

I know that science and environmentalism are linked in the minds of many with evolution, Darwin, and secularism. Let me postpone disentangling all this (I will come back to it later) and stress again: to protect the beauty of Earth and of its prodigious variety of life forms should be a common goal, regardless of differences in our metaphysical beliefs.

To make the point in good Gospel manner, let me tell the story of a young man, newly trained for the ministry, and so fixed in his Christian faith that he referred all questions of morality to readings from the Bible. When he visited the cathedral-like Atlantic rainforest of Brazil, he saw the manifest hand of God and in his notebook wrote, "It is not possible to give an adequate idea of the higher feelings of wonder, admiration, and devotion which fill and elevate the mind."

That was Charles Darwin in 1832, early into the voyage of 15 HMS *Beagle*, before he had given any thought to evolution.

And here is Darwin, concluding *On the Origin of Species* in 1859, having first abandoned Christian dogma and then, with his newfound intellectual freedom, formulated the theory of evolution by natural selection: "There is grandeur in this view of life, with its several powers, having been originally breathed into a few forms or into one; and that, whilst this planet has gone cycling on according to the fixed law of gravity, from so simple a beginning endless forms most beautiful and most wonderful have been, and are being, evolved."

Darwin's reverence for life remained the same as he crossed the seismic divide that divided his spiritual life. And so it can be for the divide that today separates scientific humanism from mainstream religion. And separates you and me.

You are well prepared to present the theological and moral arguments for saving the Creation. I am heartened by the movement growing within Christian denominations to support global conservation. The stream of thought has arisen from many sources, from evangelical to unitarian. Today it is but a rivulet. Tomorrow it will be a flood.

I already know much of the religious argument on behalf of the Creation, and would like to learn more. I will now lay before you and others who may wish to hear it the scientific argument. You will not agree with all that I say about the origins of life—science and religion do not easily mix in such matters—but I like to think that in this one life-and-death issue we have a common purpose. ∎

TOPICS FOR CRITICAL THINKING AND WRITING

1. Wilson claims to be a "secular humanist" (para. 3). How would you define that term? Are you a secular humanist? Why, or why not?

2. What does Wilson mean by "metaphysics" (para. 6)? Which if any of his views qualify as metaphysical?

3. Wilson obviously seeks to present his views in a fashion that makes them as palatable as possible. Do you think he succeeds in this endeavor? Write an essay of 500 words arguing for or against his achievement in this regard.

Index of Terms